The Currency of Desire

'As copiously erudite as it is intellectually ambitious, *The Currency of Desire* explores the long history of the "libidinal economy" as a potent, figurative force that plays at the intersection between economic rationality and psychic life – interest and identity, profit and loss, saving and spending. Metaphors are "symptoms" of survival, Bennett lucidly argues, in a striking narrative that explores the on-going struggle between economic rationality and erotic energy.'

Professor Homi K. Bhabha, Director of the Mahindra Humanities Centre, Harvard University

'It is an irresistible coupling: money and sex. David Bennett's new book displays his extraordinary erudition, which he presents with both eloquence and punch. A great read!'

Professor Joanna Bourke, Birkbeck, University of London, author of *The Story of Pain* (2015)

'Love or money, lust or labour power – what is it that makes the world go round? In *The Currency of Desire*, David Bennett offers a rich history of experiments in thinking and living according to models of monetary or libidinal circulation – from Marx to Freud, and from the early Soviet Union to nineteenth-century New England. If sexuality is like a *primum mobile* for the movements of subjective life, then how is this related to broader urges to spend or save, to put out or hold back, for individuals and for larger societies of every kind? Highly charged reading.'

Professor Rachel Bowlby, University College London, author of *Everyday Stories* (2016)

'David Bennett's ambitious survey of the political, economic and psychic currency of desire – whether for physical pleasure or, its substitute, money – is a masterpiece of historical and psychoanalytic scholarship. Always eloquent and accessible, *The Currency of Desire* takes us on a truly transdisciplinary journey, critically analysing every theoretical bump and twist in the economies of desire over the last 300 years of European history, taking us right up to the present moments of libidinally invested "saving", "investing" and "spending", now increasingly divorced from guilt, shame and, some might say, pleasure. A quite remarkable endeavour.'

Professor Lynne Segal, Birkbeck, University of London, author of *Out of Time* (2013)

The Currency of Desire:
Libidinal Economy, Psychoanalysis and Sexual Revolution

David Bennett

Lawrence & Wishart
London 2016

Lawrence and Wishart
Central Books Building
Heath Park Industrial Estate
Freshwater Road
Chadwell Heath
RM8 1RX

Typesetting: e-type
Cover design: Andrew Corbett
Cover image: Johannes Vermeer, The Procuress (detail),
bpk | Staatliche Kunstsammlungen Dresden | Elke Estel | Hans-Peter Klut.

First published 2016

British Library Cataloguing in Publication Data.
A catalogue record for this book is available from the British Library

ISBN 9781907103575

Contents

ACKNOWLEDGEMENTS

Research for this book was assisted by an Australian Research Council Discovery Project Grant. The illustration in chapter 3 is reproduced under Creative Commons license and can be found at http://goo.gl/O5na3G. The photographic illustrations in chapter 6 are reproduced with the kind permission of the Oneida Community Mansion House, and those in chapter 7 by kind permission of ADAGP, Paris and DACS, London 2016. The detail of Vermeer's painting *The Procuress* on the cover of this book is reproduced by kind permission of bpk Bildagentur archive.

I am indebted to Jenny Lee for her editorial advice and to my publishers at Lawrence & Wishart for their patience and diligence. Earlier, shorter versions of some of the material in this book have appeared in article-form as: 'Burghers, Burglars and Masturbators: The Sovereign Spender in the Age of Consumerism', *New Literary History*, vol. 30, no. 2, pp. 269-94; 'Getting the Id to Go Shopping: Psychoanalysis, Advertising, Barbie Dolls, and the Invention of the Consumer Unconscious', *Public Culture*, vol. 17, no. 1, pp. 1-25; 'Libidinal Economy, Prostitution and Consumer Culture', *Textual Practice*, vol. 24, no. 1, pp. 93-121; and 'Guilt as Capital: Psychoanalysis and the New Russians', *Journal for the Psychoanalysis of Culture and Society*, vol. 6, no. 1, pp. 123-38.

1

Introduction: Libidinal Economy Before Freud and After Neoliberalism

Since the project of this book is historical, I make no apology for beginning it with an old joke. A distinguished psychoanalyst was once asked by a new patient, 'Do you take notes?' – to which the analyst replied, 'Yes, I take notes, I take coins, I take cheques, I take anything!' Like most professional in-jokes, this one betrays an anxiety about speaking of the very subject it purports to take lightly: here, the indispensable stuff of psychoanalysis as both therapy and profession, 'filthy lucre'. Sigmund Freud once warned his colleagues never to mince their words on the two subjects about which 'civilised people' were incapable of speaking plainly: 'money matters' and 'sexual matters'.[1] The irony of that warning is inescapable: not only have psychoanalysts been much more inclined to write frankly about sex than about money, they have also habitually decoded money-talk as metaphoric sex-talk.[2] The germ of this book was a question prompted by this irony: if a cigar is sometimes just a cigar – as the pioneer of the talking cure is reputed to have

1 Sigmund Freud, 'On Beginning the Treatment', *Standard Edition of the Complete Psychological Works of Sigmund Freud*, James Strachey (ed.), Vol. 12, London, Vintage, 2001, p. 131.

2 Voices within the profession have perennially faulted it for failing to address money *qua* money since the Marxist analyst Otto Fenichel criticised Freud's and Ferenczi's 'biologising' of the origins of money and the impulse to accumulate it – as sublimations of coprophilia – in his essay 'The Drive to Amass Wealth', *Psychoanalytic Quarterly*, 7 (1938): 74. For versions of this complaint in more recent decades, see David W. Krueger, *The Last Taboo: Money as Symbol and Reality in Psychotherapy and Psychoanalysis*, New York, Brunner and Mazel, 1986; Richard Trachtman, 'The Money Taboo: Its Effects in Everyday Life and in the Practice of Psychotherapy', *Clinical Social Work Journal*, 27 (1999): 275-288; Del Loewenthal, 'Editorial: Sex, Shit, Money and Marxism – The Continued Demise of the "Third Way"', *European Journal of*

said of the phallic symbol that would cause his own death from mouth cancer – then how might an acceptance that money is sometimes just money change our understanding of psychoanalysis itself and of the 300-year-old tradition of thought about subjectivity and desire to which it arguably belongs? Could Freud's explanation of the mind as an 'economy of libido', for example, have more to do with money and the marketplace than he was ready to admit? What happens when we start to decode sex-talk as metaphoric money-talk? And what preconceptions about the capitalist economy as a system of production, exchange, accumulation, valuation and expenditure have sedimented as 'common sense' in our understandings of ourselves as embodied subjects of desire?

As this book aims to show, such questions open onto a much broader history of thought about the currency of desire and its economies than that of the psychoanalytic tradition alone. The history of what would become known in the twentieth century as 'libidinal economy' can be traced back at least to the seventeenth century and across discourses as disparate as medicine and marketing, pornography and political economy, social anthropology and literary fiction, heretical theology and revolutionary political theory.

*

In 1992 the Swedish Academy of the Sciences awarded Gary Becker the Nobel Prize in Economics for 'having extended the domain of economic theory to aspects of human behaviour which had previously been dealt with – if at all – by other social science disciplines such as sociology, demography and criminology'.[3] It

Psychotherapy and Counselling, 11, 4 (2009): 349-353; and David Bennett (ed.), *Loaded Subjects: Psychoanalysis, Money and the Global Financial Crisis*, London, Lawrence & Wishart, 2012, pp. 7-33.

3 Quoted on the late Professor Gary Becker's University of Chicago home page: http://home.uchicago.edu/~gbecker/Nobel/nobel.html (accessed 22/11/2013). The 'Official Web Site of the Nobel Prize' cites a different wording: '... for having extended the domain of microeconomic analysis to a wide range of human behaviour and interaction, including nonmarket behaviour': http://

was Becker's putatively innovative concept of 'human capital', which he had developed in collaboration with Theodore Schultz at Chicago University in the early 1960s, that had most impressed the Academy, for it had helped to teach the late twentieth century to reinterpret everything from marriage, procreation and child-rearing to education, career-choice and criminality in terms of the cost-benefit calculations of 'economic man'. It is now an orthodoxy of intellectual history, promulgated not least by Michel Foucault,[4] that it was only with the rise of Chicago School neoliberal economics in the 1960s that the mentality of *homo œconomicus* became universalised, reaching out from the 'purely' economic and juridical spheres to colonise many other domains of human experience, including the most intimately 'private' or 'personal' ones of affective ties and sexual desire. Cost-benefit calculations have no doubt always typified behaviour in the marketplace proper and the juridical sphere (where the 'just price' to be 'paid' for a crime is correlated with its perceived 'costs' to its victims and the criminal's 'debt' to society) but, with Becker's and his colleagues' promptings, it had become possible to understand the self in *all* its dimensions and relationships as an economic enterprise. Domains of action and decision once deemed remote from the logic of money and the marketplace – and more properly interpretable by ethics, religion, philosophy, psychology or anthropology – could now be explained in terms of a personal calculus of profit and loss, investment and dividend, outlay and return.

This book tells a different story. It dates the birth of 'economic man' as a fully 'psychologised' and 'sexualised' subject – the emergence of *homo œconomicus* as, at once, *homo psychologicus* and *homo sexualis* – from at least as far back as the European Enlightenment. It traces the history of the exchange or intercourse between the languages of money and sex, political economy and libidinal

www.nobelprize.org/nobel_prizes/economic-sciences/laureates/1992/ (accessed 20/12/2014).

4 See Michel Foucault, *The Birth of Biopolitics: Lectures at the Collège de France, 1978–79*, Michel Senellart (ed.), Graham Burchell (trans.), Houndsmills, Palgrave Macmillan, 2008, pp. 267-70.

economy, from the 1700s to the present, demonstrating how medical, commercial, political and pornographic representations of sexual psychology have often relied, since the beginnings of consumer society, on a shifting complex of monetary models and metaphors to explain the nature of desire and its 'value' to both the self and society.

Claims to be setting the study of sexuality, for the first time, on a 'rational' or 'scientific' footing by explaining it in economic terms have been made repeatedly over the past three centuries. Recent candidates for the credit of coining libidinal economy include a spate of studies since the 1990s by professors of law, economics and sociology, each claiming to have originated 'an economics of sexuality', a 'sexual economics' or an 'economics of erotic capital' that explains sexual desire as a quantifiable economic resource capable of being saved, spent, profitably invested or squandered. In the same year as Becker won his Nobel prize, Judge Richard Posner undertook to enlighten a benighted American legal profession as to the truth of sexuality in his book *Sex and Reason*, by providing the first 'functional, means-end, rational – in other words, economic – theory' of sexual behaviour.[5] Acknowledging his debt to Becker's work, Posner asserted that his own 'economics of sex' was the first to 'try to strip away the moral and emotional overtones, the preconceptions, the myths, the customary attitudes that make it difficult for people in our society, however well educated, to treat sex, and its regulation by law or social custom, as subjects of dispassionate scientific study'.[6] A dozen years later, in 2004, the social psychology and marketing professors Roy Baumeister and Kathleen Vohs described their own project of 'sexual economics' as 'novel' inasmuch as it applied Becker's cost-benefit analytics to the social exchange of 'sex' understood as a 'nonmaterial good' capable of being traded, stolen, purchased, hoarded or given away.[7] In the same year, two

5 Richard A. Posner, *Sex and Reason*, Cambridge, MA and London, Harvard University Press, 1992, p. 85.

6 Ibid.

7 Roy F. Baumeister and Kathleen D. Vohs, 'Sexual Economics: Sex as Female Resource for Social Exchange in Heterosexual Interactions', *Personality and Social Psychology Review*, 8, 4 (2004): 339-63.

National Bureau of Economic Research economists, David Blanchflower and Andrew Oswald, claimed to demonstrate that happiness can be precisely quantified and correlated with income, and that the dividend of happiness yielded by increasing the frequency of sexual intercourse from once-a-month to once-a-week was the equivalent of a £32,000 per annum income-rise.[8] Blanchflower and Oswald's research has been cited by the British sociologist Catherine Hakim as 'scientific' evidence in support of her own 'ground-breaking investigation into the changing nature of marriage' and sexual relationships in the neoliberal era, *Honey Money: The Power of Erotic Capital* (2011).[9] Hakim claimed to make essentially the same conceptual breakthrough with her 'economics of erotic capital' as Posner had claimed for his 'economics of sex' some twenty years earlier, but she cites as its inspiration not the economist Becker but the sociologist Pierre Bourdieu. Hakim stakes her claim to originality on her discovery of a hitherto neglected category of capital – 'erotic capital' – that she proposes adding to Bourdieu's inventory of the different forms of personal capital (economic, human, social, cultural) that an individual may inherit, acquire, exploit or lose.[10]

8 David D. Blanchflower and Andrew J. Oswald, 'Money, Sex and Happiness: An Empirical Study', Working Paper 10499, National Bureau of Economic Research, Cambridge, MA, May 2004: http://www.nber.org/papers/w10499. Cf. Stuart Jeffries, 'The sex issue: Is monogamy dead?' *The Guardian*, 10 November 2012: http://www.guardian.co.uk/lfeandstyle/2012/nov/10/sex-is-monogamy-dead.

9 Catherine Hakim, *Honey Money: The Power of Erotic Capital*, London, Allen Lane, 2011, and *The New Rules: Internet, Playfairs and Erotic Power*, London, Gibson Square, 2012, pp. 77-78. Applying Blanchflower and Oswald's findings, Hakim calculates that 'If you add the two together, an affair providing lots of sex and an enduring marriage', the result is £96,000-worth of happiness. See Catherine Hakim, 'The recipe for happiness? An enduring marriage and an affair with lots of sex' (modified excerpt of *The New Rules*), *The Telegraph*, 20 August, 2012: http://www.telegraph.co.uk/women/sex9486351/The-recipe-for-happiness-An-enduring-marriage-and-an-affair-with-lots-of-sex.html.

10 Pierre Bourdieu, 'The forms of capital', in J. Richardson (ed.), *Handbook of Theory and Research for the Sociology of Education*, New York, Greenwood, 1986, pp. 241–58.

Bourdieu himself was a committed critic of neoliberalism, castigating it in his essay 'The Essence of Neoliberalism' (1998) as 'a programme for destroying collective structures which may impede the pure market logic' and for 'conceiving of itself as the scientific description of reality'.[11] But Bourdieu also acknowledged his heavy debt to Becker's economics, and there can be little doubt that his influential introduction of non-economic categories of 'capital' into the sociological analysis of education and its reproduction of class differences has helped (despite his own politics) to legitimate the wholesale 'neoliberalising' or commoditising of higher education, academic research and 'intellectual property' that has been rapidly accelerating in our century.

As neoliberalism began to permeate the humanities and social sciences in the 1980s and 1990s, a new trend in interdisciplinary discourse-analysis became discernible: identified as 'the New Economic Criticism' by Martha Woodmansee and Marc Osteen in their 1999 anthology of that title, the research in question showed how economic concepts have increasingly shaped knowledge in the human sciences since the rise of capitalism, with terms such as 'value', 'economy', 'capital', 'exchange', 'investment' and 'debt' entering disciplines as diverse as linguistics, logic, ethics, aesthetics and literary studies – even as such disciplines were being constructed as mutually discrete and distinct from economics itself.[12] The 'New Economic Criticism' also encompasses a critical movement within economics itself – one associated most notably with the work of Donald (Deirdre) McCloskey – which uses rhetorical methods to unmask the buried metaphors and fictions that shape the language of economists.[13] Examining the homologies between language and money as systems of representation and exchange in which social relations and subjects are forged, such criticism is anti-foundation-

11 Pierre Bourdieu, 'The Essence of Neoliberalism', *Le Monde diplomatique*, English edition, December 1998: http://mondediplo.com/1998/12/08bourdieu (accessed 22/4/2013).

12 Martha Woodmansee and Marc Osteen (eds), *The New Economic Criticism: Studies at the Intersection of Literature and Economics*, London, Routledge, 1999.

13 See, e.g., Donald N. McCloskey, *The Rhetoric of Economics*, Madison, University of Wisconsin Press, 1985.

alist in the sense that it seeks to avoid privileging one discourse over another, resisting the temptation, for example, to rely on economics to 'explain' developments in other discourses of knowledge. Instead, the 'New Economic Criticism' stresses the reciprocity of influence *between* different cultural domains and discourses, and investigates the exchanges, or metaphorical transfers, that occur between them, on the assumption that exchange determines both social life and discourse about it.

A notable absence from Woodmansee and Osteen's showcase volume of New Economic Criticism, however, was any discussion of the subject of this book: the role of monetary models and metaphors in shaping the history of sexuality and psychology. And yet economic concepts have permeated the vocabularies of both popular and scientific discourses on sexual anatomy, psychology, morality and politics for several centuries. Eighteenth and nineteenth-century physicians, moralists and libertines often likened sexual energy and secretions to money, to be frugally spent, prudently saved, productively invested or pleasurably wasted. Construing the self as an economy of vital energy or desire, hypostatised in the body's 'generative fluids', they advocated regimes of self-management calculated to maximise personal health, wealth or pleasure in the emerging business culture of Enlightenment Europe and America – a culture in which desire itself was increasingly recognised as the essential currency of the consumer economy.

Since the verb 'to spend' became the standard English vernacular term for orgasm in the late seventeenth century (the earliest instance cited in the *OED* is an entry in Pepys's *Diary* of 1662),[14] economic synonyms for sexual concepts have proliferated, gaining their strongest currency in demotic language at the height of the Industrial Revolution. In vernacular English from the late sixteenth century onwards, for example, 'purse' might have meant either scrotum or vagina and 'spendings' either seminal or vaginal fluid, but it was during the later eighteenth century that 'till', 'wallet', 'money',

14 While the *OED* cites an entry in Pepys' *Diary* for 7 September, 1662, as its earliest example of 'to spend' meaning 'to ejaculate; to have an orgasm', earlier cognate examples abound, including Shakespeare's well-known trope in Sonnet 129: 'Th'expense of spirit in a waste of shame is lust in action'.

'money-box' and 'spender' all became synonyms for vagina, and in the nineteenth century that semen could be denoted by the noun 'spend' and a vagina be referred to as a 'bank' or 'budget'.[15]

As in English, so in French. Since at least the sixteenth century, French spending (*dépenser* or *épuiser*) could be erotic or pecuniary: to make a big spending or 'spend big' (*faire une grosse dépense*) was to make a lot of love (as in 'le Duc de Saux avait fait la nuit une grosse dépense avec Louise d'Arquien' – 'that night, the Duke of Saux made a big spending with Louise of Arquien').[16] In the nineteenth century, *dépenser son blanc* meant to spend semen but also money, since 'blanc' signified both.[17] To copulate was to 'pay a fine' or 'forfeit' (*le forfeit*; *forfaire*)[18] or, in eighteenth-century French slang, to be counting money (*être en argent comptant*).[19] Copulation could also be denoted by *le commerce* (business, trade) or as *la besogne*, *la carrière* or *le labeur* (employment, having a job, labour). French breasts were capital assets (*les avantages*) and a French vagina could be a coin (*pièce*), wallet (*bissac*), moneybox (*caisse* or *tirelire*),[20]

15 See Francis Grose, *A Classical Dictionary of the Vulgar Tongue*, London, S. Hooper, 1785; Richard A. Spears, *Slang and Euphemism: A Dictionary of Oaths, Curses, Insults, Sexual Slang and Metaphor, Racial Slurs, Drug Talk, Homosexual Lingo, and Related Matters*, New York, Jonathan David Publishers, 1981; Alan Richter, *Dictionary of Sexual Slang: Words, Phrases, and Idioms from AC/DC to Zig-zig*, New York, John Wiley, 1993; Gordon Williams, *A Dictionary of Sexual Language and Imagery in Shakespearean and Stuart Literature*, Vols I-III, London and Atlantic Highlands, NJ, Athlone Press, 1994; and Jonathon Green, *The Cassell Dictionary of Slang*, London, Cassell, 1998.

16 Quoted from a 1696 source in Pierre Guiraud, *Dictionnaire Erotique*, Paris, Editions Payot & Rivages, 1993, p. 202.

17 Ibid., p. 278. The following words, cited in the main text, are also listed in John S. Farmer (ed.), *Slang and its analogues past and present: a dictionary, historical and comparative, of the heterodox speech of all classes of society for more than three hundred years; with synonyms in English, French, German, Italian, etc.*, London, Printed for subscribers, 1890-1904, Volume IV, pp. 336-345: *le bissac* (wallet), *la boutique* (shop), *celui de l'argent* ([a bit of] money), *la merchandise* (merchandise or ware), *le tirelire* (money box), *la bourse à vits* (Rabelais) (prick purse), *le combien* (prostitutes/how much), *le sac* (bag or wallet).

18 Guiraud, *Dictionnaire Erotique*, p. 343

19 Ibid., p. 141.

20 Hence '*briser sa tirelire*': to smash one's piggy bank/moneybox, or lose one's virginity.

business (*affaire*), shop (*boutique*), purse (*sac* or *bourse*), stipend or stock market (*la bourse*), bread-winner (*gagne-pain*) or, as early as the 1690s, quite simply capital, as in this adage from 1695: 'On leur dit (aux petites filles) … c'est un tresor! C'est votre *capital*! Vous en laisseriez apercevoir un petit bout que le reste ne vaudrait plus rien' ('We say to the little girls … it's a treasure! It's your capital! If you let a little of it be seen the rest will be worth nothing').[21] Similarly, a French penis might be a coin (*pièce*), treasure or jewel (*bijou*) or merchandise (*marchandise*), while testicles might be jewels (*bijoux de famille*) trinkets or charms (*breloques*).[22]

German, too, has made lexical capital out of the fungibility of sex and money. In German slang, business (*Geschäft*) can mean genitals; work (*Arbeit*) can mean sex; and manual labour (*Handarbeit*) masturbation. Being in credit (*im haben*) can mean having sex or owning someone sexually; a board of management (*Vorstand*) can mean an erect penis; a business disruption (*Betriebsstörung*) can mean impotence; having an industrial accident (*Betriebsunfall*) can mean having a sexually transmitted disease; and an entertainment tax (*Vergnügungsteuer*) may be either an STD or alimony.[23] A German vagina may be a shop (*Laden*), a savings bank or savings box (*Sparkasse*), a goldmine (*Goldgrube*) or a jewel casket (*Schatulle*), while a scrotum may be a safe or bank vault (*Tresor*).[24] A wallet (*Portemonnaie*) may be a trouser fly, and expenses (*Spesen*) can mean a kiss.[25] In German pimp's slang, to be miserly (*geizen*) may mean to be sexually abstinent.[26]

It goes without saying that sex has been for sale, libido commoditised, both before and since the Industrial Revolution, but it was during the period of concern in this book – the era of a hegemonic market economy and consumer culture in Europe and North

21 Guiraud, *Dictionnaire Erotique*, p. 236.

22 Ibid., pp. 171, 186, 191.

23 See Günther Hunold, *Sexualität in der Sprache: Lexikon d. obszönen Wortschatzes*, München, Heyne, 1978.

24 Ibid., and Ernst Borneman, *Sex im Volksmund. Die sexuelle Umgangssprache des deutschen Volkes*, Hamburg, Rowohlt, 1971.

25 Ibid.

26 Ibid.

America – that the modern 'sciences' of sexual physiology, psychology and paraphilia emerged, culminating in the *fin-de-siècle* disciplines of sexology and psychoanalysis, both heavily invested in economic explanations of desire and subjectivity. The trope of the body or self as an 'economy' recurs throughout this 300-year period of 'sexual science' in both the medical literature and its lay counterparts (from literature and pornography to social-hygiene pamphlets and advice manuals), whether as 'the œconomy of love', 'the animal economy', 'the vital economy' or 'the libidinal economy'. For the eighteenth-century French vitalist and British physiological schools of medicine, the concept of the 'animal economy' (from Latin *animalis*: 'having breath', 'animate') implied nothing less than a medical investigation of life, or vitality, as such, one that supplanted the dualist vision of a body (subject to physical science) and a soul (subject to moral science) with a view of the human animal as a single, psychosomatic 'economy'.[27] (As one prominent physician and 'animal economist' put it in 1760: 'We are ignorant both of the nature of the mind and that of the body, but we know in man the two are intimately united, and that all the changes in the one are felt in the other …'[28]) 'Resolving' the mind-body problem that had vexed philosophers from Plato to Descartes and beyond, the concept of the 'animal economy' was a scheme for conceiving of the whole person as a system of production, circulation, exchange and expenditure of some vital essence or substance; and the project of 'economic' medicine was to identify the processes and practices that sustained and reproduced a healthy 'animal economy' and whose breakdown could result in 'vital bankruptcy', or death. It was a project described in the 1765 edition of Diderot's *Encyclopédie* as 'opening up a vast field of the most interesting researches

27 Cf. Philippe Huneman, '"Animal Economy": Anthropology and the Rise of Psychiatry from the *Encyclopédie* to the Alienists', in Larry Wolf and Marco Cipollini (eds), *The Anthropology of the Enlightenment*, Stanford, CA., Stanford University Press, 2007, pp. 262-76.

28 Samuel-Auguste Tissot, *Treatise on the Diseases Caused by Masturbation* (anonymous translation of *L'Onanisme*), New York, Collins and Hannay, 1832, p. 55.

concerning all the mysteries of nature most pertinent to man',[29] which generated countless popular self-help manuals with titles such as *Conversations on the Animal Economy: Designed for the Instruction of Youth and the Perusal of General Readers* (a multi-edition bestseller by Isaac Ray, M.D., first published in 1829 in Portland, Oregon) and *Medicina Gymnastica: Or, a Treatise Concerning the Power of Exercise, with Respect to the Animal Œconomy* (a manual by Francis Fuller the Younger, M.A., published in London in 1705).

While the concept of the mind-body as an 'economy' has claimed scientific status throughout the modern medical history of sexuality, the question of what the 'currency' of the vital economy might be – of exactly *what* is being exchanged, circulated, accumulated and spent – has been answered quite differently by successive schools of science or pseudoscience, their physiology inflected by different ethics and politics. Nonetheless, just as the entities traded in the money economy have become progressively rarefied, abstracted and psychologised, so there has been a progressive dematerialising, rarefying and psychologising of the presumed currency of the animal economy since the seventeenth century. As physiology became less speculative and more experimental and as successive fashions in science – including humoral medicine, neurology, electromagnetism, thermodynamics, psychoanalysis and neuroscience – have been called upon to explain the *causa vitae*, or essence of life, so candidates for the role of vital currency have ranged from 'animal spirits', 'humours' and 'nerve fluid' to 'electrical current', an abstract 'energy' and a fully psychologised 'libido' – all more or less synonymous or interchangeable with the concepts of 'desire' and 'love'.

Eighteenth-century theories of the 'animal economy' often explained it as an economy of fluids. When the Scottish-born physician and poet John Armstrong (1709-1779) addressed his blank-verse sexual advice manual, *The Œconomy of Love: A Poetical*

29 M (J.-J. Ménuret de Chambaud), 'Œconomie animale', *Encyclopédie, ou Dictionnaire raisonné des sciences, des arts et des métiers, par une société de gens de lettres, Tome XI, N–PARI*, Neufchastel, Samuel Faulche, 1765, p. 360 (my translation).

Essay, to 'Ye Youths and Virgins' in 1736, he identified the currency of love's economy variously as 'the Blood', 'the rich Moisture', 'the melting Essence', 'Nature's Power', 'the universal Power' and 'Desire'.[30] The poem portrayed the mind–body as an economy of vital fluid that circulates in and animates the organism, driving its growth until it reaches adult proportions in adolescence, when the 'rich Moisture' is channelled into growing secondary sex characteristics, exciting erotic desire, and spending itself in sexual secretions. Armstrong's narrative of how sexual desire and menstruation arise in the adolescent female body casually mixed the vocabularies of physiology and money:

> The Maid demands
> The dues of Venus, when the parting Breasts
> Wanton exuberant and tempt the Touch,
> Plump'd with rich Moisture from the finish'd Growth
> Redundant now: for late the shooting Tubes [i.e., arteries]
> Drank all the Blood the toiling Heart could pour,
> Insatiate; now full-grown they crave no more
> Than what repairs their daily Waste. But still
> There must be Loss, nor does the Superplus
> Turn all to Thrift. For from Love's Grotto now
> Oozes the sanguine Stream thro' many a Rill ...[31]

The graphic indecency of the poem damaged Armstrong's professional practice as a physician but he defended it as 'a Poem upon a subject of no inconsiderable consequence to the health of mankind',[32] and his prescriptions for optimising the health/wealth of the animal economy would be characteristic of moderate-conservative libidinal economists for centuries to come. According

30 Anon [John Armstrong], *The Œconomy of Love: A Poetical Essay* [1736], third edition, London, M. Cooper, 1739, *passim*.

31 Ibid., ll., pp. 49-59.

32 Alexander Monro (ed.) *Medical Essays and Observations*, London, T. Cadell, 1773, p. 39, quoted in Alan Budd, 'General Introduction', *John Armstrong's The Art of Preserving Health: Eighteenth-Century Sensibility in Practice*, Alan Budd (ed.), Farnham, Ashgate, 2011, p. 19.

to Armstrong, the vital currency must ultimately be spent but needs to be prudently managed: excessive expenditure, though pleasurable, impoverishes the vital economy, while indefinite hoarding ('total Abstinence') leads to a fatally stagnant, unproductive economy. The poem's tendency to equate sexual well-being with an equilibrium of input and output, supply and demand, production and expenditure, would have struck orthodox Freudian libidinal economists a century and a half later as merely rational; but, as we shall see in subsequent chapters, more radical libidinal economists than Armstrong or Freud have advocated very different models of libidinal wealth and health, whether in the name of austerity or liberation, capitalism or collectivism.

A quarter of a century after the first edition of *The Œconomy of Love* appeared, one of the most influential tracts of eighteenth-century sexual medicine, Samuel Tissot's *L'Onanisme. Dissertation sur les maladies produites par la masturbation* (1760), provided a more precise accounting for the liquid currency of the animal economy.[33] A *mélange* of medical eclecticism, anecdotage and unsupported assertion, *L'Onanisme* attested to the rudimentary state of sexual anatomy and medicine in the 1760s, but that did not prevent it from being published in almost yearly new editions and multiple translations over two decades, and being taken up by no less than Voltaire, Kant, Napoleon Bonaparte and both the *Encyclopédie* and the *Encyclopedia Britannica.*[34] *L'Onanisme*'s panic-mongering message about onanism was based on Tissot's 'humoral' theory of what he variously referred to as 'the mechanism of the body and its union with the mind', 'the animal

33 S.A.D. Tissot's treatise was first published in Latin in 1758 and rapidly translated into French as *L'Onanisme. Dissertation sur les maladies produites par la masturbation.* Tissot was evidently capitalising on the commercial success of the anonymous English tract, *Onania*, which coined the term 'onanism' and began the international panic about masturbation in the first decades of the eighteenth century. Tissot repeatedly cites *Onania* as a source and authority despite expressing strong doubts about its medical credibility. *Onania* and *L'Onanisme* are both discussed in chapter 2, below.

34 For the prestigious 'uptake' of *L'Onanisme* in Europe, see Jean Stengers and Anne van Neck, *Masturbation: The History of a Great Terror*, Kathryn Hoffmann (trans.), New York, Palgrave, 2001, pp. 79-80, 85, 90.

machine', 'the animal economy' or simply 'the economy'. (Always eclectic in his borrowings from 'authorities', Tissot indiscriminately combined the terminologies of the opposed vitalist and Cartesian mechanistic schools of medicine.) The treatise explained the 'laws' of the vital economy in terms of its production, 'perfection', accumulation and spending of 'humours', or liquids, ranked in a hierarchy of the more or less 'valuable', 'precious', or 'perfected'. At the top of Tissot's hierarchy of value was 'genital liquor' or 'seminal fluid', the essential currency of life, and below it, in descending order of value to the animal economy, came blood, milk, urine and perspiration. 'Our bodies are constantly wasting', the treatise began, and this wastage must be repaired by digestion of food, which the organism converts into different fluids whose circulation, accumulation and exchange determine the vitality of its economy. The least valuable of the 'humours', perspiration, 'an extremely thin fluid', can normally be spent without significant cost to the body – except in the sexual act: 'A person perspires more during coition than at any other time, because the power of the circulation is quickened. This perspiration … is a real loss'.[35] Fortunately, according to Tissot's physiology, the skin has both 'exhalant vessels' and 'inhalant vessels' and the sweat lost through the 'exhalant vessels' of one partner in coition is reabsorbed via the 'inhalant vessels' of the other, ensuring that, as the eighteenth-century proverb had it, a fair exchange is no robbery. The onanist, by contrast, spends perspiration without return: 'In coition, it is reciprocal, and the one inspires, what the other expires. This exchange has been verified by certain observations. In masturbation there is a loss without this reciprocal benefit'.[36]

Far more costly, and potentially fatally so for the habitual masturbator, was the body's 'wastage' of 'genital fluid', otherwise 'called the *huile essentielle*, *quintessence* of the animal fluids, or more exactly, the *rectified spirit*, the dissipation of which leaves the other humors feeble'.[37] Hoarding this vital currency in the economy of

35 Tissot, *Treatise on the Diseases Caused by Masturbation*, p. 67.
36 Ibid., pp. 67-68.
37 Ibid., p. 42.

the body that produced and 'perfected' it was as essential to its normal functioning as exchanging it with another body was essential to reproducing the animal economy. Tissot's conception of 'genital liquor' as the universal 'stimulus', without whose injection or investment no enterprise in the vital economy could grow or thrive, rendered its wasted expenditure in onanism a 'crime against nature'. He argued that storing genital fluid in the stomach was indispensable to digestion and hence to nutrition and life. While uncertain whether the 'genital fluid' was synonymous with 'the animal spirits',[38] Tissot was certain of its claim to being the vital economy's most precious currency, and he justified his calculations of the relative values of the 'humors' by pointing out:

> A robust nurse, who would be destroyed by the loss of a few pounds of blood in a single day, may supply the same quantity of milk to her child, several days in succession, without being sensibly incommoded by it; because of all the fluids, the milk is the least assimilated; it is a fluid almost foreign to the body, while the blood is essential. There is another, the seminal fluid, which has so much influence on the strength of the body and on the perfection of digestion which restores it, that physicians of every age have unanimously admitted, that the loss of one ounce of it, enfeebles more than forty ounces of blood.[39]

Nor were the costs of squandering 'genital liquid' merely a masculine hazard; the laws of thrift and investment applied equally to the female animal economy, despite the intrinsically lower value of its liquid currency: 'The symptoms which supervene in [masturbating] females, are explained like those in men. The secretion which they lose, being less valuable and less matured than the semen of the male, its loss does not enfeeble so promptly, but when they indulge in it to excess, as their nervous system is naturally weaker and more

38 Ibid., p. 5: 'It is true we are ignorant whether the animal spirits and the seminal fluid are the same; but observations show, as we shall see hereafter, that these two fluids are very analogous, and that loss of one or the other, produces the same complaints'.

39 Ibid., 'Introduction' (unpaginated).

disposed to spasms, the symptoms are more violent'.[40] Tissot's talent for sophistry came to the fore in his invention of eight different reasons why onanistic expenditure of the vital currency was necessarily self-impoverishing in a way that its spending in copulation was not, even arguing that the characteristic physical postures of the onanist, by contrast with those of the copulator, required 'the action of a great number of muscles, and this action dissipates the animal spirits'.

Coition might be medically condoned as mutually beneficial exchange, then, while onanistic spending without a return could not; but in Tissot's book and vital bookkeeping, hoarding was preferable even to exchange and always an indisputable personal good. Addressed in the first instance to the haute bourgeoisie and nobility who formed the core of his clientele in Lausanne, Tissot's tract taught its readers the imperatives of protecting their genetic and economic capital through regimes of thrift and health. As the authors of *Le pénis et la démoralisation de l'Occident* put it, Tissot taught the eighteenth century that it was 'as scandalous to spill one's sperm as it is to throw money out the window'.[41]

The bizarre idea that vitality – hypostatised in sexual secretions – either should or could be hoarded like money to ensure the well-being of the animal economy attests to the seductive power of what Weber called the Puritan 'spirit of capitalism' in the mind-sets of physicians committed to developing a materialist science of eros in the eighteenth century. In a modern economy based on paper money and interest, it could make sense to accumulate money for accumulation's sake, to withdraw it from circulation and hoard it as a store-of-value rather than use it as a medium of exchange. ('Accumulation for accumulation's sake', wrote Marx in the 1860s, 'by this formula classical economy expressed the historical mission of the bourgeoisie', before its mid-eighteenth-century

40 Ibid., p. 57.

41 Jean-Paul Aron and Roger Kempf (authors of *Le pénis et la démoralisation de l'Occident* [1978]), interview in *Nouvel Observateur*, October 23, 1978, p. 104, quoted in Stengers and Van Neck, *Masturbation*, p. 92.

embrace of consumerism.[42]) Whereas physical commodities tend to depreciate when stockpiled, paper money, signifying debt and credit, need not decay and can keep gaining in value in an interest-based economy.[43] Withdrawing money from circulation may increase demand for the medium of exchange and drive up its market value. Transposing the same economic logic into sexual physiology and psychology, physicians of Tissot's bent argued that the 'value' of the vital economy's most 'precious' fluid was increased by saving and fatally depreciated by spending, and that the longer it was hoarded and 'perfected' in the body, the greater the value of its ultimate pay-out for the purposes of reproducing the species. Both classical political economy and neoclassical economics (in contrast to Keynesianism, for example) assume that it is natural to be profligate, to want to spend as much as possible in the present,[44] and they tend to view interest as a compensation for deferred spending, a reward for delayed gratification. As Marx noted in the *Grundrisse*: 'The cult of money has its asceticism, its self-denial, its self-sacrifice – economy and frugality, contempt for mundane, temporal, and fleeting pleasures, the chase after the *eternal* treasure. Hence the connection between English Puritanism, or also Dutch Protestantism, and money-making'.[45] *L'Onanisme* and other tracts of its genre made the connections between capitalism and sexual asceticism explicit both in warning

42 Karl Marx, *Capital: A Critique of Political Economy*, Vol. 1, Frederick Engels (ed.), Chicago, Charles H. Kerr & Co., 1919, p. 652.

43 As Silvio Gesell pointed out in his radical proposal for a non-Marxist alternative to finance capitalism, hoarded money does not to depreciate in the same way as 'physical' capital, including commodities that functioned as currency before paper money, tend to do: stockpiled grain rots, iron rusts, cattle age and die, untended land reverts to wilderness, machinery and equipment break down, become obsolete, need maintenance. Gesell proposed a system (which J.M. Keynes admired) in which unspent money would also automatically depreciate at a set rate, to discourage its hoarding and keep it in circulation as a medium of exchange. See Silvio Gesell, *The Natural Economic Order*, Philip Pye (trans.), Berlin, NEO-Verlag, 1906.

44 J.M. Keynes assumed the opposite: that it was natural, especially for the working and petit-bourgeois classes, to want to hoard money. See chapters 5 and 7 for discussions of Keynesianism and libidinal economy.

45 Karl Marx, *Grundrisse*, New York, Penguin Classics, 1993, p. 230.

that 'it is … important, in medicine as in morals, to sacrifice the present for the future'[46] and in projecting, as the future reward for present austerity, the possibility of bequeathing one's hoarded/unspent vitality to the next generation, one's children. Armstrong's *Œconomy of Love* may have been less invested in the economics of austerity than *L'Onanisme* was, but they concurred in teaching that to forego the pleasure of any and all sexual spending for many years (*The Œconomy of Love* recommended 'twice ten Years'[47]) before outlaying the 'rich Moisture' for the purposes of conception, was the only guarantee of producing vigorous, healthy offspring.[48]

A less tangible currency of life and desire than Tissot's fluids was postulated by the Edinburgh professor of medicine, William Cullen (1712-90), physician and intimate friend of the political economists David Hume and Adam Smith. Preoccupied with investigating the distribution and effects of the nervous system, Cullen hypothesised that the vital currency was 'nervous power' or 'nervous energy', which 'flows' in varying quantities into 'muscular fibre' and animates it.[49] Coining the term 'neurosis' in 1769 to describe various nervous symptoms and disorders that were inexplicable physiologically, and famously arguing that 'almost all diseases considered from a certain point of view could be called nervous',[50] Cullen helped pave the way for psychoanalytic theories of neurotic illness as purely psychical in aetiology, dysfunctions of the libidinal economy understood not in physiological but in psychological terms.

46 Tissot, *Diseases Caused by Masturbation*, p. 108.

47 Armstrong, *Œconomy of Love*, l. 54.

48 Armstrong, *Œconomy of Love*, ll. 80-85, 105-7: 'Hold, Parricide, thy Hand!' Armstrong admonished would-be practitioners of 'the Vice of Monks recluse': 'if to progeny thy Views extend … / Wouldst thou behold a thriving Race surround / Thy spacious Table; shun the soft Embrace / Emasculant, till twice ten Years and more / Have steel'd thy Nerves … '

49 William Cullen, 'Physiology', *The Works of William Cullen, M.D.* [1772], John Thomson (ed.), Vol. 1, Edinburgh, Blackwood; London, Underwood, 1827, p. 74.

50 William Cullen, *Lectures on Materia Medica*, Dublin, Whitestone, 1761, quoted in Huneman, 'Animal Economy', p. 263.

Meanwhile, other 'sexual scientists' were looking to physics and emerging theories of bioelectricity for a materialist explanation of the vital economy and its currency of desire. The liquidity preference that Tissot's generation inherited from medieval and Renaissance humoral medicine (with its four key fluids: blood, phlegm, black and yellow bile) would have a diluted legacy in Freud's 'hydraulic' model of the libido, but not before another, invisible 'fluid' – electricity – had been called upon to explain the *causa vitae* and fill the role of vital currency in the animal economy.[51] As early as the 1740s, William Watson, a fellow of London's Royal Society, announced his discovery of a 'fluid' that he called 'electrical ether'; in 1778, Anton Mesmer was propounding his theory of an invisible 'animal magnetic fluid' to Parisian audiences; his contemporary, P.J.C. Maudyt de la Verenne, lecturing to Paris's Royal Society on electrical therapies, was demonstrating the properties of what he called the 'weightless fluid' of electricity; while Benjamin Franklin, who knew that water vapour could conduct electricity, had developed a natural philosophy of weather based on his empirically defined 'electric fluid'.[52] By the 1840s, the American sexual revolutionary, heretical preacher and 'Bible Communist' John Humphrey Noyes would be calling on physics, economics and theology, simultaneously, to explain the invisible currency exchanged in both sexual intercourse and the divine afflatus, concluding that it must be a 'spiritual *fluid*; having many of the properties of caloric, light, electricity, galvanism and magnetism'.[53]

51 The concept of 'animal electricity' as the *causa vitae* is said to have been first proposed by Luigi Galvani in 1791, only to be refuted two years later by Alessandro Volta. See Robert O. Becker and Gary Selden, *The Body Electric: Electromagnetism and the Foundation of Life*, New York, William Morrow, 1985, p. 63. However, my researches indicate that others, including William Watson, proposed it several decades before Galvani did.

52 Watson and Mesmer are discussed in detail, below, in chapter 6. The idea of electricity as the *causa vitae* has also been attributed to John Abernethy, *An Inquiry into the Probability and Rationality of Mr. Hunter's Theory of Life, Being the Subject of the First Two Anatomical Lectures Delivered before the Royal College of Surgeons of London in the Year 1814*, London, Longman & Co., 1814.

53 John Humphrey Noyes, *The Berean: A Manual for the Help of Those Who Seek the Faith of the Primitive Church*, Putney, VT, The Spiritual Magazine, 1847, p. 65. See below, chapter 6, for further discussion of electrical theories of sex.

How such hypotheses were translated into economic theories of electrifying sex between the eighteenth and twentieth centuries will be examined in chapter six; suffice it, here, to note the lasting influence of Tissot's 'austerity' economics on the thinking of vitalists and mechanists who had long ago abandoned his attachment to 'humours' in favour of an invisible, 'spiritual' currency of desire in the form of electricity.

Noyes's contemporary, Orson Squire Fowler (1809-87), a self-styled 'sexual scientist' and prolific author of pseudo-medical tracts on sexual health and physiology, insisted that so potent and yet rarefied was the vital currency of electricity that it could be exchanged between the sexes through the air, without bodily contact.[54] Like his admirer Walt Whitman, author of 'I Sing the Body Electric' (1855), Fowler celebrated sexual energy and pleasure as the life-force at its most intense, and he insisted that 'only something ethereal, interior, spiritual, could possibly cause or account for all the phenomena of gender, or anything like all of Nature's transmitting facts. Life is mainly mental, not physical; spiritual, not anatomical. Electricity is its chief organic agent and motor'.[55] Fowler went on to explain how 'this galvanic current', or 'sexual electricity', flows and exchanges in sexual attraction, conception, reproduction and the animal economy in general;[56] however, despite his enthusiasm for erotic exchange, he could reproduce Tissot's calculations of the cost ratios involved in sexual spending, a century after *L'Onanisme*, in his account of how onanists' wastage of electrical current 'soon renders them vital bankrupts': masturbation's 'drain on the vital forces is indeed terrible. Semen contains forty times more vital force than an equal amount of red blood right from the heart'.[57]

The tenacity of austerity economics in sexual science would still be evident in a medical manual of 1902, Moritz Platen's *Livre d'Or*

54 Orson Squire Fowler, *Creative and Sexual Science; or, Manhood, Womanhood, and Their Mutual Interrelations; Love, its Laws, Power, Etc. … as Taught By Phrenology and Physiology*, Philadelphia, E. Gately & Co., n.d. [1870]), pp. 188, 191-92.

55 Ibid., pp. 188-89.

56 Ibid., pp. 191-92.

57 Ibid., pp. 882, 891.

de la Santé, which transposed Tissot's explanation of coition as mutually beneficial exchange and onanism as wasted expenditure into an early twentieth-century register by substituting electromagnetic energy for Tissot's sweat and semen:

> A fact which is worth taking into account is that, during normal coition, a magnetic compensation occurs between the man and the woman. This magnetic contact, which culminates, at the height of the voluptuous sensation, in a shock of the entire body similar to that of an electric discharge, increases the vital force of the two partners in the sexual act. The conditions are quite different in the case of the solitary onanist who, lacking the magnetic compensation afforded by a sexual partner, weakens his vital force with each repetition of the act.[58]

With psychoanalysis's 'libidinal economy', the presumed currency of desire would be further abstracted from the tangible or empirically verifiable, despite Freud's own loyalty to the anti-vitalist, mechanistic mindset of his medical mentors. In classical and medieval Latin usage, *libido* (from *libere*, to please or be pleasing) meant desire, passion, lust, sexual appetite; hence 'libidinous', 'libidinosity' and 'libidinist', terms in common usage since the Renaissance. But the incorporation of 'libido' into medical discourse and its investment with an aura of scientific precision only occurred in the 1880s and 1890s in the work of the founding fathers of sexology, Richard Krafft-Ebing, Iwan Bloch and Albert Moll (author of *Libido Sexualis: Studies in the Psychosexual Laws of Love Verified by Clinical Sexual Case Histories*).[59] In his groundbreaking work of psychiatric nosology, *Psychopathia Sexualis* (first published in 1886), Krafft-Ebing took over the Latin term, untranslated, as simply a synonym of sexual desire, understood as a

58 P.M. Platen, *Livre d'Or de la Santé*, Dr Léon Deschamps (trans. and expanded), *Volume spéciale*, Paris: Bong & Cie, 1902, p. 602.

59 Albert Moll's *Untersuchungen über die Libido sexualis* was published in 1897-98 and translated into English, in 1933, as *Libido Sexualis: Studies in the Psychosexual Laws of Love Verified by Clinical Sexual Case Histories*, New York, American Ethnological Press, 1933.

quantitatively and qualitatively variable entity with a basis in physiology. As Krafft-Ebing saw it, the quantity of an individual's libido could normally be explained in terms of the state of development or atrophy of their 'generative organs' or 'generative glands'. Libido thus appeared to name something measurable, not least because a sufficient increase in the *quantity* of a subject's libido could produce a *qualitative* change – from normal to perverse, healthy to pathological (as Krafft-Ebing put it: 'with excessive sexual desire all manner of perversity of sexual acts become possible'.[60]) It was this quantitative character of libido that would enable it to function, like money, as a term of universal equivalence.

Both Krafft-Ebing and Moll construed libido as central to health and hence to social wellbeing, thereby staking a claim to centrality in biopolitics for their new discipline of sexology. Undertaking, like others before them, to transfer the study of sexuality from the moral and criminal domains to the medico-scientific domain, and privileging the pleasure principle of libidinal spending over the 'reproductive imperative' in their explanations of the human sexual economy, the sexologists depicted sexual desire as a powerful, universal (genderless), often unconscious force, both socially constructive and potentially destructive, which can build up in the mind-body and either be discharged compulsively or spent in moderation to conserve the body's vitality and fertility. The underlying logic of this economic ideal of equilibrium between accumulation and expenditure, input and output, which seems to contradict the capitalist practice of maximal hoarding of resources as the ultimate guarantee of security and pleasure, was spelt out by the sexologists' contemporaries, the neoclassical economists, in the theory of 'marginal utility', which holds that a commodity is most useful and hence valuable when it satisfies a need and its utility/value steadily diminishes once satiety has been achieved, rendering further accumulation pointless.[61]

60 R. v. Krafft-Ebing, *Psychopathia Sexualis with especial reference to Antipathic Sexual Instinct: A Medico-Forensic Study*, translation of the tenth German edition, London, Rebman, 1899, p. 64.

61 The parallels between neoclassical economics, sexology and psychoanalysis are discussed, below, in chapter 2.

Freud acknowledged his large debt to the sexologists at the start of his seminal 'Three Essays on the Theory of Sexuality' (1905), going on to explain that biology posits 'a "sexual instinct", on the analogy of the instinct of nutrition, that is of hunger', and while 'everyday language possesses no counterpart to the word "hunger" ... science makes use of the word "libido" for that purpose'.[62] In so far as Freud defined 'instinct' itself as 'energy', his explanation of libido as 'the energy of the sexual instincts'[63] was tautological (much like Bergson's concept of *élan vital*, of which the biologist Julian Huxley remarked that it was no better an explanation of life than explaining the operation of a railway engine by its *élan locomotif*, or 'locomotive momentum').[64] However, like the 'energy' conceptualised by physicists in the 1840s and 1850s, Freud's libido could exhibit multiple, seemingly disparate properties. Sometimes it behaves like Armstrong's 'blood', Tissot's 'seminal fluid' and Bergson's 'current of life' or 'élan vital': libido is a liquid that can flow, be channelled, dammed up, or overflow. When it fails to find an outlet, Freud explained, libido can behave 'like a stream whose main bed becomes blocked. It proceeds to fill up collateral channels which hitherto had been empty'.[65]

At other times, Freudian libido exhibits the properties of money, being capable of investment, expenditure, profit-making or loss, saving or squandering. It was primarily on his theory of what he called 'the economy of the mind' and 'the economics of the libido' that Freud staked psychoanalysis's claim to 'scientific' credibility.[66]

62 Sigmund Freud, 'Three Essays on the Theory of Sexuality', *Standard Edition of the Complete Psychological Works of Sigmund Freud*, James Strachey (ed.), Vol. 7, London, Vintage, 2001, p. 135.

63 Sigmund Freud, 'Beyond the Pleasure Principle', *Standard Edition of the Complete Psychological Works of Sigmund Freud*, Vol. 18, p. 51.

64 Julian Huxley, *Essays of a Biologist*, New York, Alfred A. Knopf, 1923, p. 33. Molière parodied the same epistemological fallacy in *Le Malade imaginaire* by having a quack answer the question, 'Why does opium cause sleep?' with 'Because of its soporific power'.

65 Freud, 'Three Essays on the History of Sexuality', p. 133.

66 See, e.g., Sigmund Freud, 'The Unconscious' (1915), *Standard Edition of the Complete Psychological Works of Sigmund Freud*, Vol. 14 p. 181; and 'Psycho-Analysis' (1926), *Standard Edition of the Complete Psychological Works of Sigmund Freud*, Vol. 20, pp. 265-66.

He was confident that physiology would sooner or later prove the truth of his psychological hypotheses by grounding his 'theory of mental functioning' in a 'sort of economics of nerve-force' based on quantitative measurements of neuronal energy.[67] The received view of Freud's libidinal economy is that he based it exclusively on hypotheses derived from his study of the 'hard sciences' of neurobiology and physics, more specifically, from the 'physicalist physiology' promulgated by Vienna's Helmholtz School of Medicine in the 1840s-70s.[68] For a six-year period Freud had been a student of the physician Ernst Brücke who, with his colleagues Herman Helmholtz and Emil du Bois-Reymond in the late 1830s and 1840s, contested vitalism with the physicalist thesis that the only forces operative in an organism are 'the common physio-chemical ones', forces that would become synonymous with the newly-forming abstraction of 'energy'. Helmholtz himself pioneered what would become the first law of thermodynamics – the law of the conservation and transformation of energy – in his influential essay 'The Conservation of Force: A Physical Memoir' (1847) and he was a key figure in arguing the case that the same laws apply to animate beings as to inanimate matter, although his essay 'The Application of the Law of the Conservation of Force to Organic Nature' (1861) left unresolved the question of whether life should be simply equated with energy, whether there is any essential difference between the vital and the physical. By the 1890s, the Russian psychologist Nicolas von Grot and the Austrian Freud were extending the Helmholtzian conception of force-as-energy, subject to the law of conservation and transformation, to the concept of 'psychic energy', subject to the same law. In von

67 See Sigmund Freud, *The Origins of Psychoanalysis: Letters to Wilhelm Fliess, Drafts and Notes, 1887–1902*, Marie Bonaparte, Anna Freud and Ernst Kris (eds), New York, Basic Books, 1954, pp. 119-20: 'I am plagued by two ambitions: to see how the theory of mental functioning takes shape if quantitative considerations, a sort of economics of nerve-force, are introduced into it; and secondly, to extract from psychopathology what may be of profit to normal psychology'.

68 See, e.g., Frank J. Sulloway, *Freud, Biologist of the Mind: Beyond the Psychoanalytic Legend*, Cambridge, MA, Harvard University Press, 1992, pp. 62-69.

Grot's words: 'The concept of psychic energy is as much justified in science as that of physical energy, and psychic energy has just as many quantitative measurements and different forms as has physical energy'.[69]

The nineteenth-century recourse to physics and economics for credibility in psychological matters has an obvious legacy in psychoanalysis, with its ambition to vest a hermeneutics of mental phenomena with the authority of a natural science. In the 1920s, C.G. Jung attempted a systematic application of the laws of classical thermodynamics to the concept of libido in his long and laboured essay, 'On Psychical Energy', concluding that the first and third laws – of energy conservation, transformation and entropy – could, indeed, be applied to the psyche understood as 'a relatively closed system'[70] (whereas others had argued that the law of entropy is inapplicable to mental energy precisely because the psyche, like the body, is an open system). Describing the concept of libido as a subcategory of 'bio-energy' and as akin in meaning to Aristotle's '*horme*', Schopenhauer's 'will' and Bergson's '*élan vital*', Jung postulated that libido and physical energy were simply different forms of the same, elusive thing – 'energy' itself being 'a hypostasised concept', an a priori logical postulate or a 'concept abstracted from experience'.[71] Jung also argued that disinvestment of libido in one part of the vital economy means that an equal 'sum of libido' or 'an equivalent value [will] spring up elsewhere', and the forms that such a re-invested 'libido-sum' may take elsewhere are multiple.[72] Psyches, he proposed, should thus be viewed as 'systems of energy susceptible of unlimited exchangeability under

69 Nicolas Von Grot, 'Die Begriffe der Seele und der Psychischen Energie in der Psychologie' (the terms of the soul and psychic energy in psychology), *Archiv fur systematische Philosophie,* IV (1898), quoted in C.G. Jung, 'On Psychical Energy', *Contributions to Analytical Psychology,* H.G. and Cary F. Baynes (trans.), London, Kegan Paul, Trench, Trubner, 1928, p. 5.

70 Jung, 'On Psychical Energy', pp. 27-28. For a discussion of attempts to correlate Freud's theory of the death instinct with the second law of thermodynamics (the law of entropy), see Sulloway, *Freud, Biologist of the Mind,* pp. 406–7.

71 Jung, 'On Psychical Energy', pp. 17, 30-33.

72 Ibid., p. 20.

the principle of equivalence' and capable of 'appear[ing] in the forms of sexual, vital, mental, moral "energy"'.[73] So persuasive was the explanatory power of the laws of thermodynamics and the science of the steam engine, that motor of the Industrial Revolution from which they were largely derived, that Jung proposed interpreting not just the psyche and the body but 'culture' itself as a 'machine' that functions as a 'converter of energy' – all of them, he said, are 'machines that make use of natural potential in order to produce work'.[74] What Jung called 'machines' in the 1920s, Jean-François Lyotard in the 1970s would call 'dispositifs' (set-ups, apparatuses, investments) in his book *Economie Libidinale*, in which he described everything from bodies, theories and works of art to social institutions and systems of financial regulation as *dispositifs* for ordering or disordering the energies of the people involved in them.[75]

For Freud, by contrast, libido could not be just *any* psychical energy. Complaining that Jung 'water[s] down the meaning of the concept of libido by equating it with psychical instinctual force in general',[76] Freud insisted that libido was a distinctively sexual form of psychic energy, synonymous with sexual desire, and traceable to 'a special chemistry of the sexual function' located in the thyroid gland and 'puberty gland', in which 'special chemical substances are produced ... [and] are then taken up in the bloodstream and cause particular parts of the central nervous system to be charged with sexual tension'.[77] Among other things, then, the 'flow' of Freud's libido is a flow of (as yet unidentified) chemicals through the bloodstream. Optimistic that the biochemistry of libido would one day be established experimentally, Freud began his 1895 manifesto, 'Project for a Scientific Psychology', by declaring: 'The

73 Ibid., pp. 23, 31.

74 Ibid., pp. 45-46.

75 Jean-François Lyotard, *Economie Libidinale*, Paris, Les Éditions de Minuit, 1974.

76 Freud, 'Three Essays on the Theory of Sexuality', p. 218.

77 Ibid. pp. 218, 215. In 1925 Freud insisted: 'I gave the name of *libido* to the energy of the sexual instincts and to that form of energy alone'. Sigmund Freud, 'An Autobiographical Study', *Standard Edition of the Complete Psychological Works of Sigmund Freud*, Vol. 20, London, Vintage, 2001, p. 35

intention is to furnish a psychology that shall be a natural science: that is, to represent psychical processes as quantitatively determinate states of specifiable material particles ...'[78] And yet neither the particles nor the quantities could as yet be specified. Freud would clarify his own usage of 'libido' in 1921 by explaining: 'Libido is an expression taken from the theory of the emotions. We call by that name the energy, regarded as a quantitative magnitude (though not at present actually measurable), of those instincts which have to do with all that may be comprised under the word "love". The nucleus of what we mean by love naturally consists (and this is what is commonly called love, and what the poets sing of) in sexual love with sexual union as its aim'.[79] Though they disagreed on its definition, Freud and Jung agreed on libido's affinity with the physicists' 'energy' in respect of the first law of thermodynamics: psychoanalysis as both a theory of mind and a diagnostic system rests precisely on the hypothesis that libidinal energy can undergo any number of metamorphoses – known as 'displacements', 'sublimations', 'transferences' and 'conversions' – into a spectrum of mental and physical behaviours, or 'symptoms', ranging from the normal to the pathological, which the analyst can trace back to their common origins in the 'libidinal economy'. As Freud's 'best pupil', the Berlin analyst Karl Abraham, pointed out: 'no one has appreciated as much as Freud the capacity of the libido to transform itself'.[80] Frustrated in its primary, sexual goal (coupling and spending), libido could manifest in a plethora of seemingly disparate activities, and its diminution or increase in one activity could be explained by its increase or diminution in another. Freud would thus 'reach the

78 Sigmund Freud, 'Project for a Scientific Psychology', *Standard Edition of the Complete Psychological Works of Sigmund Freud*, Vol. 1, p. 295.

79 Sigmund Freud, 'Group Psychology and the Analysis of the Ego', *Standard Edition of the Complete Psychological Works of Sigmund Freud*, Vol. 18, p. 90.

80 Karl Abraham, 'Review of C.G. Jung's *Versuch einer Darstellung de Psychoanalytischen Theories*' (1914), in Karl Abraham, *Clinical Papers and Essays on Psychoanalysis*, Vol. 2, Hilda Abraham (ed.), Hilda Abraham and D.R. Ellison (trans.), New York, Basic Books, 1955, p. 105. The American Psychiatric Association's *Diagnostic and Statistical Manual of Mental Disorders* implicitly tipped its cap to the thermodynamic sources of Freud's libidinal logic when it replaced the stigmatised diagnosis of 'hysteria' with that of 'conversion disorders'.

idea of a quantity of libido ... whose production, increase or diminution, distribution and displacement should afford us the possibilities of explaining the psychosexual phenomena observed'.[81] Claiming to have discovered a unified theory of the mind–body grounded in libidinal economy, he concluded that 'It should be the task of a libido theory of neurotic and psychotic disorders to express all the observed phenomena and inferred processes in terms of the economics of the libido'.[82]

The paradoxes or contradictions in Freud's libidinal logic are apparent. On one hand, he narrows down the concept of 'libido' to a specifically sexual or erotic energy, emanating from certain 'glands' that charge specific parts of the 'central nervous system' with 'sexual tension'; on the other hand, he multiplies the possible expressions or manifestations of libido to include any number of forms of its 'expenditure' or 're-investment' in a multitude of physical and mental activities, ranging from the sexual to the non-sexual, the normal to the polymorphously perverse (Freud stipulates that 'the energy which the ego employs is desexualized'.[83]) As Jacques-Alain Miller summarises Freud's libidinal economics: 'Libido is a quantity which cannot be calculated, but whose introduction enables us to equate a wide variety of activities and behavior – eating, shitting, thinking and writing too, since sublimation also attests to libido ... Freud brings about an extraordinary extension of the concept of libido and of sexual gratification which we might have thought reserved to the sexual'.[84]

Like money, then, Freud's 'libido' functions as a medium of universal exchange, establishing relations of equivalence between otherwise radically disparate phenomena in the animal economy. The common currency of libido makes the apparently incommensurable (shitting, writing) commensurable. For Freud, making

81 Freud, 'Three Essays on the Theory of Sexuality', p. 217.
82 Ibid., p. 218.
83 Sigmund Freud, 'Inhibitions, Symptoms and Anxiety', *Standard Edition of the Complete Psychological Works of Sigmund Freud*, Vol. 20, p. 161.
84 Jacques-Alain Miller, 'On Perversion', in Richard Feldstein, Bruce Fink and Maire Jaanus (eds), *Reading Seminars I and II: Lacan's Return to Freud*, Albany, NY, SUNY Press, 1996, p. 312.

economic sense of the mind–body means applying not just the laws of thermodynamics but the laws of the market – equivalence and exchangeability – to the phenomena in which libido is said to be invested or spent. And, indeed, Freud relies often enough on monetary explanations of what he called 'the domestic economy of the mind' to suggest that he was drawing as much on his enthusiasm for the Enlightenment political economists, Adam Smith and David Hume, as on his knowledge of Helmholtzian neurophysiology in elaborating his theories of libidinal economy.[85] Freud had admired Hume's political economy, in particular, since his student days and he regularly discussed 'money matters' with his economist brother Alexander, who lectured on trade policy and tariff theory as a professor at the Imperial and Royal Export Academy, precursor of the Vienna University of Economics. Famous for his lifelong preoccupation with money-making, Freud once confided to his colleague Wilhelm Fliess: 'My mood … depends very strongly on my earnings. Money is laughing gas to me'.[86]

There are frequent slippages in Freud's usage of the German words 'Ökonomie' and 'ökonomisch' (from Greek *oikonomia*: 'management of household resources') between their ergonomic and monetary meanings – between 'economy' as a (closed) system of energy, and 'economics' as the branch of knowledge concerned with the production, consumption and transfer of wealth. Psychic processes, Freud insisted, should be evaluated in terms of 'gain' and 'loss'. In *The Interpretation of Dreams* he argued that repressed sexual desire can best be understood as a form of unproductive 'capital', or sleeping asset, that requires an 'entrepreneur' with 'initiative' to invest it in a profitable enterprise;[87] and in his paper on 'Inhibitions', he argued that 'when the ego is involved in a

85 Freud uses the phrase 'domestic economy of the mind' in 'Fragment of an Analysis of a Case of Hysteria' ('Dora'), *Standard Edition of the Complete Psychological Works of Sigmund Freud*, Vol. 7, p. 43.

86 Sigmund Freud, *Complete Letters of Sigmund Freud to Wilhelm Fliess 1887*–1904, Jeffrey Masson (ed.), Cambridge, MA, Harvard University Press, 1985, p. 374. See, below, my discussion of Freud and the Viennese 'poorhouse neurosis' in chapter 2.

87 Sigmund Freud, *The Interpretation of Dreams*, *Standard Edition of the Complete Psychological Works of Sigmund Freud*, Vol. 5, p. 561.

particularly difficult task', such as suppressing 'a continual flood of sexual phantasies', 'it loses so much of the energy at its disposal that it has to cut down the expenditure of it at many points at once. It is in the position of a speculator whose money has become tied up in his various enterprises'.[88] Monetary terms and exempla recur throughout Freud's clinical and metapsychological writings, and the first-generation analysts had such frequent recourse to economics to explain the nature and behaviour of libido that, by 1911, Karl Abraham could cite 'the identification of libido and money – of sexual and pecuniary "power" – with which we are so familiar', to explain why loss of libido in states of depression commonly manifests in fear of bankruptcy or impoverishment: 'whereas other people can invest their libido in the objects of the external world he [the depressive] has no such capital to expend'.[89]

Many commentators since Freud and Abraham have made best sense of the concept of libido by parsing it as money. Investigating the libidinal economy of groups in the 1960s, for example, the sociologist Philip Slater reflected on Freud's model of libidinal energy being transformed from somatic sources (chemical and cellular components) into 'psychic energy' in the ego, that 'from this it would seem to follow that libido is "psychic" energy only after it is drawn into the "reservoir" of the ego and assimilated to that structure, just as ... money becomes public only when it is collected in a governmental treasury'. What, then, happens to libidinal wealth when an individual dies? Appearances to the contrary, Slater argued, neither energy nor wealth can 'die': when the organism or psyche of an individual dies, libido merely 'reverts to its somatic components, ultimately to cellular and chemical components. The loss seems total, so impressive are the accomplishments of organic structures: we are similarly impressed with the way in which a money economy collapses when the political

88 Sigmund Freud, *Inhibitions, Symptoms and Anxiety*, *Standard Edition of the Complete Psychological Works of Sigmund Freud*, Vol. 20, p. 90.

89 Karl Abraham, 'Notes on the Psycho-analytical Investigation and Treatment of Manic-Depressive Insanity and Allied Conditions' (1911), *Selected Papers on Psychoanalysis* (1927), New York, Basic Books, 1953, p. 148. The German word translated here as 'power' is *Vermögen*: capital, wealth, capacity, potency.

entity which supports it is dissolved. Yet wealth does not vanish, but only becomes latent and fragmented, and the same is true of libidinal energy'.[90]

Libidinal economy is today sometimes distinguished from, and even opposed to, political economy, as it was by Lyotard in his iconoclastic *Economie Libidinale* (1974), in which he disavowed the Marxism and Freudianism that had shaped his political philosophy before the May 1968 uprising and argued for an analysis of the texts of Freudianism and Marxism – as of economic and class politics – in terms of the 'libidinal intensities' that could be sensed in them, rather than their logics of representation.[91] But 'libidinal economy' is also sometimes used to refer to a recent stage in the development of capitalist biopower in which the primary resource that corporations trade in and governments must manage is *affect*, in the so-called 'attention economy'. This is how the French philosopher Bernard Stiegler uses the term, offering his analyses of mass-mediated libidinal economy to the European Union as a foundation for what he proposes should be its defining political economy and constitution, which he says should aim for political control of 'the technologies of thought' and their associated industries in ways that will put them 'in the service of individuation, thereby reversing the current tendency towards a loss of individuality/ation'.[92] In his essay 'Pharmacology of Desire', Stiegler undertakes to rethink the relationship between economics and psychoanalysis from a twenty-first-century perspective, following the penetration of the global economy by a psychoanalytically-informed marketing industry whose exercise of 'psychopower' has turned libidinal dis-investment into the norm. Stiegler stresses that consumer culture has produced an economy of disposability and disinvestment, in which the goal is not the satisfaction of desire or its investment in an object, but the production of an ever-restless, unsated desire that no sooner focuses on one object/commodity

90 Philip E. Slater, 'On Social Regression', *American Sociological Review*, 28, 3 (June, 1963): 344-45.

91 See my discussion of *Économie Libidinale* in chapter 4.

92 Bernard Stiegler, 'Constitution and Individuation', *Ars Industrialis*: http://arsindustrialis.org/node/2927.

than it must move on to another. Attention-deficit disorders are the characteristic pathology of this culture of disinvestment, in everything from Internet browsing to financial speculation and derivatives trading. Consumerist marketing and information technology produce a restless attention or desire that can be channelled and packaged by mass-media technologies and marketed as itself a commodity, for sale to big brands and e-platform providers. Characterising this state of affairs as 'a libidinal dis-economy', Stiegler explains it as 'a destruction of the libido as the power of binding the drives'. Inflecting Freud's theory of the evolutionary origins of repression and sublimation with his own theories of 'prosthesis' and 'technics', Stiegler contends apocalyptically that the 'industrial exploitation' of libidinal economy 'through the use of the psychotechnologies of psychopower' can 'destroy' that economy, indeed, destroy desire itself and hence individuality, in so far as we are individuated by the singularity of our desires. Stiegler warns that the 'self-destructive character' of the capitalist 'libidinal dis-economy' has both psychopathological and sociopathological consequences, threatening the disintegration of community (with its dependence on binding, intergenerational relationships based on idealisation and identification) and, with it, 'our economic ruination', or the catastrophic destruction of 'the capitalist libidinal economy' as such.[93] No Lyotard, Stiegler seems anxious to contribute his understanding of libidinal economics to preserving a fast-disappearing stage of capitalism.

Like most uses of the concept of 'desire' in post-Lacanian, post-Deleuzean theory, Stiegler's usage of 'libido' has strayed a long way from the specificity and 'scientificity' with which Freud and Jung attempted to vest the term when grappling with the question of psychosexual energy's relationship with the thermodynamic concept of energy in the 1920s. In Slater's gloss on group libidinal economy, quoted above, the relationship posited between libido and wealth seems to be merely analogical; indeed, the very notion

93 Bernard Stiegler, 'Pharmacology of Desire: Drive-Based Capitalism and Libidinal Dis-economy', in David Bennett (ed.), *Loaded Subjects: Psychoanalysis, Money and the Global Financial Crisis*, London: Lawrence & Wishart, 2012, pp. 232-45.

of libidinal economy may strike sceptics as resting on nothing more than a forced analogy between sexuality and money, between the 'animal economy' and the wealth economy. But the links between energetics and economics are more literal than analogical, as demonstrated by the pivotal role of the steam engine in generating the wealth of the Industrial Revolution – and providing Jung with a model of the mind. In a sense, we owe the nineteenth-century abstraction 'energy' to the steam engine in so far as it depended on the discovery of how to convert one form of 'energy' (heat) into another (steam pressure) and another (mechanical momentum). Much of the refinement of the laws of energy-conservation and transformation in the 1840s and 1850s derived from attempts to maximise the efficiency of the steam engine, by minimising its heat-loss, in order to maximise profits. Work-power is earning-capacity, and efficiency – or more output for the same input – is profit.

If the definition of physical energy as the ability to perform work is applied to the animal economy, then 'life' is defined as the capacity for work, and the individual becomes understandable as an enterprise or 'economy', subject to economic laws or 'imperatives', such as the imperative of productivity, a 'productive life'. As Howard Caygill has pointed out: 'the work of the definition of energy emerged from the same context as industrial wage labour and is not inconsistent with the productivism of the capitalist mode of production and with the view of the body as an analogue of the engine understood above all as a vehicle for the performance of work'; 'indeed, the assumption that to live is to do work informs modern economic, social and political institutions ... [W]ork understood in terms of the product of force, mass and distance does not differ in essence from work as the accomplishment of wage labour'.[94] (The equation of life with work is not exclusively 'modern', of course; it informs the Judaeo-Christian creation myth in *Genesis*'s account of God cursing Adam, Eve and their offspring with life-as-work.)

And yet, for all Freud's and Jung's efforts at forging literal links

94 Howard Caygill, 'Life and Energy', *Theory, Culture & Society* 24, 19 (2007): 20-21.

between libido, thermodynamics, economics, the work ethic and money, there is a sense in which the concept of libido could only ever be mythical and the language of libidinal economy only ever figurative. Like the 'life' and 'desire' for which it functions as a synonym, libido is ubiquitous and yet invisible, knowable only in its effects, not 'in itself', and hence only representable metonymically or metaphorically. Everywhere manifest and nowhere measurable or identifiable *in se*, libido performs the essentially mythological role of a *primum mobile* – as Jacques Lacan concluded when spelling out the epistemological implications of the term in his seminar on 'The Ego in Freud's Theory':

> Libido allows one to speak of desire in terms which involve a relative objectification. It is, if you wish, a quantitative measurement. A quantity which you don't know how to measure, whose nature you don't know, but which you always assume to be there ... You assume an undifferentiated quantitative unit susceptible of entering into relations of equivalence.[95]

But, Lacan continues: 'There is a fundamental ambiguity in the use we make of the word "desire". Sometimes we objectify it – and we have to do so, if only to talk about it. On the contrary, sometimes we locate it as the primitive term in relation to any objectification'; for 'the desire in question is prior to any kind of conceptualisation – every conceptualisation stems from it'.[96] Lacan concludes: 'In the end, at the existential level, we can only talk about the libido satisfactorily in a mythical way',[97] because, in his reading of Freud, libido is the prime mover or afflatus, prior to any objectification or subjectivation; it is the desire that brings all objects and subjects into being, since we can only desire what we lack and that lack/desire is what opens up the gap between subject and object:

95 Jacques Lacan, *The Seminar of Jacques Lacan, Book II: The Ego in Freud's Theory and in the Technique of Psychoanalysis, 1954–1955*, Jacques-Alain Miller (ed.), Sylvana Tomaselli (trans.) with notes by John Forrester, New York and London, W.W. Norton, 1991, p. 221.

96 Ibid., p. 225.

97 Ibid., p. 227.

> [Freudianism] starts by postulating a world of desire. It postulates it prior to any kind of experience, prior to any considerations concerning the world of appearances and the world of essences ... The Freudian world isn't a world of things, it isn't a world of beings, it is a world of desire as such ... Desire, a function central to all human experience, is the desire for nothing nameable. And at the same time this desire lies at the origin of every variety of animation.[98]

As we have seen, Freud, like other animal economists before him, hoped and expected that one day the biochemistry of desire would be discovered experimentally, thereby anchoring his psychology in the more 'literal' truth of natural science; but he could also accept that the discipline of psychology was condemned forever to work with metaphors. In *Beyond the Pleasure Principle* he acknowledged that, even at their most scientific, psychologists 'are obliged to operate with the figurative language peculiar to psychology' and that without it 'we could not otherwise describe the processes in question at all, and indeed could not have become aware of them'. Speculating that 'the deficiencies in our description would probably vanish if we were already in a position to replace the psychological terms with physiological or chemical ones', Freud quickly qualified that hope with another reflection: 'It is true that they too are only part of a figurative language; but it is one with which we have long been familiar'.[99] For all his positivism, then, Freud seems capable of sharing Nietzsche's celebrated insight that all language, however scientific, is inherently metaphorical and that what passes for literal truth-statement at a given time is simply dead metaphor – or, as Nietzsche himself tropically put it, defaced coinage:

> What then is truth? A mobile army of metaphors, metonyms, and anthropomorphisms ... which after long use seem firm, canonical, and obligatory to a people: truths are illusions about which one has forgotten that is what they are; metaphors which

98 Ibid., pp. 222-23.
99 Sigmund Freud, *Beyond the Pleasure Principle*, p. 60.

> are worn out and without sensuous power; coins which have lost their pictures and now matter only as metal, no longer as coins.[100]

The resurrection of dead metaphors, or the resuscitation of unconscious ones, with a view to ensuring that they no longer 'seem firm, canonical, and obligatory', is one way of characterising the broad aim of the chapters that follow. There are several existing studies of key metaphors Freud employed to explain the project of psychoanalysis and the mental processes it analyses – metaphors of archaeology,[101] surgery,[102] cartography,[103] writing,[104] forensic detection,[105] and the camera obscura[106] – but there has been no sustained study, hitherto, of how economic tropes have shaped theories of the mind-body and their links with both the business and the politics of sexual desire in consumer culture. The narratives developed in the following chapters seek to destabilise, by historicising, the language of what became identified in the early twentieth century as libidinal economy – a language that has sedimented as common sense in much of our thinking about ourselves as embodied subjects of desire, irrespective of our awareness or ignorance of psychoanalysis.

Any doubt that the tropes of libidinal economy have become 'firm, canonical, and obligatory to a people' can be quickly dispelled by browsing the public e-sphere with a couple of search terms

100 Friedrich Nietzsche, 'On Truth and Lie in an Extra-Moral Sense', *The Portable* Nietzsche, Walter Kaufmann (ed. and trans.), Harmondsworth, Penguin, 1976 [42-47], pp. 46-47.

101 See Donald P. Spence, *Narrative Truth and Historical Truth*, New York, W.W. Norton, 1984; R.H. Armstrong, 'The Archaeology of Freud's Reading', *International Review of Modernism*, 3, 1 (1999): 16-20.

102 Paul E. Stepansky, *Freud, Surgery, and the Surgeons*, New York, The Analytic Press, 1999.

103 Jim Hopkins, 'Psychoanalysis, Metaphor, and the Concept of Mind' (1999), in M. Levine (ed.), *The Analytic Freud*, London, Routledge, 2000.

104 Douwe Draaisma, *Metaphors of Memory: A History of Ideas About the Mind*, Cambridge, Cambridge UP, 1999.

105 Michael B. Buchholz (ed.), *Metaphernanalyse*, Göttingen: Vandenhoeck & Ruprecht, 1993.

106 Sarah Kofman, *Camera Obscura of Ideology*, Ithaca, NY, Cornell University Press, 1999.

(love+money, for example, or relationship+investment) that will conjure the countless advertisements for psychological goods and services promising to help us manage our libidinal-economic anxieties while reinforcing our self-images as responsible entrepreneurs of our libidinal capital, or desire. Consider just two, randomly selected examples, the first promoting the services of a self-styled emotional 'Baggage Reclaim' consultant –

> **Return On Investment** (ROI) within relationships refers to the ratio of what you've gained or lost against what you invested into a relationship. This is not about financial or material gain or loss. This is about **The Three Es: Emotion, Esteeem, and Energy**. If you're not generating a return on investment and at the very least breaking even, the balance of negativity is way out of whack and you are effectively throwing The Three Es at a bad investment that is not going to generate a return. It is very difficult for you to take the relationship out of negative equity – that rather uncomfortable place where your investment is now worth less than what it was when you started ...[107]

– and the second promoting the services of a self-styled 'healing facilitator', specialising in 'Healing Compulsive Spending':

> Money is love. Wherever you focus your energy is where love multiplies. Many people love to buy things, they love to spend money. There is nothing bad about spending money. Remember that when you do, you are focusing love ... Time is love too, as it is a focusing of your life force, of your love and your very essence ...[108]

107 Natalie Lue, 'Return On Investment in Relationships', 14 November 2007, *Baggage Reclaim*: http://www.baggagereclaim.co.uk/return-on-investment-in-relationships/ (accessed 20/01/2016) (emphases in original). Ms Lue introduces herself as a London-based relationship counsellor, blogger and author of the books, *Mr Unavailable and the Fallback Girl* and *The No Contact Rule*, which 'help people to offload their emotional baggage and reclaim themselves'.

108 Linda White Dove 'Healing "compulsive spending"', *New England Holistic*, http://www.neholistic.com/articles/0042.htm (accessed 19/10/04).

And so on.

Resurrecting dead metaphors or reanimating unconscious ones is akin to the function that the Russian Formalist critics attributed to literature: that of *ostranenie*, of defamiliarising or denaturalising the language of everyday communication and its representational paradigms, in order to foreground their artifice and conventionality (the contrary of the natural or inevitable), with a view to reopening to challenge and change habits of thought and expression that have sedimented in the cultural unconscious as second nature.[109] Having learned Viktor Shklovsky's term *ostranenie* during a visit to Moscow in 1935, Bertolt Brecht translated it as the *Verfremdungseffekt* (alienation-effect)[110] – the defining effect of modernist art – foreshadowing the tactics of postmodern anti-consumerist activists known as culture-jamming, guerrilla communication or 'subvertising', tactics that entail inhabiting the medium of communication (e.g., advertising) that they seek to scramble or decommission. The aim of this book is to denaturalise (Shklovsky would have said 'de-automatise') the language of libidinal economy and reopen it to critique by historicising, rather than parodying, it. Organised thematically around key *topoi* in the history of psychosexual economics, the chapters investigate moments when economistic models of subjectivity and desire seem to shift their status between the metaphoric and the literal and directly shape policies and practices in medicine, commerce and politics. Their investigations are interdisciplinary in two senses, in the obvious sense that they draw variously on psychology, medicine, economics, literature, philosophy and politics for their analyses of intellectual history, but also in the sense that they present something like an archaeology of the emergence, separation and interaction of certain discourses *as* disciplines, each with its distinctive criteria of truth and rationality, each addressing or

109 See Viktor Shklovskij, 'Art as Technique', in Julie Rivkin and Michael Ryan (eds) *Literary Theory: An Anthology*, Malden, Blackwell Publishing, 1998.

110 Brecht learned the term *ostranenie* from Pavel Tretyakov during a visit to Moscow in 1935 and translated it as *Verfremdungseffekt* in his 1936 essay, 'Alienation Effects in Chinese Acting', in J. Willet (ed. and trans.), *Brecht on Theatre: The Development of an Aesthetic*, London, Methuen, 1974, pp. 93-99.

projecting a distinctive 'subject', such as *homo œconomicus* or *homo psychologicus*.

The Nietzschean insistence that language is inherently figurative and literal truth simply moribund metaphor does not preclude different *degrees* of metaphoricity being perceptible at different historical moments. (To call a penis a 'yard' in the twenty-first century, for example, might seem hyperbolically metaphorical, whereas 'yard' had served as a literal naming of the organ for at least half a millennium before 1693, when *Blancard's Physical Dictionary* provided an English common-language definition of the arcane Latinate word, '*Penis*, the Yard, made up of two nervous Bodies, the Channel, Nut, Skin and Fore-Skin'.[111] 'Penis' itself was already metaphoric in so far as its original Latin meaning was 'tail'.) To suggest, for example, that Tissot or Noyes employed economic 'metaphors' to explain sexual physiology and psychology in the eighteenth or nineteenth centuries is to interpret their discourses anachronistically from the perspective of a later historical moment, following the 'disciplining' of discourse in the latter nineteenth century that constructed physiology, psychology, economics and physics as discrete sciences, each with its own professional credentials and distinctive discursive objects and subjects. As we shall see in chapter six, however, the tracts in which Noyes elaborated the Oneida Association's principles of 'free love' and 'Bible Communism' present a fascinating instance of a historical moment (and discursive matrix) in which not only could science and religion seem natural allies, rather than enemies, but the vocabularies of what we now distinguish as the disciplines of theology, thermodynamics, economics, sexology and political science could all cohabit in a single discourse, purporting to speak literal truths of one and the same human subject.

Metaphoricity becomes apparent, then, when a concept regarded as belonging to one discourse and subject is used to designate a different and disparate one, and such was the case with the discourses of *homo œconomicus* and *homo psychologicus* by the turn of the nineteenth century. 'Economic man', the isolated, rational,

111 See the *OED*'s definitions of 'penis'.

self-interested subject of neoclassical and neoliberal economics, was constructed by a systematic process of separating economic 'science' from political and psychological 'sciences' that began in John Stuart Mill's seminal essay 'On the Definition of Political Economy, and on the Method of Investigation proper to It' (1836). Mill's political-economic subject was a calculated fiction or abstraction, designed to bracket-out questions of culture, community and ethics that he deemed too complex for political economy to analyse. According to Mill's definition, political economy dealt with the human considered 'solely as a being who desires to possess wealth'; who can work out rationally how best to obtain it; who is averse to labour, desires luxury, and has a reproductive or sexual drive.[112] In other words, Mill's *homo œconomicus* travelled fairly light, unburdened by matters of conscience, sympathy, duty, religious scruple or public-spiritedness, let alone such psychological refinements as neuroses, perversions or psychoses. It was during the 1880s that Mill's critics put the term 'economic man' into circulation when disparaging his political economy for dealing (as one of them complained) 'not with real but with imaginary men – "economic men" … conceived simply as "money-making animals"'.[113] And yet it would be an even more psychologically impoverished version of Mill's 'economic man', stripped of all cultural and mental baggage except for a narrowly defined 'reason' and 'self-interest', that the neoclassical theorists would define as the proper subject of a 'scientific' economics in the late nineteenth and early twentieth centuries. The architects of marginal utility theory stipulated that the fundamental premise of political economy is that individuals act rationally on self-interest;[114] thus *homo œconomicus*, construed as a self-determining, tirelessly rational and self-interested calculator of the

112 J.S. Mill, 'On the Definition of Political Economy; and on the Method of Investigation Proper to It' (1836), *Essays on Some Unsettled Questions of Political Economy by John Stuart Mill*, London, Longmans, 1874, pp. 97, 99.

113 John Kells Ingram, *A History of Political Economy* (1888); New York, Augustus M. Kelley, 1967, p. 218, quoted in Joseph Persky, 'The Ethology of *Homo Economicus*', *Journal of Economic Perspectives,* 9, 2 (Spring 1995): 222.

114 William Stanley Jevons, *The Theory of Political Economy* (1871); London, Penguin, 1970, p. 90.

marginal utility of goods, became a subject whose appetite for consumption could be predicted mathematically with 'indifference curves'. Vilfredo Pareto could consequently insist that a 'pure political economy', based on rational-choice and discovered-preference principles capable of being modelled mathematically, had 'a great interest in relying as little as possible on the domain of psychology' and could attain 'the rigor of rational mechanics'.[115]

Meanwhile, psychoanalysis was defining itself as a science of the irrational. Psychology had been a branch of philosophy until the 1870s and was only constituted as an independent scientific discipline based on experimental principles when Wilhelm Wundt founded the first laboratory dedicated exclusively to psychological research in Leipzig in 1879. Ironically, the school of psychology most indebted to monetary concepts and committed to 'economising' our understanding of the subliminal layers of the mind that it claimed to be discovering – Freudian psychoanalysis – was also the school most intent on decoding 'money matters' as metaphorical 'sexual matters', while explaining the economy itself as a realm of illusion, neurosis, phantasy and psychopathology, unconsciously determined by infantile experiences of anal and genital eroticism.

For much of the last 150 years, then, *homo œconomicus* and *homo psychologicus* have been mutually indifferent subjects, following discrete evolutionary trajectories; hence the plausibility of viewing the language of libidinal economy as merely metaphorical, as simply drawing descriptive analogies between libido and capital, desire and money, that need not be taken too seriously. And yet, since concrete individuals must live the subjectivities of both *homo psychologicus* and *homo œconomicus* simultaneously or serially (harmoniously or contradictorily), the competition between their

115 Vilfredo Pareto, *Manual of Political Economy* (1909); New York, Kelley, 1971, Ch. 3, §36b. Cf. Luigino Bruni and Robert Sugden, 'The Road Not Taken: How psychology was removed from economics, and how it might be brought back', *The Economic Journal*, 117 (January 2007): 146-173. See also my discussion of attempts by behavioural economists to heal the historical rift between economics and psychology: '*Homo oeconomicus* vs *Homo psychologicus*: A Critique of Pure Reason in Economics and Psychoanalysis', in *Loaded Subjects: Psychoanalysis, Money and the Global Financial Crisis*, David Bennett (ed.), London, Lawrence & Wishart, 2012, pp. 7-33.

respective discourses for the authority to define who we are and how we inter-relate is all-too-serious.

Michel Houellebecq, that most doggedly melancholic libidinal economist of contemporary French letters, has remarked that 'Man, at a certain stage, needs metaphors and legends. Matter itself was a necessary myth, to put an end to God'.[116] Perhaps the Freudian myth of 'libido' and its 'economy' were necessary to put an end to Mesmer's myth of 'animal magnetism', which helped put an end to Tissot's myth of 'humours', which helped challenge the poetic tradition's myths of romantic love with a materialist science of eros, which helped to contest (when it didn't reinforce) the hegemony of religio-moral discourse on sexuality – the language of virtue and vice, sin and innocence, duty and depravity, love and lust, bestiality and godliness – with a secular, putatively scientific discourse in which physiology and economy were fused. But no discourse is inherently more literal or metaphorical than another, except history makes it so – by temporarily promoting one discourse to the rank of a master-discourse or metalanguage, authorised to speak the 'literal' or 'scientific' truth that others can only gesture toward figuratively or metaphorically.

As Bourdieu pointed out in 'The Essence of Neoliberalism': 'neoliberal discourse is not just one discourse among many. Rather, it is a "strong discourse" – the way psychiatric discourse is in an asylum ... It is so strong and so hard to combat only because it has on its side all of the forces of a world of relations of forces, a world that it contributes to making what it is'.[117] Bracketing the economy off from other social realities and explaining it 'purely' in terms of the rationality of the market, *while at the same time* promoting market discourse to the status of a metalanguage or general theory of social and psychical life, neoliberalism 'constructs, in reality, an economic system conforming to its description in pure theory'.[118]

116 Michel Houellebecq and Bernard-Henri Levy, *Public Enemies*, London, Atlantic Books, 2011, p. 144.

117 Bourdieu, 'The Essence of Neoliberalism'.

118 Ibid. 'Purity' is a by-word in the neoclassical tradition of economics. Maffeo Pantaleoni, one of the founders of 'pure economics', entitled his major work *Principii di Economia pura* (English translation: *Pure Economics*), which

The following chapters contribute to challenging the metalinguistic status of market discourse by researching the history of its penetration and permeation of our mind-body images, its role in forging our self-images as entrepreneurs of libidinal capital.

Most commentary on the idea of libidinal economy assumes that eroticising the economy is something that only post-Freudian intellectuals such as Georges Bataille and Lyotard do – it being one way of challenging the economists' own paradigms of 'rationality' and proposing other, more generous ways of looking at human exchange than the categories of 'utility' and 'interest' that dominate both classical political economy and neoclassical economics. But as the following chapters illustrate, the business and politics of eroticising the economy has a much longer history, to which thinkers as disparate as Tissot and Sade, Fourier and Parent-Duchâtelet, Marx and Gandhi, Reich and Marcuse have contributed, and any understanding of 'libidinal economy' today needs to take that history into account.

in turn inspired Vilfredo Pareto's stipulations that 'pure political economy' should dissociate itself from 'the domain of psychology'. See Vilfredo Pareto, *Manual of Political Economy* (1909); New York, Kelley, 1971, Ch. 3, §36b.

2

Consumer Culture and the Sovereign Spender: Sade, Freud, Bataille and Lawrence

'Erotic conduct', Georges Bataille tells us in his study of Sade, 'is the opposite of normal conduct as spending is the opposite of getting'. Glossing the rigorous anti-rationalism of the libertine doctrine, Bataille goes on:

> If we follow the dictates of reason we try to acquire all kinds of goods, we work in order to increase the sum of our possessions … use all means to get richer and to possess more. Our status in the social order is based on this sort of behaviour. But when the fever of sex seizes us we behave in the opposite way. We recklessly draw on our strength and sometimes in the violence of passion we squander considerable resources to no real purpose. … [W]e always want to be sure of the uselessness or ruinousness of our extravagance. We want to feel as remote from the world where thrift is the rule as we can.[1]

By contrast with the so-called 'producer ethic', which preaches the ascetic virtues of frugality, sobriety and the self-repressing postponement of pleasure in the interests of productive labour, the so-called 'consumer ethic' stimulates the economy by promulgating the values of spending not saving, self-gratification not self-denial, the pleasures of consumption rather than the dignity of labour. The emergence of consumerist culture in the West has been variously

1 Georges Bataille, 'De Sade's Sovereign Man', *Erotism: Death and Sensuality*, M. Dalwood (trans.), San Francisco, 1986, p. 170.

dated from the 'decadent' 1890s, the 'modernist' 1920s, and the 'countercultural' 1960s – the decade when Hefner's *Playboy* and Penguin's *Lady Chatterley* helped to turn countercultural recreational sex into what has been called the 'dominant pornographic culture' of contemporary transatlantic consumerism.[2] However, by identifying the 'decisive discovery' of 'what spending can really mean' with a Sade pictured as being struck by this 'violent truth' in the loneliness of the Bastille as he watched the guillotine at work from his cell window, Bataille dates the emergence of the consumer ethic – and of the spender as 'sovereign' – from the very moment of the Bourgeois Revolution itself.[3]

It is with the figure of the 'sovereign' spender that this chapter is concerned: a figure ambiguously positioned on the dividing-line between law and the underworld, between 'legitimate' and 'black' economies, in the writings of early twentieth-century sexual psychologists such as Freud and D.H. Lawrence, whose inconclusive efforts to separate a discourse of desire from the discourse of economics reveal the profound complicity of the consumer and producer ethics in the early twentieth-century moment of that other 'long revolution', the sexual revolution, which is coterminous with modernity itself.

Like Lawrence, Freud prided himself on plain-speaking. In 1913 he warned his colleagues that there were two subjects that 'civilised people' will always treat 'with the same inconsistency, prudishness and hypocrisy', and about which psychoanalysts must insist on speaking with 'the same matter-of-fact frankness': 'money matters' and 'sexual matters'.[4] An ironic warning, you may think, since it was psychoanalysis that taught the twentieth century the *impossibility* of speaking plainly about money: taught it that speech about money is invariably metaphoric, to be decoded into speech about sex – taught it, in other words, a cardinal principle of the consumer ethic: the imperative of eroticising money, never economising on sex. Freud's case histories continually 'dematerialise' economic

2 See, for example, Susan Griffin, *Pornography and Silence: Culture's Revenge Against Nature*, New York, 1982.

3 Bataille, 'De Sade's Sovereign Man', pp. 169, 171.

4 Freud, 'On Beginning the Treatment', p. 131.

relationships – the relationships of unequal property and power enacted in the taking, giving, lending or withholding of money – decoding them into symbolic expressions of erotic desire and denial, secondary transcriptions of a truth anterior to money, the originary truth of sex. This, at least, is the familiar Freud, the one whose 'overvaluation of sexuality', as Jung put it, 'has brought upon him the justified reproach of pan-sexualism'.[5] But now consider how the opposite process can also occur in Freud's writing.

Addressing fellow clinicians in his 1913 paper 'On Beginning the Treatment', Freud explained why the bourgeois patrons of his new therapeutic technique were making a sound investment in spending their income on the unorthodox practice of purchasing a daily hour of the doctor's time. Laying down what he called the 'rules of the game' for psychoanalysis – including 'the strict principle of leasing by the hour', the charging of high fees, the refusal of credit to patients, and the denial of gratis treatment no matter how deserving or desperate the case – Freud acknowledged that by his rules 'analytic therapy is almost inaccessible to poor people'.[6] He settled his conscience on this score, however, with the observation that 'perhaps there is truth in the widespread belief that those who are forced by necessity to a life of hard toil are less easily overtaken by neurosis', and indeed that neurosis in the poor typically functions as a screen for indolence, enabling the malingerer to claim 'by right of his neurosis the pity which the world has refused to his material distress, and … [to] absolve himself from the obligation of combating his poverty by working'.[7] For the bourgeois client, by contrast, the expense of psychoanalysis was 'excessive only in appearance', and not because health is priceless but, on the contrary, because health is synonymous with 'efficiency', and 'efficiency' with 'earning capacity'. Proving himself as canny a salesman of his services as any insurance broker, Freud points out that the relatively 'modest financial outlay' involved in an analytic cure compares favourably with 'the unceasing costs of nursing homes

5 Jung, 'On Psychical Energy', p. 19.

6 Freud, 'On Beginning the Treatment', pp. 123, 127, 132.

7 Ibid., pp. 132-33.

and medical treatment', and if we 'contrast them with the increase of efficiency and earning capacity which results from a successfully completed analysis, we are entitled to say that the patients have made a good bargain. Nothing in life is so expensive as illness …'[8] For those who can afford it, in other words, psychoanalysis is not a sacrifice of material for mental well-being, an exchange of wealth for health, but a pragmatic investment in increased earning-power, a hedge against depreciation of one's human capital. Reminding his colleagues of 'the familiar fact that the value of treatment is not enhanced in the patients' eyes if a very low fee is charged', Freud justifies his rule that the analyst should never 'act the part of the disinterested philanthropist' on the grounds that free treatment would increase the temptation to phantasmatic transference-effects: 'the absence of the regulating effect offered by the payment of a fee to the doctor', he says, would mean that 'the whole relationship is removed from the real world … '[9]

Like the 'normal conduct' that Bataille identifies with the 'rationality' of acquisition rather than the unproductive expenditure of pleasure, Freud's 'real world' is governed by the producer ethic: it is the world of *homo œconomicus*, of the citizen as property-owner and worker, a world constituted in the division of labour between fee-paying clients, for example, and wage-labouring analysts. And this world of the producer ethic, whose 'reality principle' checks and defers the 'pleasure principle' of consumption, no more begins, for Freud and his patients, outside the consulting-room door than it begins with the employer-employee relationship into which patient and doctor enter in the business of psychoanalysis. The 'real world' of the market economy, the world that Hegel called 'civil society',[10] inhabits our very dreams, governs the productive mechanisms of what Freud tellingly termed 'the dream-*work*' and what he would come to call 'the economics of the libido'

8 Ibid.

9 Ibid., pp. 131, 132.

10 See G.W.F. Hegel, 'Civil Society', Part 3, Section 2 of *The Philosophy of Right*, in *The Philosophy of Right, The Philosophy of History*, T.M. Knox and J. Sibree (trans.), Chicago, London, Toronto, Encyclopaedia Britannica, 1952, pp. 64-80.

and 'the domestic economy of the mind' itself.[11] (Commenting, in *Civilization and Its Discontents*, on 'the significance of work for the economics of the libido' – and specifying that by work he meant 'the ordinary professional work that is open to everyone' – Freud argued that 'No other technique for the conduct of life attaches the individual so firmly to reality as laying emphasis on work'.[12] He had earlier maintained that the addition of 'the *economic* point of view' to 'the dynamic and the topographical points of view' was 'the consummation of psychoanalytic research'.[13])

In *The Interpretation of Dreams* (1900), published more than a decade before his paper 'On Beginning the Treatment', Freud had developed an elaborate simile for the unconscious which struck him as sufficiently definitive to be worth quoting, without further explanation, in his case history of 'Dora' (1905). Illustrating the mechanisms of dream-work, he suggested that the role played by the day's residue of conscious wishes in triggering deep-seated unconscious desires in dreams

> may be explained by an analogy. A daytime thought may very well play the part of *entrepreneur* for a dream; but the *entrepreneur*, who, as people say, has the idea and the initiative to carry it out, can do nothing without capital; he needs a *capitalist* who can afford the outlay, and the capitalist who provides the psychical outlay for the dream is invariably and indisputably, whatever may be the thoughts of the previous day, *a wish from the unconscious.*
>
> Sometimes the capitalist is himself the *entrepreneur*, and indeed in the case of dreams this is the commoner event: an unconscious wish is stirred up by the daytime activity and proceeds to construct a dream. So, too, the other possible variations in the economic

11 Freud uses the phrase 'economics of the libido' repeatedly in *Civilization and Its Discontents*, *Standard Edition of the Complete Psychological Works of Sigmund Freud*, James Strachey (ed.), Vol. 21, London, Vintage, 2001, pp. 59-243. The phrase 'domestic economy of the mind' is from Freud, 'Fragment of an Analysis', p. 43.

12 Freud, *Civilization and Its Discontents*, p. 80 n.

13 Freud, 'The Unconscious', p. 180.

> situation that I have taken as an analogy have their parallel in dream-processes. The *entrepreneur* may himself make a small contribution to the capital; several *entrepreneurs* may apply to the same capitalist; several capitalists may combine to put up what is necessary for the *entrepreneur*. In the same way, we come across dreams that are supported by more than one dream-wish; and so too with other similar variations, which could easily be run through ... [14]

There are no coincidences in the unconscious, according to Freud, and it seems more than coincidental that this analogy should have occurred to him during a discussion of some dream-work performed by one of his own, most gnawingly persistent conscious wishes, which he identifies as 'my cherished desire' 'at long last [to] become a Professor Extraordinarius'.[15] (The professorial title carried no salary but was valued for its prestige and the higher fees it commanded; in Freud's words, 'it elevates the physician in our society into a demigod for his patients'.[16]) For the impecunious Freud, who once described himself as 'a mere money-acquisition-machine' and a 'day-labourer',[17] the prospect of promotion to Professor Extraordinarius meant both the fee levels and the patient numbers that would finally free him from his life-long neurotic anxieties about money (from which, in the event, the disappointing sales of *The Interpretation of Dreams* itself brought none of the hoped-for relief).[18] Hence the latent analogy that is at once 'capitalised' upon (as Freud has it) and screened by the manifest one that Freud actually offers us in his text: the role of the day's residue in exploiting the 'capital' or 'capitalist' of unconscious desire bears an

14 Freud, *The Interpretation of Dreams*, p. 561.

15 Ibid., p. 560.

16 Peter Gay, *Freud: A Life for Our Time*, London, Macmillan, 1989, p. 136.

17 Unpublished letter to Lilly Freud Marlé, March 14, 1911, quoted in Gay, *Freud*, p. 160.

18 Freud's promotion to Professor Extraordinarius, after seventeen years as *Privatdozent*, eventually came in February 1902, following his decision to abandon moral scruple and rely on the system of patronage, influential connections and occasional bribery known as *Protektion*. Freud's self-confessed 'fear of poverty' nonetheless remained with him for the rest of his career.

uncanny resemblance to the role of the entrepreneurial analyst who knows how to profit from the repressed desires encoded in his bourgeois patients' dreams and symptoms. Freud all but brings this latent meaning to the surface of his analogy in his Postscript to 'Dora' – the case history with which he hoped to prove the truth, and so boost the poor sales, of *The Interpretation of Dreams*, thus securing his promotion to Professor Extraordinarius.[19] Reflecting on this case history rich in monetary references, and whose narrative dénouement is the canny analyst's triumphant discovery of what he calls the 'key' to the jewel box of his patient's dream and to her nervous fingering of her real money-purse, Freud claims in his Postscript that it is by means of his psychoanalytic technique 'alone [that] the pure metal of valuable unconscious thoughts can be extracted from the raw material of the patient's associations'.[20] If the analyst can be pictured as an industrious miner of the rich vein of his patient's unconscious desire or 'capital', his clinical technique can also be pictured as an 'underworld' one in another sense, the criminal sense. Writing about 'Dora' (Ida Bauer) to Fliess, Freud likened psychoanalysis to the technique of burglary: 'I have a new patient', he reported, 'a girl of eighteen; the case has opened smoothly to my collection of picklocks'.[21]

In the popular view of Freudianism as a reductionist hermeneutic, which decodes economic and social relationships into disguised repetitions of archetypal erotic ones, the 'other' of Freud's 'real world' of *homo œconomicus* is the so-called 'private' world of the family – that traditionally cooperative realm (an economy of love, not money) which intellectuals from Hobbes to Marx contrasted with the competitive domain of the social, inhab-

19 Reviews of *The Interpretation of Dreams* early in 1900 had criticised it for not providing detailed case material that clearly showed how dream interpretation could remedy a neurosis. 'Dora' became a patient of Freud's late in 1900 and her two dreams promised interpretative material that might prove incontrovertibly the theories of what Freud regarded as his unacknowledged masterpiece, as well as his unrecognized claim to the professional respect and reputation that should gain him promotion and the increase in clientele and fees it would bring.

20 Freud, 'Fragment of an Analysis', p. 112.

21 Freud, *The Origins of Psychoanalysis*, p. 325.

ited by possessive individuals. But in an era when marriage was still predominantly conceived as an economic contract[22] – when, as Lawrence put it, 'marriage has been found the best method of conserving property and stimulating production'[23] – and when father-daughter relationships, as 'Dora's' own muted testimony suggests, could also be conducted as property-relationships, the 'other' of Freud's 'real world' of the market economy was not so much the 'private' world of family-life, but the underworld, the burglar's world. It is in the underworld, according to Bataille, that the producer ethic has no purchase. Bataille prefaces his study of Sade in *Erotism* with an essay on 'Kinsey, the Underworld and Work', in which he argues that the most significant finding of the Kinsey Reports was that America's criminal population enjoyed, on average, five times as many orgasms per week as its working population.[24] In showing that class background, religion and age were relatively insignificant influences on the quantity of an individual's sexual spending compared with the overriding factor of *work*, the Kinsey Reports confirmed Bataille's intuition of a deep affinity between eroticism, crime and Nature, linked as they are by their marginality to what Freud called the 'real world' of productive labour.

'[G]enuine pornography is almost always underworld', Lawrence explained in 'Pornography and Obscenity', his broadside against the forces of law and order that had confiscated his paintings of nudes from the Warren Gallery Exhibition in 1929 and publicly burned the Methuen edition of *The Rainbow* for 'indecency' fourteen years earlier, in the name of the English war-

22 Under the Austrian civil code in the 1890s, for example, a husband could forbid his wife to take employment; had the legal right to decide unilaterally the family's domicile; and had the power to administer his wife's property unless a legal agreement to the contrary had been arranged. See John W. Boyer, 'Freud, Marriage, and Late Viennese Liberalism: A Commentary from 1905', *Journal of Modern History*, 50, 1 (March 1978): 89.

23 D.H. Lawrence, 'A Propos of Lady Chatterley's Lover' (1930), in *Lady Chatterley's Lover and A Propos of Lady Chatterley's Lover*, Michael Squires (ed.), Cambridge, Cambridge University Press, 1993, p. 319.

24 Georges Bataille, 'Kinsey, the underworld and work', *Erotism*, p. 157.

effort.[25] Like Bataille, but with very different sympathies, Lawrence propounded the intrinsic links between crime, pornography and unproductive expenditure. Paring away what he took to be the confusion of customary definitions of obscenity and pornography, he narrowed down his own definition of the 'genuine pornography' that circulates in the black economy of the underworld to material intended as 'a direct provocative of masturbation': 'an invariable stimulant to the vice of self-abuse, onanism, masturbation, call it what you will'.[26] Describing masturbation as 'the one thoroughly secret act of the human being, more secret even than excrementation', Lawrence went on to characterise it, notoriously if unexceptionally for his time, as 'the deepest and most dangerous cancer of our civilization ... certainly the most dangerous sexual vice that a society can be afflicted with, in the long run'. Why? Because:

> The great danger of masturbation lies in its merely exhaustive nature. In sexual intercourse, there is give and take. A new stimulus enters as the native stimulus departs. Something quite new is added as the old surcharge is removed. And this is so in all sexual intercourse where two creatures are concerned, even in the homosexual intercourse. But in masturbation there is nothing but loss. There is no reciprocity. There is merely the spending away of a certain force, and no return. The body remains, in a sense, a corpse, after the act of self-abuse. ... There is what we call dead loss. ... the self becomes emptier and emptier, till it is almost a nullus, a nothingness.[27]

25 D.H. Lawrence, 'Pornography and Obscenity', *Phoenix: The Posthumous Papers of D.H. Lawrence*, Edward D. McDonald (ed.), London, William Heinemann, 1936, p. 175. The National Purity League's instigation of the prosecution of *The Rainbow* was part of a generalised campaign against pornographers, pimps and prostitutes in Britain during the Great War, a campaign that represented them as the enemy at 'the heart of the Empire', treasonously sapping the fighting strength of England's soldiers and having what the Bishop of London described as 'the insolence to try and make money out of the weakness of our boys'; 'shooting is not good enough for them', the Bishop said. For commentary on the political context of this war-time campaign, see Cate Haste, *Rules of Desire – Sex in Britain: World War I to the Present*, London, Chatto & Windus, 1992, pp. 50-57.

26 Lawrence, 'Pornography and Obscenity', p. 178.

27 Ibid., pp. 179-80.

If there is a criminal aspect to masturbation – that vice most injurious to the social body – it is the crime of spending without receiving a return on one's outlay. As for the bourgeois investor in Freud's economical therapy, so for Lawrence's 'healthy' individual, desire as capital is that form of personal property that should create more capital. Few terms in Lawrence's lexicon of invective were more damnatory than 'masturbation', understood as the epitome of the uncreative or unproductive; the term could be applied, by metaphoric extension, to all of his *bêtes noires*, not least Freudian 'science' itself. (In his 1929 essay, 'Introduction to These Paintings', Lawrence attaches the stigma of 'masturbation' to physics, astronomy, Christianity and most of post-Renaissance European visual art.[28] When identifying and deploring 'niggling analysis, often self-analysis', as the cultural 'manifestation of masturbation' in 'Pornography and Obscenity', he clearly has in mind Freudian psychology as well as Proustian and Joycean literary modernism.[29]) The question of when the social 'cancer' of masturbation first began to attack European civilisation was one that teased Lawrence's historical imagination; when introducing his own paintings of nudes, he traced its emergence to a pervasive fear of sexual intercourse consequent on the arrival of syphilis in England and Europe from the New World in the late sixteenth century;[30] but in 'Obscenity and Pornography' he proposed that 'The real masturbation of Englishmen began only in the nineteenth century' and 'has continued with an increasing emptying of the real vitality and the real *being* of men, till now people are little more than shells of people … incapable of either giving or taking. And this is masturbation result' (*sic*).[31] If the 'masturbation result' could be traced in England to the nineteenth century, so, too, can Lawrence's own thinking on the exchange-value of sexual intercourse, which has much in common with the popular wisdom of the 1850s studiously documented by the pseu-

28 D.H. Lawrence, 'Introduction to These Paintings', in *Phoenix: The Posthumous Papers of D.H. Lawrence*, Edward D. McDonald (ed.), London, William Heinemann, 1936, pp. 551-84.

29 Lawrence, 'Pornography and Obscenity', p. 180.

30 Lawrence, 'Introduction to These Paintings', pp. 551-52.

31 Lawrence, 'Pornography and Obscenity', p. 180.

donymous 'Walter' in *My Secret Life* – that pornographic epic of prodigious, underworld spending, as much by the countless prostitutes who are Walter's partners in sexual 'crime' as by the near-bankrupted autobiographer himself. As Walter understood it, (re)productive sexual exchange depended on simultaneous spending by both partners. In his own words: 'If the man alone spends in the woman's cunt, it will not do it – If the woman spends alone, it will not do it – If they spend some time after each other, it may or may not do it'.[32] Only if both parties to the transaction spend simultaneously can they be sure that – as the work-shy Walter put it – 'the job is done'.[33] By contrast with the libertine author of *My Secret Life*, dedicated to consumption not production, Lawrence regarded simultaneous orgasm as 'the only evidence of a perfect union': a central dissatisfaction in his early sexual relations with his wife Frieda, as in Mellors' relations with Bertha Coutts and Connie's with Michaelis in *Lady Chatterley's Lover*, was their failure to spend together.[34] (Lawrence – or his characters – may have been reading Marie Stopes's 1918 bestseller, *Married Love: A New Contribution to the Solution of Sex Difficulties*, which fervently advocated the benefits of simultaneous orgasm and the importance to health of the mutual exchange of bodily fluids in sex.[35] It was the latter thesis that in the 1920s inspired the pharmaceutical production of pills containing sexual fluids, for use by women whose husbands wore condoms.[36]) Bataille suggests that 'if one calculates the ratio between energy consumed and the usefulness of the results, the pursuit of pleasure

32 Anon, *My Secret Life*, abridged with an introduction by G. Legman, New York, Grove, 1966, p. 367.

33 Ibid.

34 Compton Mackenzie (in *My Life and Times: Octave Five (1915-1923)*, London, Chatto & Windus, 1966, pp. 167-68), reports that 'What worried him [Lawrence] particularly was his inability to attain consummation simultaneously with his wife, which according to him must mean that their marriage was still imperfect in spite of all they had both gone through. I insisted that such a happy coincidence was always rare, but he became more and more depressed about what *he* insisted was the only evidence of a perfect union'.

35 Marie Stopes, *Married Love: A New Contribution to the Solution of Sex Difficulties*, London, Putnam, 1918.

36 See Paul Ferris, *Sex and the British: A Twentieth Century History*, London, Michael Joseph, 1993, p. 81.

even if reckoned as useful is essentially extravagant; the more so in that usually pleasure has no end product ... '[37] Pointedly indifferent though the spendthrift Walter was to end-products, his calculative bourgeois mind was fascinated by the precise quantities of expenditure involved in erotic pleasure. His onanistic researches revealed that a man's average outlay of *élan vital* was a large teaspoonful (a finding that suggests a new meaning for J. Alfred Prufrock's melancholy reflection, 'I have measured out my life in coffee spoons'[38]); and as for the amount of expenditure that could be contained by a woman, Walter found that it amounted to exactly four guineas-worth. A financial-cum-erotic compact with a favourite prostitute revealed that her 'infundibular cavern', or vagina, could hold no less, but no more, than eighty-four silver shillings – an achievement that entitled her to keep the coins on condition that she provide her services gratis to Walter on two future visits.[39] The 'sovereign' spender of the underworld libidinal economy measured his outlay in shillings.

The fetishistic association of sexual with fiscal expenditure, so insistently foregrounded in the underworld libidinal economy of *My Secret Life*, was mediated for Victorians by a third term, that of 'energy', typically figured as a liquid currency, which is the manifest content of the economic models of the libido that both Freud and Lawrence inherited from early nineteenth-century sexual 'science'. If Lawrence was right, in a sense, that 'the real masturbation of Englishmen began only in the nineteenth century', it was not because the so-called 'secret vice' hadn't begun to be pathologised as a dangerous wastage of personal resources, or capital reserves of energy, at least a century earlier. The institutionalised repression of masturbation that began in England in the early eighteenth century, spread rapidly to the Continent and North America, and lasted for some two hundred and fifty years, has been extensively documented – the seminal study, so to speak, being René Spitz's 'Authority and Masturbation: Some Remarks on a Bibliographical Investigation',

37 Bataille, 'De Sade's Sovereign Man', p. 168.

38 See T.S. Eliot's poem, 'The Love Song of J. Alfred Prufrock' (1915).

39 Anon, *My Secret Life*, p. 526.

published in the *Psychoanalytic Quarterly* in 1952.[40] Spitz's researches showed that while belief in the harmful effects of excessive expenditure of semen can be traced back at least to Hippocrates, Celsius and Galenus, the association of excessive expenditure specifically with masturbation (rather than with heterogenital intercourse, for example) only arose in the early 1700s, with the publication in English, and rapid translation into several other languages, of a moralistic pamphlet attributed to one 'Dr Bekkers' and entitled *Onania; Or the Heinous Sin of Self-Pollution, And All its Frightful Consequences, in both Sexes, Consider'd, with Spiritual and Physical Advice to those who have already injur'd themselves by this abominable Practice.*[41] It was in this tract of very dubious medical authority but widespread prurient interest that the word 'onanism' itself was coined, and Bekkers' inventory of the frightful consequences of 'self-abuse' – ranging from epilepsy, impotence and arrested growth in men, to consumption, hysteric fits and sterility in women – set

40 René A. Spitz, 'Authority and Masturbation: Some Remarks on a Bibliographical Investigation', *Psychoanalytic Quarterly*, 21 (1952): 490-526. The voluminous literature on the history of masturbation phobia includes: E.H. Hare, 'Masturbatory Insanity: The History of an Idea', *Journal of Medical Science*, 108, 452 (January 1962): 1-21; Robert H. MacDonald, 'The Frightful Consequences of Onanism: Notes on the History of a Delusion', *Journal of the History of Ideas*, 28, 3 (1967): 423-24; G.J. Barker-Benfield, *The Horrors of the Half-Known Life: Male Attitudes Toward Women and Sexuality in Nineteenth-Century America*, New York, Harper and Row, 1976, pp. 163-74; G.J. Barker-Benfield, 'The Spermatic Economy: A Nineteenth-Century View of Sexuality', in Michael Gordon (ed.), *The American Family in Social-Historical Perspective*, second edn, New York, 1978, pp. 374-402; Thomas W. Laqueur, 'Credit, Novels, Masturbation', in Susan Leigh Foster (ed.), *Choreographing History*, Bloomington and Indianapolis: Indiana University Press, 1995, pp. 119-28; Thomas W. Laqueur, 'Sexual Desire and the Market Economy During the Industrial Revolution', in Donna C. Stanton (ed.), *Discourses of Sexuality – From Aristotle to AIDS*, Ann Arbor, University of Michigan Press, 1992, pp. 185-215; Thomas W. Laqueur, *Solitary Sex: A Cultural History of Masturbation*, New York, Zone Books, 2003; and Jean Stengers and Anne Van Neck, *Masturbation: The History of a Great Terror*, K. Hoffmann (trans.), New York, Palgrave, 2001.

41 Spitz dates the first publication of this anonymous pamphlet from 1700, whereas Laqueur dates the first edition from 1711, and Stengers and Van Neck date it from 1715 in *Masturbation*, p. 35. Tissot appears to have been the first to attribute *Onania*'s authorship to a 'Doctor Bekkers', in his *Tentamen de morbis ex manustupratione* of 1758. See Stengers and Van Neck, *Masturbation*, p. 38.

the terms for the vast outpouring of medical and moral literature on the personal and social costs of masturbation for the next two and a half centuries. By the time the self-proclaimed *médecin–philosophe* (physician–philosopher) S.A.D. Tissot published his own famous *Treatise on the Curse of Onan* some fifty years after Bekkers', the symptomatology of masturbation had swollen to include blindness, imbecility, insanity, rheumatism, female homosexuality and premature death for both sexes. (Bekkers had apologised for adopting a masculine Biblical name, Onan, for the disease that he invented for the benefit of both sexes.[42]) As Spitz shows, however, prescribed remedies for 'self-abuse' during the first century-and-a-half of masturbation phobia were often anodyne – typically, dieting, exercise and hydrotherapy (cold baths) – and it was only around 1850 that severe punishment and restraint, combined with surgical measures like circumcision, clitoridectomy, infibulation and cauterisation to the spine, thighs and genitals, became the preferred methods for suppressing masturbation and remained so in all European countries for the next thirty years, lingering on in parts of Europe and America till as late as the 1930s and 1940s. (Writing, as he was, for the *Psychoanalytic Quarterly*, Spitz attributed the decline of such 'sadistic' methods of treatment in the earlier twentieth century to the progressive influence of psychoanalysis, especially Freud's *Three Essays on the Theory of Sexuality*, which overhauled much of the received medical wisdom about infantile sexuality and dissociated guilt and anxiety neuroses from organic diseases.[43]) Measured by its

42 Anon, *Onania; Or the Heinous Sin of Self-Pollution, And All its Frightful Consequences, in both Sexes, Consider'd, with Spiritual and Physical Advice to those who have already injur'd themselves by this abominable Practice*, 4th edn, London, printed for the author, and sold by N. Crouch, P. Varenne, and J. Isted; n.d. Preface to the fourth edition, p. iii.

43 Freud himself, nonetheless, attributed the aetiology of Dora's hysteria to the habit of masturbation, and his attitudes to the practice reflected mainstream nineteenth-century medical wisdom in various ways. See his contributions to a 'discussion on the harmfulness of masturbation' conducted by the Vienna Psychoanalytic Society in 1910, in Herman Nunberg and Ernst Federn (eds), *Minutes of the Vienna Psychoanalytic Society, Volume II: 1908–1910*, M. Nunberg (trans.), New York, International Universities Press,1967, pp. 542–72. See also Hannah S. Decker, *Freud, Dora, and Vienna 1900*, New York, Free Press, 1991, pp. 96–97, 237.

frightful medical consequences, then, the 'real masturbation' of Europeans only began in the 1850s, when the medical profession ensured that castration anxieties were more than phantasmatic.

It was also in the nineteenth century that the economic costs of onanism became an insistent literal, as much as metaphoric, theme of anti-masturbation literature. One of the genres of *de facto* pornography used by Georgian and Victorian self-abusers was, ironically, the aptly-named self-help manual, written by assorted doctors, clergymen and hacks, designed to provide young people with systems of self-discipline to prepare them for success in the competitive world of the modern business economy, and documenting the dangerous practice and effects of masturbation, which they figured as a debilitating drain on the economy of the working body. The incorporation of narratives and confessions of male and female self-abusers, either debilitated by or cured of the affliction, invested such manuals with pornographic appeal. It was to screen his account of masturbation from prurient eyes that one of the most successful American exponents of the genre, the Reverend John Todd, had recourse to Latin in a chapter of his bestselling guide to regimes of character-building for self-made males, *The Student's Manual*, which went through scores of editions in the USA following its publication in 1835 and sold more than a hundred thousand copies in Europe by 1854.[44] Todd's theme was the need to maximise the vital personal resources – of energy, time, money and information – indispensable to success in the most 'advanced' because most democratic and business-driven of nineteenth-century societies. Bodily energies in general and sperm in particular were like time and money: to be 'save[d] with the utmost care, and spen[t] with the greatest caution'.[45] Todd figured energy and semen, like time and useful knowledge, as liquid, mutually exchangeable currencies, convertible into profit or pleasure, success or failure. In his model of the

44 John Todd, *The Student's Manual*, Northampton, Hopkins, Bridgman, 1835. See Barker-Benfield, *Horrors*, p. 135.

45 See Todd, *Student's Manual*, p. 168: 'A miser will frequently become wealthy – not because he has a great income, but because he saves with the utmost care, and spends with the greatest caution'.

body, universal business competition was internalised: the self was an economy of energy in which personified interests like Ambition and Sloth, Procrastination and Fantasy competed for limited reserves of the vital currency, and it was as a prodigal wastage of these reserves that Todd indicted (in Latin) what he called 'the practice of pouring out by the hand (the vicious act of Onan)'.[46] As another exponent of the so-called 'fundamental law of the animal economy' advised in a manual on *Mental Hygiene* in 1863, one's bodily resources were valuable assets that should be 'managed' 'so as to ensure the greatest possible return'.[47] Masturbation could threaten the nation, jeopardising, as it did, the body economic, both individual and collective. The English Christian campaigner, Alfred S. Dyer, president of the 'movement for social purity and national righteousness' and editor of *The Sentinel*, claimed to have already sold fifty thousand copies of his manual *Facts for Men on Moral Purity and Health, Being Plain Words to Young Men Upon an Avoided Subject*, when he published the 1884 edition of his manual, in which he declared that 'History testifies that no sin has been more disastrous to public life' than 'impurity' or 'self-abuse', such was its degenerative impact on the nation's libidinal economy: 'Young men who wish well to their country; young men who in the natural course of events will in a few years be responsible for the destiny of this nation, should not be thoughtless on this momentous subject':

> When such things permeate the life of a whole people, it is inevitable that the nation must sink … I shall not stop to illustrate this subject by an appeal to the histories of Greece and Persia. We may come down to our own day and learn the lesson of contemporary events. The nations on the Continent of Europe that are receding, are the ones that are most given up to licentiousness.[48]

46 Ibid., p. 146.
47 Isaac Ray, *Mental Hygiene* (1863), New York, Hafner, 1968, pp. 68, 89.
48 Alfred S. Dyer, *Facts for Men on Moral Purity and Health, Being Plain Words to Young Men Upon an Avoided Subject; Safeguards against Immorality, & Facts that Men Ought to Know*, London, Dyer Brothers, 1884, pp. 5, 13, 14.

It is no accident that the period in which such advice manuals proliferated – the 1830s and 1840s – also saw the establishment of classical thermodynamics as a science of energy defined as capacity for work. The pseudo-scientific conception of sexuality that prevails in self-help literature of Todd's and Dyer's kind is at once economic and thermodynamic: an application of the laws of the conservation and transformation of energy, and of the entropy that Lawrence called 'dead loss', to the monadic economy of the self. (We saw in the previous chapter how Freud and Jung negotiated the legacy of this tradition of 'vital economics' for psychoanalysis.) While physicists and engineers like Carnot, Joule and Clausius were formulating the first two laws of classical thermodynamics in the 1830s and 1840s, readers of Dr Amariah Brigham's *Remarks on the Influence of Mental Cultivation and Mental Excitement upon Mental Health* (1832) were being taught that a 'fundamental law of the distribution of vital powers [is] ... that when they are increased in one part, they are diminished in all the rest of the living economy ... to increase the powers of one organ it is absolutely necessary that they should be diminished in all the others'.[49] Among the organs in question were the penis and the brain, and a pressing concern of eighteenth and nineteenth-century self-help manuals was to exhort young men and women not to expend in masturbation vital energies that might be profitably invested in manual or mental work. Productive labour, the antithesis of masturbatory waste, was a common homeopathic cure for the 'disease'. An article in the *New Orleans Medical and Surgical Journal* of 1855 reported the case of a 'young man of fine physical development who wrote good verses and practiced masturbation to excess. [He] asked for medical advice ... [and] was persuaded to try severe manual labor, he cleared six acres of heavily timbered beech and sugar tree bottoms – was cured and rose to distinction in civil life'.[50]

49 Amariah Brigham, *Remarks on the Influence of Mental Cultivation and Mental Excitement upon Mental Health* (1832), Boston, Marsh Capen and Lyon, 1833, p. 16.

50 Quoted in Barker-Benfield, *Horrors*, p. 176. Contributing to a 'discussion on the harmfulness of masturbation' conducted by the Vienna Psychoanalytic Society in 1910, Wilhelm Stekel, by contrast, cited the case of two brothers

The mounting stress on the economic costs of 'wasted' libidinal expenditure in onanism was a corollary of the anti-onanists' own pursuit of profit, their promotion of an epidemic of anxiety about masturbation and its 'costs' that could be converted into a desire to spend money on 'sovereign remedies' for the vice. In other words, the masturbator's shameful outlay in the libidinal black economy could be converted into respectable profits in the 'legitimate' market of medical publishing. On one hand, the anti-onanists' tracts functioned as incitements to the sin they condemned, straddling the genres of quack medicine and pornography by incorporating detailed narratives of the sexual practices of young men and women whom the doctor-author claimed to have treated and whose confessional letters were stitched into ever-expanding new editions of their tracts. On the other hand, the tracts functioned as advertisements for the patent medicines, tinctures, tablets and personalised diagnostic advice dispensed by the author and his bookseller or publisher. (A *Supplement to the Onania*, running to twice its number of pages and designed to be bound into its seventh and subsequent editions, advertised itself as 'Containing many remarkable, and indeed surprizing Instances of the Health being impair'd, and Genitals spoil'd, by that filthy Commerce with ones self, which is daily practised, as well by Adults as Youth, Women as Men, Married as Single, as their Letters inserted manifest'.[51]) Purportedly scandalised by the profits being reaped by such literature and possibly seeking to share in them, one 'Philo-Castitatis' published a refutation of *Onania* in 1723, critiquing Bekkers' credentials as physician and theologian, exposing the flaws in his knowledge of anatomy and of 'the Animal Œconomy it self', in a tract entitled *Onania Examin'd, and Detected; or, The Ignorance, Error, Impertinence, and Contradiction of a Book call'd ONANIA,*

who were his patients: 'The one who looked fresh and vigorous turned out to be a masturbator, whereas the other one, who looked pale and sickly, timid and embarrassed, did not masturbate but has intercourse regularly'. See Nunberg and Federn (eds), *Minutes of the Vienna Psychoanalytic Society, Volume II*, p. 554.

51 Anon, *A Supplement to the Onania, Or the Heinous Sin of Self-Pollution, And all its frightful Consequences, in the two Sexes, consider'd, Etc … to be bound up with either the 7th, 8th, 9th, or 10th Editions of that Book*, London, T. Crouch and J. Isted, n.d. The quotation is from the title page.

Discovered, and Exposed.[52] Philo-Castitatis explained that he was moved to write his refutation by witnessing the rapid succession of new editions of Bekkers' best-seller and its merely venal motivation: 'the Author of ONANIA seems to be Master only of some flat, senseless, erroneous, and, in some Things, pernicious Conceptions, all flowing from a Mercenary Principle, which made his Pen go for money'.[53] Bucking the trend that *Onania* had set, Philo-Castitatis himself reported the case of an exceptionally chaste and industrious young man who suffered severe painful distemper arising from the build-up of 'seed' in his 'seed-bladders', which all the attempted remedies of bed-rest, bleeding and purging had failed to cure: 'After a long Time spent, and the Man nothing better, at last Masturpation [*sic*] was allowed, whereby, upon two or three copious Discharges, the Vessels became flaccid, the Patient quickly restored, and quickly after marry'd'.[54]

Why masturbation phobia should have begun to grip the minds of moralists and medical men in the early 1700s is still subject to debate (rarely mentioned in this debate is the enormous increase in the availability of printed erotica all over Europe in the period after 1660.[55]) Thomas Laqueur has proposed interpreting it as one of a trio of cognate inventions that coincided in the second decade of the eighteenth century: the medical invention of onanism as a disease (with the publication of *Onania* in 1711), the invention of the novel as a literary genre (with *Robinson Crusoe* in 1719), and what was in effect a third invention of the same decade, that of history's first credit market crashes – the bursting of the Mississippi Bubble in France and the South Sea Bubble in England, both early in 1720.[56]

52 Philo-Castitatis, *Onania Examin'd, and Detected; or, The Ignorance, Error, Impertinence, and Contradiction of a Book call'd ONANIA, Discovered, and Exposed*, London, Joseph Marshall, 1723.

53 Ibid., 'Preface' (unpaginated).

54 Ibid., p. 99.

55 See Lynn Hunt (ed.), *The Invention of Pornography, 1500–1800*, New York, Zone Books, 1993.

56 See Laqueur's 'Credit, Novels, Masturbation' and 'Sexual Desire and the Market Economy During the Industrial Revolution'. Laqueur appears to be drawing extensively on the arguments of Barker-Benfield's *Horrors* and 'The Spermatic Economy' in developing his thesis in these essays.

The common denominator, Laqueur suggests, is the element of fictiveness, or inauthenticity. Fantasy was deemed the invariant accompaniment, if not cause, of masturbation; like the new 'vices' of novel-reading and financial speculation in the credit market, masturbatory fantasies were focused on purely imaginary objects, implicated with a dangerous unreality. Eighteenth-century moralists identified all three phenomena with the evils of an over-stimulated imagination, which removed those who yielded to its temptations from the constraints of the natural world, with potentially fatal results. Nervous of economistic explanations, as 'new historicists' invariably are, Laqueur prefers to see masturbation phobia as part of a 'much more general and far-reaching eighteenth-century debate' about the pathological powers of the imagination, rather than as arising directly from the correlation of semen, money and energy and a perception that all were in short supply, to be profligately spent at the wastrel's peril.[57] In particular, Laqueur questions why anxieties about excessive expenditure should have arisen precisely at the time when, with the rapidly expanding factory-production made possible by the Industrial Revolution, economic theorists were beginning to recognise the possibility of a widespread surplus of commodities. Why, in other words, should an ideology of scarcity coincide with an economy of abundance, or a potential surfeit of unsold goods? In Laqueur's words, there is a 'difficulty' 'inherent in trying to construe onanism within an economy of scarcity – of semen, of nervous energy – when the danger lay in an economy of surfeit, of excess, of the "supplement"'.[58]

A solution to Laqueur's 'difficulty' can be found by reconsidering the classical view of scarcity from the perspectives of the so-called 'sciences' of neoclassical economics and sexology, which developed in tandem with one another in the last decades of the

57 Laqueur, 'Credit, Novels, Masturbation', pp. 126, 121. The traditional association of the imagination with gold – an association whose history stretches from the Elizabethans to Palgrave's *Golden Treasury* and beyond – does not feature in Laqueur's analysis. For a discussion of the identification of imagination with gold, and of the conflation, rather than polarisation, of the tropes of the 'Golden Age' and 'an age of gold', see K.K. Ruthven, 'Keats and *Dea Moneta*', *Studies in Romanticism*, 15, 3 (Summer 1976): 445-59.

58 Laqueur, 'Credit, Novels, Masturbation', p. 123.

nineteenth century, and whose own models of scarcity and desire help to explain the ambiguous status of the spender, as both waster and winner, in Freud's and Lawrence's discourses on desire.

Scarcity as a universal economic condition was certainly an invention of the Enlightenment, but it was the relative scarcity of *goods* seen against the background of an infinite abundance of *desire*. In eighteenth-century London – centre of what Neil McKendrick has called the 'Consumer Revolution' of the eighteenth century[59] – the Industrial Revolution had created high-volume, standardised production, which in turn produced a pattern of high-volume, standardised consumption, driven by the social imperatives of fashion.[60] Eighteenth-century entrepreneurs like Josiah Wedgwood and Matthew Boulton discovered what the neoclassical economists would later call the elasticity of demand, or the idea that stimulating consumer desires for new commodities could indefinitely expand domestic markets. Fashion, or social emulation, was the motor of this demand: as the provincial gentry and merchant classes aped what they took to be (and the entrepreneurs calculatedly portrayed as) aristocratic patterns of consumption, their tastes were progressively refined, and this upward mobility of taste, combined with the downward mobility of successive fashions, could ensure that desire was endlessly renewable, and thus demand infinitely elastic. For the Scottish Enlightenment thinkers, David Hume and Adam Smith, the functional distinction between need and desire, or necessities and superfluous goods, became unsustainable: the natural species-needs to which Rousseau's unspoilt Savage was subject, and which labour was previously thought to meet, became conceptually indistinguishable from the fashion-driven demands for 'trinkets' that Adam Smith criticised in the tastes of eighteenth-century consumers. It was in the context of

59 Neil McKendrick, 'Introduction' and 'The Consumer Revolution of Eighteenth-Century England', in Neil McKendrick, John Brewer and J.H. Plumb, *The Birth of a Consumer Society: The Commercialization of Eighteenth-Century England*, Bloomington and Indianapolis, Indiana University Press, 1985.

60 See Nicholas Xenos, *Scarcity and Modernity*, London and New York, Routledge, 1989, p. 8.

this vision of the desire-to-spend as an insatiable, infinitely renewable resource that a theory of the fundamental scarcity of goods arose as a universal postulate of economics.

Although the coveted objects of fashion-driven desire might be intrinsically worthless, the very coveting of them was seen by classical economists as contributing to the progressive cultural 'refinement' of the middle classes, and thus to the 'civilising' of society as a whole. Bernard Mandeville's summary of this process in his 1705 poem, 'The Grumbling Hive: or, Knaves turn'd Honest' (subsequently republished in his book *The Fable of the Bees: Or, Private Vices, Publick Benefits*), anticipated Smith's 'trickle-down' defence of the taste for useless luxuries by more than half-a-century: 'whilst Luxury / Employ'd a Million of the Poor, And odious Pride a Million more: / Envy itself, and Vanity, / Were Ministers of Industry; / Their darling Folly, Fickleness, / In Dyet, Furniture and Dress ... was made / The very Wheel that turn'd the Trade'.[61] It was this sententious view of consumer culture, still grounded in moral philosophy, that ceased to be a legitimate consideration for a 'scientific' economics in the 1870s, when neoclassical theorists such as Carl Menger in Austria, Leon Walras in France, Stanley Jevons and Alfred Marshall in Britain launched the so-called 'marginalist revolution' in economic theory, overhauling the productivist ethos of classical political economy maintained by Mill, Ricardo and Marx.[62] Reinterpreting production as simply a deferred or indirect form of consumption (driven as it was by a vision of the future consumption for which it provided), the 'marginal utility' theorists stressed the primacy of consumer tastes and desires in the potential growth of any manufacturing enterprise. 'It is surely obvious', Jevons insisted,

61 Bernard Mandeville, *The Fable of the Bees: Or, Private Vices, Publick Benefits*, 5th edn, London, J. Tonson, 1728, p. 10.

62 My overview of neoclassical economics, or 'marginal utility theory', draws on Nicholas Xenos, *Scarcity and Modernity*, London and New York, Routledge, 1989, and Lawrence Birken, *Consuming Desire: Sexual Science and the Emergence of a Culture of Abundance, 1871–1914*, Ithaca and London, Cornell UP, 1988. For a related discussion, see Wolfgang Fritz Haug, *Critique of Commodity Aesthetics: Appearance, Sexuality and Advertising in Capitalist Society*, Robert Brock (trans.), Cambridge, Polity, 1971.

> that economics does rest upon the laws of human enjoyment; and that, if those laws are developed by no other science, they must be developed by economists. We labour to produce with the sole object of consuming, and the kinds and amounts of goods produced must be determined with regard to what we want to consume. Every manufacturer knows and feels how closely he must anticipate the tastes and needs of his customers: his whole success depends on it; and, in like manner, the theory of economics must begin with a correct theory of consumption.[63]

Bracketing the question of the social value, and even the social determinants, of consumer desires, the marginalists postulated only that such desires exist and treated them as idiosyncratic, essentially individual in origin. Production, conceived by some Enlightenment theorists as the meeting of normal species-needs, was rethought as merely the satisfaction or frustration of desires that could be capricious and individualistic, and to which the use-value of commodities could be marginal or irrelevant. Neoclassical economics thus replaced utility, as the universal yardstick of the comparative value of goods, with a universally exchangeable desire. *Homo œconomicus*, or the citizen as producer and property-owner, became *homo desiderans*, the citizen-consumer, the capricious subject of a desire to spend, and a crucial concern for manufacturers and advertisers became the kinds and quantities of desire that could be stimulated, intensified and channelled into consumption of any given commodity. Generating this 'capital' of desire was, of course, the function of the advertising industry (the focus of the next chapter), which developed increasingly sophisticated techniques during the nineteenth century for what Rosalind Williams has described as the 'arousal of free-floating desire'.[64] (Writing of the art of advertising in

63 W. Stanley Jevons, *The Theory of Political Economy* (1871), London, Penguin, 1970, pp. 102-3.

64 Rosalind H. Williams, *Dream Worlds: Mass Consumption in Late Nineteenth-Century France*, Berkeley and Los Angeles, University of California Press, 1982. Williams emphasises the advertising function of the new department stores established first in London and later in Paris, describing them as 'places … where arousal of free-floating desire is as important as immediate purchase of particular items' (p. 67).

1929, D.H. Lawrence observed that it was the advertising industry's discovery of how to construct commodities as objects of individualised desire rather than of general utility that accounted for the 'very skilfully poetic' quality of American advertisements, rendering advertising the true 'poetry' of desire.[65])

From the early eighteenth century onwards, then, what came increasingly to be perceived as in demand, and thus as potentially 'scarce', was not so much commodities, or potential objects of desire, but desire itself. We can illustrate this shift of emphasis in visions of scarcity by contrasting Hume's famous commentary on 'wants' in *The Treatise of Human Nature* (1739-40) with the neoclassical economist, Alfred Marshall's commentary in his *Principles of Economics* (1890). Locating the origins of society in scarcity and sexual desire, Hume argued that 'cruel' nature had burdened the human animal with 'numberless wants and necessities' and 'slender means' of satisfying them; but by entering into society and the division of labour, 'man' overcomes his scant personal means and 'is able to supply his defects', 'and tho' in that situation his wants multiply every moment upon him, yet his abilities are still more augmented ... '[66] For Hume, in other words, increased productive capacity doesn't satisfy, but rather increases, the desire for further consumption: desires multiply even as productive abilities are 'augmented'. Compare this vision of a constantly renewable desire-to-spend with Alfred Marshall's stress on the fundamentally ephemeral and capricious nature of consumer desires in his explanation of neoclassical economics in 1890:

> It is an almost universal law that each several want is limited, and that with every increase in the amount of a thing which a man has, the eagerness of his desire to obtain more of it diminishes; until it yields place to the desire for some other thing, of which perhaps he had hardly thought, so long as his more urgent wants were still unsatisfied. There is an endless variety of wants, but there is a limit to each separate want.[67]

65 Lawrence, 'Pornography and Obscenity', pp. 171-72.

66 David Hume, *A Treatise of Human Nature* (2nd edn), L.A. Selby-Bigge and P. Neddich (eds), Oxford, Clarendon, 1978, pp. 484-85.

67 Alfred Marshall, *Principles of Economics*, London, Macmillan, 1890, p. 155.

One way of reading marginalist theory that suggests a solution to Laqueur's 'difficulty' is as an inversion of the relationship between goods and desires postulated in the classical model of scarcity – an inversion always inherent in that model, as entrepreneurs like Boulton and Wedgwood attested. When desire for any given object is perceived as limited and exhaustible, capable of burning itself out at any moment, what seems to be in demand in an economy of scarcity is desire itself – the desire that Freud figured as 'capital' in *The Interpretation of Dreams* and as the 'valuable' 'metal' to be 'extracted' from his client's word-associations in 'Dora'. Channelling this potentially scarce and unreliable desire into profitable exchange in the legitimate market of 'civil' society – preventing its 'wastage', or what Lawrence called its 'dead loss', in the 'secret', underworld economy of pornographers and prostitutes, masturbators and fornicators – was clearly one of the motives for the intensified campaign against 'unproductive' expenditure mounted during the increasingly consumerist eighteenth and nineteenth centuries. The celebrated Manchester sanitary reformer, Dr Kay-Shuttleworth, explicitly made the link between unregulated sexual spending in the 'black' economy and diminished consumer-desire in the legitimate economy when he argued in the 1830s that a population given to sexual licentiousness becomes 'politically worthless as having few desires to satisfy, and noxious as dissipators of capital accumulated'.[68]

To dispose of Laqueur's other arguments for favouring a Kantian-idealist over a libidinal-economic explanation of eighteenth-century masturbation-phobia: his would-be clinching argument is that half the population – namely, women – fall outside the 'seminal economy', whereas 'contemporary literature insists that the practice was every bit as dangerous for women, who, as everyone agreed by this time, produced no semen'.[69] Laqueur's scholarship lets him down here, for there are countless instances of 'semen', 'semina', 'sperm' and 'seed' being used to refer to both female and male

68 James Phillips Kay-Shuttleworth, *The Moral and Physical Condition of the Working Classes employed in the Cotton Manufacture in Manchester* (1832), Manchester, Morton, 1969, p. 155.

69 Laqueur, 'Credit, Novels, Masturbation', p. 122.

sexual secretions up until the turn of the nineteenth century. A case in point was the Scottish medical entrepreneur and celebrity sexologist *avant-la-lettre*, Dr James Graham, who wrote of male and female 'semen', 'male-semina' and 'the semina contained in the ovarum', in his *Eccentric Lecture on the Art of Propagating the Human Species* (1783), seven decades after the appearance of Bekkers' tract.[70] *Onania* itself, the *fons et origo* of masturbation-phobia, stresses from the outset that women and men are equally disposed to the vice, which in men 'rob[s] the Body of its balmy and vital Moisture' and in women 'drain[s] away all the radical Moisture'.[71] So widely accepted was it in early modern medicine that vaginal secretion of 'semen' during coitus was as indispensable as male ejaculate to conception that the abbé Tomàs Sanchez, in his exhaustive inquiry into the physiology of orgasm in *Aphorismi Thomae Sanchez de matrimonio* (1629), could pose the question: 'Did the Virgin Mary emit semen in the course of her relations with the Holy Spirit?'[72] An advertisement at the back of the fourth edition of *Onania*, 'for the Medicines mentioned by the Author in this Treatise', explains to the reader in considerable anatomical detail how a 'Strengthening Tincture' works on both male and female glands and genitals to restore the weakened or lost 'seed' in both sexes, guaranteeing that 'This Cordial Draught will be found an exceeding Comforter and Nourisher of the Genital Parts, in both Sexes, supplying all Defects or Want of seminal Matter, which it also enriches and Spiritualizes'.[73] The prodigal wastage of vital fluid in onanism, then, was said to impoverish or bankrupt male and female libidinal economies alike. Bekkers nonetheless acknowledged that a total thwarting of the healthy young body's natural impulse to expend its sexual fluids can also lead to disease, as a consequence of dammed-up moisture or energy. It would seem

70 James Graham, *An Eccentric Lecture on the Art of Propagating the Human Species, and Producing a Numerous and Healthy Offspring, &c.*, London, A. Roger, G. Lister and other Booksellers, 1783.

71 Anon, *Onania*, pp. 19, 21.

72 Quoted in Pierre Darmon, *Trial by Impotence: Virility and Marriage in Pre-Revolutionary France*, Paul Keegan (trans.), London, Chatto & Windus, 1985, p. 4.

73 *Onania*, pp. 84-88.

that for Bekkers and his countless followers, youth is damned if it does spend and dammed if it doesn't, the implication being that the true villain in libidinal economy is not spending as such but *unproductive* spending.

If neoclassical economics was an attempt to investigate the desire of the 'sovereign' spender 'scientifically', the new discipline of sexology that developed alongside it in the 1880s and 1890s was no less an attempt to put the study of spending-desire on a 'scientific' footing. The uncanny parallels between the concerns of the two movements have been suggested by Lawrence Birken in his book *Consuming Desire*, and can only be sketched briefly here. Like the neoclassical economists, the sexologists treated desire as a universal, but its manifestations as essentially capricious and individualistic, irreducible to a limited set of species-needs, and to be studied 'scientifically' across a spectrum of polymorphous perversity. (Thus the sexological debates of the 1880s and 1890s between Krafft-Ebing and 'associationist' psychologists like Alfred Binet and Albert von Schrenk-Notzing focused on the question of whether congenital factors or personal associations with chance events in childhood were what determined a given individual's distinctive sexual pathology, his or her unique form of fetishism, homosexuality, sadism or masochism.[74]) Just as the marginalists bracketed questions of ethics from a 'scientific' economics,[75] so the sexologists undertook to establish an 'objective', 'scientific' study of polymorphous desires, freed, in principle at least, from moralistic judgements of the kind that had justified the sadistic 'cures' of campaigns against practices like masturbation. Introducing his own path-breaking study of auto-erotism in

74 See Sulloway's overview of these debates in *Freud, Biologist of the Mind*, pp. 283-87.

75 Carl Menger, for example, went out of his way, by contrast with Marx, to reject any notion that the morality of rent or interest should be of any concern to a 'scientific' economics: 'One of the strangest questions ever made the subject of scientific debate is whether rent and interest are justified from an ethical point of view or whether they are "immoral" ... But it seems to me that the question of the legal or moral character of these facts is beyond the sphere of our science'. Carl Menger, *Principles of Economics*, J. Dingwall and B.F. Hoselitz (trans.), New York and London, New York University Press, 1981, p. 173.

1897, Havelock Ellis pointed out that 'psychologists, medical and non-medical alike', had hitherto treated masturbation in 'a dogmatic and off-hand manner which is far from scientific'; and as for the current state of medical knowledge about sex, 'it can safely be said that in no other field of human activity is so vast an amount of strenuous didactic morality founded on so slender a basis of facts'.[76] For the 'sexual scientists', as for the economic 'scientists', the number of potential objects of desire is unlimited, but desire directed toward any one object soon falls off, because desire itself is scarce[77] (the revolutionary credentials of the contrary view are examined in chapters 4 to 6.) Figuring desire as energy, sexologists like Ellis equated erotic pleasure with the depletion or spending of nervous energy, and they distinguished sexual practices 'scientifically' on the basis of the speed with which this expenditure occurred: masturbation was equated with immediate discharge, or what we would now call impulse-spending; homosexuality with less instant but still rapid spending; and what Ellis termed 'normal', 'civilized', heterogenital love with long-delayed expenditure, or prolonged periods of abstinence in which the quantity of available energy mounted up, projecting a correspondingly greater value onto the object of desire. The protracted courtship rituals that Ellis equated with 'civilized' love thus resembled an interest-bearing deposit account, in which capital reserves of spending-power keep accumulating the longer expenditure is delayed, increasing the investment-value of the ultimate 'discharge'.[78] (Ellis meanwhile anticipated Lawrence's and Bataille's equation of 'wasted' expenditure with crime when he noted that the 'very striking analogy' between sexual spending-desire and the 'impulse to evacuate an excretion' had a special 'appeal' to 'the criminal mind', which associates orgasm with the pleasure of expelling bodily waste, as evidenced by the fact that 'in the slang of French criminals the brothel is *le cloaque*'.[79])

76 Havelock Ellis, *Studies in the Psychology of Sex*, Vol. 1, 3rd edn, Philadelphia, Davis, 1910, pp. 163 and ix-x.

77 See Birken, *Consuming Desire*, p. 48.

78 Havelock Ellis, 'Analysis of the Sexual Impulse', *Studies in the Psychology of Sex*, Philadelphia, Davis, 1908, pp. 1-55.

79 Ellis, 'Analysis of the Sexual Impulse', pp. 13, 3.

Freud, whose profound influence on the sexologists Ellis acknowledged and who recorded his own debt to their researches in his *Three Essays on the Theory of Sexuality* (1905),[80] had already defined the impulse to spend energy as the primary, 'pleasure principle', which is necessarily checked by the secondary, 'reality principle', or the exigencies of civilisation, which demand the postponement of pleasure, this deferral of spending being the precondition for the continued existence of the nervous system as a form of congealed energy, or 'capital'. Viewing object-love as a series of successive displacements of a singular libidinal energy (from self to same-sex parent to someone of complementary gender, for example), Freud was figuring libido not as an inexhaustible, endlessly expendable quantity, but as a potentially scarce resource that could be variously channelled, diverted, dammed up or discharged.[81] The law of the pleasure principle was that this libidinal energy tended to discharge itself via the shortest possible path; hence the conservationist principle of diverting it along 'the defiles of the signifier' (Lacan), or the symbolic displacements ('sublimations') that Freud identified with civilisation. When sexual energy was so dammed that spending was permanently delayed, it appeared to Freud to transform itself into pathological symptoms – civilisation's discontents. Uninvested capital, so to speak, burns a hole in one's trouser pocket.[82] (It might also burn a hole in the seat of the trousers. The association of reckless spending with crime, which we

80 See, for example, Ellis's preface to his one-volume *Psychology of Sex*, London, Heinemann, 1933, pp. vii-viii, and Freud's note to the title of the first of his 'Three Essays on the Theory of Sexuality', p. 135 n.

81 Though Freud rejected (in *The Future of an Illusion* [1929] and *Civilization and Its Discontents* [1930]) communism's view of the private property system as the historically contingent origin of human aggression, he conceived the libido – from which, he argued, aggression emanates – as itself a kind of private property: as genderless, certainly, as capital (which Marx called 'the eunuch of industry') and as polymorphously exchangeable as money, but ultimately limited in quantity and the basic resource of the self as human capital.

82 Weighing 'the advantages' against 'the harmful effects' of masturbation, Freud pointed out that 'masturbation counteracts abstinence and, after all, does represent a sexual gratification that discharges the sexual tension that otherwise would often have a pathogenic effect' (Nunberg et al., *Minutes of the Vienna Psychoanalytic Society, Volume II*, p. 563).

have already encountered in Bataille, Lawrence and Ellis, is also at the core of Freud's symbolic equation of money with faeces. In his 1908 paper on 'Character and Anal Erotism', Freud argued that psychoanalysis is an especially effective form of treatment for even the most 'refractory and long-standing' cases of constipation, but only on condition that the analysis brings the patient's 'money complex' into consciousness. Adult parsimony and avarice, he argued, are reaction-formations against infantile faecal incontinence and anal erotism; hence, to uncover the 'treasure' of repressed infantile anal-erotic desires, the analyst must first pick the lock of the patient's 'money complex'.[83] The impulse to spend recklessly, it seems, encounters the Law at all of the body's orifices.)

The Freudian theory of primary narcissism, which Lawrence found so antipathetic, yields a model of delayed expenditure, or the deferred pleasure principle, which in fact corresponds quite closely to Lawrence's image of profitable exchange in sexual love. Dependent on others as the human infant is for its survival, narcissism is unable to satisfy itself through itself, and so invests pleasure in others as a roundabout means of satisfying its own original desires: investment of desire in others is really an investment in the self, an expenditure that yields a return – or as the marginalists would say, production is simply an indirect and deferred form of consumption. (As we have seen, the marginalists were far from original in this perception of consumer culture: it was anticipated by Mandeville in 1705, and was spelt out by Benjamin Franklin in a letter of 1784, which would be quoted in a J. Walter Thompson advertisement of the 1950s promoting the view that it is economically and socially desirable to be a spender not a saver, a disinhibited, self-gratifying, hedonistic consumer of luxuries.[84] In what the advertisement characterised as 'a mature afterthought', the Franklin famous for advocating saving rather than spending points out: 'Is not the hope of being one day able to purchase and enjoy luxuries a great spur to labor and industry?

83 Sigmund Freud, 'Character and Anal Erotism' (1908), *Standard Edition of the Complete Psychological Works of Sigmund Freud*, James Strachey (ed.), Vol. 9, London, Vintage, 2001, pp. 172-74.

84 The advertisement is described in William H. Whyte, *The Organization Man*, New York, Simon & Schuster, 1956, pp. 448-49.

May not luxury therefore produce more than it consumes, if, without such a spur, people would be, as they are naturally enough inclined to be, lazy and indolent?'[85]) Similarly, Lawrence explained object-love as the 'self-outpouring' of 'that strange effluence of the self' upon 'the treasured object', which is then taken back ('introjected', in Freudian terminology) as part of the self, which 'verily builds its own tissue of such treasure': 'It is really self-devoting love, not self-less'.[86]

Sexology and neoclassical economics were complementary, 'scientific' moments in a broader redefinition of the citizen-individual during the eighteenth and nineteenth centuries as primarily a subject of desire rather than of labour – a unit of spending-power rather than work-power. Freud and Lawrence were among the early twentieth-century sexual psychologists whose writings participated in this centring of desire – understood as the impulse to spend (more or less 'recklessly') rather than to produce – in the definition of the social subject, which is to say in 'civil' society. Outspoken critics of the industrial work ethic and advocates of libidinal release, or (measured) expenditure, as a means of alleviating civilisation's discontents, they represented the urge to spend as a biological or natural imperative, anterior to the social, and as such irreducible to – and ultimately irrepressible by – socio-economic or cultural determinations. There are certainly many echoes of the terms and concerns of early Victorian self-help psychology in Lawrence's conceptions of masturbation, education, and the novel as an agent of self-education. Like the Reverend Todd, Lawrence habitually figured energy as an expendable bodily liquid ('that strange effluence of the self', a 'flux', 'stream', 'sheer effluent'[87]) which masturbation criminally wasted and which

85 Benjamin Franklin, 'On Luxury, Idleness, and Industry' (from a letter to Mr. Benjamin Vaughan, dated July 26, 1784), in *The Works of Benjamin Franklin: Containing Several Political and Historical Tracts Not Included in Any Former Edition, and Many Letters, Official and Private, Not Hitherto Published; with Notes and a Life of the Author, with Notes and a Life of the Author, by Jared Sparks, Volume II*, Boston, Hilliard, Gray, 1840, pp. 448-49.

86 D.H. Lawrence, *Psychoanalysis and the Unconscious*, in *Fantasia of the Unconscious and Psychoanalysis and the Unconscious*, London, Heinemann, 1961, pp. 235-36.

87 See D.H. Lawrence, *Fantasia of the Unconscious*, in *Fantasia of the Unconscious and Psychoanalysis and the Unconscious, passim.*

it was the purpose of education to stimulate and maximise in the animal economy;[88] and he conceived of the novel as a genre of self-help manual, an instrument of mental hygiene and character-building, whose function was to channel the flow of vital energies away from 'dead loss' toward 'healthy' goals, 'cleansing and refreshing' the stream of consciousness, as he puts it in *Lady Chatterley's Lover*.[89] But in construing the desire to spend as a natural, organic imperative, Lawrence repudiated the economism of both productivist and consumerist images of the body. In 'A Propos of *Lady Chatterley's Lover*' he complained that 'Now the body is at best the tool of the mind, at worst, the toy'; his illustration of the body as profit-producing tool was that of 'the business man [who] keeps himself "fit", that is, keeps his body in good working order, for the sake of his business'; and his illustration of the body as pleasure-yielding toy was that of 'the usual young person who spends … time on keeping fit … out of self-conscious self-absorption, narcissism' (narcissism being Lawrentian code for masturbation).[90] *Lady Chatterley's Lover* itself is unsparing in its indictments both of the industrial producer ethic that transforms English woodlands into profitable timber – Nature into commodities – and of the English working class's pleasure in its newfound spending-power, which the novel represents as having transformed pre-war England into a class-less population of hedonistic consumer-spenders, the undifferentiated 'moneyboys and moneygirls' of Tevershall, Mayfair and Kensington, as devoted to the pleasures of conspicuous spending as they are resistant to saving or investing.[91]

Sex, for Lawrence, was an originary psychical truth, irreducible to either the profit or the pleasure principles, and to *speak* sex was

88 See, for example, the 'First Steps in Education' chapter of *Fantasia*, in which Lawrence warns teachers and parents: 'There should be no effort made to teach children to think, to have ideas. Only to lift them and urge them into dynamic activity', ibid., p. 74.

89 Lawrence, *Lady Chatterley's Lover and A Propos of Lady Chatterley's Lover*, Michael Squires (ed.), Cambridge, Cambridge UP, 1993, p. 101.

90 Lawrence, 'A Propos of *Lady Chatterley's Lover*', p. 310.

91 See Mrs Bolton's and Connie's commentaries on the new consumerism of the post-war working class in Chapter 9 of *Lady Chatterley's Lover*.

to speak the Truth with a capital-t: 'Sex is the one thing you cannot really swindle ... Once come down to sex, and the emotional swindle must collapse ... Sex lashes out against counterfeit emotion, and is ruthless, devastating against false love'.[92] Putting this truth 'back' into 'civil' circulation meant bringing it up from the underworld, out of the legal closet of the family or marriage vows, and stripping away the screens of Latin, blue book covers, and the stigma of 'obscenity' from a plain-speaking sex – just as for Freud it meant freeing polymorphous desires, in the name of scientific reason, from the medical and moral stigmas of 'perversion' which had pathologised masturbation as an unnatural and immoral wastage of potentially profitable energies. Projecting their own, literary and scientific discourses on desire as the very type of plain-speaking truth meant denouncing the prevailing 'civil' discourses of sex as inherently euphemistic (products of the 'centuries of obfuscation' surrounding sexual knowledge that Lawrence saw his own paintings and novels as defying,[93] or of 'the prudishness and hypocrisy' with which Freud's 'civilized' patients invariably treated 'sexual matters'). And yet, even as they construct sexual desire as *the* originary truth of subjectivity, Freud and Lawrence irresistibly convert it into the currency of other truths. Sexology and psychoanalysis borrowed much of their aura of scientificity from the putatively non-ethical discourses of thermodynamics and economics: the one, however, a theory of energy defined as capacity for work, the other a theory of desire defined as the motor of industrial expansion. The repressed voice of the producer ethic thus returns in the putatively 'neutral' discourse of 'science'. (The language of science is the language of reason and, as Bataille remarks, 'Reason is bound up with work and the purposeful activity that incarnates its laws', or with calculating 'the ratio between energy consumed and the usefulness of the results'.[94]) Lawrence famously repudiated the scientism of psychoanalysis, insisting on the 'untranslatable

92 Lawrence, 'A Propos of Lady Chatterley's Lover', p. 313

93 Ibid., p. 308.

94 Bataille, *Erotism*, p. 168.

otherness' of unconscious desire,[95] but even as he stresses the unfakeable, unexchangeable truth of sex, his terms threaten to convert it into the very monetary interests from which he wanted it freed: sex is that which cannot be 'swindled', it drives the 'counterfeit' off the market, 'collapses' the 'false' economy – as if sex were the only authentic currency, the one true coin, Freud's 'pure metal of valuable … associations'.

In my reading of Freud's analogy between the unconscious and capital, psychoanalysis undertakes to put the sleeping asset of blocked libido to work, to bring it up from the unconscious, out of the closet of the symptom, into the open market of profitable exchange – profitable alike to analyst and analysand as investors in the economy of desire, the desire to be economical. This is one way of reading psychoanalysis's contribution to that 'putting-into-discourse' of sex which the nineteenth century defined as a secular medical imperative, and which Lawrence helped to define as a twentieth-century literary imperative (both of them avatars of the Christian confessional). Like Freud's rhetorical devices, Lawrence's can be read against their grain – his manifest metaphors interpreted as latently literal. Of *Lady Chatterley's Lover* he writes: 'this is the real point of this book. I want men and women to be able to think sex, fully, completely, honestly, and cleanly. Even if we can't act sexually to our complete satisfaction, let us at least think sexually … Now our *business* is to *realize* sex'[96] (italics added) – as if the conversion of sex into words, the legitimate currency of social exchange, were a matter of 'realizing' hidden assets, which, indeed, is how Lawrence represents his own linguistic business in reclaiming what he terms 'the evocative power' of 'the so-called obscene words' from the underworld and putting them back into 'honest' circulation in 'civil' society, or middle-class conversation and highbrow fiction. (It was Lawrence's literary use of the vernacular Anglo-

95 D.H. Lawrence, *The Symbolic Meaning: The Uncollected Versions of 'Studies in Classic American Literature'*, A. Arnold (ed.), Fontwell, Arundel, Centaur, 1962, p. 17. In applying the phrase 'untranslatable otherness' to the unconscious, I am following Anne Fernihough's example in *D.H. Lawrence: Aesthetics and Ideology*, Oxford, Clarendon, 1993, pp. 67-68.

96 Lawrence, 'A Propos of *Lady Chatterley's Lover*', p. 308.

Saxon words for sexual organs and acts, which he insisted are the psyche's 'natural' language of sex, in contrast to the Latinate language of medical and legal regulation of sex – vagina, copulation, penis, etc. – that set *Lady Chatterley's Lover* on its collision-course with the British censors.) More impecunious even than Freud, and hence sorely tempted to accept pay-offs from publishers and distributors of pirated editions of his novel,[97] Lawrence nonetheless resisted their invitations to become part of the libidinal black economy of pornographers and the self-wasting, 'secret' spenders they served – refused, in other words, to be complicit in the continued 'underworlding' of the desire-to-spend that the work ethic had defined as marginal to a 'public' sphere identified with productive labour, and to the 'private' sphere of a family identified with reproductive labour.

In my reading of the stubborn traces of economism and productivism in Freud's and Lawrence's discourses on desire, however, I don't mean to imply either that a *non*-metaphoric language of desire might be possible or that Freud and Lawrence were closet opponents of the deregulation of the desire-to-spend, the libertarian or 'consumerist' revolution in sexuality. Notwithstanding my focus on the irresistible returns of repressed 'money matters' in their discourses on 'sexual matters', I want to suggest something more than that the producer ethic continues to inhabit the thinking of sexual psychologists who were committed critics of the industrial work ethic and, in their time, notorious advocates of sexual spending as an antidote to its alienations or discontents. To put what both writers represented as the repressed or 'secreted' truth of erotic desire 'back' into circulation in 'civil' society meant sacrificing its 'untranslatable otherness', opening it up to exchange. Freud was the first to admit the inevitability of this exchange, or what he described as the unavoidably 'figurative language, peculiar to psychology':[98] for, any attempt to give unconscious desire a voice, to know the unknowable, cannot

97 Ibid., p. 306.

98 Freud, 'Beyond the Pleasure Principle', p. 60. In observing that psychologists are 'obliged to operate with the scientific terms, that is to say with the figurative language, peculiar to psychology', Freud goes on to describe the discourses of physiology, chemistry and biology as themselves 'figurative' languages.

but substitute a simulacrum for the original, or as Jacques Derrida put it in a reading of Freud that Lawrence is said to have anticipated, the unconscious is 'a text nowhere present, consisting of archives which are *always already* transcriptions'.[99]

But if unconscious desire is always already metaphoric, money is no less inherently metaphoric: to be 'realized' it needs to be translated or exchanged – as Marx illustrated when in order to speak plainly about economic relationships he translated them into erotic ones. In the first volume of *Capital* (1867), Marx tells us that 'commodities are in love with money', they ogle it with their price, 'casting wooing glances' at consumers' pockets;[100] and in his *Economic and Philosophical Manuscripts*, he describes capital as 'the eunuch of industry', arguing that 'no eunuch flatters his despot more basely or uses more infamous means to revive his flagging capacity for pleasure, in order to win a surreptitious pleasure for himself, than does the eunuch of industry ... in order to ... coax the gold from the pocket of his dearly beloved neighbour'.[101] Here, Freud's monetary metaphor (repressed sexual desire as 'capital') is Marx's sexual metaphor (capital as frustrated, or castrated, sexual desire). The 'economising' of sex and the eroticising of money, it seems, are two sides of the same metaphoric coin. On the face of it, the pervasive use of economic metaphors by sexual psychologists during the nineteenth and twentieth centuries has the effect of extending market logic to the psychic domain, incorporating the most intimately 'private' and 'personal' in the public sphere of the market economy. But the discourse of erotic expenditure is inherently ambiguous and duplicitous: what appears in one aspect to be an 'economising' of sexual desire appears in the other to be an eroticising of money. Flip the coin, so to speak, and the productivist and consumerist ethics of sex become indistinguishable.

99 Jacques Derrida, 'Freud and the Scene of Writing', in *Writing and Difference*, Alan Bass (trans.), Chicago and London, University of Chicago Press, 1978, p. 211. For the suggestion that Lawrence anticipated Derrida's deconstruction of Freud, see Fernihough, *D.H. Lawrence*, p. 69.

100 Marx, *Capital, Vol. 1*, pp. 121, 124.

101 Karl Marx, 'Economic and Philosophical Manuscripts', *Early Writings*, Harmondsworth, Penguin, 1974, p. 359.

The story of the recourse by post-Enlightenment economic theory to the language of sexual attractions, courtship and seduction to explain the logic of money and the 'fetishism of commodities' deserves its own investigation, but if, as I am suggesting, the discourses of money and sex became inseparable at a certain historical moment (and quite possibly remain so), then neither discourse can ultimately claim to 'demystify' the other, or explain the other historically – neither discourse, in other words, can securely establish itself as the literal, rather than the metaphoric, voice of history, as *the* language of historical facts, not rhetorical figures.

Which is not, of course, to disclaim the project of historiography as such – including the historiography of promiscuously inter-embracing discourses like those of sex and money. Historicising what became known in the early twentieth century as libidinal economy, demonstrating the cultural relativity of the 'truths' that its discourse articulates, and insisting on the metaphoricity of terms that have now sedimented as commonsensical, 'literal' descriptions of our everyday experience, is central to the project of this book. Such discourse-analysis can find fertile metaphoric ground in the 1980s and 1990s, for example, in Reagonomics and its synonyms. The rhetoric of Reagonomics told us that too much spending-power and spending-desire had been closeted for too long in the underclass economy of welfare mothers or 'welfare queens', and that it should be released into the 'free' market – the phallic economy – where it can, so to speak, get fucking. But the story of the genderings and ungenderings of spending-power (the story, for example, of how Walter's attribution of the power to 'spend profusely' to both sexes, equally, should have come to seem in the mid-twentieth century at once anatomically naïve and economically realistic, and later, in the era of internet pornography, both anatomically and economically realistic)[102] is too complex to be addressed here and

102 J. Lowndes Sevely and J. W. Bennett, 'Concerning Female Ejaculation and the Female Prostate', *The Journal of Sex research*, 14, 1 (February 1978): 1-20, shows how medical authorities – as well as pornographers – recognised female ejaculation up until the early twentieth century, but that 'bipolar

must wait until the following two chapters. Nonetheless, it is clear that the Bataillеian notion of the 1950s that the reckless spending of desire, careless of any return, represents a 'criminal' repudiation of capitalism – or Nature's revenge on the social – is now as quaint as the notion that perversely polymorphous, or queerly individualistic and nomadic, desire might represent a force of resistance to what Gilles Deleuze and Félix Guattari term capitalism's ceaseless decoding and recoding of desire-flows. As Eugene Holland glosses the thesis of Deleuze and Guattari's *Anti-Oedipus*: 'In opposition to savage "coding" and despotic "overcoding" … the semiotic process governing the Symbolic order under capitalism is "decoding", market society's aggressive elimination of all pre-existing meanings and codes'.[103] If avant-garde queer theory here meets Madison Avenue and Wall Street,[104] the dialectic of money and sex that I have been describing in psychological theory is an earlier moment in the same semiotic process. Psychoanalysis may have attracted what Jung called 'the justified reproach of pan-sexualism'[105] by insistently decoding economic relationships – such as those of master-servant, employer-employee, client-contractor, analyst-analysand – as expressions and repressions of erotic desire, but it also, as we have seen, practices the reverse exchange, decoding sexual relationships as economic ones. If erotic desire can be recoded as 'capital', or converted into money, money can be exchanged for sexual desire, and it is the very volatility and visibility of this exchange-relation that makes for the increasing inseparability of the discourses of money and sex since the eighteenth century, and the apparent inability of one interpretative discourse to demystify or

thinking' about sexual difference subsequently demoted the phenomenon to a pornographers' fiction.

103 Eugene Holland, 'Schizoanalysis', in L. Grossberg and C. Nelson (eds), *Marxism and the Interpretation of Culture*, Urbana and Chicago, University of Illinois Press, 1988, p. 407.

104 See Rosemary Hennessy, 'Queer Theory, Left Politics', *Rethinking Marxism* 7, 3 (1994): 105: 'Challenges to naturalized notions of identity and difference emanating from Madison Avenue and Wall St share a certain ideological affiliation with avant-garde queer theory'.

105 Jung, *Contributions to Analytic Psychology*, p. 19.

'trump' the other. No doubt money has always been exchanged for sexual desire, and sexual desire for money, but what is relatively new is the obscene visibility of this exchange, in the Baudrillardian sense of the 'obscene' as the over-exposed, the hyper-visible; it is now definitively *out* of the bourgeois closet, *up* from the criminal underworld.

Coda: Depathologising Onanism as 'autonomous hedonism'

One of the four men to whom an intellectually lonely Freud sent postcards in 1902, inviting them to form a small coterie to discuss psychoanalytic work at his home on the Berggasse once a week (the famous 'Wednesday evenings' in the Freud family apartment, from which the Vienna Psycho-analytic Society would be born) was a dashing young doctor, Wilhelm Stekel, who had attracted Freud's attention with his publication of a study of *Coitus in Children* that seemed to offer supporting evidence for Freud's controversial seduction theory. Seeing his work cited in Freud's paper on the 'Etiology of Hysteria', the young Dr Stekel had approached Freud for professional help with a problem of his own, one of sexual impotence, not unconnected with his wife's scornful reproaches concerning the diminutive size of his income.[106] Stekel's marriage had reached a stalemate; from its outset 'his wife had become anxious about his small income and had reproached him one day' for having a much smaller one than a colleague of his had.[107] Stekel protested that the size of his income was sufficient for their modest marital requirements and, when his wife later asked for something beyond his means, he assured her that it would certainly grow bigger in time – an assurance to which she reacted by pouring abuse on

106 See Wilhelm Stekel, *The Autobiography of Wilhelm Stekel*, Emil A. Gutheil et al. (eds), New York, Liveright, 1950, pp. 77 and 91; and Vincent Brome, *Freud and His Early Circle: The Struggles of Psychoanalysis*, London, Heinemann, 1967, pp. 19-21. Brome's inference from hints in Stekel's autobiography and from interviews with his friends and acquaintances is that the problem he took to Freud was, indeed, one of 'psychological impotence'.

107 Brome, *Freud and His Early Circle*, p. 20.

his head and calling him a miser. The horror of the scene took up residence in Stekel's unconscious and he would later tell Freud, who naturally prescribed a psychoanalytic cure for this case of 'psychic impotence', that 'many things that happened later [in the marriage] may have been due to a desire to avenge this unwarranted insult'.[108] Among the things that happened was that, in Stekel's words: 'One day I was no longer a man. I tried everything to overcome my weakness but I failed'.[109] Whether his eight analytic sessions with Freud restored his manhood – or whether their cost simply diminished the size of Stekel's means still further, adding to his economic impotence – is unclear. But another of the things that happened, due perhaps to Stekel's desire to avenge his wife's unwarranted insult of his diminutive means, was that he became a regular member of Freud's Wednesday evening group. Stekel's developing interest in psychoanalysis and his desire to free himself from general practice in order to specialise in psychiatry antagonised his wife on two grounds: she said of the study of psychology, 'I can't go along with you in this matter, it's like a swindle'; and as for Stekel's desire to give up lucrative general practice for psychiatry, she rejected it as threatening their marriage with penury.[110] In the event, Stekel would be all but bankrupted by divorce from his wife, a cripplingly expensive process under Viennese legal conditions.[111] It was partly to escape the emotional poverty of his marriage that he became a member of the Wednesday circle, many of whose meetings in 1908 were occupied with the subject of 'psychic impotence in the male'. At a meeting on 6 May, 1908, Stekel presented 'Some Remarks on the Genesis of Psychic Impotence', focusing on impotence that appears at a later age for unconscious reasons, and he summarised the four theses of his book *Nervous Anxiety States and Their Treatment*, one of which linked impotence to guilt-feelings that are 'actu-

108 See Stekel, *Autobiography*, p. 77, and Brome, *Freud*, p. 20.

109 Stekel, *Autobiography*, p. 77

110 See ibid., p. 124, and Brome, *Freud*, p. 21.

111 Brome, ibid., p. 221.

ally remorse about masturbation':[112] 'consciousness of guilt has an inhibitory influence. This consciousness of guilt is remorse for masturbation';[113] 'the impotence is partly a punishment and is voluntarily retained from unconscious motives of penance for the criminal phantasies' that accompany masturbation.[114] (In Freud's view, it was 'the cheapness and easy availability of the sexual act' in masturbation that led to 'the general debasement of sexual life' for masturbators, who are 'thereafter unable to have intercourse with persons whom they love and esteem …'[115]) Stekel was famous for his ability to hypnotise patients at will and he reported numerous successes in treating cases of impotence and masturbation-neurosis psychoanalytically; but he claimed that his real satisfaction came mainly from writing his book *Onanie und Homosexualität*, in which he concluded that masturbation 'freed men and women or boys and girls, from the "social obligations of gratitude". The masturbator gave himself or herself great pleasure with an organ which society expected him to employ exclusively in marriage'.[116]

Contrary to the proverbial view of onanism as 'self-abuse', then, Stekel redefined it as self-enrichment, a gift to the self, or a form of pleasurable spending on the self freed from indebtedness to others or any obligation to spend on them. Such an act of self-gratification – the sexual epitome of the 'autonomous hedonism' that Colin Campbell identifies as the core of consumer psychology[117] – had

112 Nunberg et al. (eds), *Minutes of the Vienna Psychoanalytic Society, Volume I*, pp. 392-93; and Wilhelm Stekel, *Conditions of Nervous Anxiety and Their Treament*, Rosalie Gabler (trans.), London, Kegan Paul, Trench, Trubner, 1923, chapter 24, 'Dread of the Railway, Dread of Getting Cold, Dread of Examinations, and Psychic Impotence', pp. 241-55.

113 Stekel, *Conditions of Nervous Anxiety*, p. 249.

114 Ibid.

115 Nunberg et al. (eds), *Minutes of the Vienna Psychoanalytic Society, Volume II*, p. 562. Like Lawrence, Freud could represent the masturbator as antisocial; he claimed that one of the 'injuries' associated with masturbation comes about 'through loosening the individual's interconnections with his fellow men; masturbatory gratification is an antisocial act; it brings the individual concerned into opposition to society' (ibid., pp. 561-62).

116 Brome, *Freud*, p. 218.

117 Colin Campbell, *The Romantic Ethic and the Spirit of Modern Consumerism*,

been freighted with guilt for centuries in a culture permeated by Protestant morality and industrial capitalism's 'producer ethic'. The psychoanalytic movement both attested and contributed to the discrediting of masturbation-phobia in the twentieth century, by demonstrating no organic cause, merely guilt, for masturbation's unwanted 'side-effects' – the neurotic guilt that Stekel claimed psychoanalysis alone could alleviate. Stekel's *Auto-erotism: A Psychiatric Study of Masturbation and Neurosis* maintained that onanism was normal, universal, self-rewarding and in many ways socially beneficial. In a fifty-page chapter entitled 'The Social Function of Onanism', which recounted numerous cases of masturbation-neurosis treated by psychoanalysis, Stekel presented his readers with four stark conclusions, intended to impose closure on two-and-a-half centuries of masturbation-phobia and to identify onanism not only with health but with the will-to-live, or life-force, itself:

1. *Masturbation is not the cause of the neuroses. The neuroses break out when masturbation is given up.*
2. *Masturbation owes its psychic significance to the accompanying specific phantasies.*
3. *When masturbation is given up, the will to live itself is disturbed in many cases.*
4. *The mental and physical dangers of masturbation exist only in the imagination of ignorant physicians.*[118]

Arguing that 'masturbation is the representative of all guilt',[119]

Oxford, Blackwell, 1987, *passim*. Barker-Benfield glosses 'autonomous hedonism' as 'the capacity freely to take pleasure in one's own feelings, aroused by fantasy, in the privacy of one's own imagination, enjoyed under the new conditions of literal privacy – feelings, fantasy, and privacy all sponsored by the rise of commercial capitalism'. See G.J. Barker-Benfield, *The Culture of Sensibility: Sex and Society in Eighteenth-Century Britain*, Chicago and London, University of Chicago Press, 1992, p. 340.

118 Ibid., p. 60.

119 Wilhelm Stekel, *Auto-erotism: A Psychiatric Study of Masturbation and Neurosis*, introduction by Frederic Wertham, J.S. Van Teslaar (trans.), London, Peter Nevill, 1951, p. 117.

Stekel charged psychoanalysis with the task of de-pathologising it; his motto was: '*Lust ohne Schuld*, pleasure without guilt'.[120] Normalising pleasurable spending on the self (an expenditure that might be guiltily withheld from a spouse, such as Frau Stekel, but guiltlessly bestowed on the self) was, in turn, indispensable to reinforcing the precepts of the 'consumer ethic'. The next chapter explores the role of psychoanalytically inspired advertising in this 'normalisation' of pleasurable, guiltless spending.

120 Ibid., p. 118.

3

The Libidinal Economy of Advertising: Psychoanalysis and the Invention of the Consumer Unconscious

Following the rumour that oniomania, otherwise known as compulsive spending or shopaholism, would be recognised as a clinical disorder in the fifth edition of the American Psychiatric Association's diagnostic manual (*DSM-5*), watchdogs of the mind-control industries were quick to note the 'coincidence' that a Stanford University research team's recent discovery of a pharmaceutical 'cure' for oniomania was funded by a pharmaceutical company.[1] Compulsive shoppers were to be encouraged to make one more purchase: a daily pill to make it all better. Marketing a cure for a new disorder – itself an effect of excessive marketing – means first marketing the disorder. Some critics of the pharmaceutical companies' power to create simultaneous supply and demand for products like the shopaholic pill have responded by advocating the more traditional and personally 'empowering' recourse of psychotherapy – varieties of the 'talking cure' – as the better response to oniomania. Such was the approach of the TV talkshow programme

1 The company in question was Forest Laboratories Inc., whose antidepressants, Celexa and Lexapro, were tested on shopaholics by the Stanford University Medical Centre. Press reports of the research include Anne Marie Chaker, 'For Antidepressant Makers, Shopaholics Are a New Market', *The Wall Street Journal*, 2 January 2003, and Richard Luscombe, 'Anti-Depressant Drug on Offer to Shopaholics', *The Scotsman*, 18 July 2003. In the event, the *DSM* contributors voted against including 'compulsive buying disorder' in the manual's fifth edition (belatedly published in 2013) on the grounds quoted at the end of this chapter.

Oprah when it tackled compulsive spending as a self-help issue in 1994. Oprah's guest expert was writer Neale Godfrey, coauthor of *Money Doesn't Grow on Trees*, who talked his audience through various cognitive and behaviour-modification strategies to deal with an inability to control their spending. However, as Jane Shattuc complained of Oprah's programme in her book *The Talking Cure: TV Talk Shows and Women*: typically, 'there was no attempt to ascertain the sources of unrestrained buying'.[2]

This chapter revisits a neglected episode in the cultural history of the 'talking cure' when psychoanalysis was tied to compulsive spending as a patriotic duty;[3] when Freudian analysis, conceived not as a cure but as a catalyst for unrestrained buying, was harnessed to the production of a new kind of citizen-subject, a type of what Georges Bataille called the 'sovereign spender';[4] when the market-research and advertising industries, falling under the spell of Freud's 'economics of the libido', set about eroticising commodities and addressing the consumer not as *homo œconomicus* – the rational, self-interested decision-maker of classical political economy and neoclassical economics – but as a subject driven by unconscious sexual desire. It was a period in the development of consumer culture when, to talk loosely, Freud fathered the Barbie Doll and American advertisers set about getting the id, rather than the ego, to do the shopping.

The period begins – at least in my account of it – in Austria in the 1930s and officially ends in America in the 1960s – but only offi-

2 Jane M. Shattuc, *The Talking Cure: TV Talk Shows and Women*, New York and London, Routledge, 1997, p. 117.

3 The journal publication of an earlier version of this chapter ('Getting the Id to Go Shopping', *Public Culture*, 17, 1 (January 2005): 1-25) apparently sparked interest in this previously forgotten episode of psychoanalytic history: a year after my article's appearance, the 'First International Conference on Ernest Dichter and Motivation Research' was held at the University of Vienna (December 2005), with a selection of its papers appearing five years later in Stefan Schwarzkopf and Rainer Gries (eds), *Ernest Dichter and Motivation Research: New Perspectives on the Making of Post-war Consumer Culture*, Basingstoke, Palgrave Macmillan, 2010. A trade book reprising some of the same material as my article has also been published: Lawrence R. Samuel, *Freud on Madison Avenue*, Philadelphia, University of Pennsylvania Press, 2010.

4 Bataille, 'De Sade's Sovereign Man', p. 171.

cially. My account of this intriguing episode in the history of Freudianism's intercourse with consumerism focuses on the career and influence of an Austrian psychoanalyst who left Vienna in the 1930s to join the flux of European Jewish émigrés to the USA, where he would become the world's highest-paid and most (in)famous market researcher – and who meant something quite different from Oprah's guest expert when he later commented in his autobiography: 'I am interested in Money Therapy. We talk about sex much more openly today than we talk about the role money plays in our lives. An important problem that many people seem to have, at least I do, is to enjoy one's money by spending it … To enjoy expenses that are plain luxury and unnecessary may be recognized as an important experience. It could lead to a liberation from the domination of money'.[5]

The advocate of uninhibited spending as the best medicine for Cold-War America's economy was Dr Ernest Dichter (1907-91), who enjoyed international notoriety in the late 1950s as the protagonist of Vance Packard's best-selling exposé of subliminal advertising and propaganda techniques, *The Hidden Persuaders* (1957) – a notoriety that would explain the subsequent fading of his name from the textbooks of market research and advertising lore, and what I shall suggest has been a re-branding of his theories by other names in our own century.[6]

Addictive shopping first entered the psychiatric textbooks in 1915 (in the eighth edition of Emil Kraepelin's *Psychiatrie*, where it figures among manias such as kleptomania, pyromania and anonymous letter-writing[7]), but it was only in the 1990s that it became the subject of a raft of psychological theories and therapies offering to explain and address the emotional needs and person-

5 Ernest Dichter, *Getting Motivated by Ernest Dichter: The Secret Behind Individual Motivations by the Man Who Was Not Afraid to Ask 'Why'*, New York, Pergamon Press, 1979, p. 139.

6 Dichter's name has also been strangely absent from histories of psychoanalysis. It is puzzling, for example, to find no mention of him in Eli Zaretsky's otherwise comprehensive history, *Secrets of the Soul: A Social and Cultural History of Psychoanalysis*, New York, Alfred A. Knopf, 2004.

7 Emil Kraepelin, *Psychiatrie: Ein Lehrbuch Für Studierende und Ärzte*, Leipzig, Verlag von Johann Ambrosius Barth, 1915, p. 1911.

ality traits assumed to give rise to compulsive spending. Critiques of consumer culture have often called on psychoanalytic theory to explain the psychology of consumption and commodity fetishism, but my concern in this chapter is with a different aspect of the Freudianism-consumerism nexus: the use of psychoanalytic theory by market researchers and advertisers themselves to construct their campaigns, design their commodities, interpellate consumers and influence their behaviour through the mass media in ways they conceived of as 'social engineering'.[8] In short, my concern is with the use of psychoanalysis in the discursive *production* of consumer subjectivity, rather than in its diagnosis or 'cure'.

As Rachel Bowlby has pointed out in *Shopping With Freud*: 'It is commonplace to talk about the "economic" model in Freud, but this is never, as far as I have seen, put into relation with either the economics of his time or the psychological preoccupations of that economics in the area of marketing'.[9] As we shall see, it was the revolution in marketing theory largely initiated by Dichter that introduced Freudian concepts into the self-consciously hardnosed, rationalistic culture of American business and advertising during the Cold War. 'Spending' being the Victorian vernacular term for orgasm, Dichter's project could be described in a nutshell as the revival of a dead metaphor. His challenge to the prevailing wisdom of the market-research and advertising industries depended on a literal interpretation of Freud's metaphoric description of the psyche as an 'economy' of sexual spending-power, and its translation into a theory of consumer spending. This theory was intended both to bolster American corporate capitalism in its Cold War with communism and to help form a new kind of citizen or social subject – one resistant to the lures of either communism or fascism to the extent that it was addicted to the 'erotic' pleasures of spending in consumer society.

8 Ernest Dichter, *The Strategy of Desire*, Garden City, New York, Doubleday, 1960, p. 59.

9 Rachel Bowlby, *Shopping With Freud*, London and New York, Routledge, 1993, p. 114.

The Background: Psychoanalysis and Money in the 1930s

The year 1934 was not the most auspicious moment to start a psychoanalytic practice in Vienna, even for an ambitious young psychologist like Ernest Dichter, with a doctorate in psychology from Vienna University, a training analysis with a member of Freud's inner circle, and rooms on the Berggasse directly opposite the professor's own famous apartment. The Nazi bonfires of Jewish and left-wing literature staged outside the Berlin Opera House the previous year had included Freud's books, and some sixty psychoanalysts were among the first German Jews to leave their country. Over the border, many of their Austrian Jewish colleagues were preparing to follow suit, though Freud himself resisted friends' entreaties to him to emigrate, believing that the worst Austria could expect was what he called 'a moderate fascism', that the League of Nations would surely intervene if Austrian Nazis introduced anti-Semitic laws, and that France and its allies would prevent an *Anschluss* between Germany and Austria.[10] (Proven wrong on all counts, of course, Freud would be forced to leave Vienna by the German invasion four years later, in 1938.) Meanwhile, the Depression that followed the October 1929 New York stock market crash – and that was so conducive to the psychology of fascism – was hitting Austrians hard.[11] Vienna's largest commercial bank, the Creditanstalt, was forced to report insolvency in May 1931 and by the time Hitler became German Chancellor in January 1933, unemployment in Austria had soared to 27 percent. The following month, Austria's Christian Social chancellor, Engelbert Dollfuss, gave the Viennese a foretaste of Austrian fascism when he brutally repressed a Socialist-led political strike in Vienna, only to be murdered, in turn, by Austrian Nazis in an abortive coup of July 1934 that was to have been followed by Hitler's invasion. A self-declared 'old-fashioned liberal', Freud showed little pity for the victims of Dollfuss's brutality, expecting, as he put it, 'no salvation

10 Gay, *Freud*, pp. 593-94.

11 For a 1930s Freudian analysis of the psychology of the Great Depression by a Viennese psychoanalyst, see Paul Federn, 'Factors in the World Depression', *The Journal of Nervous and Mental Disease*, 79, 1 (1934): 43-58.

from Communism' and regarding German invasion of Austria as an inevitability had the Socialist revolution succeeded.[12]

But while he was apprehensive of his country's political prospects, Freud was better insulated than many of his compatriots against the economic hardships of the Depression. While the Austrian mark was plummeting daily and most citizens were turning to barter as the bigger factories and offices began issuing their own money, Freud was making a large enough income in hard foreign currency from psychoanalysis to allay even his acute case of the then-common bourgeois Viennese affliction known as the 'poorhouse or money neurosis' – an anxiety-neurosis described by Peter Drucker as the pervasive tendency of the Viennese bourgeoisie to misrepresent themselves as underpaid and in constant financial distress.[13] Since the early 1920s, Freud had become an international, household name (often paired, as a byword of genius, with Einstein, whose books were also burned outside the Berlin Opera House) and psychoanalysis's popularity had been spreading like wildfire, fanned as much by faddists, profiteers and charlatans as by its dedicated practitioners and patrons in the medical community. An indication of its fashionability in England was a 1921 advertisement by an 'English Psycho-Analytic Publishing Company' offering postal lessons in psychoanalysis, at four guineas for an eight-lesson course, with the promise of £1,000-a-year earnings from psychoanalysis for anyone who completed the course.[14] Nowhere was the 'talking cure' more fashionable than in the country Freud called 'Dollaria', home of the greenback, a nation he believed had 'no time for libido', being completely 'enslaved to that favorite product of anal adults, money'.[15] Yet Americans might have been forgiven for mistaking psychoanalysis itself as primarily a money-spinner, or the epitome of what Lacan, speaking of American ego psychology, would later call the psychology of free

12 Gay, *Freud*, p. 595.

13 Peter F. Drucker, *Adventures of a Bystander*, London, Heinemann, 1979, pp. 83-99.

14 See Ernest Jones, *Sigmund Freud: Life and Work, Volume III, the Last Phase, 1919-1939*, London, Hogarth Press, 1957, p. 50 n.

15 Gay, *Freud*, pp. 568, 570.

enterprise, which, after all, was how it was also officially regarded in Bolshevik Russia from the late 1920s until the 1980s.[16] As we noted in the previous chapter, Freud himself had declared that the 'consummation of psychoanalytic research' had been his discovery of the 'economic view' of the mind, which explained the psyche as an economy of libidinal energy capable of being pleasurably spent in sexual activity, productively invested in work, or unprofitably dammed up in the unconscious by neurosis; and he defended the expense of psychotherapy as a cost-effective investment for bourgeois neurotics interested in freeing their blocked libidinal 'capital' for productive investment in their business or professional work.

Still, it is unlikely that Sam Goldwyn was familiar with Freud's penchant for economic explanations of the psyche when, in 1924, he made his much-publicised offer of $100,000 to the professor, as 'the greatest love specialist in the world', to 'commercialize his study' by writing a romantic screenplay for Hollywood – or that the Hearst Press and *Chicago Tribune* had anything more in mind than capitalising on the public fascination with psychoanalysis when, in the same year, they offered Freud any fee he cared to name, plus a specially chartered liner, to bring him to Chicago to analyse two high-society thrill-killers then standing trial.[17] However, poorhouse neurosis or no poorhouse neurosis, Freud could afford to resist the seductions of Dollaria. By the early 1930s he was making enough money from part-time analytical work not only to support his large, extended family (including providing living allowances for sons-in-law whose businesses were failing in the Depression) but to accumulate capital at the same time. By then, most of his clients were foreign trainee analysts keen to join him in the lucrative profession of psychotherapy and able to pay his steep fee of US$25 per analytic hour in hard cash.

Economically, then, if not politically, psychoanalysis might have seemed an attractive career in 1934 for an ambitious young Jewish

16 See Jacques Lacan, *Écrits: A Selection*, Alan Sheridan (trans.), London, Tavistock Publications, 1982, p. 38; and, below, chapter 8 of this book.

17 See 'To Ask Freud to Come Here', *New York Times*, 21 December 1924, sec. 7, p. 3; and Ernest Jones, *Sigmund Freud: Life and Work, , Vol. III, the Last Phase, 1919-1939*, London, Hogarth Press, 1957, pp. 108-9.

Viennese psychologist. Such were the conditions – a booming international market for psychoanalysis and a looming, anti-Semitic fascism in Austria, fuelled by soaring inflation and unemployment – in which the twenty-seven-year-old Dichter started up his own psychoanalytic practice in his family apartment over the street from Freud's. When reflecting in his autobiography on the need for 'Money Therapy' or 'a course in hard cash psychotherapy' to help people learn to spend guiltlessly, Dichter would look back fondly on his experience of hyperinflation in Austria during 1929-30 as the period of most anxiety-free spending in his life: as he explained, a high inflation rate is the ideal condition for encouraging uninhibited spending, since money has to be spent instantly or it quickly becomes worthless.[18]

'Getting Motivated': Marketing (to) the Unconscious

Dichter had left school at fifteen to become the family breadwinner, and while his younger brothers were growing up socialists, he was identified as the family capitalist. While studying for the Vienna University entrance exam he worked as a window-dresser in his uncle's department store and saved enough money to spend a year in Paris (1929-30), where he registered at the Sorbonne for courses in literature and philosophy, became romantically infatuated with a socialist psychology student, and switched his study to psychology. In 1934 he graduated with a PhD in psychology from Vienna University, where he claims to have been one of 'two star pupils' of his statistics teacher, Paul Lazarsfeld, the pioneer sociologist and psychologist of mass communications, with whom he would later work in market research for CBS after they had both emigrated to America. During an impoverished year after graduating, Dichter set himself up as a lay psychoanalyst, having been analysed free of charge by an American analyst in exchange for German lessons.[19]

18 Dichter, *Getting Motivated*, p. 142.

19 Ibid., pp. 10, 43, 24. Dichter's sketchy accounts of his own analysis are inconsistent. He mentions working with Wilhelm Stekel at this time (*Getting Motivated*, p. 11) and also being analysed by a member of Freud's original circle (see Daniel Horowitz, 'The Émigré as Celebrant of American Consumer Culture: George Katona and Ernest Dichter', in *Getting and Spending:*

Still cash-strapped in 1936, however, he accepted work with Vienna University's Psychoeconomic Institute, conducting interviews on the milk-drinking habits of the Viennese, during which he and several of his colleagues were arrested and jailed for a month by the Austrian police on suspicion of spying. After a week's incarceration he discovered that the Institute had been used by socialists as a secret mailing centre during the Dollfuss and Schuschnigg Fascist rule of Austria. In his autobiography he recalls: 'The next morning the papers were full of stories about how market research and public opinion research had been used to cleverly disguise the subversive socialist activities of the underground. The Social Democratic Party leaders and all the union leaders had either fled months before or were in jail'.[20] A few days after his arrest, the official Nazi newspaper in Germany, the *Volkische Beobachter*, published a list of 'subversives' that included the names of Freud, Einstein, Marx, Engels and Dichter himself. This, combined with the growing number of Nazis in the Austrian police, bureaucracy and professions, and his bleak employment prospects as a Jew, persuaded Dichter to leave what he claimed was his then 'burgeoning psychoanalytic practice'[21] and move to Paris, where he found work as a travelling salesman for a labels factory and made his seminal discovery that sales depended not on customers' actual needs but on the power of the salesman to motivate them to spend. In 1938, the same year that Freud escaped Vienna via Paris to England, Dichter escaped Vienna via Paris to Dollaria, arriving in New York, where his first job was with a market research company, analysing the milk-drinking habits of Americans.

American marketing theory in the 1930s was tied strictly to questionnaire-based statistical research on consumer preferences – an approach that Lazarsfeld had helped to develop but which struck the Freudian Dichter as 'naïve empiricism' and tantamount to what in psychoanalysis would be 'the mistake of self-diagnosis'.

European and American Consumer Societies in the Twentieth Century, S. Strasser, C. McGovern and M. Judt (eds), Cambridge, Cambridge University Press, 1998, pp. 149-66). But neither Stekel nor, presumably, any of Freud's other close associates would have required German lessons from Dichter.

20 Dichter, *Getting Motivated*, p. 17.

21 Ibid., p. 23.

Likening consumption, ironically, to disease, Dichter would later recall in an interview with *The Journal of Marketing Research*: 'What struck me, coming from clinical psychology and psychoanalytic research, was that people were being asked through questionnaires why they were buying milk … and I just couldn't swallow that. It was almost comparable to asking people why they thought they were neurotic or to a physician asking a patient whatever disease he thought he had. I started fighting against that'.[22] As Dichter saw it, the questionnaire-approach to researching consumer motivation could only yield answers clouded by unanalysed transference, in which consumers projected a flattering self-image of rational, needs-based, economic decision-making ('The last thing I should do', he said, 'is let the person who behaves in one form or another interpret his or her behavior … because you cannot get reliable answers that way. You get rationalized answers'.[23]) His own approach, by contrast, was not to solicit answers to a predetermined set of marketing questions but to encourage his interviewees 'to talk in a free-associative way' about their everyday habits and tastes; by interpreting the subtext or latent meaning of their discourse, he would develop psychoanalytic hypotheses about the subliminal motivations of consumers, their unconscious relations of desire and identification with commodities. In short, his concern was with what the title of one of his books called *The Strategy of Desire*.[24]

Marrying his talent for self-salesmanship with his experience of researching both Austrian and American milk-drinking habits, Dichter then wrote to six big American companies, introducing himself as 'a young psychologist from Vienna' with 'some interesting new ideas which can help you be more successful, effective, sell more and communicate better with your potential clients'. In 1939 he landed himself an assignment with the magazine *Esquire* – the *Playboy* or *Penthouse* of its day – researching why men read the magazine. His unsurprising discovery was 'something that

22 Rena Bartos, 'Ernest Dichter: Motive Interpreter' (interview with Dichter), *Journal of Advertising Research*, 26, 1 (February/March 1986): 15.

23 Dichter qtd in Bartos, 'Ernest Dichter', pp. 16-17.

24 Ibid., p. 18; and Dichter, *The Strategy of Desire*.

everybody knew but nobody dared to put down on paper', namely, that the magazine's major attraction was its photographs of naked women. Ever the shrewd salesman, however, Dichter managed to 'sell' this research finding to the reluctant magazine proprietors by arguing that sexually arousing images dilated the pupils of readers, thus making them more susceptible to visual advertising; hence what *Esquire* should be selling to its potential advertisers was precisely the increased effectiveness of its ads.[25]

From this modest success, Dichter proceeded to make himself $200 by discovering the auto-erotic associations of toilet-soap lather for the Compton Advertising Agency and its client, Ivory Soap. Observing that 'one of the few occasions when the puritanical American was allowed to caress himself or herself was while applying soap', he conducted 'a hundred non-directive interviews where people were permitted to talk at great length about their most recent experiences' with soap[26] – a technique that he would later dub 'the depth interview', modelled on the psychoanalytic session. The depth interview's free-association technique could be supplemented with another technique from the psychoanalytic armoury, called the 'psychodrama', which he described as 'penetrat[ing] just a few pegs deeper than the depth interview', and 'where we ask people to act out a product': 'You are a soap, let's say … How old are you? Are you feminine? Are you masculine?'[27] He would later demonstrate the technique of 'psychodrama' before a TV audience of millions on *The David Frost Show*, in which a woman from the studio audience was asked to impersonate a typewriter.[28]

It was when researching Ivory Soap that Dichter rediscovered Marx's insight into the fetishisation of commodities, or the process whereby a social relation between workers appears as a social relation with or between their products, the commodities they buy and sell. Dichter's own insight into commodity fetishism came in the form of his groundbreaking 'concept of the "personality" or "image" of a product' – a notion now banally familiar but one that

25 Dichter, *Getting Motivated*, pp. 33-35.
26 Ibid., and Dichter, *The Strategy of Desire*, p. 33.
27 Dichter qtd in Bartos, 'Ernest Dichter', p. 17.
28 Dichter, *Getting Motivated*, p. 53.

was as novel to American business in the 1930s as the whole 'philosophy' of 'branding' that would soon be built on it. Through canny listening to his free-associating interviewees, Dichter discovered that toilet soap acquires more value by association with washing before a special occasion, such as a romantic date, when people bathe longer, more carefully and more luxuriously; hence, the more erotic a soap's connotations or the more sexual its 'personality', the greater its perceived value and the more likely the consumer is to spend on it. Dichter's report to the Compton Advertising Agency was that Ivory Soap, in 1939, 'had more of a somber, utilitarian, thoroughly cleansing character than the more glamorous personalities of other soaps such as Cashmere Bouquet ... '[29]

The 'personalities' of cars also proved to be fundamentally sexual. From Ivory Soap in Chicago, Dichter drove to the Chrysler Corporation in Detroit in 1939 to help sell its Plymouth car by conducting 'depth-interviews' with car buyers. His method of Motivational Research (MR) – as he came to call his psychoanalytic probings – revealed that men unconsciously regard sedans as symbolic wives and convertibles as symbolic mistresses; and while middle-aged men might buy a convertible to indulge 'their secret wish for a mistress' 'without the expense and guilt of having a live mistress', most men, influenced in their purchasing decisions by their real wives, settled for 'the sedan: the "wife", comfortable and safe'. Hence Dichter's recommendation to Chrysler that 'it was psychologically desirable and effective ... to use a convertible as ... the "bait"' in the showroom window to lure in the male buyer – an advertising strategy that dramatically boosted Chrysler's sales of sedans. The dividend for Dichter himself came in the form of a publicity coup that launched him as a budding celebrity in the American advertising industry: a two-column article in *Time Magazine*, captioned 'Viennese Psychologist Discovers Gold Mine for Chrysler Corporation', and describing him as 'the first to apply to advertising the really scientific psychology' that tapped 'hidden desires and urges'.[30]

29 Dichter, *Strategy of Desire*, p. 34.

30 Dichter, *Getting Motivated*, pp. 38, 40-41; Horowitz, 'The Émigré as Celebrant of American Consumer Culture', p. 159.

The car as castrato: advertisement for 1958 Edsel Full Line Prestige. *http://goo.gl/O5na3G: (in the public domain)*

At the level of manifest, if not latent, content, Dichter's finding for Chrysler might seem at odds with his later research for Ford into the failure of its Edsel car, in which he reported that 'sex was responsible for a half-billion dollar blunder'. The problem he found with the Edsel was that 'some designer who knew little about human motivations' had inadvertently 'castrated the car. It had a gaping hole at the front end' where its nose should have been: 'Our survey showed that the otherwise inhibited Americans were referring to this oval-shaped opening either as a lemon or, the more outspoken ones, as a hole which needed a bit of pubic hair around it to make it more real. This was a major reason for the flop'. To resolve the apparent contradiction between the success of Chryslers as mistress-symbols and the failure of Fords as castrati or vulva-symbols required only a modicum of psychoanalytic insight, for the 'personality' of the sportscar as mistress reflects precisely the sexual potency of the owner whom the Edsel was symbolically castrating. As Dichter put it: 'The fact that most cars either resemble or have names which have something to do with aggression and, if you want to be psychoanalytic, with phallic symbols, is now fairly well known. Whenever a car does not correspond to this concept of penetrating the highway, or moving aggressively forward, it becomes a flop. The failure of the Edsel … was due to a misunderstanding of the soul of a car'. That objects have 'souls' was another of Dichter's insights, underpinning his construction of 'personalities' for commodities. Under the title 'The Soul of Things', he explained, 'People on the one hand, and products, goods, and commodities on the other, entertain a dynamic relationship of constant interaction. Individuals project themselves into products. In buying a car they actually buy an extension of their own personality'.[31]

While working for the same agency that had landed the Chrysler contract, Dichter also researched the psychology of smoking, surreptitiously photographing smokers at ice-skating rinks, analysing their behaviour and concluding that, nicotine-addiction aside, 'smoking, of course, is oral satisfaction': 'holding a cigarette in your mouth is comparable to sucking at the nipples of a gigantic world breast and deriving from it the same type of satisfaction and tranquilizing effect that the baby does when being nursed'.[32] Dichter's Freudianism proved no less marketable for being of the vulgar variety. Among his numerous other findings in the same vein were: that lipstick could be a subliminal invitation to fellatio ('In a study on lipsticks, we found that the more phallic the lipstick and the packaging appeared, the more it attracted women'); that life insurance could be sold to newly-married young men as a form of symbolic resistance to the phallic mother and economic proof of their sexual potency or spending-power; that 'tractors and steam shovels take on [female] sexual characteristics when filtered

31 Dichter, *Getting Motivated*, pp. 94, 126; Dichter, *The Strategy of Desire*, p. 86.

32 Dichter, *Getting Motivated*, p. 42. Cf. Ernest Dichter, *The Psychology of Everyday Living*, New York, Barnes & Noble, 1947, p. 88.

through the engineer's emotions'; and that a German necktie-manufacturer's sales could be substantially boosted by an advertisement that contrasted an 'old, very wrinkled, and limp tie ... hanging on an old man', with 'a new tie – smooth, colourful, erect, and manly', hanging on the same man ten years younger.[33] (A fellow market researcher similarly reported that men's belts could be sold more successfully to wives when displayed on a shelf rather than hanging limply from a rack. As he explained: 'Marketing tests and experience have shown that ... hanging belts do not arouse a woman's interest. A hanging belt has no attraction power. It is limp, unstimulating and undesirable. To the normal, healthy, energetic woman a hanging belt is not a symbol of virility or quality. It cannot possibly be associated with her man'.[34]) Dichter also lifted a typewriter manufacturer's sales by arguing that the body of a typewriter should be modelled on the female body, 'making the keyboard more receptive, more concave', and he claimed to have 'laid the groundwork for the symbolism' of Esso's 'Tiger in the Tank' ad campaign by decoding one of his patients' dreams of fighting with a powerful animal, which he recognised as 'a symbolic way of fighting and loving his father' – an insight that could be translated into a petrol ad's appeal to the subliminal desire to incorporate the father, or the father's power, cannibalistically. As Dichter explained:

> The 'Tiger in the Tank' [w]as another worldwide, successful translation of sex into sales. A gas tank is mysterious and dark like a womb. It can be fertile or sterile. The hose of the gas pump resembles you-know-what. Rational? Who cares? The symbol of power, of virility, of strength, goes through the oddly shaped nozzle into the receptive womb and gives it power and strength. It worked practically around the world. I want you to realise that

33 See Ernest Dichter, *Packaging, the Sixth Sense? A Guide to Identifying Consumer Motivation*, Boston, Cahners Books, 1975, p. 100; Dichter, *The Strategy of Desire*, pp. 216-217, 157; Dichter, *Getting Motivated*, p. 93.
34 Louis Cheskin, *Why People Buy: Motivation Research and Its Successful Application* (1959) 2nd edn, with an introduction by Howard D. Hadley, London, Business Publications Ltd, 1960, p. 219.

> I am as amazed as the infidels are. How can such a contrived mixture between sexual allegories, mysticism, and caveman symbolism result in millions of dollars of very unmysterious cash through increased sales?[35]

Louis Cheskin, a colleague of Dichter's in the motivational research industry, described him admiringly in 1959 as 'the "total psychoanalyst" of marketing' who 'looks for Freudian symbolism in every product and libidinous meanings in every human action. Nearly every utterance attributed to him that has come to my attention indicates an almost complete preoccupation with Freudian symbolism and libidinous connotations'.[36]

Perhaps the symbolic culmination of Dichter's work was his marketing campaign for Mattel Toys' Barbie doll, in which, with spectacular success, he combined his 'sex sells' or 'sex into sales' principle with his strategy of investing commodities with 'personality', as a result of which a Barbie doll is reputedly sold somewhere in the world every half-second. When the founders of Mattel Toys (Ruth and Elliott Handler, parents of a real-life Barbara and Ken) commissioned him to design a sales campaign for the toy in 1958, Dichter was so besieged with commissions that he was delegating many of them to his staff, but he kept the Mattel project for himself. The fruits of his six-month motivational research into toys – based on depth-interviews with 357 children and 58 parents and encompassing dolls, guns, holsters and rockets – included his findings that 'big guns are like penises' and that the unconscious motivation of child's play with toys is to relieve psychic tension and maintain a child's '"psycho-economic equilibrium" in the face of growing knowledge, growing bodies and growing pressure from the adult world'.[37]

The marketing industry's rediscovery of the child-as-consumer in post-World War II America was indispensable to Barbie's success, and Dichter argued that one of the functions of an adver-

35 Dichter, *Getting Motivated*, pp. 53, 80, 93.

36 Cheskin, *Why People Buy*, p. 155.

37 M. G. Lord, *Forever Barbie: The Unauthorized Biography of a Real Doll*, New York, William Morrow & Co., 1994, p. 40.

tising campaign was to provide children with arguments that could be used to persuade a parent to purchase the commodity for them or to allow them to buy it themselves. Probing 'the gift psychology of adults' and the purchasability of a child's love, Dichter recognised the potential of the doll's sexually racy persona (epitomised in her 'Mount Rushmore breasts'[38]) as a medium in which a child could play out her rebellion against her parents, and he recommended a win-win marketing formula to Mattel: Barbie's sexual maturity, self-display and social independence would speak to the child's desires, while her elaborate wardrobes and grooming needs spoke to the mother's anxieties about how to turn an unkempt, tomboyish daughter into a marriageable 'poised little lady'.[39] On the strength of Dichter's research findings and recommendations, Mattel decided to break with tradition and market the toy as a 'personality' with a 'life that was as glamorous and American as possible' ('We never mentioned the fact that she was a doll', a copywriter reported. 'The positioning from the very first commercial was that she was a person'.[40]) Constructing the doll not as the generic infant of little girls' maternal or oedipal fantasies, but as a teenage fashion model-cum-Hollywood denizen with a lifestyle as remote as possible from the contemporary American suburban family's, Dichter and Mattel produced what many first-generation Barbie owners experienced as a 'revelation' of what the girl-as-fancy-free-consumer might become – even, for some, 'a sort of feminist pioneer'. (As one Barbie owner said, 'She didn't teach us to nurture, like our clinging, dependent Betsy Wetsys and Chatty Cathys ... She taught us independence ... She could invent herself with a costume change ...'[41]) Happily unmarried, parent-free and child-free, Barbie was a successful career-girl and sexual free-agent whose social mobility required as many (profit-generating) outfits as there were social occasions – from 'Easter Parade' to 'Roman

38 Gail Caldwell, 'Major Barbie: She's the plastic miniature of everything good, bad and ugly about American culture', *Boston Globe*, 27 November 1994, A13.

39 Dichter qtd in Lord, *Forever Barbie*, p. 40.

40 Lord, *Forever Barbie*, p. 41.

41 Interviewee qtd in Lord, *Forever Barbie*, p. 9.

Holiday' and 'Gay Parisienne', from beach dates to high state occasions.[42] Between them, Dichter and the Handlers had constructed an object of female childhood desire that was a prototype of the compulsive spender and guiltless consumer driven by desublimated sexual desire.

Expounding the theory of his increasingly lucrative practice, Dichter published numerous (usually ill-written) articles and books promoting the philosophy of Motivational Research. Selling his methods to American businessmen in the 1930s and 1940s meant challenging their attachment to that cornerstone of neoclassical economics, the *homo œconomicus* model of the shopper as a rationally calculating, self-aware consumer, and displacing it with a desire-centred model of consumption. Dichter's persuasive reasoning was that the 'science' of MR, which undertakes to tap or desublimate repressed sexual desire and convert it into monetary spending, was the answer to a crisis of over-supply in the post-war American consumer marketplace. During the war, with scarcity of goods, rationing, and demand in excess of supply, there was little need for understanding consumer psychology; but as the sellers' market ended and the mass-production techniques stimulated by the war rapidly increased supply till it far-outstripped demand, marketers had to rely more and more heavily on branding and advertising, which, in turn, entailed analysis of consumer desires. Dichter argued that in an economy of scarcity and need, consumers make rational choices – in Freudian terms, the ego does the shopping; but in an economy of abundance and desire, rather than scarcity and need, consumer motivation is largely subliminal: the id goes shopping – or, at least, it needed to be *persuaded* to go shopping by a marketing technique designed to generate that scarcest and most valuable resource in an economy of surplus-production, namely, desire itself, the desire to spend.[43] Motivational Research,

42 It was only under pressure from consumers' demands for a boyfriend for Barbie that Mattel released its Ken doll in 1961, two years after Barbie's release.

43 As Dichter's fellow motivational researcher, Louis Cheskin put it: 'Motivation research deals with the unconscious mind, and as long as we have an economy of abundance in which brands are competing for the consumer's dollar, we need research into the unconscious motives of the consumers. You

in other words, was the ruse of a marketing industry faced with the challenge of selling new brands of otherwise indistinguishable goods to consumers whose conscious needs were already more than met by the existing brands.

As a strategy for uncovering hidden desire and putting it into profitable circulation in the market economy, Motivational Research bore more than a mere resemblance to the psychotherapeutic technique Freud described in his 1913 paper, 'On Beginning the Treatment', in which he depicted the goal of psychoanalysis as the liberation of libido from blockage in neurosis for productive investment in the patient's business or professional activities. If Dichter was unpacking Freud's economic metaphors by literalising them, it was something Freud himself had already done. The major difference was that where Freud's technique was production-oriented and driven by the work ethic, Dichter's was consumption-oriented and governed by the pleasure-principle of spending. As Dichter argued in *The Psychology of Everyday Living*, the pleasure-yield, rather than use-value, of commodity-consumption becomes paramount in an economy in which labour is monotonous, repetitious, mechanical, de-individualising, and not itself a source of pleasure or self-satisfaction.[44]

Dichter's *Packaging, The Sixth Sense? A Guide to Identifying Consumer Motivation* (1975) provided 'packaging engineers' with a rudimentary lesson in Freud's 'dissection of the psychical personality',[45] explaining that the most effective advertising must speak to all three of the psychic zones or functions distinguished by Freud, disarming 'the parent-surrogate, prohibitionist ... conscience-embodying superego', while flattering the 'rational, reflective, reality-oriented ego', in order to give free rein to the 'instinctual,

have to be sure that your product has favorable psychological connotations before it is put on the market, because the actual product may be about the same in performance as competing product' (Cheskin, *Why People Buy*, p. 102).

44 Dichter, *Psychology of Everyday Living*, p. 67.

45 See Sigmund Freud, 'The Dissection of the Psychical Personality', *New Introductory Lectures on Psychoanalysis*, *Standard Edition of the Complete Psychological Works of Sigmund Freud*, James Strachey (ed.), Vol. 22, London, Vintage, 2001, pp. 57-80.

pleasure-seeking … amoral id['s]' basic urge to spend. Here is how theory could be translated into packaging practice by the tobacco industry, disguising its promise of nipple-sucking pleasure from the censorious superego and the rational ego:

> In cigarette packaging … the combination of filter and pleasure-appeals attempts to communicate with both the rational ego bent on preserving health and with the id clamoring for sensuous gratifications. A third kind of appeal, which currently stresses the 'sociability' of smokers, even appeals to the superego. Here one attitude, 'cigarette is a vice', is combated by another: 'cigarette creates a bond among people'.
>
> Theoretically it should be possible to subdivide the whole cigarette market and the way cigarettes are packaged into predominantly ego, superego, and id markets and fashion symbolic appeals according to the main demands of each category … The most powerful, the most penetrating symbols are those that reach and act upon all three layers of the human personality.[46]

Selling such theory and praxis to the US marketing industry in the 1930s and 1940s was itself a triumph of marketing savvy. Before Dichter's intervention, American market research was dominated by the hardnosed, 'masculine' ethos of number-crunching statistical analysis, in contrast to the 'feminine', because intuitive and 'psychological', 'qualitative' approach of Motivational Research. And while Freudianism may have been high fashion and fad with the American public and press in the 1920s, it took another a decade or two for Dichter and his fellow motivational researchers to persuade American business culture to embrace psychoanalytic concepts. Evidence of their success, however, was the fact that by the late 1950s there were eighty-two organisations registered with the US Advertising Research Foundation (ARF) that were conducting motivational research,[47] and its vogue was

46 Dichter, *Packaging*, pp. 125-26.

47 Barbara Mostyn, *Motivational Research, Passing Fad or Permanent Feature?*, Bradford, UK, MCB Books, 1977, p. 1.

such that in 1953 the ARF's Committee on Motivational Research published a book-length dictionary of psychological terms for use by market researchers – glossing everything from 'abreaction', 'anal eroticism' and 'analysand' through 'memory-trace' and 'mother-fixation' to 'wish-fulfilment' and 'word-association test', and stipulating that 'the only comprehensive and systematic approach to a study of motivation is based on Freudian concepts'.[48] So hotly was MR selling in the 1950s that there was fierce competition to own the brand. Various contenders among Dichter's colleagues in the psychological marketplace published their own manifestos, with titles like *Introduction to the New Science and Art of Motivation Research* and *Why People Buy: Motivation Research and Its Successful Application*, claiming the discovery of MR for their own companies, and in one case dating its invention as early as 'circa 1914'.[49]

The Breaking/Making of Motivational Research

MR's greatest publicity coup, however, was what would soon be read as its obituary: the publication of a book that quoted Dichter (often unacknowledged) on nearly every page and that topped the US non-fiction bestseller list for six weeks in 1957 and continued to sell well, internationally, for another two decades. This was *The Hidden Persuaders* – Vance Packard's demonising exposé of subliminal selling techniques, which helped to 'prove' their scientific credentials even as it discredited them morally. Claiming that America had moved 'into the chilling world of George Orwell and his Big Brother', Packard reported that 'the use of mass psychoanalysis to guide campaigns of persuasion has become the basis of a multimillion-dollar industry'; 'large-scale efforts are being made,

48 Joseph W. Wulfeck and Edward M. Bennett, *The Language of Dynamic Psychology As Related to Motivation Research*, New York, Toronto, London, McGraw-Hill, 1954, p. 7.

49 In his book *Introduction to the New Science and Art of Motivation Research*, Liverpool, Bell Press, n.d. [1958], J. George Frederick, President of the Business Bourse in New York, attributed the discovery of motivational research to his own organisation as far back as 'circa 1914'. In *Why People Buy* (p. 102), Louis Cheskin, a specialist in the psychological effects of colours and packaging, claimed to have been a pioneer of 'unconscious level testing' in the 1930s.

often with impressive success, to channel our unthinking habits, our purchasing decisions, and our thought processes by the use of insights gleaned from psychiatry and the social sciences' (Packard was hazy on the differences between psychiatry and psychoanalysis). 'The sale to us of billions of dollars of United States products is being … revolutionized by this approach', which 'marketers call "motivation analysis"'; moreover, it was also being used by professional politicians to manipulate voters, by fund-raisers 'to wring more money from us', and by public-relations experts to '"engineer" our consent to their propositions'.[50]

The scandal was partly sexual, in Packard's account: Motivational Research verged on pornography, if not statutory rape. He reported that a Chicago advertising agency had 'been studying the housewife's menstrual cycle and its psychological concomitants in order to find appeals that will be more effective in selling her certain food products … Seemingly, in the probing and manipulating nothing is sacred. The same Chicago ad agency has used psychiatric probing techniques on little girls'.[51] In a later edition of his book, Packard would report how Dichter's subliminal 'sex into sales' principle was being applied in the most literal fashion by advertisers who were embedding subliminal messages in printed advertisements for products such as cosmetics and liquor, consisting simply of the word *sex*, or occasionally *fuck*, barely discernible in the shadow-pattern of ice cubes in a gin ad, for example, and making pervasive use of blatant sexual symbolism in packaging, such as the use of penis-shaped containers for women's stockings.[52]

So seductive was the idea of 'subliminal seduction' to Cold-War American capitalism that even revelations of its groundlessness could not diminish its appeal. Six years after Packard's book reported that a New Jersey cinema had dramatically boosted its sales of food and drink by flashing subliminal commands to film-viewers to 'EAT POPCORN' and 'DRINK COKE', his source for the story, James

50 Vance Packard, *The Hidden Persuaders*, New York, McKay; London, Longmans, Green, 1957, pp. 3-5.
51 Ibid., p. 5.
52 Vance Packard, *The Hidden Persuaders* [revised edition], Harmondsworth, Penguin, 1981, p. 234.

Vicary, founder of Subliminal Production Inc., admitted he had bamboozled Packard and that no such experiment had ever occurred.[53] As Hal Shoup, executive director of the American Association of Advertising Agencies, observed in 2000, subliminal advertising 'is a myth that has been perpetrated for the last thirty or forty years'[54] – but its perennial exposure *as* myth hasn't stopped US department stores embedding subliminal anti-shoplifting messages in their muzak, nor American consumers spending $50 million per year on self-help tapes designed to teach them to quit smoking, speak a foreign language or lose weight while they sleep – nor George W. Bush from slinging subliminal mud at Al Gore in a $2.5 million presidential election campaign-ad that flashed the word 'RATS' on the screen when Gore's policies were mentioned.[55] (The revelation of Bush's skulduggery seemed to leave no more of a dent in his reputation than Vicary's revelation of his original hoax dented the reputation of subliminal selling itself.)

With enemies like Packard, Dichter and his fellow motivational researchers hardly needed friends. *The Hidden Persuaders* made the careers of both its author and its prime suspect, Dichter, whose company – now called the Institute for Motivation Research[56] – increased its staff from six to sixty and opened offices in eleven different countries to cope with all the contracts that flowed in as a result of Packard's 'adverse' publicity.[57] Dichter began receiving consultancy and speaking invitations from as far afield as India and Australia and appeared on numerous TV and radio programmes in discussions with his 'opponent', Packard, debating the morality of his business of 'manipulating and persuading people with mysterious means to do things that they never intended to do'.[58] Much

53 Richard Glen Boire, 'Laced Media', *The Journal of Cognitive Liberties*, 1, 3 (2000): 73.

54 Qtd ibid.

55 Ibid., p. 72.

56 Dichter initially called his company the Institute for Mass Motivation Research but dropped the 'mass' because of its unwanted associations with Communism.

57 Dichter, *Getting Motivated*, p. 105.

58 Ibid., pp. 82-83.

like Freud, Dichter acquired a reputation for mantic powers to penetrate and manipulate people's unconscious – powers he was paid to apply to the election campaigns of politicians such as US Vice President Hubert Humphrey, the Chancellor of Austria, Bruno Kreisky, and the Leonist party of Venezuela. He also used sex to sell the Christian Democrats to Italian voters and, after the Vietnam War, was commissioned by the Pentagon 'to prepare a secret plan' for motivating veterans to volunteer for another war and prepare the American public to accept involvement in it.[59] Dichter was also consulted by Stanley Kubrik on the appropriateness of using humour in his anti-atomic war film, *Dr Strangelove*, and commissioned by an Italian publisher to write a book on the unification of Europe, called *The Disease of Nationalism.*

On the other hand, civil libertarians, soon to be joined by feminists, were up in arms against MR following Packard's revelations, which did seemingly irreparable damage to its reputation in the textbooks of American marketing theory – if not in much actual advertising practice – for the rest of the twentieth century. MR's official demise seemed sealed in 1963 by the publication of Betty Friedan's *The Feminine Mystique*, which acknowledged Dichter ('this most helpful of hidden persuaders'[60]) and his Institute's archives as a prime source for its information. Friedan laid the blame for a disastrous return of patriarchal stereotypes of femininity to American popular culture and education in the 1940s squarely at the doors of the popularisers of applied psychoanalysis, who pushed the barrow of Freud's pansexualism and his anatomy-is-destiny gender-essentialism in everything from marketing theory to anthropology to marriage-guidance manuals. In her chapter on 'The Sexual Sell', Friedan depicted Dichter and his fellow hidden persuaders, American ad-men, as crucial agents in the fabrication and marketing of 'the feminine mystique', selling to American women the self-image of housewife, mother and consumer and persuading them, as the preeminent shoppers, that spending money

59 Ibid., pp. 97-102, 148.
60 Betty Friedan, *The Feminine Mystique*, London, Victor Gollancz, 1963, p. 208.

on commodities could give them 'the sexual joy they lack', along with 'the sense of identity, purpose, creativity, the self-realization' they also lacked.[61] America had become the centre of the psychoanalytic movement as Freudians, Jungians and Adlerians fled Vienna and Berlin to live on the lucratively multiplying neuroses of Americans, and Friedan saw Freudianism as installing itself in the hollow core of American consumer subjectivity, performing the same function as the religious revival. 'The Freudian mania in the American culture', she wrote, 'filled a real need in the forties and fifties: the need for an ideology, a national purpose, an application of the mind to the problems of people. Analysts themselves have recently suggested that the lack of an ideology or national purpose may be partially responsible for the personal emptiness which sends many men and women into psychotherapy … '[62] As prime perpetrators of the 'Freudian mania', Dichter and his ilk were filling that emptiness with sexual desire (they were responsible, Friedan charged, for 'the mounting sex-hunger of American women', their successful reduction 'to sex creatures, sex-seekers'[63]), helping to produce a citizen who, now convinced that her behaviour as spender and consumer was motivated by repressed sexual desire, was prepared to buy psychoanalysis itself.

It was partly in response to Packard's and Friedan's ethically stigmatising, if profit-generating, exposés of his 'hidden' influence that Dichter elaborated his defence of MR as a contribution to democracy and the survival of capitalism in its Cold War with Communism. In his 1960 book, *The Strategy of Desire*, Dichter described himself as a 'social scientist' engaged in 'social engineering' through advertising: his projects included strengthening the capitalist economy through the trickle-down effect of conspicuous consumption and retraining conformist American citizens, who had been moulded by the Fordist mass culture of the 1930s and 1940s, in autonomous decision-making and hence individualism through consumer-choice – the antithesis of communism's and fascism's Party-made decisions and social

61 Ibid.
62 Ibid., pp. 187-88.
63 Ibid., p. 261.

conformity. By presenting Americans with a potentially dazzling variety of individuated 'brand images' or 'brand personalities'[64] to choose among, MR's programmatic fetishisation of commodities encouraged them to define their mutual differences, and construct their own personalities as individuals, through their purchasing decisions. As Dichter had put it in his 1947 book, *The Psychology of Everyday Living*: 'Possessions expand our personality', and for Americans, who lack European noble titles, 'the trademark products they own' are a 'modern source of distinction'.[65] Democracy, according to Dichter, imposed an unwanted burden of responsibility on conformist Americans that he called 'the misery of choice': 'one of the basic tasks of modern life is to learn to decide. Democracy represents one of the most difficult forms of life adjustment … Yet few of us have learned to make decisions. Contrary to what we think, changing one's brand, one's [political] candidate, one's jobs, are all miseries of choice rather than pleasures'.[66] The role of the marketer as social engineer was to invest these choices with libidinal pleasure, liberating the consumer from both social conformity and 'masochistic' self-denial into guiltless spending.[67] Training in such individualism could mean everything from being offered individual-sized packages of butter, jam, sugar and salt in restaurants and hotels to learning to live guiltlessly with excess, a superfluity of commodities.[68]

The Psychology of Everyday Living anticipates by more than four decades the world of Bret Easton Ellis's *American Psycho* in its vision of identity as a function of designer labels, its prediction that 'it may soon be customary to describe an individual's personality not by referring to him as one who is timid or self-conscious or characterized by any other traits, but rather, for example, as one who wears an Adam hat, drives a Plymouth car, drinks PM whiskey, and wears Arrow ties and shirts'.[69] Dichter's book also anticipates by half a century the marketing theorist Tom Peters'

64 Dichter, *The Strategy of Desire*, p. 231.
65 Dichter, *Psychology of Everyday Living*, p. 212.
66 Dichter, *The Strategy of Desire*, p. 242.
67 Dichter, *Getting Motivated*, p. 185.
68 Dichter, *Packaging*, p. 75; Dichter, *Getting Motivated*, p. 185.
69 Dichter, *Psychology of Everyday Living*, p. 213.

advocacy of what he terms 'personal branding', or 'The Brand Called You'. 'Big companies understand the importance of brands', Peters wrote in 1997, 'Today, in the Age of the Individual, you have to be your own brand. Here's what it takes to be the CEO of Me Inc ... '[70]

Dichter's market populism also reads like an uncanny echo – from within the advertising machine itself – of the Frankfurt School's critique of mass culture, social conformity and fascism, and its celebration of individualism. The logical outcome of MR's investing of otherwise indistinguishable goods with individuated 'personalities' was the breakup of a single mass market, regulated by a mass culture, into a plurality of niche-markets, regulated by the so-called 'segment-making media', along lines of sex, age, region, race, class and so on. The rhetoric of self-defining citizens and subcultures differentiating themselves by distinctive patterns and practices of consumption – the rhetoric so seductive to post-modern cultural studies – can thus be seen as the legacy of a Cold-War advertising industry solving the 'problem' of surplus production and insufficient consumer-desire through the multiplication of brand identities or 'personalities'.

Sexual Desire: The Catalyst or the Commodity?

One possible conclusion to be drawn from the episode of cultural history I have been describing is that the 'unconscious' of structuralist cultural studies might be Motivational Research itself – in other words, that behind the tendency of French cultural theorists to shrug off Marxism in favour of the semiotic analysis of consumer society in the 1970s lies the success of the marketing and advertising philosophy that Dichter promoted. Jean Baudrillard, for example, used Dichter as a whipping-boy when he embarked on his structuralist analysis of consumer culture at the end of the 1960s, but he wasn't above repeating many of Dichter's own themes. In *La Société de consommation*

70 Tom Peters, 'The Brand Called You', *Fastcompany Magazine*, August 1997, p. 1. For a discussion of Peters' marketing theory, see Thomas Frank, *One Market Under God*, London, Vintage, 2002, *passim*.

(1970), Baudrillard dismisses the economists' notion of rationally calculating, self-aware, self-interested *homo œconomicus* as a purely mythic creature,[71] without considering that mid-twentieth-century marketers had been working very hard indeed to *make* this creature obsolete or mythic and to 'sell' to American business, to the public and to cultural theorists alike, the image of a consumer driven by an irrational desire to spend beyond any satisfiable need. (That desire is always in excess of its object was, and is, a fundamental tenet of psychoanalysis, which thus appears to naturalise or biologise and universalise greed, the reputed cause of global financial crises such as the 2008 one.) Dismissing *homo œconomicus* as myth, Baudrillard postulates two bedrock 'truths' about subjectivity: that desire is insatiable and that social subjects *need* difference, a 'need' they pursue and communicate by consuming commodities as signs (messages, images) rather than for their utility.[72] In Baudrillard's account, it is as if the Cold-War marketing industry's 'dematerialising' of goods and displacing of their use-value with a constructed sign-value, or 'brand-image', had simply produced a new or expanded language in which the human 'need' for social difference could be infinitely pursued. Again, Baudrillard's semiotics seems to naturalise the appetite for symbolic difference, whereas, arguably, it was the marketing and advertising industries themselves that worked to produce symbolic difference *as* a commodity, or marketable good, and train consumers to desire it. Such training meant persuading citizen-consumers to discover in themselves a desire they didn't know they had, an unconscious desire. In order to sell to the id, however, the consumer had first to be psychologised, or Freudianised, and this is what both MR and Packard's exposé of its scandal achieved. The discrediting of subliminal selling as a sinister commercial practice was part of the successful marketing to consumers of the belief that they *had* repressed desires which might be variously manipulated, symbolically satisfied, neglected or frustrated – in other words, the selling

71 Jean Baudrillard, *The Consumer Society: Myths and Structures*, London, Sage, 1998, pp. 68-69.
72 Ibid., pp. 77-78.

to consumers of a personality radically different from, indeed antithetical to, *homo œconomicus*. In so far as these unconscious desires were understood to be fundamentally sexual, then the care of the self in consumer society meant care of one's sexual desire – hence the pervasive eroticisation of consumer culture, which purports to 'speak' to the individual's interiority, or unconscious, by providing the symbolic goods that realise its 'fantasies'.

But what is speaking here, of course, is neither Desire nor the Unconscious, but rather psychoanalytic culture itself, in its banalised, commercialised, mass-mediated form. And if eroticised advertising refers not to unconscious desires, but rather to psychoanalytic culture as it has entered into the everyday, then what this psychoanalytic culture in turn connotes or signifies is self-cultivation as liberation from repression – a new way of relating to, or understanding, the self as a domain of complexity and contradiction. *The Feminine Mystique* and *The Hidden Persuaders* established the terms of debate about eroticised advertising as a struggle between those who would plumb and manipulate subliminal desires and those who would censor the former's advertisements in order to protect the personal unconscious from exploitation by commerce, capital, the mass media. But the real conditioning to which consumers are subjected by what Baudrillard calls 'the machinery of erotic advertising' is not some '"deep-level" persuasion or unconscious suggestion',[73] but rather their blinding to the fact that the meanings into which goods have been transformed are all *on the surface*, constructed not by the individual's primordial hidden drives but by the culture that is accused (not least by Freudianism itself) of disciplining, 'distorting', or denying those drives. In short, to make a Baudrillardian point, the whole Dichter-Packard 'scandal' served to deflect attention from the fact that the codes of commodities and advertising, the whole codified play of sexual signs, had no reference – not only no 'deep' meaning, but no reference at all (except to themselves). Thus the sexual came to *stand in* for reference or meaning. Psychoanalysis having established that the hidden, the unconscious, was essentially sexual, the sexual itself came to stand for hidden meaning, the elusive truth or

73 Ibid., p. 148.

value which the consumer desires. And if a commodity (a new brand of petrol, say, or tyres) had no meaning, then a pseudo-secret meaning, a symbolically 'disguised' one, could be invented for it by advertising that eroticised it. Once sexualised, it became meaningful, and by this means, sexuality became synonymous with meaning itself. So, to saturate society or the self with meaning must be to sexualise it. The circularity or self-referentiality of the process was precisely what Dichter was defending in arguing that selling brand-images or brand-personalities to consumers was the way to invent a society of individuals with interiority, depth, or desire for more in life than mere means of subsistence.

This is the process by which the catalyst to consumption or spending – sex – becomes the commodity, or object of consumption. (The corollary of the 'sexual sell' was what Friedan identified as a new tendency of suburban housewives in the 1950s to seek fulfilment and identity in sex, including sexual promiscuity. As another commentator observed in 1950: 'More than before, as job-mindedness declines, sex permeates the daytime as well as the playtime consciousness. It is viewed as a consumption good not only by the old leisure classes but by the modern leisure masses'.[74]) Dichter set out to make money from repressed sexual desires, which, being repressed and only manifest in 'disguised' or symbolic form, could be satisfied by the symbolic means of the eroticised commodity – Ivory Soap, the Plymouth car and so forth. Perhaps it was inevitable that the disguise should be shed and the catalyst become the commodity – such that what consumers learned to desire as a token of their belonging in consumer culture was an insatiable quantity of sexual desire itself.

The After-life of Motivational Research

By 1990, the official verdict of the academic marketing profession was that, 'after the early 1960s Dichter gradually faded into irrelevance', leaving 'no original, usable scientific legacy or methodology', and the fashion for MR gave way to a style of marketing

74 David Riesman, *The Lonely Crowd*, New Haven, Yale University Press, 1950, p. 172, qtd in Friedan, *Feminine Mystique*, p. 391.

analysis much more indebted to Lazarsfeld than to Dichter, one that 'increasingly reflected the hard sciences: formal experimental designs, operations research, mathematical modelling and multivariate analysis ...'[75] But intellectual fashions rotate rapidly in the industry whose business it is to keep manufacturers and retailers interested by dreaming up ever-new fashions. In other words, novelty and amnesia are close kin in advertising, and one of the putatively 'postmodern' turns that marketing theory has taken in the twenty-first century amounts to a reinvention of Dichter's wheel by other names. During the past two decades, a few brave professors of marketing have begun elaborating the concept of 'hedonic consumption', acknowledging that hitherto 'desire has been a taboo word in consumer research'. Apparently unaware of MR, Dichter and Packard, they have postulated subliminal, desire-driven consumer motivations and pleasures, even drawing analogies between consumer spending and orgasm.[76] Under the title, 'The Missing Streetcar Named Desire', professors Belk, Ger and Askegaard explain that their theory of 'hedonic consumption' presupposes that the material objects on which desire temporarily focuses are not only secondary to their symbolic meanings, but that 'commodity advertising can cater for the desire to desire, or that the arousal of desire can function as an end, a source of pleasure, in itself'.[77] This 'new' turn – or return – to libidinal economy in consumer research has been depicted as a 'postmodernising' of marketing theory under the intellectual influence of such intellectuals as Debord, Derrida, Deleuze, Jameson, Jencks and Lyotard, giving rise to putatively new perceptions of a new kind of consumer: 'the postmodern buyer' for whom brands serve multiple goals simultaneously, including 'things such as fulfilling the consumer goal of "self-indulgence" and enabling consumers to

75 Ronald A. Fullerton and Barbara B. Stern, 'The Rise and Fall of Ernest Dichter', *Werbeforschung und Praxis*, 35, 6 (June 1990): 210-11.

76 Russell W. Belk, Güliz Ger and Søren Askegaard, 'The Missing Streetcar Named Desire', in S. Ratneshwar, David Glen Mick and Cynthia Huffman (eds), *The Why of Consumption: Contemporary Perspectives on Consumer Motives, Goals, and Desire*, London and New York, Routledge, 2000, pp. 98-103.

77 Belk et al., 'The Missing Streetcar', p. 107.

act out fantasy identities in their leisure time'.[78] The proponents of hedonic consumption point out that 'for Lacan, as for Freud, sexual desire is not simply a metaphor for other forms of desire, the libido, or the striving for *jouissance*, is the underlying source of all desire', and they stress that desire is something that may 'overcome', 'torment', 'suffuse', 'enchant', 'blind', 'tease' or 'arouse' a subject, and that 'we battle, resist, and struggle with, or succumb, surrender, and indulge our desires. Passionate potential consumers are consumed by desire'.[79]

Another marketing academic who has evidently repressed all memory-trace of Dichter and MR is the Harvard Business School professor, Gerald Zaltman, who reinvents Dichter's wheel under the fashionable sign of neuroscience in *How Customers Think: Essential Insights into the Mind of the Market* (2003), a book that undertakes to show 'how to unlock the hidden 95 per cent of the customer's mind that traditional marketing methods have never reached', by employing a 'practical synthesis of the cognitive sciences' that combines 'academic rigor with real-world results to offer highly accessible insights' and 'an all-new tool kit'. The cover blurb of his book goes on to tell us: 'Zaltman provides research tools – metaphor elicitation, response latency, and implicit association techniques, to name a few – that will be all-new to marketers and demonstrates how innovators can use these tools to get clues from the subconscious when developing new products and finding new solutions, long before competitors do'.[80]

Those who forget history may be condemned to repeat it, but the signs of a twenty-first-century revival of the Cold War fashion for MR may be merely a formal academic rehabilitation of assumptions long naturalised in the actual practices of marketing, a rehabilitation by professors who are finally catching up with the twentieth-century mutations in consumer subjectivity that were not so much discovered by MR as engineered by the marketing and advertising practices

78 Craig J. Thompson, 'Postmodern Consumer Goals Made Easy!' in S. Ratneshwar et al. (eds), *The Why of Consumption*, pp.120-21.

79 Belk et al., 'The Missing Streetcar', p. 99.

80 Cover text of Gerald Zaltman, *How Customers Think: Essential Insights into the Mind of the Market*, Boston, Harvard Business School Press, 2003.

it helped to inspire. Such assumptions have now sedimented as commonsense in a pervasively sexualised consumer culture in which the catchphrases 'sex sells' and 'retail therapy' have become vernacular clichés rather than the provocative slogans of a revolutionary new 'science' of consumption. Contemporary marketing theory's contributions to the overhauling of classical *homo œconomicus* – its role in redefining the consumer as a subject of irrational, subliminal or 'supraliminal' desires, rather than of rational, self-interested, cost-benefit calculations – may now go by such names as 'hedonic consumption', 'metaphor elicitation' and 'neuromarketing research', rather than 'Motivational Research', but it makes much the same claim to be unmasking what its advocates describe as 'the substantial role played by unconscious processes (and the minimal role played by deliberate, effortful processes) in psychological and behavioral phenomena'.[81] The difference is that today's industry professionals are more likely to genuflect to neuroscience than to psychoanalysis, citing research data such as the finding that MRI (magnetic resonance imaging) scanning shows greater brain activity in subjects who think they are drinking Coca Cola than in those who think they are drinking Pepsi, despite their inability to taste any difference between the brands when drinking them 'blind' (a finding reported in the distinguished neuroscience journal *Neuron*, in 2004, under the title 'Neural Correlates of Behavioral Preference for Culturally Familiar Drinks').[82] As we have seen, brand-imagineering was developed as a way of stimulating consumer demand in a market 'over-supplied' with otherwise indistinguishable, mass-produced goods, that is, as a way for manufacturers to protect their products from price-competition by making shoppers more brand-loyal and less price-sensitive. As a corporate partner of Starbucks points out: 'Nobody buys a ten-cent cup of coffee for $4 unless they're buying a brand'.[83]

81 John A. Bargh, 'Losing Consciousness: Automatic Influence on Consumer Judgment, Behavior, and Motivation', *Journal of Consumer Research*, 29, 2 (2002): 280-86.

82 Samuel M. McClure et al., 'Neural Correlates of Behavioral Preference for Culturally Familiar Drinks', *Neuron*, 44, 2 (October 2004): 379-87.

83 Quoted in Robert Levine, 'Would You Like an Extra Shot of Music with that Macchiato', *New York Times*, 3 November 2004, p. E3.

Dichter's theories of subjective identification and individualisation through brand-identification have meanwhile been extrapolated into new practices of 'hidden persuasion' in the contemporary advertising industry. Packard's project of demystification and consciousness-raising – what today would be called teaching consumers media-literacy – presupposed that the ego, or rational consciousness, could master the id and hence defend it from the 'hidden persuaders'. Bypassing the media-savvy twenty-first-century consumer's conscious defences against advertising is a challenge to which the industry has risen with an arsenal of fresh tactics designed to thwart the public's ability to spot and evade branded messages, such as by embedding them in infotainment content, diaristic blogging or everyday conversation that is not legally defined, nor therefore regulated, as commercial – tactics known as 'guerrilla' marketing, or buzz, stealth or word-of-mouth marketing. (WOMMA, the Chicago-based Word of Mouth Marketing Association founded in 2004, describes itself as 'the official trade association dedicated to word of mouth and social media marketing'.) As finely-honed techniques of niche-marketing, predicated on theories of self-differentiation and tribal identification through brand-choice, such strategies divide up 'the market' (the citizenry) along all sorts of fault-lines other than class and in ways seemingly calculated to render class-distinctions and class-perceptions obsolete. 'Subliminal' niche-marketing thus has an obvious affinity with neoliberalism's promotion of competitive individualism, its repression of class-consciousness, and its vision of the individual as author of his/her own economic fate.

Meanwhile, Dichter's identification of shopping with patriotism has been forcefully reaffirmed in the twenty-first century, not least by politicians such as President George Bush, Jr when encouraging patriotic Americans to keep shopping after the atrocity of '9/11'. In the 1950s, William Whyte had pointed out that the 'Protestant Ethic' of thrift had been 'becoming a little unAmerican' since the beginning of the twentieth century, and that 'the same man who will quote Benjamin Franklin on thrift for the [corporate] house organ would be horrified if consumers took these maxims to heart and started putting money into savings and less into instalment purchases'.[84] Whyte cast as a moral conundrum the question of how to stimulate consumer spending in the 1950s without offending America's Puritan ethic, citing Dichter's view that 'one of the basic problems' of prosperity is 'the problem of permitting the average American to feel moral ... even when he is spending, even when he is not saving'.[85]

Neoliberalism recasts the moral/immoral distinction as a rational/irrational one, reinforcing the bonds between economic and psychiatric rationality. As national economies continue to lurch between inflation and recession in the twenty-first century, the question of how much credit-fuelled spending is rational or irrational, healthy or unhealthy, for any nation at any given moment continues to divide economists, just as the question of how much shopping might be rational or irrational, healthy or pathological, for any individual divides psychiatrists.

It thus seems reasonable to presume a connection between the perennial *in*decisiveness of economists and the recent decision of the American Psychiatric Association *not* to include 'shopping addiction' as a recognised mental disorder in its latest *Diagnostic and Statistical Manual.* While the *DSM-5* editors decided to retain 'kleptomania' (defined as 'the recurrent failure to resist impulses to steal items even though the items are not needed') in their manual and to add 'gambling disorder' under a new heading of 'Addictive Disorders', they explain their decision against including 'groups of repetitive behaviors, which some term *behavioral addictions*, with such subcategories as "sex addiction", "exercise addiction", or "shopping addiction"' on the grounds that there is 'insufficient peer-reviewed evidence to establish the diagnostic criteria and course descriptions needed to identify them'.[86] Evidently, the psychiatric profession disagrees with itself on the quantitative measure of pathological shopping, or the boundary between economic sanity and

84 William H. Whyte, *The Organization Man*, New York, Simon and Schuster, 1956, p. 17.

85 Ibid.

86 American Psychiatric Association, *Diagnostic and Statistical Manual of Mental Disorders*, Fifth Edition, DSM-5, Washington, D.C. and London, American Psychiatric Publishing, 2013, p. 481.

unreason, for the *DSM* editors made their decision despite the *American Journal of Psychiatry*'s publication of the results of a 2006 survey, using 'a clinically validated screening instrument, the Compulsive Buying Scale', that found that at least 5.8 per cent of Americans suffer from 'compulsive buying behavior'.[87]

Despite divisions among and between economists and psychiatrists on the indices of rational shopping, it was precisely the medicalising of compulsive shopping as a pathological threat to the virtues of thrift and capital accumulation in the nineteenth and twentieth centuries that inspired a counter-tradition of radical libidinal economists to celebrate the compulsive spender as a quasi-heroic figure of refusal of what Marx called 'the historical mission of the bourgeoisie', namely, 'accumulation for accumulation's sake, production for production's sake'.[88] It is to that history of pathologisation and radicalisation that the next chapter turns.

87 Lorrin M. Koran, Ronald J. Faber, Elias Aboujaoude, Michael D. Large and Richard T. Serpe, 'Estimated Prevalence of Compulsive Buying Behavior in the United States', *American Journal of Psychiatry*, 163 (1 October, 2006): 1806.
88 Marx, *Capital*, Vol. 1, p. 652.

4

Compulsive Spending and the Trope of the Prostitute as Proto-Revolutionary: Parent-Duchâtelet, Reich, Bataille, Marcuse and Lyotard

In his infamous essay 'On Women' (1851), Arthur Schopenhauer observed that 'women in their hearts think that men are intended to earn money so that they may spend', and their 'greater inclination to extravagance … sometimes borders on madness'.[1] The history of the medicalisation of compulsive spending as a psychosexual disorder is intimately bound up with another history, that of Victorian social anthropology's pathologising of the female prostitute as a hereditary character-type predisposed to reckless spending. In this chapter I shall be tracing the changing fortunes of this figure of the spendthrift prostitute – and her relationship, as a woman *of* the street, to the average woman *in* the street – in discourses of libidinal economy ranging from pornography to anthropology to psychoanalysis, and from Freudo-Marxist revolutionary theory to the post-political anti-theory of Jean-François Lyotard, author of the only book actually called *Libidinal Economy.*

The Victorian medical profession's pathologising of all but the most frugal and (re)productive sexual spending – its stigmatising of onanism and fornication as the wasted expenditure of a precious energy-resource, vital to the economy of both the

1 Arthur Schopenhauer, 'On Women' (1851), *Essays and Aphorisms*, R.J. Hollindale (introd. and trans.), Harmondsworth, Penguin, 1973, full text available at https://ebooks.adelaide.edu.au/s/schopenhauer/arthur/essays/chapter5.html

working body and the wealth of nations – represented only one side of the coin of the emerging 'science' of libidinal economics. The other side of the coin was nineteenth-century erotica's unashamed celebration of the sexual big-spender. In pornography's black economy, the pleasure-yield of spending rarely comes at a damaging cost to the consumer. One of the stock-types of the erotic-memoir genre of Victorian pornography is that of the narrator-hero who embarks on a career of libertinism with a fortune as large as his libido – as well-endowed with monetary as with sexual spending-power – and happily remains that way, undiminished by pleasurable spending. Nor was prodigal spending the exclusive preserve of male characters in Victorian erotica, any more than the term 'sperm' was reserved for male 'spendings'. The editors of the pornographic journal *The Pearl*, published for the Society of Vice in London in the late 1870s, made something of a fetish of big-spending women in its stories. In the space of a single page of its August 1879 issue, the autobiographical narrator of one tale recounts how a female character 'deluged me with her warm glutinous spendings', then 'came again in another luscious flood of spendings', and a third time 'seemed to boil over in spendings'.[2] Pornography being (etymologically speaking) writing of harlots, it seems appropriate that *The Pearl*'s biggest female spenders should be prostitutes. A pseudo-memoir in the Christmas 1879 issue recounted a visit to a brothel whose Madame exhorts the narrator to 'Watch Marie when she spends, and she is going to. It is worth seeing, I only know two people who can emit as copiously at one discharge as that girl. What she will do when she is full grown I do not know'.[3] Marie duly spends what the author describes as 'a deluge of sperm', but not before the Madame has whispered to the narrator to observe another prostitute: '"See! See! … look at Celestine", and sure enough I saw … the sperm spout hotly from

2 Anon, 'Sub-Umbra, or Sport Amongst the She-Noodles', *The Pearl, a Journal of Facetiae*, 2 (August 1879): 34-35.

3 Anon, 'The Passenger's Story', *Swivia; or, the Briefless Barrister. The Extra Special Number of* The Pearl, *Containing a Variety of Complete Tales, with Five Illustrations, Poetry, Facetiae, Etc.*, (Christmas 1879): 46.

her quim as she spent most profusely'.[4] What American slang of the stag-film era would come to know as 'the money shot' was as much the prostitute's prerogative as her male client's in the libidinal economy of Victorian erotica.[5]

And, indeed, it was precisely the prostitute's presumed prodigality with money – her inability to save it, her compulsion to spend it – that was at the core of the pathological character-type constructed for the female prostitute by the European and American medical professions in the early nineteenth century. While masturbators were censured for wastefully draining their own libido and hence the productive energy needed to build commerce and industry, many Victorian social hygienists focused their anxiety about wasted libidinal expenditure on prostitutes, believing it was mainly they who drained men's seminal fluid and that at the bottom of the slippery slope on which the masturbator embarked was the brothel.[6]

The seminal study of the 'public prostitute' and 'her world' was the French physician and specialist in drains and sewers, Dr A.J.B. Parent-Duchâtelet's *Prostitution in the City of Paris* of 1836, a masterwork of Enlightenment social anthropology whose statistical methods and research findings were replicated in numerous subsequent studies of prostitution in cities from Marseilles to Edinburgh, London to

4 Ibid.

5 The relationship of female sexual spending to pleasure, on one hand, and reproduction, on the other, had been exercising the imaginations of the medical profession for centuries. In his *Libido Sexualis* (1897-98), the sexologist Albert Moll undertook to put matters on a scientific footing by identifying the physiology of female ejaculation, explaining it as a 'secretion originating in the glands of Bartholin and perhaps also in the mucous glands of the uterus'; he thus concluded that 'since ejaculation in woman is not for the purpose of expelling sex cells as in man, it must be assumed from the very outset that ejaculation for her in intercourse is not as important as in man'. Moll added: 'I have been assured, however, that some women may reach the highest pitch of orgasm with a feeling of complete satisfaction without ejaculation' (*Libido Sexualis*, p. 27). For a review of the relevant physiology and its history, see Lowndes Sevely and Bennett, 'Concerning Female Ejaculation and the Female Prostate'.

6 See Carolyn Dean, *Sexuality and Modern Western Culture*, New York, Twayne Publishers, 1996, p. 4.

Boston.[7] Parent-Duchâtelet described prostitutes as 'a people apart', 'differing as much in their morals, their tastes, and their Habits from the society of their compatriots, as the latter differ from the nations of another hemisphere'.[8] While studies of this 'people apart' lamented the social factors that contributed to prostitution, they invariably treated it as a trans-historical and incurable social evil, and hence to be regulated rather than eradicated, not least because they found a distinctive personality-type, or hereditary psychology, to be decisive in a woman's fall into prostitution. This was what Parent-Duchatelet termed the 'libidinous temperament', in which 'hereditary debauchery' combined with a catalogue of other traits antithetical to the values of the time: the prostitute was by nature a sexually licentious, work-shy, improvident, compulsive shopper, addicted to spending both libido and money.[9] The stereotypes inscribed in Parent-Duchâtelet's research findings would prevail in commentaries on prostitutes for the next century and a half – among them, Dr Julien Jeannel's *De la prostitution dans les grandes villes au XIXe siècle et de l'extinction des maladies vénériennes*, which concluded that: 'Laziness, greed, disorder, hereditary debauchery … utter abandonment, and a distaste for work, these are the true sources of public prostitution'.[10] Another medical author, Dr H.A. Frégier, in his 1842 study of 'the dangerous classes' of big city populations, called

7 A.J.B. Parent-Duchâtelet, *De la prostitution dans la ville de Paris considérée sous le rapport de l'hygiène publique de la morale et de l'adminstration ouvrage appuyé de documents statistiques*, Paris, J.B. Baillière, 1836. Studies indebted to Parent-Duchâtelet's include such monuments to statistical and taxonomical method as Bracebridge Hemyng's 'Prostitution in London,' in *London Labour and the London Poor*, Vol. 4, Henry Mayhew (ed.), [1861], London, Frank Cass & Co., 1967, and William Acton's *Prostitution, considered in its moral, social and sanitary aspects in London and other large cities*, London, John Churchill, 1857.

8 A.J.B. Parent-Duchâtelet, *Prostitution in Paris, Considered Morally, Politically and Medically: Prepared for philanthropists and legislators from statistical documents, translated from the French by an American physician*, Boston, C.H. Brainard, 1845, pp. 19-20.

9 See Alain Corbin, *Women For Hire: Prostitution and Sexuality in France after 1850*, Alan Sheridan (trans.), Cambridge, MA and London, Harvard University Press, 1990, p. 7.

10 Julien F. Jeannel, *De la prostitution dans les grandes villes au XIXe siècle et de l'extinction des maladies vénériennes*, Paris, J.B. Baillière, 1862, p. 174.

upon the police superintendents to try to persuade prostitutes to mend their prodigal ways and save money by banking their earnings.[11] The prevailing view was that prostitutes shared with criminals the hereditary character of 'unproductiveness', which itself was 'anti-social' and hence 'a form of criminality'.[12]

However, in conflict with the aim of imposing frugality on constitutionally spendthrift prostitutes was that key mechanism of Adam Smith's 'trickledown effect': consumer culture's fashion system. As Parent-Duchâtelet explained:

> Vanity and the desire of dress, together with idleness, is a very active cause of prostitution, particularly at Paris; when the simplicity and *a fortiori* the shabbiness of clothing is considered truly as a reproach, is it astonishing that so many young girls are seduced, by a desire for dress which will elevate them from the position in which they are born, and which permits them to mingle with that class who have looked on them with contempt? Those who know to what extent the love of dress is carried among women, can easily appreciate the influence of this cause of prostitution at Paris.[13]

Reputedly attracted to prostitution in the first place by an insatiable appetite for consuming the ephemera of women's fashions – the epitome of wasteful expenditure for economists from Adam Smith to Alfred Marshall[14] – the prostitute was the prototypical conspicuous consumer: a figure in whom pleasure in sex and shopping,

11 H.A. Frégier, *Des classes dangereuses de la population dans les grandes villes, et des moyens de les rendre meilleures*, Vol. 2, Paris, J.B. Baillière, 1840, p. 259.

12 Havelock Ellis cites this view in 'Sex in Relation to Society', *Studies in the Psychology of Sex*, Vol. 6, Philadelphia, Davis, 1910, quoted in Lucy Bland and Laura Doan (eds), *Sexology Uncensored: The Documents of Sexual Science*, Cambridge, Polity Press, 1998, p. 248.

13 Parent-Duchâtelet, *Prostitution in Paris*, p. 51.

14 See A.C. Pigou (ed.), *Memorials of Alfred Marshall*, London, Macmillan, 1925, p. 325; J.M. Lipkis, 'Historians and the History of Economic Thought: A Response to Lawrence Birken', *History of Political Economy* 25, 1 (1993): 94. Lipkis remarks: 'No-one can read much Marshall without encountering his favourite *bête-noire*, the epitome of wasteful expenditure — woman's fashions'.

in libidinal and monetary spending, were *causally* combined. G.B. Shaw's Mrs Warren was echoing a Victorian anthropological platitude when she explained to her daughter, in 1894, that her profession in prostitution 'means a new dress every day', whereas her daughter's wage-labour as a barrister's bookkeeper meant 'toiling and moiling early and late for your bare living and two cheap dresses a year'.[15]

The regulationist project, which Parent-Duchâtelet was the first to expound, was the 'Foucaultian' project of enclosing in order to observe, in order to know, in order to supervise and control, prostitutes. It included legal requirements that prostitutes register their identities and addresses with the police, that they submit to regular medical examinations, reside in certain areas ('red light districts'), and other stigmatising measures designed to mark them as 'a people apart', segregated from the rest of the population.[16] However, as Alain Corbin has shown in his study of French attitudes to prostitution during the Third Republic, the anxiety that increasingly animates medical and sociological writing on prostitutes during the nineteenth century is a fear that the regulationist project was failing, that segregation wasn't working and the disease of prostitution was in danger of corrupting the social organism as a whole.[17] Fashion was a crucial factor in this fear that women of the street might become indistinguishable from the average woman *in* the street. Not only were many women attracted to prostitution for the ready cash it provided for spending on the latest fashions, but the casual or 'public' prostitute, like the mistress or kept woman, was seen as offering a model of luxury, idleness and conspicuous consumption seductive to working girls and women in general (this is a central theme of Bracebridge Hemyng's monumental 1861 study of 'Prostitution in London', which documents in detail how prostitution and the fashion industry went hand-in-hand).[18]

The link between shopping and prostitution, then, was established early in the history of the 'psychologisation' of the prostitute,

15 George Bernard Shaw, *Mrs Warren's Profession* (1894), *Plays Pleasant and Unpleasant*, Vol. 1, London, Constable, 1931, p. 242.

16 Parent-Duchâtelet , *Prostitution in Paris*, pp. 19-20.

17 Corbin, *Women For Hire*, p. 22.

18 See Hemyng, 'Prostitution in London,' pp. 216-17, 220.

and the regulationists' worst fears seemed confirmed to at least one observer, Charles Desmaze, when he reported in 1881 that:

> In the past, prostitution was limited to certain women: they were known, registered, wore gilt belts, and were confined to certain districts. Nowadays, in Paris, they are everywhere, filling the streets, wearing whatever they like. *In the past debauchery could be enumerated by a certain fixed figure*; now, its name is legion and its ranks are swollen each day, by the shops, factories, and theaters.[19]

If the prospect of a growing 'prostitutionalisation' of the female population as a whole threatened the morals and health of the nineteenth-century bourgeoisie, it also threatened their pockets. For just as prostitutes had been seen by commentators from St Augustine to Parent-Duchâtelet as a seminal drain, carrying away men's excess libido,[20] so the *femmes galantes* (loose women), the *mangeardes* (women who 'eat up' men's money), the female 'parasites', the vamps who prey on men's capital, were seen as a drain on the economy of saving and productive investment. Women of easy morals were partly responsible for what one writer described in 1872 as the 'extraordinary mobility of money'.[21] Fear that the ruling classes would be contaminated – in their morals, their health, and their racial stock – by contact with the 'prostitute class'[22] extended to a fear of contamination by easy money. For, loose morals and loose money – fast-circulating, freely-spent money –

19 Charles Desmaze, *Le crime et la débouache à Paris: Le divorce*, Paris, G. Charpentier, 1881, p. v, quoted in Corbin, *Women For Hire*, p. 377 n. 101.

20 See Corbin, *Women For Hire*, p. 24; Parent-Duchâtelet , *Prostitution in Paris*, Vol. 2, p. 23: 'Prostitutes are as inevitable, where men live together in large concentrations, as drains and refuse dumps'; and Saint Augustine, *De ordine* 2.4.12, quoted in Corbin, *Women For Hire*, 372 n.11: 'Abolish the prostitutes and the passions will overthrow the world',.

21 Maxime du Camp, *Paris: ses organes, ses fonctions et sa view dans la seconde moitié du XIX siècle*, Vol. 3, Paris: Hachette, 1872, p. 460, quoted in Corbin, *Women For Hire*, p. 24.

22 The term 'prostitute class' is used by Hemyng, 'Prostitution in London', pp. 210-226.

went literally hand-in-hand, as did the liberalisation of sexual morality and the extension of consumerism to the lower classes.

Psychoanalysing the Prostitute/Shopper

How the prostitute as compulsive spender could be assimilated to Freudianism's economic view of the psyche was demonstrated by the founder of the Berlin Psychoanalytic Society, Karl Abraham, in his 1917 paper, 'The Spending of Money in Anxiety States'. Noting that Freud and other analysts had hitherto focused their money-interests on 'anal' character-traits – 'neurotic avarice and the anxious retention of money' – Abraham chose instead to focus on 'the opposite behaviour of many neurotics, the excessive spending of money', a tendency which, he said, 'appears suddenly in many neurotics, like a kind of attack, and stands in conspicuous contrast to their usual parsimony'.[23] This behaviour was typical of agoraphobic women, whose libido is fixated on a parent-figure and who are consequently 'in a state of permanent infantile dependence on the parental home and ... attacked with depression or anxiety as soon as they are away from it. The patients themselves say that the spending of money relieves their depression or anxiety' by increasing their self-confidence and providing distraction; but Abraham's analysis revealed that 'female patients who suffer from street anxiety are heavily burdened with unconscious, at times even conscious, phantasies of prostitution. Their unconscious wants to yield without restraint to every person they meet; but their conscious anxiety restricts the transference of their libido within the narrowest bounds, so that they become incapable of making free use of it'.[24] Suppressing a strong impulse to spend their libido on any and every person they meet in the street,

23 Karl Abraham, 'The Spending of Money in Anxiety States', *Selected Papers of Karl Abraham, M.D.*, Douglas Bryan and Alix Strachey (trans.), introduction by Ernest Jones (1917), London, Hogarth Press and institute of Psycho-Analysis, 1927, p. 299.

24 Abraham, 'The Spending of Money', pp. 299-300. See also Karl Abraham, 'On the Psychogenesis of Agoraphobia in Childhood', *Clinical Papers and Essays on Psycho-Analysis* (1913), London, Maresfield Reprints, 1979, pp. 42-43.

they deal unconsciously with the anxiety it arouses by 'giving out *money* instead of *libido*'. Their compulsive spending on objects of no intrinsic interest to them 'deceives them as to the want of freedom of their libido and thus relieves them for a short time of the painful feeling of sexual insufficiency'. In Abraham's analysis, the female shopaholic is unconsciously both prostitute and john, at once 'transferring [her] libido in rapid succession to an unlimited number of objects' (i.e., persons) and using 'money [as] the means of obtaining transitory and easily changed relationships'.[25]

The other side of the coin of Abraham's diagnosis of compulsive spending as a displacement of fantasies of prostitution was the psychoanalytic and psychiatric explanation of the 'disease' of kleptomania as a displacement of sexual frustration, a symbolic refusal of the thwarting of a woman's urge to spend. Kleptomania was gendered feminine in much nineteenth- and early twentieth-century medical and legal writing on shoplifting, and it was also class-specific.[26] Whereas working-class women shoplifters were merely thieves, middleclass women shoplifters were kleptomaniacs suffering from one of the monomanias that were still – millennia after the ancient Egyptian or Greek invention of hysteria as a disease of the unruly womb, or of woman's rebelliously 'irrational' sexuality – being diagnosed as symptoms of 'uterine disease' or 'pelvic disease'.[27]

Kleptomania was also a pathology whose invention by the medical profession coincided with the retail industry's invention of that theatre of seduction and temptation (primarily of women), the department store. The French criminal anthropologist, Paul Dubuisson, dubbed kleptomania 'magasinitis' (*magasin*: shop) in his 1901 article, 'Les Voleuses des grands magasins'.[28] For Walter

25 Abraham, 'The Spending of Money', p. 301.

26 See Elaine S. Abelson, *When Ladies Go A-Thieving: Middle-Class Shoplifters in the Victorian Department Store*, New York and Oxford, Oxford University Press, 1989.

27 See Mark S. Micale, *Approaching Hysteria: Disease and Its Interpretations*, Princeton, Princeton University Press, 1995.

28 Paul Dubuisson, 'Les Voleuses des grands magasins', *Archives d'Anthropologie Criminelle: De criminologie et de psychologie normale et pathologique*, Vol. 16 (1901): 1-20.

Benjamin, famously, the 'street' in 'streetwalker' would be the shopping arcade, and if the shopping arcade was the public space dedicated to arousing the desire to spend, it was the presence of the 'public prostitute' that made explicit the sexual aetiology of that desire: 'The arcade is a street of lascivious commerce only; it is wholly adapted to arousing desires'.[29]

Kleptomania, in contrast to working-class theft, was potentially treatable by surgery. Surgical intervention was attempted in the celebrated case of Mrs Walter Castle, prosecuted for industrial-scale shoplifting in London department stores while on holiday from San Francisco with her wealthy husband in 1896 and defended in court by a team of medical experts who redefined a criminal act as a gendered medical problem – 'disordered menstruation, haemorrhoids, and uterine irregularities' – thus securing her speedy release by the British Home Secretary, but not before Dr Arthur Conan Doyle had written a letter to *The Times* insisting that Mrs Castle belonged not in a prison cell but in the physician's consulting room.[30] As early as 1851, Schopenhauer had remarked on the prevalence of compulsive shoplifting in 'On Women', citing kleptomania as simply one among many other manifestations of woman's biologically determined 'falseness, faithlessness, treachery': 'From time to time there are repeated cases everywhere of ladies, who want for nothing, secretly pocketing and taking away things from shop counters'.[31]

It was to Freudianism's credit that it 'psychologised' the diagnosis of hysteria in general in the 1890s, linking the 'disease' to the socio-psychic repression of female sexuality rather than to the organic nerve lesion to which the legendary neurologist Jean-Martin Charcot attributed hysteria.[32] Similarly, psychoanalysis

29 Walter Benjamin, *The Arcades Project* (1927-1940), Rolf Tiedemann (ed.), Howard Eiland and Kevin McLaughlin (trans.), Cambridge, MA, Harvard University Press, 2002, p. 42.

30 See Abelson, *When Ladies Go A-Thieving*, pp. 173-87.

31 Schopenhauer, 'On Women'.

32 Josef Breuer and Sigmund Freud, *Studies on Hysteria* (1893-1895), *Standard Edition of the Complete Psychological Works of Sigmund Freud*, James Strachey (ed.), Vol. 2, London, Vintage, 2001.

de-biologised kleptomania, redefining it as a symptom not of deformity of the womb, damage to the central nervous system, or simply the XX chromosome as such, but of thwarted female sexual desire. If woman could not give vent to the urge to spend her desire freely, then she would have to steal the pleasure of spending, and she stole this pleasure in the psychically and socially disguised form of shoplifting. Such was the diagnosis made by orthodox first-generation Freudians such as Abraham, Stekel and Otto Gross. Stekel's overview of psychoanalytic research into the disease, 'The Sexual Root of Kleptomania', which spelled out the diagnosis and its debt to Gross's research, appeared in the July, 1911 issue of the *Journal of the American Institute of Criminal Law and Criminology*.[33] In the same year, Pierre Janet's 'La Kleptomanie et la depression mentale' identified the association of shoplifting with sensations and emotions akin to orgasm,[34] an association similarly asserted in many contemporary shopaholics' descriptions of their sensations of libidinal release at the moment of purchase, after which they report quickly losing interest in the objects purchased, just as Stekel's kleptomaniacs lost interest in their stolen goods. (It seems more than a coincidence that Ernest Dichter, whose Freudian 'revolution' of the advertising industry we examined in the preceding chapter, claimed to have received lessons in psychoanalysis from Stekel in Vienna in the 1930s[35]).

Spending for Revolution: The Prostitute as Proto-Revolutionary

It was spending on the scale that seemed to come naturally to *The Pearl*'s prostitutes, and which Abraham's shopaholics unconsciously longed to enjoy, that the Freudian heretic, Wilhelm Reich, believed communism would make available to all by abolishing the institution of private property that enabled a patriarchal elite to

33 Wilhelm Stekel, 'The Sexual Root of Kleptomania', *Journal of the American Institute of Criminal Law and Criminology*, 2, 2 (July 1911): 239-46.

34 Pierre Janet, 'La Kleptomanie et la depression mentale', *Journale de psychologie, normale et pathologique*, 8ème Année (1911): 97-103.

35 Ronald A. Fullerton, '"Mr MASS motivations himself": Explaining Dr Ernest Dichter', *Journal of Consumer Behavior*, 6 (2007): 373.

monopolise libidinal spending-power, denying it to others. Despite Reich's bad press as the clinically paranoid, cloud-busting, orgone-box-salesman prosecuted for quackery by the FDA in the 1950s, his early thinking retains a powerful currency in left-wing libidinal economy that figures the sex-drive and the urge to spend as a potentially subversive force in capitalist society. His influence is palpable in the work of thinkers such as Herbert Marcuse and Norman O. Brown; he fuels Deleuze and Guattari's critique of 'familialism' in *Anti-Oedipus* (Reich's term for the disease was 'familitis') and their trope of the unconscious as factory, not theatre; and, as we shall see, Reich's insistence on returning to Freud's early notion of libidinal energy as a kind of cosmic currency, not tied to genital drives, also animates Lyotard's Nietzschean riffing on 'intensities' in *Economie Libidinale*.

Reich's theory of 'orgastic potency' as the key to both personal and collective health constructed orgasm as a universal, natural right, which a genuinely egalitarian society would protect. He defined 'orgastic potency' as the capacity for 'complete' orgasm, for spending all one's accumulated libidinal energy, without reserve. In Reich's self-styled 'sex-economic theory', libidinal thrift produced neurosis at best, cancer and fascism at worst (malignant tumours, he would argue, are the result of undischarged sexual energy). The unspent energy of incomplete orgasm turned into what Reich called 'character armour', libido hoarded in the body as a defence, but functioning as a prison for the natural urge to spend. 'Compulsory sexual morality' – including the institutions of monogamy, premarital chastity, extramarital abstinence, and the incest and masturbation taboos – fatally compromised the universal right to orgastic potency, denying it to children, adolescents, the unmarried, even to married women, and it went hand-in-hand with patriarchal property-rights, reserving free sexual spending-power for the head of the bourgeois 'patriarchal-authoritarian family', which in turn was the building-block of the fascist state.[36]

36 See, e.g., Wilhelm Reich, 'The Problem of Sexual Economy', *Sex-Pol: Essays 1929-1934*, Lee Baxandall (ed.), introduction by Bertell Ollman, Anna Bostock, Tom DuBose and Lee Baxandall (trans.), New York, Random House, 1972, pp. 226-49; and Wilhelm Reich, *Geschlechtsreife, Enthaltsamkeit,*

Under the umbrella of the KPD (German Communist Party) in the early 1930s, Reich's Sex-Pol movement claimed some 30,000 supporters among German workers and youth intent on providing the sex-education, law-changes, contraception and abortions that would make 'orgastic potency' available to all, thereby achieving the 'Sexual Revolution' (the title of one of his books) that Reich saw as the promise of Soviet Communism in the early 1920s, before Stalin instituted the 'state-capitalism' and 'Red Fascism' that quickly put an end to the ideal of a society founded on the pleasure-principle of free, equal and universal sexual spending.[37]

It was Reich's activism on behalf of the orgasmic rights of children, adolescents and workers that got him expelled from the Austrian, German and Danish communist parties (he was never actually a member of the Danish party but was expelled from it nonetheless). And it was what Freud called his 'bolshevism' that got Reich expelled from the International Psychoanalytic Association in 1934. But, even setting aside Freud's dreams of an apolitical, because 'scientific', psychoanalysis, his and Reich's economics were fundamentally at odds. An admirer of Smith and Hume, Freud transferred political economy's 'quantitative' method from the public sphere to the private sphere of the psyche, 'introjecting' the classical economics of scarcity as a model for the psyche, and translating political economy's moralistic distinction between productive and unproductive consumption into a distinction between productive and unproductive desire. His libidinal economy presupposed a potentially infinite supply of desirable objects and a relative scarcity of desire itself – such that what is spent in orgasmic pleasure becomes unavailable for sublimation and hence for civilisation.[38] By contrast, Reich's libidinal economy preached unreserved libidinal spending as the key to

Ehemoral (sexual maturity, abstinence and marital fidelity), Vienna, Muensterverlag, 1930.

37 See Wilhelm Reich, *The Sexual Revolution*, Theodore P. Wolfe (trans.), (1936; 1945), New York, Farrar, Strauss and Giroux, 1971, and *Wilhelm Reich Speaks of Freud*, Mary Higgins and Chester M. Raphael (eds), Harmondsworth, Penguin, 1975, p. 11.

38 As Freud puts it in *Civilization and Its Discontents*, p. 103: 'Since man does not have unlimited quantities of psychical energy at his disposal, he has to accomplish his tasks by making an expedient distribution of his libido'.

the psychic and economic health of both the individual and society, and, indeed, as a natural law of the cosmic economy of energy. For Reich, libidinal thrift produced neurosis and a corresponding stagnation of the collective economy of energy – the currency of life. Only spending without reserve (and by all equally), which kept libido in constant circulation and exchange, could keep the economy healthy and productive, obviating the depressions, recessions and economic collapses that resulted from the hoarding of libido and the unequal distribution of its spending in class-society.[39] Reich deemed prostitution a perversion, but only because the easy-come, easy-spend mentality for which the prostitute was historically stigmatised should have been common to all in a society in which money and libidinal spending-power were equitably distributed – as they were, Reich believed, in the primitive matriarchal societies described by Malinowski.[40]

In 1936, after turning his back on the political parties that had turned their backs on 'orgastic potency', Reich attributed what he claimed was his unique success in fusing Freudianism and Marxism to his discovery of their common currency: namely, the energy that Freud called 'libido' and that Marx had recognised as 'the living commodity "work-power"' but which Reich himself identified as 'cosmic orgone energy'.[41] 'Orgone' (connoting orgasm, organism and ergonomic) was the currency of the cosmos, physically measurable, Reich insisted, and universally exchangeable, manifest in living organisms as bio-energy and in inanimate matter as a radiating blue light.[42] And a fundamental natural law of a healthy

39 See D.Z. Mairowitz, *Reich for Beginners*, London, Unwin, 1986, p. 56.

40 Wilhelm Reich, *The Sexual Struggle of Youth. The Invasion of Compulsory Sex Morality* (1932), London, Socialist Reproduction, 1972.

41 Wilhelm Reich, *People in Trouble*, Philip Schmitz (trans.), New York, Farrar, Strauss and Giroux, 1976, p. 71.

42 See Wilhelm Reich, *The Bion Experiments* (1938), New York, Farrar Straus Giroux, 1979, and Myron Sharaf, *Fury on Earth: A Biography of Wilhelm Reich*, London, Hutchinson, 1983, p. 223. Cf. Wilhelm Reich, *The Bioelectrical Investigation of Sexuality and Anxiety*, Marion Faber (trans.), Mary Higgins and Chester Raphael (eds), New York, Farrar, Straus and Giroux, 1982, p. 126: 'Sexual excitation is functionally identical to bioenergetic charge of the erogenous zones ... The concept of "libido" as a yardstick of "psychic energy"

cosmic economy was that this energy should be constantly expended or consumed, not trapped in clouds or bodies – an idea that Georges Bataille would develop in his theory of general economy in the 1940s, pointing to the fiery sun expending its energy 'with absolute generosity' and without return.[43]

Bataille's prostitute in *L'Erotisme* (1957), like Marcuse's in *One-Dimensional Man* (1964), is a figure of glorious, gratuitous, unproductive expenditure, and hence a heroic figure of negation, of what Marcuse called 'the Great Refusal' of 'the order of business' and the bourgeois imperatives of parsimony, accumulation and investment. *One-Dimensional Man*'s prostitute is a marginal figure who challenges the instrumental rationality of advanced industrial society, apparently by cheating its rules of investment and return, its imperatives of alienated labour, time and sexuality. For Marcuse, the prostitute's 'avoidance' of 'work', her refusal to support herself with wage-slavery, renders her a heroic figure with the same 'power of negation' as the work of art possesses in a 'two-dimensional culture'.[44] Marcuse values precisely the 'subversive force' of prostitution that its critics traditionally feared, oddly implying that the prostitute is somehow living, or spending, her desire more authentically than are those whose sexuality and libido have been fully assimilated to bourgeois society – as if the prostitute expressed 'a gratification that would dissolve the society which suppresses it'.[45]

But back to Bataille. Under titles that might have been coined by Reich, such as 'The Dependence of the Economy on the Circulation of Energy on the Earth' (1949), Bataille expounded his theory of energy as wealth that must be wastefully spent, arguing in the 1930s and 1940s that a Copernican revolution in economic thinking was necessary to accommodate the fact that the Industrial Revolution

is no longer a mere metaphor, but applies to energetic processes. Thus, the sexual function is one of the general electrical (orgonotic) processes that occur in nature'.

43 Fred Botting and Scott Wilson (eds), *The Bataille Reader*, Oxford, Blackwell, 1997, p. 18.

44 Herbert Marcuse, *One-Dimensional Man*, London, Sphere Books, 1968, pp. 62-63.

45 Ibid., pp. 60-61.

had produced a surplus of productive power and commodities, a surplus wealth that would have to be 'surrendered without return', not reinvested in production. Nor was this a historically contingent truth, peculiar to post-nineteenth-century Europe, for what we call 'the economic activity of men' is merely a local application of a 'cosmic phenomenon', 'the circulation of energy ... in the universe'; and the law of this energy is that a large part of it must ultimately be consumed 'without any possible profit'.[46]

Eroticism figures in Bataille's writings on economy as the prototype of such spending, a self-wasting drive of ecstatic, gratuitous expenditure; and the epitome of spendthrift eroticism was the prostitute, described by Bataille as 'dedicated to a life of transgression', 'to violating the taboo' against 'the sacred or forbidden aspect of sexuality', that aspect being the deathly drive to total, self-consuming spending, without product or profit.[47] In his chapter on prostitution in *L'Erotisme*, Bataille argues that if the 'original', 'sacred' 'prostitute received sums of money ... these were originally gifts ... which she would use for extravagant expenditure':

> This exchange of gifts was not a commercial transaction. What a woman can give outside marriage cannot be put to any productive use, and similarly with the gifts that dedicate her to the luxurious life of eroticism. This sort of exchange led to all sorts of extravagance rather than to the regularity of commerce. Desire was a fiery thing; it could burn up a man's wealth to the last penny, it could burn out the life of the man in whom it was aroused.[48]

During the 1930s and 1940s, then, against the background of the Great Depression, and with the sun as their witness, Reich and Bataille elevated the spending of libidinal energy for its own sake to the status of a universal natural principle, a law of physics, burying their economics in nature, just as Freud had claimed to extract his economics from physics. Freud's politically conservative libidinal

46 Georges Bataille, 'The Meaning of General Economy', *The Accursed Share*, Robert Hurley (trans.), Vol. 1, New York, Zone Books, 1991, p. 25.

47 Bataille, *Erotism*, pp. 132-33.

48 Ibid.

economy had produced a petit-bourgeois psyche, managing its economy of energy as a self-employed businessman must: spending only frugally, whenever possible re-investing in increased productivity, eschewing conspicuous consumption and credit – treating desire, or libidinal energy, as a relatively scarce resource, not as surplus. It took psychoanalysis's anti-bourgeois exponents, the communist-affiliated Reich and Bataille, to develop libidinal economy in the direction of a fully-fledged consumerist culture that celebrated spending for spending's sake, as an end in itself. And by 'naturalising' gratuitous, wasteful expenditure – construing it as a cosmic principle that trumped capitalism's imperative of accumulation and productive investment – left-wing libidinal economists such as Reich and Bataille were paradoxically dissolving any residual distinction between natural and unnatural desires, which classical economics had distinguished on the basis of natural species-need and the artificial wants and tastes that capitalism's fashion-cycles generate. They were also, therefore, helping to naturalise consumerist psychology.

We shall return to Bataille near the end of this chapter, but now let's leap forward, over May 1968, to 1974, and consider another prostitute, the late Marx's prostitute as revisited and patronised by Jean-François Lyotard in a 'scandalous' tract that insists that political economy is always already libidinal economy. Lyotard's eccentric book *Economie Libidinale* (1974) argues that there is no point of libidinal opposition outside of capital, and that any notion of a primitive society in which libido was not already 'scrambled' or alienated by exchange and book-keeping is a myth.[49] His book cost Lyotard friendships on the Parisian Left for its scathing attacks on the two traditions of theoretical critique of capital, those of Marxism and psychoanalysis, that had linked him with other members of the *Socialisme ou Barbarie* group. In it he undertakes a 'libidinal' re-reading of Marx's political economy, or what he terms 'The Desire Named Marx', and the prostitute figures so often and

49 Jean-François Lyotard, *Libidinal Economy*, Iain Hamilton Grant (trans.), London, Athlone Press, 1993, pp. 108-9. Cf. Jean-François Lyotard, *Just Gaming*, Wlad Godzich (trans.), Minneapolis, University of Minnesota Press, 1985, p. 4.

in so many guises in the book that it seems fair to charge Lyotard with 'projection' in the case he brings against Marx for trafficking with prostitution.

Marx's mid-nineteenth-century prostitute was not, of course, the subversive figure of negation that she would become in Bataille's or Marcuse's thinking a century later. In the *1844 Manuscripts* Marx's prostitute is none other than money itself: 'Money is the common whore', he explains, 'the common procurer of people and nations'; rendering everything exchangeable and alienable, it is 'the distorting and confounding of all human and natural qualities'.[50] No Marcusean sentimentalism there. But the figure of the prostitute becomes prodigiously promiscuous in Marx's hands: not only is bourgeois marriage and its attendant 'affairs' a practice of 'private prostitution', as reprehensible as working-class 'public prostitution', but insofar as we have intercourse with capital we are *all* prostitutes in Marx's estimation:

> Prostitution is only a particular expression of the general prostitution of the worker, and because prostitution is a relationship which includes both the person prostituted and the person prostituting – whose baseness is even greater – thus the capitalist, too, etc. is included within this category.[51]

In short, for Marx in the 1840s, prostitution is the master-trope of alienation, epitomising all the alienations wrought by capital: the alienation of 'nature from man', of 'man from himself', of labourer from product, sexuality from subjectivity, and so on. Nonetheless, by reading Marx 'libidinally' rather than for the truth-value of his political economy, Lyotard concludes that Marx himself was unconsciously in love with the prostitute of capital, besotted by the object he loved to hate, and unable to break off his perverse affair with it; hence the endlessly proliferating pages of *Capital*,

50 Karl Marx, *Economic and Philosophic Manuscripts of 1844*, 5th edn, Moscow, Progress Publishers, 1977, p. 131.
51 Karl Marx, 'Private Property and Communism,' *Karl Marx Selected Writings*, David McLellan (ed.), Oxford, Oxford University Press, 1977, p. 90 n.

which Marx, despite his best intentions, couldn't bring himself to finish. Having devoted his life to analysing the perversions of the unspeakable prostitute of capital, he was unable to give up the libidinal pleasure of his text. In Lyotard's reading of what he terms the 'libidinal geography' of Marx's work, Marx takes on the job of prosecuting the pervert and conceiving a suitable object of desire, a loveable body of the proletariat; but he is as fascinated by the accused as he is scandalised by it (or her), devoting thousands of pages to microscopic analysis of the aberrations of capital.[52] And Lyotard's Marx discovers in the *endlessness* of his research 'a strange *jouissance*', the 'perverse' intensity of *postponed* orgasm: 'So much so', says Lyotard, 'that the prosecutor charged with obtaining proof of the pornographic ignominy of capital repeats ... this same "Don't come yet" – so to speak – which is simply another modality of *jouissance*, which is found in the libidinal *dispositif* of capital'.[53] In other words, Marx can't 'come' – can't or won't spend his desire in the conception of a loveable Socialism; instead, like a Victorian shopkeeper, he hoards his desire and gets off on the intensity of his own frustration or postponement of spending – here conceived as a form of necessary suffering and expiation, even martyrdom, which 'pays' for the revolution-to-come.[54]

Like Reich, Lyotard distinguishes two models of desire in Freud: desire-as-wish (implying phantasy, representation of an absent object, and hence reference and meaning) and desire-as-force (the energetic component of the unconscious, pure energy, libido, primary process) and it is *for* and *with* this latter desire that Lyotard seeks to re-read Marx reading capital.[55] Lyotard is interested, here, not in meaning or reference, which always posits an absent object or lost origin, but in process – what he calls 'conduction' rather than communication – conduction of 'libidinal intensity', which,

52 Lyotard, *Libidinal Economy*, p. 97.

53 Ibid., p. 99. Lyotard's usage of *dispositif* combines the meanings of *set-up* and *apparatus* with *investment* and *cathexis* or *disposition to invest.*

54 Ibid., pp. 99-101.

55 See Jean-François Lyotard, 'On a Figure of Discourse', *Toward the Postmodern*, R. Harvey and M.S. Roberts (eds), Atlantic Highlands, NJ, Humanities Press, 1993, p. 13.

like Reich's orgone, does not *mean* or *represent*, it just *is*.[56] As Lyotard puts it, 'desire is energetic, economic, non-representative', and he proposes that 'what would be interesting would be to stay put, but quietly seize every chance to function as good intensity-conducting bodies. No need for declarations, manifestos, organizations, provocations, no need for *exemplary actions*'.[57] If this seems remarkably modest as a politics of desire, it follows from Lyotard's conclusion that the 'repressive hypothesis' and the whole libido-*versus*-capitalism opposition – traditionally figured, as we have seen, as an opposition between spending and saving, wasting and accumulating, nature and culture – is essentially mythic, and capitalism is always already invested with libido, political economy always libidinal economy.[58]

Lyotard dismisses the Maussian or Bataillian 'primitive' 'society of the gift and counter-gift', which plays the role of a lost referent in critiques of capital, as no more than a projection of 'Western racism and imperialism', a variant of 'ethnology's good savage, slightly libidinalized'.[59] And as for the idea of a nature that capitalism denatures or alienates from humans: the notion of a (good) rebellious nature before or outside the (bad) market is mere 'phantasy'.[60] In Lyotard's reading, the very notion of alienation only arises from the posture of theoretical critique that Marx adopts; he tells us: '*There is no alienation* from the instant one escapes the critical relation. *There is as much libidinal intensity in capitalist exchange as in the alleged "symbolic" exchange*'.[61] And Lyotard unmasks this intensity of desire, of the urge to spend energy, in some of the least likely places. For example, what political economy traditionally wrote as alienation and destruction of

56 In *Des Dispositifs pulsionnels*, Lyotard describes words as objects formed of energy: *utterances* are energy-events, whereas *written* or *recorded* words are stored energy 'that is always reactualizable, re-vivable'. See Lyotard, 'On a Figure of Discourse', p. 18.

57 Lyotard, *Libidinal Economy*, pp. 22, 262.

58 Ibid., pp. 104, 108.

59 Ibid., p. 106.

60 Ibid., p. 107.

61 Ibid., p. 109.

the proletarian body and self, Lyotard scandalously rewrites as *jouissance*, an insane delight in losing the (organic) self to the machine of capital – the depersonalised, fragmented, mechanical actions of the productive process that made prostitutes of the proletariat itself:

> the English unemployed did not become workers to survive, they – hang on tight and spit on me – *enjoyed* the hysterical, masochistic, whatever exhaustion it was of *hanging on* in the mines, in the foundries, in the factories, in hell … enjoyed the mad destruction of their organic body … the decomposition of their personal identity … the dissolution of their families and villages … [62]

The *jouissance* of spending the (proletarian) self by prostituting it, hiring out the erogenous zones of its labouring body – this *jouissance*, or libidinal intensity, is the very currency of capitalism itself, flowing freely, according to Lyotard, in every direction, energy in a state of continuous nonlinear movement.[63]

In sum, Lyotard suggests that Marx's 'horror … of the world of capital as the *Milieu* of universal prostitution … is the *horror* of (and therefore the lust for)' money's perverse fluidity.[64] But the very process of liquefaction that Marx feared seems to be what Reich and his heirs among the disillusioned *soixante-huitards*, including Lyotard, come to desire:[65] namely, the uninhibited

62 Ibid., p. 111.
63 Ibid., pp. 120; 111-12.
64 Ibid., pp.137-138.
65 Lyotard was caught up in the '*événements*' of 1968: he was a lecturer at Nanterre University when the student 'Movement of March 22' occupied the administration building in protest against the arrest of leaders of the anti-Vietnam War movement, and he undertook to write a history or 'antihistory' of the radically disruptive energy-event that he considered such revolutionary political moments to be. See Jean-François Lyotard, 'March 23,' in *Political Writings*, Bill Readings and Kevin Paul Geiman (trans.), foreword by Bill Readings, London, UCL Press, 1993, pp. 60-67; and David Bennett, 'May '68, ÉVÉNEMENTS', in Stuart Sim (ed.), *The Lyotard Dictionary*, Edinburgh, Edinburgh University Press, 2011, pp. 138-41.

circulation or free exchange of the currency of desire in an economy of spending without saving – not energy or libido locked up in an object, constituting that object's 'natural' value, but the free-flowing desire that Freud described as the 'polymorphous perversity' (and Lyotard the polymorphous *di*versity) of childhood sexuality. When libido is hoarded or locked up, not spent, it creates oppressive structures: Freud's neurotic symptoms, Reich's 'character armour', the patriarchal family, the authoritarian state, grounded in the institution of property understood as frozen desire, blocked spending-power, not liquidity. Lyotard equates 'extravagant *jouissances*' with 'expenditure as pure loss', those 'outpourings of pulsional intensities' that yield no 'return'.[66] And it is precisely for such sterile, profitless spendings, which simply keep desire/money in circulation, that the client pays the prostitute:

> The prostitute therefore redeems perversion (the diversion of the pulsions) by replacing its product, not semen exactly, but its equivalent, money, not in the entry to her uterus … but in the entry to the goods market, and therefore to society … And just as the client pays money for the fruitlessness of whatever *jouissance* he may derive … so the citizen pays by the semen he deposits in the woman's genitalia for this truly sterile *jouissance*.[67]

As for critique of capital, Lyotard's political activists are passive conductors of intensities, and his 'anti-philosophy' of abandoning critique and opposition to capitalism and making oneself into a good conductor of 'intensities' – helping to put libido into constant circulation – seems to boil down to a species of revelling in the process famously encapsulated by the *Communist Manifesto* in the phrase, 'all that is solid melts into air': the deliquescent process by which the bourgeois revolution rendered everything insubstantial and motile by making it exchangeable for money. *Economie Libidinale* appears to advocate giving oneself to this bourgeois revolutionary process in the hope that exacerbating capitalism's

66 Lyotard, *Libidinal Economy*, p. 201.
67 Ibid., p. 157.

own revolutionary tendencies, rather than seeking to reform them – that is, accelerating, not obstructing, exchange or the circulation of money/desire – might somehow precipitate an as-yet-unimaginable transformation, if not actually an end, of capitalism.

Thus, by the time Lyotard comes to re-read Marx through the lens of libidinal economy, after the failure of the socialist revolutionary desire called 'May 1968', libidinal spending of the not-for-profit or wasteful variety has been thoroughly rehabilitated in what Lyotard calls 'the world of capital as the *Milieu* of universal prostitution'.[68] The figure of the prostitute as compulsive spender has lost all oppositional force and is again synonymous, as she was for Marx more than a century earlier, with the logic of money itself. But the difference between Lyotard and Marx, here, is that Lyotard's libidinal fixation on the prostitute is shameless and uninhibited by dreams of a 'purer' alternative. If Lyotard rejects what he terms Marx's 'characterization and rejection of capitalism and wage earners as arising out of prostitution', it is only because, for Lyotard, prostitution wears no scarlet letter, carries no stigma, for 'intensities are lodged here no less than in every other possible network', and also because prostitution epitomises the *jouissance* of expending libido for its own sake, not for production or reproduction.[69] Likening the psychoanalyst to the prostitute, Lyotard represents them both as converting intensity into cash, rendering *jouissance* exchangeable, closing the gap between desire and money.[70]

Since all that seems to matter to Lyotard is that desire, like money, should circulate as quickly and polyvalently as possible, he unsurprisingly approves of hyperinflation, because it excites intense exchange-activity among traders anxious not to be caught holding worthless currency. In a discussion of hyperinflation in Moscow of the 1920s, Lyotard writes approvingly of John Maynard Keynes as 'a true libidinalist' for describing as a 'period of fantastic intensity' what other economists 'would hypocritically call "velocity of circulation"'.[71]

68 Ibid., p. 139.
69 Ibid., p. 143, 141.
70 Ibid., p. 185.
71 Ibid., p. 231.

Economics 'Proper'

Mention of Keynes brings us to the discourse of economics proper, which clearly also deserves some credit for the twentieth-century rehabilitation of spending-for-spending's sake. The other side of the story of libidinal economy outlined here is the story of how the mid-twentieth-century marketing and advertising industries challenged the orthodoxies of neoclassical 'marginal utility theory' and its premise of *homo œconomicus* by rediscovering that the desire to spend, for its own sake, could itself be marketed; it could also could be elaborated into influential theories of economic salvation through spending by economists such as Keynes in the 1930s and George Marshall, architect of the Marshall Plan, in the 1940s. It was against the same background of the Great Depression to which Reich and Bataille were responding that Keynes (himself well-acquainted with the psychoanalytic movement through the Bloomsbury Set) developed his own theory of salvation through spending rather than saving or investing. In his 'iconoclastic' book, *The General Theory of Employment, Interest and Money* (1936), Keynes challenged the neoclassical supposition of a necessary equilibrium between consumer-desire and supply, and hence wages and employment, by reviving the 'underconsumption' theory of economic slumps and arguing that only an increase in spending as such – by consumers and government alike – could reflate the economy and solve the more intractable problems of the Great Depression.[72] It was during the 1930s and 1940s, when the neoclassical economists' faith in a consumer desire-driven, self-regulating market was being challenged by Keynesianism's insistence on the need for governments to intervene in the market and stimulate spending if unemployment were not to keep growing exponentially, that Bataille's and Reich's theories of libidinal spending as an end in itself came into their own in psychology and anthropology.

72 John Maynard Keynes, *The General Theory of Employment, Interest and Money*, London, Macmillan, 1936. Anxiety about 'underconsumption' or 'overproduction' has been a common theme in economic analyses since the sixteenth century, contested though it has been by advocates of 'Say's Law', which holds that 'supply creates demand'. See Jean-Baptiste Say, *Traité d'Economie Politique*, Paris, Horace Say, 1803.

Contrary to political economy, Bataille – his thinking permeated by the psychoanalysis that he believed had saved his sanity in 1927 – argued that the word 'expenditure' should be reserved for 'unproductive forms' of spending only: 'the principle of loss, in other words, of unconditional expenditure, no matter how contrary it might be to the economic principle of balanced accounts (expenditure regularly compensated for by acquisition)'.[73]

The heyday of Keynesianism in international economic policy followed World War II, during which Keynes played a key role in establishing the IMF; and it was also in the immediate post-war years that the erstwhile communists Reich and Bataille were paradoxically reconciling their own libidinal economics with American capitalism.[74] In his preface to the revised, 1952 edition of his book *The Sexual Revolution* (first published in 1936), Reich would admit that, contrary to his original predictions, the sexual revolution was actually occurring in the capitalist USA, not in the putatively socialist USSR. Four years earlier, Bataille had argued that the deliberate 'squandering of profits', the 'lavish' spending, 'without return', of 'that energy, which constitutes wealth', was something America should engage in if 'the industrial development of the entire world' was to be assured and further war avoided.[75] Bataille's thinking seems to have lost some of its radical edge: his theory was already lagging behind capitalist practice.[76] For this was in 1949, two years *after* US Secretary of State George Marshall outlined the extravagant potlatch scheme that became known as the Marshall Plan, which pumped thirteen billion American dollars into war-wrecked Europe purely as a gratuity, though also to help prevent post-war poverty leading Europe in the direction of communism. Earlier still, in 1932, the *Business*

73 Georges Bataille, 'The Notion of Expenditure' (1933), *Visions of Excess: Selected Writings, 1927-1939*, Allan Stoekl with Carl R. Lovitt and Donald M. Leslie, Jr (eds and trans.), Minneapolis, University of Minnesota Press, 1985, p. 169.

74 Bataille was a member of the Democratic Communist Circle from 1931 to 1934.

75 See Bataille, 'The Meaning of General Economy', pp. 25-26.

76 Cf. Jean-Joseph Goux, 'General Economics and Postmodern Capitalism', *Yale French Studies* 78 (1990): 206-24.

Week economist, Virgil Jordan, had told the Pennsylvania Chamber of Commerce: 'Just as we saved our way into depression, we must squander our way out of it'.[77]

In short, the 'subversive' and liberating exhortation to spend for the sheer pleasure of it – once conceived as a 'Great Refusal' of the self-alienating order of business and the capitalist imperatives of thrift and investment – comes uncannily to resemble precisely the imperatives that twentieth-century economists and marketers themselves were issuing for the survival of liberal capitalism in its wars, hot and cold, with fascism and communism.

Today, more than half a century later, the desire to spend for its own sake, which is essentially the desire to desire, goes by the banal names of 'retail therapy' and 'Viagra' rather than Marcuse's 'Great Refusal', and is evidence of capitalism's success in marketing a new idea of the mass consumer – not as *homo œconomicus* (constantly calculating a commodity's marginal utility relative to its cost), but as *homo desiderans* or *homo sexualis*, a subject in whom desire exceeds reason and is always in excess of any potential object. (According to Say's Law, which holds that 'supply creates demand', the capitalist economy supplies in order to create desire, rather than seeking to satisfy a desire already known by the person who experiences it. The department-store principle of marketing, developed in Western Europe at the end of the nineteenth century, relies on the premise that you didn't know you wanted it until you saw it in the shop. By contrast, socialism's centrally planned economy begins with a postulate of demand – understood as an expression of rational or reasonable need – and responds to that postulated demand with supply.)

Perhaps the whole tradition of heroising sexual desire or libido as a force for subversion is merely a variant of the old cliché of the uncontrollable male sex-drive, which was regarded in the eighteenth century as an explanation of the inevitability of prostitution – prostitutes being the receptacle or drain for excess male libido that could not be satisfied or expended with a respectable partner

77 Quoted in William L. Anderson, 'Say's Law: Were (Are) the Critics Right?', in *Austrian Scholars Conference 7: Proceedings* (Auburn, Alabama: Ludwig von Mises Institute, 2001), http://www.mises.org/upcomingstory.aspx?Id=15.

in marriage.[78] But what I have been suggesting in tracking the trope of wasteful spending and the prostitute through Reich, Marcuse, Bataille and Lyotard is a history of libidinal economy in which the drive to spend, rather than to invest, is redefined not as the libidinous subversion of capitalism but as its very currency, and in which the currency of this desire becomes embedded in nature, as a cosmic fact, apparently no longer subject to interpretation.

If we insist on interpreting it nonetheless, one way of understanding this drive to naturalise unproductive spending as a cosmic principle, or law of physics, is as a symptom of the universalisation and banalisation of the imperative to compete in unproductive consumption in 'post-bourgeois' or 'post-industrial' society, in which the licence to waste (conspicuously) has finally 'trickled down', in economic theory, from Adam Smith's *haute bourgeoisie* to the lowest classes. 'Post-industrial society', in other words, has witnessed a democratisation of waste. Bataille's ennobling sacrifice of reckless, unproductive squandering has become prosaic 'retail therapy' in a culture that guiltlessly embraces what Bataille calls 'the moral indifference of capitalism', or political economy's abandonment of any moral distinction between useful and useless commodities in favour of a definition of utility as simply that which sells, that for which a desire (to spend) has been found or invented. Consumerist society becomes more legible as a 'post-bourgeois' capitalism after the sexual and countercultural 'revolutions' of the 1960s, when 'dropping out' and 'turning on' became the recreational route to full integration with consumer capitalism for the middle classes, who were finally bidden to abandon their self-definition as more repressed, more self-denying, more self-disciplining than the so-called 'working masses'.[79]

78 See Joanna Brewis and Stephen Linstead, *Sex, Work and Sex Work: Eroticizing Organization*, London, Routledge, 2000, p. 191.

79 On self-disciplining and repression as, primarily, aspects of bourgeois self-care, see Michel Foucault, *History of Sexuality Volume 1*, Robert Hurley (trans.), Harmondsworth, Penguin, 1978. However, as John Levi Martin points out in 'Structuring the Sexual Revolution', *Theory and Society* 25 (February 1996): 115, thrift, industry and chastity were not capitalist values or virtues as such, but the virtues of the shopkeeper, or petit-bourgeois.

Postmodern Prostitute Chic

As for the trope of the prostitute as prototypical consumer, history appears to have come full circle, realising, once again, in the recent fashion for 'prostitute chic', the fears of the early regulationists that the prostitute might one day become indistinguishable from Everywoman. In the Spring of 2005, the London department store Selfridges developed its seasonal marketing theme of 'Las Vegas' into window-displays resembling the prostitute arcades of Amsterdam or Gent, in which women in scanty underwear sit in shop windows grooming themselves before mirrors in order to attract the window-shopping 'johns' who walk the arcades inspecting the 'goods'. In a setting of mirrors and makeup bottles, Selfridges' mannequins displayed the G-strings, lacy bras, heavy makeup and big hair-pieces of the 'Vegas hooker look' – except that, in this case, the target-market was not so much 'johns' as women shoppers themselves, invited to discover their own reflections in the mirrors of the harlot's dressing-room. Selfridges' windows were selling lingerie, cosmetics, hairpieces – but, above all, the *image* of the show-girl or call-girl preparing for a trick. The belatedness of this down-market advertising strategy by the up-market Selfridges can be gauged by the fact that three and a half decades had already passed since Yves Saint Laurent scandalised the Milan catwalks by introducing the 'happy hooker look' in 1971, and that it was half-a-decade since the 'trickledown' of prostitute-chic from *haute couture* to *prêt à porter* had been hastened by such pop-cultural icons as Britney Spears and Christina Aguilera. Indeed, if the American press was to be believed, the fashion had already waned before Selfridges got around to hailing its well-heeled shoppers as show-girls or whores. According to the *San Francisco Examiner*, Aguilera had 'dumped her "hooker look"' two seasons earlier, in June 2004,[80] while the *Potomac Times* reported that middle-American moms in Virginia were already voicing their relief that the hooker-look fashion had lost its grip on their sub-teen daughters.[81]

80 See Bill Picture, 'X-tina's image makeover', *San Francisco Examiner*, July 7, 2004, http://www.examiner.com/article/index.cfm/i/070704c_scoop.
81 Penelope M. Carrington, 'Hooker look is out', *Potomac News*, January

Postmodern 'prostitute-chic', alias 'stripper chic', 'porno-chic',[82] the 'hooker look', and 'raunch culture',[83] along with the mass suburban market for prostitute memoirs[84] and such hands-on manuals as *How to Make Love like a Porn Star*, represent a very different kind of cultural or semiotic rehabilitation of the prostitute from that undertaken by the prostitutes' rights-campaigners who were intent on legalising prostitution *as work* in the 1970s and 1980s. The feminist prostitute Carol Leigh claims to have coined the term 'sex *worker*' in 1980 and to have thought it comically paradoxical, 'mostly because sex is funny' whereas work is serious.[85] 'Sex-work' became a (contested) rallying-cry for women (and their male clients) wanting to 'respectabilise' prostitution as a selling of time and skills on a par with any other form of commoditised labour: a legitimate exploitation of labour-power and talent in a service sector of the capitalist economy. Such campaigns culminated, symbolically, in the world's first legal unionisation of prostitutes in Australia, in 1996, when the Liquor, Hospitality and Miscellaneous Workers Union began signing-up brothel-workers to its membership and seeking an 'award' that would guarantee them minimum wages and conditions, including job-security and professional training, and reintegrate them into civil society as 'productive' because taxable – that is, state-recognised – income-earners.

28, 2005, http://www.insidenova.com/servlet/Satellite?pagename=WPN/HTMLPage/WPN_HTMLPage&c=HTMLPage&cid=1031777505020&tacodalogin=no

82 For a survey of turn-of-the-century porno-chic, see Brian McNair, *Striptease Culture: Sex, Media and the Democratisation of Desire*, London, Routledge, 2002.

83 Ariel Levy, *Female Chauvinist Pigs: Women and the Rise of Raunch Culture*, Melbourne, Black Inc., 2005.

84 Jeanette Angell, *Callgirl: Confessions of a Double Life*, Sag Harbour, NY, Permanent Press, 2004; Belle de Jour, *The Intimate Adventures of a London Call Girl*, London, Weidenfeld & Nicolson, 2005; Kate Holden, *In My Skin: A Memoir*, Melbourne, Text Publishing, 2005. Jenna Jameson's *How to Make Love Like a Porn Star*, New York, William Morrow, 2004 remained on the US bestseller list for six weeks.

85 Carol Leigh, 'Inventing Sex Work', in *Whores and Other Feminists*, Jill Nagle (ed.), New York and London, Routledge, 1997, pp. 226, 230.

The modernist re-invention of sexual intercourse as *work* was a watershed in the history of the normalisation, or depathologising, of un(re)productive libidinal expenditure: it countered the centuries-old stereotype of the prostitute as a constitutionally lazy, workshy drain on the capitalist economy, the female genetic counterpart of the male hereditary criminal, each as unproductive as the other. The re-invention of sex as work was a bid to bring prostitution out of the so-called 'unproductive', black economy and challenge the stigmatisation of prostitution as an evasion of the work ethic, a means of easy money-making for anti-social women.

But what is clear about postmodern prostitute-chic is that its market appeal (its retail-therapeutic promise) is based on an association of sex *neither* with the dignity of labour *nor* with alienated work, but with pleasure and consumption, or the two forms of spending that the prostitute is deemed to have more of: sex and shopping, libidinal and fiscal spending. Consumer culture's fashion-cycle has come full circle, confirming Parent-Duchâtelet and the Victorian regulationists' worst fear: the fear that the 'streetwalker' would become indistinguishable from the average woman-in-the-street. A journalist covering the 2003 Toronto Film Festival reported attending a festival party at which, she said:

> I suddenly realized I was surrounded by hookers. From the skin-tight trousers that revealed a part of the rear anatomy normally reserved for builders to the skimpy tops that put a smile on my husband's face, these women had all the requisites – except they weren't prostitutes. They were average young women out for a good time.
>
> Later, on TV, I caught comedian Bill Maher on the issue. 'Over here, over here, it's me, I'm the real whore', Maher screeched, portraying the difficulty the genuine hooker is having these days, distinguishing herself from ordinary girls.[86]

86 Barbara Sumner Burstyn, 'Hooker Look in Fashion as Porn Becomes de Rigueur', *Dissident Voice*, November 3, 2003, http://www.dissidentvoice.org/Articles9/Burstyn_Hooker-Look.htm.

Or, as Jeanette Angell, the Boston postgraduate divinity student-cum-prostitute, university lecturer and author, put it in her bestselling memoir, *Callgirl: Confessions of a Double Life* (2004):

> They want callgirls to be different, identifiable. That keeps them safe.
>
> But the reality, of course, is that usually we're not … [C]allgirls – women who work for escort services, especially expensive ones, especially those run by other women – we don't look any different than anyone else. Not even always prettier. So we're scary: because, you know, we could be you, too.
>
> Maybe we are.[87]

87 Angell, *Callgirl*, p. 5.

5

'Revolution is the orgasm of history':[1] Two Theories of Revolutionary Libidinal Economy

In the previous chapter we saw how the socially liminal figure of the prostitute, stigmatised by Victorian anthropologists as a criminal 'drain' on capitalist society, could be re-cast as a proto-revolutionary figure in a tradition of Freudo-Marxist libidinal economy. In this and the following chapters, we turn to the tradition of sexual revolution proper and consider how two opposed models of libidinal economy, answering to the producer and consumer ethics respectively, have shaped the ideologies and *Realpolitik* of revolutionary movements that have concerned themselves integrally with sexuality.

Numerous books have been written on the subject of sexual revolution, three of the best-known being John Heidenry's *What Wild Ecstasy: The Rise and Fall of the Sexual Revolution* (1977), Linda Grant's *Sexing the Millennium: A Political History of the Sexual Revolution* (1993) and David Allyn's *Make Love, Not War: The Sexual Revolution: An Unfettered History* (2001). Notice the recurring formula in the subtitles of these books, with its misleading definite article: 'the' sexual revolution. Commentators on the subject often ask whether 'the sexual revolution' ever really happened ('So, *has* there been a sexual revolution?' asks Grant, by way of introducing *Sexing the Millennium*, a book that confines its ambit almost exclusively to the two decades between *Time* maga-

1 A widespread graffito of the 1960s, cited in Linda Grant, *Sexing the Millennium: Women and the Sexual Revolution*, London, Harper Collins, 1993, p. 172.

zine's 1964 heralding of a 'World Sexual Revolution' and its 1984 announcement: 'the revolution is over'[2]). A better, if unanswerable and hence merely rhetorical, question might be: how *many* sexual revolutions have there been? The history of radical shifts in the kinds and conditions of human sexual relating is unimaginably long, and there can be no justification for limiting the historical and cultural reference of the term 'sexual revolution' to that notoriously elastic decade, the 1960s, nor to the Western edge of Europe and North America. Judaeo-Christian myth *begins* with a story of sexual revolution, the Temptation and Fall of Man – at least as the *Book of Genesis* was read in the 1830s by the Perfectionist preacher and sexual liberationist, John Humphrey Noyes. Modern ethnography posits a no less mythical, originary revolution in its story of how patriarchy must have overturned the 'primitive matriarchal societies' – the gynocracies and free-love regimes – that Bronislaw Malinowski postulated were pervasive features of the Neolithic era, and which such twentieth-century sexual radicals as Otto Gross, Wilhelm Reich and Georges Bataille (all readers of Malinowski's *Argonauts of the Western Pacific* [1922]) imagined as blueprints for sexually liberated societies of the future. Forty years before Malinowski's book appeared, Frederick Engels had hypothesised the same prehistorical sexual revolution in his *The Origin of the Family, Private Property and the State* (1884): 'the overthrow of the mother right *was the world historical defeat of the female sex*'.[3]

In short, history inherits the very notion of sexual revolution from prehistory. And whether or not Noyes was right to interpret the Biblical Fall as a story of world-changing transgressive sexual desire, it did have four specific consequences that all utopian-socialist sexual revolutions have been trying to put right ever since: namely, the curses of shame, toil, the pains of motherhood, and woman's subservience to male desire – God's four curses on Adam and Eve for tasting the fruit of knowledge (*Genesis* 3: 6-24).

2 Ibid., p. 18.

3 Fredrick Engels, *The Origin of the Family, Private Property and the State* [1884], introduction by E.B. Leacock, New York, International Publishers, 1972, p. 120 (emphasis in original).

Like other millenarians, the eighteenth-century Shakers solved the problem of toil by abolishing private property, collectivising their wealth, and instituting gender-equality in the division of labour, and they eliminated sexual shame and the pains of motherhood by practising a strict code of celibacy – a solution revealed in a vision to their leader, Mother Ann Lee (revealed to the Shakers in 1770 as God's second and female incarnation), following her own harrowing experience of four traumatic deliveries and four infant deaths. The Shakers' consequent reliance on recruitment, not reproduction, to maintain their community (children were recruited into its communal 'families' through adoption or conversion) has not stopped it lasting some 260 years – the most successful countercultural movement in American history, judged by longevity. The Shakers' putatively matriarchal model has been invoked by many radical-feminist historians since the eighteenth century as a prototype for women seeking gender equality and prepared to practice chastity, or the withdrawal of sexual labour, to achieve it. In April of 2009, Kenya's Federation of Women Lawyers famously organised a nationwide boycott of heterosexual intercourse by Kenyan women, taking a leaf out of Aristophanes's 411 BC comedy, *Lysistrata*, to force resolution of a factional impasse in Kenya's male-dominated government. But the strategy has also been advocated as a genuinely revolutionary one, never more sincerely than by the radical lesbian feminist activist, Sheila Jeffreys, in her verdict on the 1960s sexual revolution as 'anticlimactic' for women. In 1990 Jeffreys concluded her book, *Anticlimax: A Feminist Perspective on the Sexual Revolution*, by arguing that the only way for women to dismantle male privilege and power was to practice lesbianism as a political choice, withdrawing their 'most valuable energies' from men.[4] By the 1970s, many straight women who were sexually active in the 1960s were arriving at a similar conclusion: better that eroticism be put on hold till gender and class relations are overhauled than that women become the tea-makers, typists and bed-mates of another masculinist sexual revolution.

4 Sheila Jeffreys, *Anticlimax: A Feminist Perspective on the Sexual Revolution*, London, Women's Press, 1990, pp. 291, 293.

Celibacy and sublimation have figured large in other revolutions, but the founder of the second most-celebrated countercultural experiment in early American history took the opposite view to Mother Ann Lee's, arguing that the Shakers had freed women from the burden of motherhood at unnecessary cost: the cost of the sexual pleasure for which God created Eve as companion to Adam before banishing them both from Eden with the curse of parenthood ('in sorrow thou shalt bring forth children'). This was the heretical theologian and Owenite socialist, John Humphrey Noyes, who coined the term 'free love' in the 1840s and founded what would become the 300-strong Oneida Community, which successfully practised sexual and economic communism for some forty years in New York State before disbanding in 1881 and turning itself into Charles Fourier's ideal of unalienated labour, a joint-stock company. The Oneida experiment has been an inspiration for countercultural communes and sexual-liberation movements ever since. Noyes's repudiation of celibacy and sublimation in favour of polyamory and 'free love' provides one of the case histories in libidinal communism to be examined in subsequent chapters; but it represents only one side of the coin of revolutionary libidinal economy.

There are two basic models of the libidinal economy of revolutionary movements, which we might characterise as the Freudian and the Reichian, or the petit-bourgeois and the utopian-socialist, or the Calvinist and the Keynesian models – the former based on a vision of (libidinal) spending as depletion or loss, the latter on a vision of spending as *generating* (libidinal) wealth.

Mahatma Gandhi was an advocate of the petit-bourgeois or Freudian theory of libidinal economy, spelling out its implications in his 1927 treatise, *Self-Restraint versus Self-Indulgence*. In a chapter devoted to a long and laudatory review of a book entitled *Towards Moral Bankruptcy*,[5] Gandhi warned his fellow Indians and would-be revolutionaries that the doctrine of 'free love' was fundamentally misconceived and that 'the true sexual emancipation' consists in 'perpetual restraint', or life-long continence. (Readers of his chapter

5 M.K. Gandhi, 'Towards Moral Bankruptcy' (review of the English translation of Paul Bureau's *L' Indiscipline des moeurs*), *Self-Restraint versus Self-Indulgence*, Ahmedabad, Navajivan Press, 1930, pp. 1-49.

'On the Necessity of Continence' were assured that 'no other chapter is nearly as important as this'[6]). Citing both medical authority and personal experience as evidence for his case, Gandhi argued that the expenditure of 'vital energy' in orgasm is 'positively injurious to health' – 'all the strength of body and mind that has taken long to acquire is lost all at once by a single dissipation of energy'[7] – and that the 'economic security and success' of any society depends on conserving and hoarding this vital energy, hard though this might be for Indians who suffered, as a population, from what he called the 'almost incurable disease' of sexual 'merry-making'. Unless Indians learned to conserve their libidinal energies and invest them in industry and politics instead of squandering them in onanism, promiscuity and unplanned pregnancies, they would never throw off the yoke of British imperialism: 'When we are engaged in a death grip with a powerful government, we shall need all the strength physical, material, moral and spiritual. We cannot gain it unless we husband the one thing which we must prize above everything else. Without this personal purity of life, we must remain a nation of slaves'.[8] Anticipating Foucault's critique of the 'repressive hypothesis', Gandhi insisted that it was the British national habits of 'sexual continence and self-denial' that had enabled the imperialists to accumulate sufficient vital energy to subjugate and colonise the sensual Indians; and if anti-colonial revolutionaries like himself were ever to win the struggle for self-rule, India would need to achieve the same percentage of celibates among its population as the Western European nations could boast:[9]

> Let us not deceive ourselves by imagining, that because we consider the system of government to be corrupt, Englishmen are to be despised as competitors in a race for personal virtue. Without making any spiritual parade of the fundamental virtues, they practise them at least physically in abundant measure.

6 Ibid. pp. 32-33; and M.K. Gandhi, 'On the Necessity of Continence' (1927), *Self-restraint versus Self-indulgence*, p. 71.

7 Ibid., p. 73

8 Ibid., pp. 109-10.

9 Ibid., p. 73.

> Among those who are engaged in the political life of the country, there are more celibates and spinsters than among us. Spinsters among us are practically unknown, except the nuns who leave no impression on the political life of the country, whereas in Europe, thousands claim celibacy as a common virtue.[10]

For the Mahatma, as for Freud, libido spent in erotic pleasure becomes unavailable for sublimation and hence for civilisation – or for Gandhi's revolutionary project of postcolonial nation-building.[11]

Much to Wilhelm Reich's dismay, it was this same view of libidinal economy that the Bolsheviks would adopt when they started rolling back the sexual revolution they had introduced in Russia immediately after the October Revolution with a raft of progressive laws on gender equality, sexual freedom, women's rights, divorce, abortion, state-provided childcare and the decriminalisation of homosexuality. Intent on overcoming gender inequality and dismantling the traditional patriarchal nuclear family, the Bolshevik reformers were progressive not least in formulating their policies on sexual and gender issues in social terms, rather than medicalising or biologising them and thus handing them over to a scientific elite for deliberation. Treating the sexual as permeated by the social and hence as available to political transformation, the Bolsheviks were being true to Engels's analysis of the superstructural dependence of gender-relations and sexual morality on property-relations in *The Origin of the Family*. But this social-constructivist approach to sexuality could also turn into a politically convenient, 'vulgar' economic determinism, according to which the state had no real need to concern itself with sexual reforms and freedoms as such, since the 'new sexuality', like the 'New Man' and 'New Woman' (reconstructed as 'socialised' subjects), was supposed to follow automatically from the abolition of private property.

Already over-stretched by the task of managing the simultaneous economic, educational and cultural modernisation of Russia, the

10 Ibid., p. 110.

11 For parallels between Freudianism and Gandhi's Hindu philosophy of continence, see Erik H. Erikson, *Gandhi's Truth: On the Origins of Militant Nonviolence*, London, Faber & Faber, 1970, pp. 246-47.

Soviet authorities decided they could shelve the issue of sexual revolution for Soviet youth, since sexual problems would simply wither away in the transformed conditions of revolutionary society. This view was compounded by what has been called 'Stalinist sexophobia', an important strand of Stalin's 'cultural revolution' or counterrevolution in the early 1930s, which 'aimed at liquidating social and cultural diversity and at establishing total control over the personality'.[12] By the mid-1920s, Bolshevik moralists such as Aron Zalkind were stigmatising 'free love' as a decadent bourgeois doctrine, deploring the degeneracy of Soviet university students, and blaming the remnants of the bourgeois class for injecting 'the laboring masses with a sexual narcotic'.[13] Ironically, party-line Soviet sexual ideology began to echo the most conservative Victorian marriage-advice manuals in maintaining that sexual intimacy had no other purpose than the 'creation of healthy, robust descendants', as Dr A.L. Berkovich argued in his plan for the complete 'rationalisation of sex', published in *The Young Guard* in 1923.[14] Stalin's sexual counterrevolution included the re-criminalising of homosexuality and culminated in 1945 in his prohibition of abortion.[15] Gregory Carleton cites as 'the crowning statement of Bolshevik asceticism' in the 1930s a sentiment voiced by a newly converted communist character in Nikolai Ostrovsky's classic socialist-realist novel, *How the Steel Was Tempered* (1932): 'Mama, I've sworn to myself not to chase girls until we've knocked off the bourgeoisie in the whole world'.[16]

While the Western press was demonising the Bolsheviks' free-love regime for desecrating the sanctity of marriage and the dignity of womanhood, then, the Bolsheviks themselves were concluding that the physical and emotional demands, or libidinal costs, of civil war and revolution required them to conserve scarce energies rather

12 Igor S. Kon, *The Sexual Revolution in Russia: From the Age of the Czars to Today*, J. Riordan (trans.), New York, Free Press, 1995, p. 266.

13 Gregory Carleton, *Sexual Revolution in Bolshevik Russia*, Pittsburgh, University of Pittsburgh Press, 2005, p. 57.

14 Ibid., p. 62.

15 Martin, 'Structuring the Sexual Revolution', p. 124.

16 Carleton, *Sexual Revolution in Bolshevik Russia*, p. 222.

than squander them in sexual experimentation. From 1922 onwards, therefore, the Bolsheviks began offering Soviet youth the examples not of sexual liberationists but of celibate great men – Leonardo, Beethoven, Newton and Kant – as models of productive sublimation. Driving sex underground, Soviet asceticism ensured that sex of any kind became, in Igor Kon's words, 'a sign of social protest and a refuge for individuals from the totalitarian state. Forbidden erotica became a strong anti-Soviet and anti-Communist symbol, pressing the people to make their choice'.[17] One outcome of the Communist Party's systematic suppression of all things sexual – sex research, sex education, 'erotic' art and literature – would be Russia's second abortive sexual revolution in the twentieth century, the one that followed *perestroika* in the late 1980s, when rigid government control gave way to a deregulated market in unclassified pornography and commoditised sex, which delivered the long-desired sexual liberation in the form of de-romanticised and commercialised, anarchic and alienated, obscene and trivialised sex.

It was also the petit-bourgeois or Freudian model of libidinal economy – promulgating thrift, frugality and productive investment or 'sublimation' as economic necessities – that would be imported from psychoanalysis into Western sociology in the late 1990s, when questions of desire, affective ties and sexual relationships were reintroduced into group-behaviour research and theory after a long period of being repressed from paradigms that stressed the *rational* character and goals of social movements. Just as psychological analyses of consumer desire – as distinct from statistical analyses of consumer choices – became officially unfashionable in the market research and advertising industries following Packard and Friedan's exposés of the 'hidden persuaders' in the 1960s, so 'desire' had become an unfashionable concept among group-behaviour sociologists who were reacting against 'the tendency of "classical" collective-behaviour theory to view social-movement participants as irrational, expressive, and highly manipulable'.[18] As

17 Kon, *The Sexual Revolution in Russia*, pp. 266-67.

18 Jeff Goodwin, 'The Libidinal Constitution of a High-Risk Social Movement: Affectual Ties and Solidarity in the Huk Rebellion, 1946 to 1954', *American Sociological Review*, 62 (February 1997): 54.

one sociologist remarked in the late 1990s: 'If the modern era is characterised by [what Foucault termed] "a veritable discursive explosion" about sexuality, then social-movement theory remains deeply embedded in the ancien régime'.[19] Systematically neglecting what Freud called the 'libidinal constitution' of social movements, the dominant paradigms of group-behaviour theory resemble neoclassical and neoliberal economics in stressing the relentless rationality of *homo œconomicus*, allowing little room for the sexual relationships and affectual ties that bind groups and complicate exchange-relations. However, when desire and libido do resurface in a psychoanalytically-informed sociology of group behaviour, the libido/money analogy or equation, central to the history of libidinal economy that we are investigating, also resurfaces.[20] Calling for a return of repressed desire in social-movement research in the *American Sociological Review* in 1997, Jeff Goodwin illustrated how the sociologist Philip Slater's psychoanalytically-oriented theories of libidinal economy could be applied to analysis of 'affectual ties and solidarity' in 'a high-risk social movement', or revolutionary political movement, such as the post-World War II Huk Rebellion in the Philippines – a Communist-led peasant insurgency against the occupying US authorities and their allies, the Filipino landed oligarchy, between 1946 and 1954.

Slater's approach to social-group analysis focuses on the institutions and practices designed to prevent 'libidinal withdrawal' – the withdrawal of emotional energy – from the group, on the premise that the available libido is always finite and can only be invested or spent in a limited number of ways.[21] As Goodwin puts it: 'a fundamental premise of a libidinal-economy analysis is that individuals cannot make unlimited emotional investments in even a relatively

19 Ibid., p. 53.

20 As we saw in chapter 3, desire and libido were also rediscovered in marketing theory in the twenty-first century by a generation of theorists more familiar with the names of Deleuze, Derrida and Lyotard than with those of Freud and Dichter.

21 Philip Slater, *Footholds: Understanding the Shifting Family and Sexual Tensions in Our Culture*, Wendy Slater Palmer (ed.), Boston, Beacon Press, 1977.

small number of object-choices; the distribution of cathexes is always a potential source of social conflict because, as Coser notes, "human beings possess only finite libidinal energies for cathecting social objects"'.[22] Dennis Wrong has commented of this 'scarcity' model of libido:

> A more fundamental criticism of Freud is that his theory of the necessary repression of Eros presupposes his 'hydraulic' conception of psychic energy. If the individual possesses only a limited quantum of libidinal energy, clearly it must be rationed among the various tasks and objects to which he or she is committed or attached. If it is fully discharged in pleasurable sexual relations or in family attachments, there will not be enough left over for the wider public obligations entailed by membership in a larger society. Such a view of a limited supply of available energy is a relic of Freud's nineteenth-century physicalism or materialism. Yet Freud may have been right in substance even if the doctrinaire terms of his metapsychological theory are no longer convincing.[23]

Slater identifies three kinds of libidinal 'threats' to group solidarity, three forms of 'emotional withdrawal' or 'libidinal disinvestment' from the community, which he calls 'dyadic', 'familial' and 'narcissistic withdrawal', and which the institutions of the incest taboo, marriage and socialisation, respectively, are designed to regulate.[24] 'Dyadic withdrawal' is the disinvestment of libido from groups and its exclusive investment in a sexually intimate couple-relationship ('an intimate dyadic relationship always threatens to short-circuit the libidinal network of the community and drain off its source of sustenance').[25] 'Familial withdrawal' 'occurs whenever a nuclear family becomes emotionally or libidinally sufficient unto itself'; while 'narcissistic withdrawal' is the onanistic investment of libido in

22 Goodwin, 'The Libidinal Constitution', pp. 55-56.

23 Dennis H. Wrong, *The Problem of Order, or What Unites and Divides Society*, Cambridge, Mass., Harvard University Press, 1995, p. 139-40

24 See Slater, 'On Social Regression', pp. 339-364; and Slater, *Footholds*, p. 116.

25 Slater, 'On Social Regression', p. 348.

self-love and self-interest, with no effectual or emotional investment in others.[26] Goodwin hints at how libidinal-economic group-theory can tend to denaturalise and pathologise the *homo œconomicus* model of purely self-interested motivation – promulgated as a human universal by neoclassical and neoliberal economists – when he observes of Slater's 'narcissistic withdrawal' that 'self-interested social action, in this view, is not some natural psychological predisposition, but is a consequence of the "libidinal opportunity" associated with particular positions in social networks'. In other words, *homo œconomicus*'s 'narcissistic withdrawal' is predicated on the social privilege of *apparent* self-sufficiency. 'More specifically', Goodwin adds, 'it is the structural possibility of libidinal withdrawal from all groups and dyads that allows for "the complete economic man, motivated solely by rational self-interest"'.[27] Slater demonstrated in persuasive detail how the institutions of marriage, the incest taboo and socialisation serve to limit and regulate the three kinds of libidinal disinvestment from groups, and – developing the Freudian model of an economy of libidinal scarcity – explained the economy at stake by elaborating on Talcott Parsons' suggestion 'that pleasure was the money of the body'.[28] Positing a causal relationship between libido and the money-economy – arguing that 'money and its institutions are modelled after the organisation of pleasure in the body'[29] – Slater maintained that pleasure functions as a universal equivalent in the corporeal economy, a psychosomatic currency or medium of exchange that enables inherently disparate, or qualitatively incommensurable, actions, experiences and sensations to be rendered quantitatively comparable: 'Pleasure is a kind of *lingua franca* for the body that, like money for a social system, translates a variety of *qualitatively* different stimuli into a single *quantitative* dimension of value. This enables us to organize a uniform hierarchy of value out of

26 See ibid., and Slater, *Footholds*, p. 116.

27 See Slater, 'On Social Regression', p. 345; and Goodwin, 'The Libidinal Constitution', p. 56.

28 Talcott Parsons, 'Some Reflections on the Problem of Psychosomatic Relationships in Health and Illness' (unpublished essay), quoted in Slater, *Footholds*, 175.

29 Slater, ibid.

a heterogeneous chaos of unique experiences and events'.[30] It is thus the economy of pleasure, or the currency of the pleasure-principle in libidinal economy, that enables an organism to choose between two qualitatively different actions, each with its own unique set of appeals: 'pleasure is a unitary concept, reducing all these unique events to a single quantitative standard'.[31] (Freudian libidinal economics shares its utilitarian philosophical basis with neoclassical economics: the economist Francis Edgeworth, in his major work *Mathematical Psychics* [1881], stated as an axiom that 'Pleasure is measurable, and all pleasures are commensurable', and that 'the rate of increase of pleasure decreases as its means increase'[32]).

Freud himself had constructed orgasm as the universal yardstick of value in the corporeal economy of pleasure. *Civilization and Its Discontents* develops the thesis that 'it is simply the pleasure-principle which draws up the programme of life's purpose ... What is called happiness in its narrowest sense comes from the satisfaction – most often instantaneous – of pent-up needs which have reached great intensity'; 'sexual love gives us our most intense experience of an overwhelming pleasurable sensation and so furnishes a prototype for our strivings after happiness'; 'in that modified sense in which we have seen it to be attainable, happiness is a problem of the economics of the libido in each individual'. To this exposition of the orgasmic spending of pent-up energy as the prototypical pleasure and universal measure of value in libidinal economy, Freud added a characteristic caveat, implicitly advocating sublimation: 'Just as a cautious business-man avoids investing all his capital in one concern, so wisdom would probably admonish us also not to anticipate all our happiness from one quarter alone'.[33]

Elaborating on the relationship between money and pleasure, political economy and libidinal economy, Slater argued that 'the societal equivalent of genital orgasm in the body is war. In war the total society prevents decentralization by the discharge of

30 Ibid.

31 Ibid., p. 177.

32 Francis Edgeworth, *Mathematical Psychics* (1881), New York, Kelley, 1967, p. 16.

33 Freud, *Civilization and Its Discontents*, pp. 91-104.

surplus wealth through destruction – a highly inelegant genital mechanism, it must be admitted'.[34] Slater also noted that healing of the body (politic) occurs through libidinal investment in the damaged or painful (unpleasurable) part, and that 'a gifted healer is one who can get the psychic economy rolling – swiftly acquiring some emotional spending money, spending it, getting it back and spending more'.[35] Positing an equivalence of libido with money raises the question of what happens to libidinal wealth when a subject dies. Slater's argument, as we noted in chapter one, is that, contrary to appearances, neither energy nor wealth can 'die': when the individual psyche dies, libido merely reverts to its somatic components, ultimately cellular and chemical ones, just as, when a money economy collapses, 'wealth does not vanish, but only becomes latent and fragmented, and the same is true of libidinal energy'.[36]

But what has Freudianised social-movement theory to do with 'the orgasm of history', as revolution was dubbed by a ubiquitous graffito of the 1960s? Goodwin illustrates the application of Slater's theses to the Huk Rebellion, pointing out that libidinal withdrawal was explicitly discussed and 'politicised' (though not in strictly psychoanalytic terms) by the Huk activists, as recorded in the Filipino Communist Party's (PKP's) records, which were captured by the Philippine government in October, 1950. The PKP produced two parallel documents, one on the problems of 'Sex Opportunism', also known as 'the Sex Problem', the other, 'Finance Opportunism: Its Basic Causes and Remedies'. The documents addressed the question of how to prevent libidinal and economic resources from being privatised, or invested/expended in personal and familial interests rather than in the movement's interests. Recognising that 'sexual relations raised the possibility of divided emotional commitments that could weaken the Huk movement', Goodwin reports, 'the PKP felt obliged to oversee and regulate the sexual relations of Huk activists'.[37] Among other measures, Huk marriage

34 Slater, *Footholds*, p. 177.
35 Ibid. p. 185
36 Slater, 'On Social Regression', pp. 344-45.
37 Goodwin, 'The Libidinal Constitution', p. 60.

ceremonies were recast as ritual affirmations of the couple's joint loyalty and commitment to the struggle, with the couple joining hands on a pistol. The PKP leadership also drew up a policy statement entitled 'Revolutionary Solution of the Sex Problem', identifying the problem as the combination of heightened sexual excitement associated with front-line living, and 'sex opportunism', or the practice of married men (remote from their home villages and families) informally taking second wives in the Huk camps. The document reviewed the historical costs of 'private' libidinal expenditure to previous revolutionary movements in the Philippines and canvassed possible ways of preventing such libidinal wastage, not excluding surgical 'removal of the organs from which the desire is generated'. However, the PKP document concluded that neither celibacy nor eunuchism offered 'scientifically' correct solutions to the Huk movement's sex problem, and that it had to be approached with neither 'feudal' nor 'bourgeois' notions of sexual morality. Instead, the 'sex problem' demanded a revolutionary solution in which the Party would determine exactly when or whether a particular extra-marital relationship would or would not serve 'the interests of the movement', weighing such factors as the effects of sexual frustration on the health and efficiency of the cadre and alternative possibilities for sublimation. Such a pragmatic, revolutionary morality, geared entirely to the interests of the Party and its day-by-day struggle, would 'lay the foundations of future communist sex morality'.[38]

Politically relativistic and historically 'open-minded', then, the PKP's rationalised view of sexual morality as libidinal-economic book-keeping was nonetheless predicated on the same, 'scarcity' model of libido as the Soviet sexual counter-revolution, whose ethos was pithily encapsulated in the vernacular name for the Stalin Prize novel: 'Boy Meets Tractor' fiction. According to this Freudian model of libidinal economy, adopted alike by Stalinist and Gandhian revolutionaries and social-movement theorists: libido expended in sexual pleasure is necessarily privatised; 'invested' in the self or family, as a form of private capital, it becomes unavail-

38 Ibid., p. 62.

able to the collectivity; its expenditure in sexual pleasure, as opposed to its sublimation, impoverishes the group and threatens its survival or disintegration. The logic of this model arguably reflects a specifically petit-bourgeois conception of fiscal wisdom and wealth, rather than the inherent ethic of capitalism itself, which can entertain contradictory imperatives, including those of the producer and consumer ethics, the one advocating saving and investment, the other spending, as the key to economic health or wealth.

There is, then, another tradition of revolutionary libidinal economy, predicated on the opposite view of sexual spending: the view that the more eroticised or sexualised the relationships within a group, and the more libido is pleasurably spent or circulated among its members, the greater the libidinal wealth that will be generated for the group. This utopian-socialist or Reichian vision of libidinal economy is also one whose Keynesian credentials we shall be examining in a later chapter. Keynes, of course, was neither utopian nor socialist, but much as Reich's politico-intellectual career saw him exchanging a youthful commitment to Eastern European communist movements for a disillusioned embrace of American capitalism in late middle-age, so the utopian-socialist model of libidinal economy could turn out, uncannily, to be no less co-optable by, or compatible with, the logic of advanced consumer capitalism than was the 1960s sexual revolution that Reich would help to father.

While Reich was not the coiner of the term 'sexual revolution', his name is now inextricably linked to it (the first usage of the term has been traced to Wilhelm Heinrich Dreuw's 1921 book, *Die Sexual-Revolution: Der Kampf und die Staatliche: Bekämpfung der Geschlechtskranheiten* [The sexual revolution: the struggle for the state: combating sexually transmitted diseases], which advocated a 'revolution' in legal thinking about prostitution and venereal disease[39]). Reich keenly followed the early Bolshevik experiment with sexual revolution and he returned from a lecture tour in Russia in 1929 impressed by progressive institutions such as the State

39 Wilhelm Heinrich Dreuw, *Die Sexual-Revolution: Der Kampf und die Staatliche: Bekämpfung der Geschlechtskranheiten*, Leipzig, Ernst Bircher Verlag, 1921. See Martin, 'Structuring the Sexual Revolution', p. 107.

Psychoanalytic Orphanage-Laboratory, in which children of Party members, including Joseph Stalin's son, were raised without guilt-inducing judgement or punishment for sexual behaviour, with a view to obviating all sexually derived problems in their later lives.[40] At the same time, Reich was depressed by the early signs of the Soviet retreat from sexual liberalisation,[41] and he authored several mutating editions of a two-part study entitled, in 1936, *Die Sexualität im Kulturkampf: zur sozialistischen Umstrukturierung des Menschen* (Sexuality in the culture struggle: for the socialist restructuring of humans) and re-titled, from the 1945 English edition onwards, *The Sexual Revolution: Toward a Self-Governing Character Structure*. Part I of the book was dedicated to analysing the failure of attempted sexual reforms in bourgeois society to overhaul the institutions of monogamy and the patriarchal family that sustained capitalism, while Part II tracked the rise and fall of the Soviet sexual revolution. Reich's career as an ideologue of sexual liberation spanned both of the decades popularly identified with sexual revolutions in the West – the so-called 'Roaring Twenties' and the 1960s – but it was the early Marxist Reich whose thinking would shape the revolutionary calls to arms issued by 1960s theorists of sexual liberation such as Marcuse and Norman O. Brown, rather than the cloud-busting exponent of orgone theory that Reich became during the McCarthy era.[42]

Like his fellow psychoanalyst and would-be revolutionary, Otto Gross, Reich was a classical Freudian to the extent that he based his revolutionary theory on the 'hydraulic' model of liberation, positing that 'natural', 'healthy', 'instinctual' erotic drives were psychically repressed by introjected 'foreign' authorities, in the form of the superego, with pathological consequences – and that exorcising the most pathogenic of those introjected authorities, using psychoanalytic techniques, was the only route to salvation. The sadistic conscience or superego was the internalised representative of the

40 Alexander Etkind, *Eros of the Impossible: The History of Psychoanalysis in Russia*, Boulder, CO, Westview, 1997, p. 203. See, below, chapter eight.
41 Sharaf, *Fury on Earth*, pp. 142-43.
42 Reich, *The Function of the Orgasm*, New York, Farrar, Strauss and Giroux, 1973, pp. 368-93

patriarchal head of the bourgeois nuclear family and the authoritarian state, institutions that propped up class society and its exploitative divisions of labour and wealth.[43] (According to Max Weber, who rejected an article Gross sent to his journal for publication, Gross insisted that 'every suppression of emotion-laden desires and drives leads to "repression" and therefore calls for revolution' – a naive and dangerous view, in Weber's judgement, making no allowance for the fact that the ethical life always entails some repression.[44]) In *The Sexual Revolution* Reich insisted that individual neurosis and 'pathological' or 'irrational mass behaviour' can invariably be traced to the same source, sexual repression, which he explained as an unconscious conflict between instinctual drives for erotic gratification and 'the moral pressure which is needed to keep the dammed-up energies under control'.[45] The outcome of this conflict is that 'the natural capacity for sexual gratification' is thwarted, either 'entirely destroyed' or displaced into 'sadistic concepts of the sexual act, rape phantasies, etc'.[46] As the ego arms 'itself against the instinct as well as the outer world', libidinal energy congeals into a form of 'character armour' that functions as a prison to the instinctual drive to release or spend libido in orgasm. Only by 'eliminat[ing] the genital inhibitions and genital anxiety' that are instilled in individuals by the ages of four or five through the taboos against masturbation, incest and infantile polymorphous sexuality, and reinforced by the institutions of the patriarchal family, premarital chastity and life-long monogamy, could both individual neurosis and mass pathology be cured.[47] Carolyn Dean summarises Reich's logic: 'healthy sexuality leads to democracy and perverted sexuality leads to fascism'.[48] Nor was

43 Wilhelm Reich, *The Sexual Revolution: Toward a Self-Governing Character Structure*, revised Theodore P. Wolfe (ed. and trans.), New York, Farrar, Straus and Giroux, 1969, chapter 5: 'The Compulsive Family as Educational Apparatus', pp. 71-79.

44 Zaretsky, *Secrets of the Soul*, p. 86.

45 Reich, *The Sexual* Revolution, pp. 3-4.

46 Ibid., p. 4.

47 Ibid., pp. 116-49.

48 Dean, *Sexuality and Modern Western Culture*, p. 60.

Freud correct in positing that 'culture always owes its existence to instinctual repression and renunciation ... that cultural achievements are the result of sublimated sexual energy'; for 'there is historical evidence', Reich insisted vaguely, 'of the incorrectness of this formulation':

> there are in existence highly cultured societies without any sexual suppression and a completely free sex life. What is correct in this theory is only that sexual suppression forms the mass-psychological basis for a certain culture, namely, the patriarchal authoritarian one, in all of its forms.[49]

Marcuse would refine this challenge to Freud's pessimistic, ahistorical, universalist conception of repression with his theory of 'surplus repression', developed in what became one of the key philosophical handbooks for sexual revolutionaries in the 1960s, *Eros and Civilization* (1955). In Marcuse's view, oedipalisation was the disciplinary process by which the body and its senses became organised around work or utility, rather than around instinctual gratification or sensual pleasure, and it necessitated a contraction of the erotogenic zones of the body to the single zone of the genitals, thereby 'freeing' the rest of the body for labour. Marcuse described this process as 'the desexualization of the organism required by its social utilization as an instrument of labour';[50] but he argued that the material abundance that the Industrial Revolution had delivered to first-world societies in the form of labour-saving technology should have rendered much of traditional work – and hence the repression and sublimation by which libidinal energy is channelled into work – redundant. If such repression was still being exacted by civilisation, Marcuse argued, it was only because of the exploitative division of labour in class society, which demands 'surplus repression' from the so-called 'working', or 'dominated', classes, allowing the dominant to enjoy a corresponding deficit in repression.

49 Reich, *The Sexual Revolution*, p. 10.

50 Herbert Marcuse, *Eros and Civilization* (1955), Boston, Beacon Press, 1966, p. 39.

Marcuse's utopian vision was of a non-repressive society of material abundance, in which the body would be fully restored to its 'natural' potential for unsublimated erotic pleasure diffused across all its surfaces, senses and organs.[51]

Construing repression as a blockage of the body's instinctual drive to discharge libidinal energy, then, Reich advocated its antithesis: to spend all one's hoarded libidinal energy without reserve was the revolutionary key to psychic and economic health, both personal and collective. Nor was such a programme based tenuously on a form of metaphorical sophistry, or the forcing of an analogy between libido and the productive capacity – and hence material wealth – of a community or continent. Reich's laboratory experiments with patients in Scandinavia in the 1930s-40s, in which he put what he called his 'orgasm theory' to the test of biochemical and electrocardiographical analyses, proved to his satisfaction that 'the concept of "libido" as a yardstick of "psychic energy" is no longer a mere metaphor'; instead, 'libido' could now be regarded as a literal naming of the bioelectrical charge that his laboratory apparatuses had measured in his sexually aroused patients, thereby proving that 'the sexual function is one of the general electrical processes that occur in nature'.[52]

In classical psychoanalytic theory, the contrary of the pleasurable release of banked-up libido in orgasm is anxiety, a state that inhibits spending in the interests of self-defence. Freud himself had attempted to explain anxiety symptoms 'economically', as redirected or misdirected libido, before later linking anxiety and self-punishment to his hypothesis of a death-instinct locked in a struggle with the life-instinct or Eros: 'Formerly, I regarded anxiety as a general reaction of the ego under conditions of unpleasure. I always sought to justify its appearance on economic grounds and I assumed, on the strength of my investigations into the "actual" neuroses, that libido (sexual excitation) which was rejected or not utilized by the

51 Ibid., pp. 34-35.

52 Wilhelm Reich, *The Bioelectrical Investigation of Sexuality and Anxiety*, Mary Higgins and Chesterfield M. Raphael (eds), Marion Faber with Derek and Ince Jordan (trans.), New York, Farrar, Straus and Giroux, 1982, p. 126.

ego found direct discharge in the form of anxiety'.[53] What Reich claimed to demonstrate and quantify in his laboratory experiments was the extent to which the bodies of patients in states of 'unpleasure, anxiety, annoyance, pressure, etc.' generate *less* bioelectricity than when they are in a resting state, whereas the bodies of patients in pleasurable states of sexual excitation generate a *higher* bioelectrical charge than when not aroused ('sexual excitation is functionally identical to bioenergetic charge of the erogenous zones').[54] In short, sexual excitation does not simply 'use up', 'deploy' or 'consume' bioelectricity, it *creates* it, generating more bioenergy than was there before. It therefore follows that maximising the amount of sexual excitation in a community means maximising not only its capacity for pleasure but also its productive capacity, its energy – worthy goals for any revolutionary movement.

Reich spelled out his findings in his 1945 book *The Bioelectrical Investigation of Sexuality and Anxiety*, which stressed that his 'orgone biophysics' was firmly based in empirical observation and experimental testing, that it filled 'many gaps in natural science' while proving, for the first time, that 'objective natural processes are concretely linked with subjective emotional life'.[55] An appendix of the book reproduced the 'electrophotographic data' showing correlations between bioelectrical activity on the skin-surface of his patients' erogenous zones and their states of depression, erotic excitation, fear and so on, while the final chapter enumerated 'some theoretical conclusions', such as:

6. Sexual friction is a biological activity which is governed by the alternation of charge and discharge. Discharge is always pleasurable; charge is always pleasurable, provided it is followed by discharge ...
7. *The intensity of the pleasurable sensation corresponds to the quantity of electrical surface charge, and vice versa* ...

53 Sigmund Freud, 'Inhibitions, Symptoms and Anxiety', *Standard Edition of the Complete Psychological Works of Sigmund Freud*, James Strachey (ed.), Vol. 20, London, Vintage, 2001, p. 161.

54 Reich, *The Bioelectrical Investigation of Sexuality*, p. 126.

55 Ibid., p. xii.

9. Since only vegetative sensations of pleasure are accompanied by an increase in peripheral charge, and since unpleasure, anxiety, annoyance, pressure, etc., cause a shift toward negative potentials, we are justified in assuming that erogenous excitation represents the specifically *productive* process of the living organism ... *The sexual process, then, is the biological-productive process per se.* Anxiety is the opposite fundamental biological direction, which is congruent with that of dying, without being identical to it ... [56]

Reich recalled the etymological origins of 'economy' (Greek *oikonomia*: management of household resources) when concluding that, as a result of his empirical investigations of the 'biological electrolyte and membrane system' of his patients in varying moods, 'the way in which the sexual (pleasure, biological energy) household is regulated, and the sex-economic relations between individuals, all assume a greater significance than in the past'.[57] Reich had come to psychoanalysis from a background in the physical sciences, having studied electronics, quantum mechanics and relativity theory. While his psychoanalytic colleagues were focusing on the representational or semiotic contents of their patients' mental processes, Reich was preoccupied with questions and quantities of energy, the somatic sources of neurosis – hence the dominant meaning of his term 'sex economy'. In positing that the bioelectricity generated by erotic excitation was continuous with the cosmic energy ('orgone') emitted by the solar system, he was reviving in the 1930s a thesis whose revival in the 1760s had earned the German physician Franz Anton Mesmer his doctorate. Mesmer's thesis, *De influxu planetarum in corpus humanum*, revived the ancient idea that the planets of our solar system exude invisible rays that affect our bodies, rays that Mesmer called 'magnetic fluid', producing the effect he called 'animal magnetism' – a thesis sufficiently persuasive, at the time, for Mesmer to found a school on it, in Vienna, dedicated to healing diseases by the application of magnets to patients' bodies (a proce-

56 Ibid., pp. 128-29.
57 Ibid., pp. 129, 126.

dure later practised by Freud's mentor, the neurologist Jean-Martin Charcot).[58]

Meanwhile, in Marcuse's analysis, Reich's increasingly single-minded focus on orgasm as the instrument of liberation and on the individual's political duty to pursue revolutionary orgasms – along with the whole psychotherapeutic industry that would develop in the later twentieth century around the promise of delivering orgasmic release and satisfaction to anorgasmic patients – these were part of the problem, not a revolutionary solution to it. With Reich and Eric Fromm, Marcuse may have helped provide the socio-political philosophy for those who like to take their sexual liberation with a dose of theory, but he also provided an explanation of why sexual liberation movements were counterrevolutionary or anti-revolutionary. In what Marcuse called two-dimensional society, the art and literature of a once economically marginal 'high culture' kept alive the utopian vision against which technocratic, industrial-capitalist society could be critically measured and found wanting: this high culture's 'authentic works expressed a conscious, methodical alienation from the entire sphere of business and industry, and from its calculable and profitable order'.[59] One-dimensional society abolishes this critical alienation, collapsing yesterday's 'high culture' into today's 'popular culture' with its techniques of mass reproduction and pre-digestion, resolving difference and conflict into harmonious pluralism, and one of its strategies for achieving this is its 'repressive desublimation' of libido: 'sexuality is liberated (or rather liberalized) in socially constructive forms'; 'repressive desublimation ... operates as the byproduct of the social controls of technological reality, which extend liberty while intensifying domination':

> advanced industrial civilization operates with a great degree of sexual freedom – 'operates' in the sense that the latter becomes a market value and a factor of social mores. Without

58 See, for example, Antoine Faivre, *Access to Western Esotericism*, Albany, NY, State University of New York Press, 1994, p. 77.

59 Marcuse, *One-Dimensional Man* (1964), London, Sphere Books, 1968, p. 59.

> ceasing to be an instrument of labour, the body is allowed to exhibit its sexual features in the everyday work world and in work relations ... Sex is integrated into work and public relations and is thus made more susceptible to (controlled) satisfaction.[60]

In developing his concept of repressive desublimation, Marcuse seems nostalgic for a lost historical moment when a libido denied satisfaction by a more Puritanical, less hedonistic consumer culture might, 'hydraulically' as it were, have burst its fetters and shaken the institutional pillars of class society to the ground. Instead, the 'negativity' of libido – its socially destructive, oppositional, 'unproductive' potential – is neutralised by commoditising sexual satisfaction and incorporating it in the everyday experience, the business, of organised work and play. From this melancholic Freudo-Marxist critical perspective, the 1960s 'sexual revolution', for the vast majority of its beneficiaries who turned on, tuned in, dropped out and then returned to bourgeois careers when the money ran out or the communes disbanded due to internal rivalries – the 1960s sexual revolution merely served to bind its baby-boomers more effectively to a late capitalism that now delivered commercial quantities of sexual pleasure as entertainment and leisure. As the Situationist International leader, Raoul Vaneigem, put it in a chapter on 'Spurious Opposition' in his book *The Revolution of Everyday Life* (1967): 'The more the requirements of consumption come to supersede the requirements of production, the more government by constraint gives way to government by seduction'.[61]

Nonetheless, it would be premature to grant the Marcuse of *One-Dimensional Man* the last word on revolutionary libidinal economy. Some of the most radical and economically viable experiments in libidinal communism long predated the liberationist movements of the so-called Golden Age of Capitalism, the post-

60 Ibid., pp. 69-71.

61 Raoul Vaneigem, *The Revolution of Everyday Life: Survival and false opposition to it*, Situationist International Text Library, 1967: http://library.nothingness.org/articles/SI/en/display/60

World War II decades of global economic expansion. In analysing the biopolitics of one such pre-twentieth-century movement in the next chapter, we shall unavoidably revisit the tensions between Marcuse's and Reich's libidinal economics.

6

Libidinal Communists and Sexual Revolutionaries, Part 1:

The Oneida Community (1848–1880), With a Digression on Electrifying Sex

'Totalitarianism or Biopolitics?', the title of an influential essay by the Italian political philosopher Roberto Esposito,[1] might have served as the title of this chapter, which examines utopian-socialist sexual-revolutionary movements that have attempted to reinvent sexualities, subjectivities and socio-economic relationships wholesale. Hannah Arendt argued in 1950 that the Nazi concentration camps made no sense either politically or economically: representing a massive drain on the resources of a nation at war, they could only be explained as an experiment in stripping humanity back to bare life and seeing whether it could be reconstructed, from scratch, as a bundle of conditioned reflexes. In other words, the camps were a nightmarish culmination of the social-constructivist tradition of Western thought – a grotesque experimental testing of the idea that culture, not nature, is the determining condition of human character, and hence that jewishness, gypsy-ness, homosexuality and so forth might be stripped away from the human animal, and that animal reinvented as Pavlov's dog ('We know that the object of the concentration camps was to serve as laboratories in training people to become bundles of reactions, in making them behave like Pavlov's dog …').[2] It is therefore unsurprising that the

1 Roberto Esposito, 'Totalitarianism or Biopolitics? Concerning a Philosophical Interpretation of the Twentieth Century', Timothy Campbell (trans.), *Critical Inquiry*, 34, 4 (Summer 2008): 633-44.

2 Hannah Arendt, 'Social Science and the Study of Concentration Camps', *Jewish Social Studies*, 12, 1 (1950): 242.

totalitarianism that established and administered the camps should have had at least something in common with the 'progressive' experiments in reinventing the human animal as a sexual, economic and political subject – that is, in redesigning *bios* – undertaken by the two utopian-socialist, 'free love' movements we shall be examining in this and the next chapter. Those movements are the Oneida Association, founded in mid-nineteenth-century America, and the Friedrichshof Commune in late twentieth-century Austria – just two of the scores of radical experiments in sexual and economic communism of the past two centuries that have seen themselves as leading the world by example, providing a pattern of the peaceful revolutionising of capitalist society, sexuality and subjectivity that the rest of the world would inevitably wish to follow. The Friedrichshof Commune was also known as *Das Paradies Experiment* – one of its numerous connections with the Oneida Community's vision of itself as paradise regained, a realisation of heaven on earth that 'took the waiting out of wanting' (to borrow the slogan that launched one of the first credit cards).[3] And yet a 1999 television documentary about the Friedrichshof experiment would be aptly entitled *Slaves in Paradise*.[4]

From the outset, socialism has treated the question of sex as a question of property – as institutionalised in monogamy, in which the patriarchal male claims a monopoly on the body, labour-power and libido of the female. For Marx, as we have seen, bourgeois marriage was not the contrary of prostitution but its epitome, while Emma Goldman could reflect on her own, fleeting experience of the institution: 'Marriage is primarily an economic arrangement, an insurance pact … Its returns are insignificantly small compared with the investments'.[5] In a defence of socialist 'free love' that got him into trouble with the London *Times* in 1906, H.G. Wells

3 'Taking the waiting out of wanting' was the slogan with which a consortium of British banks launched the Access Card, one the earliest credit cards, in 1972.

4 Soul Purpose Productions, 'Slaves in Paradise' (TV documentary), Madonna Benjamin (prod. and dir.), UK Channel Four Television Corporation, 1999.

5 Emma Goldman, 'Marriage and Love', *Anarchism and Other Essays*, New York, Mother Earth Publishing, 1910, p. 234.

explained: 'Essentially the Socialist position is a denial of property in human beings; not only must land and the means of production be liberated, but women and children, just as men and things must cease to be owned'.[6]

The classic statement of the liberal philosophical view of the body as property owned by a subject is John Locke's, in his *Second Treatise of Government* (1689):

> Though the earth and all inferior creatures be common to all men, yet every man has a property in his own person; this nobody has any right to but himself. The labor of his body and the work of his hands, we may say, are properly his. Whatsoever then he removes out of the state that nature has provided and left it in, he has mixed his labor with, and joined to it something that is his own, and thereby makes it his property.[7]

While classical liberalism posits the individual as owner of her/his body as a form of private property that can be used (as in labour), traded (as in marriage), leased (as in prostitution) or refashioned (cosmetically, athletically, transsexually) by a subject as ideally free as the market should be,[8] utopian socialism undertakes to abolish the property-relation altogether, and with it the view of libidinal economy as private enterprise and the desiring subject as an entrepreneur of libido. Perhaps never more rigorously has the abolition of sexual property-relations been undertaken than by the Oneida Association and its self-conscious heir in the tradition of sexual revolution, the Friedrichshof Commune. Inspired by their visions of a de-commodified sexuality and a fully 'collectivised' libido, both communities set about exorcising *homo œconomicus* from

6 H.G. Wells, *Socialism and the Family*, quoted in J.H. Bottomley, *A Popular Lecture of Socialism, Atheism, and Free Love, Explained and Exposed by J.H. Bottomley, Esq.*, St Helens, St Helens and Prescot Reporter Ltd., 1907, p. 12.

7 John Locke, *Two Treatises of Government*, Peter Laslett (ed.), Cambridge, Cambridge University Press, 1988, p. 291.

8 For an insightful discussion of the ethics of viewing the body and its parts as exchangeable or disposable commodities, see Margaret Jane Radin, *Contested Commodities: The Trouble with Trade in Sex, Children, Body Parts, and Other Things*, Cambridge, Mass, Harvard University Press, 1996.

homo sexualis, quarrying-out capitalism from the most intimate recesses of subjectivity, thus throwing open the question of what new kinds of freedom and, indeed, new conceptions of subjectivity or selfhood a sexual liberation movement might entertain.

The managed libidinal economy – as distinct from the libidinal free market – is a biopolitical economy, and regimes that undertake to regulate the intimate lives of their citizens' bodies have been identified by Esposito with a tradition of biopolitics ideologically opposed to the traditions of democracy and communism. In 'Totalitarianism or Biopolitics?', Esposito opposes two kinds of totalitarianism, Nazi and Communist, arguing that Nazism belongs ideologically on a continuum with liberalism, whereas communism is cognate with democracy. Communist and democratic ideologies are both 'universalist and egalitarian': they address persons as a totality of equal subjects endowed with rational will and abstracted from the specificity of their bodies and those bodies' distinctive desires and needs. Communism, according to Esposito, simply carries this abstracting, disembodying, universalising ideology to excess: he describes communist totalitarianism as arising from 'a surplus of democracy', not a deficit of it, suggesting that 'communism is both democracy's dream and its nightmare'.[9] On the other hand, biopolitics, whether in its liberal or its Nazi forms, is anti-egalitarian and particularist, concerning itself with the different 'natures' of embodied persons, whose desires and 'needs' are both the object and the subject of politics. Esposito's thesis is that democracy had already died as a meaningful ideology in Europe by the 1920s or 1930s, when it was superseded by biopolitics, first in its fascist form and then, after Nazism's defeat in the Second World War, in its liberal form:

> If man for Nazism is his body and only his body, for liberalism, beginning with Locke, man is the possessor of his own body and therefore can use it, transform it, and sell it, as if the body were a slave. In this sense liberalism ... turns the Nazi perspective inside out, transferring the property of the body [from] the state

9 Esposito, 'Totalitarianism or Biopolitics?', p. 638.

> to the individual, but within the same biopolitical lexicon ... [I]t is precisely the biopolitical character of liberalism that separates it from democracy.[10]

In Esposito's view, then, European history of the past eighty-odd years has been shaped by two, opposed kinds of biopolitics: the biopolitics of the state, as in Nazism, where the body is the property of the state; and the biopolitics of the individual, as in liberalism, where the body is the property of the individual – who can maximise its health, beauty, utility, reproductive capacity and so on, with a plethora of commodified services and products. It is this latter, liberal model of biopolitics that has prevailed in libidinal economy that treats libido as an economic resource that the individual can productively invest, pleasurably spend or prudently hoard. But if Esposito is right in opposing liberal and totalitarian biopolitics to democracy and communism, what are we to make of the long tradition of sexual-revolutionary movements predicated on a *fusion* of communism and biopolitics – indeed, on understanding utopian socialism as *necessarily* a form of biopolitics? How should we situate such movements, ideologically and historically, in relation to totalitarianism, liberalism and democracy?

Esposito ends his essay by insisting that we need to jettison all our old 'conceptual paradigms' and existing 'philosophies of history' if we are to begin to imagine what he calls 'a democratic biopolitics ... that is capable of being used not on bodies but in favor of bodies' – a politics 'for' life instead of 'over' life, which treats 'the body as subject, not object' – and he suggests that we have not yet even begun to 'glimpse the outlines' of such a project.[11] Like the Marcuse of *Eros and Civilization* in 1956, then, Esposito represents as a yet-to-be-imagined, future project what this book's investigation of sexual revolution addresses as a long-established countercultural tradition, an often-repeated historical experiment.

10 Ibid., p. 641.
11 Ibid., p. 644.

The Oneida Association, 1836-1881[12]

The Oneida Association was one of about a hundred utopian communes founded and disbanded in America during the nineteenth century. It was formally established in the revolutionary year of 1848 by the charismatic preacher and utopian socialist John Humphrey Noyes (1811-1886), who developed his heretical doctrine of 'perfectionism' while training in theology at Dartmouth, Andover and Yale theological colleges. Noyes maintained that a close reading of the Bible revealed that Christ's second coming had already occurred (he dated it in 70 A.D.) and that those who, like himself, were receptive to this second coming were reconciled with God, purged of sin and shame, and hence capable of perfection in this world. Noyes's heresy cost him his licence to preach (he was expelled from Yale) but his message that his new relationship with God freed him from both the laws of the church and the moral conventions of society helped attract a group of followers equally committed to realising perfection in this life. Calling themselves the Putney Bible Society, the group started with members of Noyes' extended family in Putney, Vermont, in 1836; they went on to establish a formal communal organisation in 1844 and practised group marriage until their Putney neighbours became too disapproving of their unorthodox living arrangements

12 Sources of information about the Oneida Association include the following (full details are provided in the bibliography): John Humphrey Noyes, *The Berean: A Manual for the Help of Those Who Seek the Faith of the Primitive Church* (1847); J.H. Noyes, *Male Continence* (1872); J.H. Noyes, *Essay on Scientific Propagation* (1875); J.H. Noyes, *The Way of Holiness* (1838); J.H. Noyes, *History of American Socialisms* (1870); George W. Noyes, *The Religious Experience of John Humphrey Noyes* (1923); Oneida Association, *Bible Communism* (1853); *Handbook of the Oneida Community* (1867); John B. Ellis, *Free Love and Its Votaries; or, American Socialism Unmasked* (1870); Charles Nordhoff, *American* Utopias (1875 and 1993); Louis J. Kern, *An Ordered Love: Sex Roles and Sexuality in Victorian Utopias* (1981); John Stewart Sill, 'Utopian Group Marriage in the 19th and 20th Centuries: Oneida Community and Kerista Commune' (1990); Maren Lockwood Carden, *Oneida: Utopian Community to Modern Corporation* (1998); Robert S. Fogarty, *Special Love, Special Sex: An Oneida Community Diary* (1994); Robert S. Fogarty Fogarty (ed.), *Desire and Duty at Oneida* (2000); Spencer Klaw, *Without Sin: The Life and Death of the Oneida Community* (1993); Lawrence Foster, *Women, Family, and Utopia: Communal Experiments of the Shakers, the Oneida Community, and the Mormons* (1991).

and Noyes was indicted on two counts of adultery, prompting the group to leave Vermont for Oneida in New York, where one of their members owned a farm. The Oneida Association grew rapidly, peaking at more than 300 members in 1878, with several satellite communities being established in Connecticut, New Jersey and Vermont.[13] The Association lasted until 1881, and for much of its thirty-odd years of successful 'Bible Communism', so called, the community owned a thousand acres of prime farmland, built and shared communal living and sleeping quarters known as the Mansion House (with a library, museum and chapel), built and ran a range of profitable factories (including steel trap, cutlery and china factories), published their own books and newspapers (including *The Circular* and *The American Socialist*), and mounted extensive educational and cultural programmes.

John Humphrey Noyes, c. 1850. (OCMH B8 #25, SUL 192) *Courtesy of the Oneida Community Mansion House*

13 The primary leader of the Community between 1848 and 1854 was John Miller, rather than Noyes. Noyes took over the leadership after Miller's death in 1854 and consolidated what were half-a-dozen scattered groups at that stage.

Oneida Community members, 1863 (OCMH b7 #15, SUL 104). *Courtesy of the Oneida Community Mansion House*

The Mansion House from the South Lawn, 1871 (OCMH B7 #39, SUL 29). *Courtesy of the Oneida Community Mansion House*

The Oneidans combined gender-equality in all aspects of community life, work and governance with a principle of collective ownership that extended from property to persons to sexual desire, or libido, itself. As a 'homegrown' American socialism, the movement distinguished itself from what Noyes called the 'imported socialisms' of Owenism and Fourierism, as well as from homegrown Shakerism, by preaching and practising six principles, set out in three main publications: Oneida's theology was expounded in Noyes's treatise, *The Berean: A Manual for the Help of Those Who Seek the Faith of the Primitive Church* (1847), and its social, economic and political theory in a volume of community reports and manifestos entitled *Bible Communism* (1853) and in Noyes's *History of American Socialisms* (1870). The defining principles of the Association were known as: (1) 'Communalism' (2) 'Complex Marriage' (3) 'Stirpiculture', or 'Scientific Breeding' (4) 'Male Continence' (5) 'Mutual Criticism' and (6) 'Ascending Fellowship'. 'Communalism' meant the abolition of private property, both in things and persons, objects and subjects ('Communism of property goes with Communism of persons'[14]). As a utopian socialist, Noyes argued that monogamy both contradicted the natural law of desire – which can never be satisfied by a single partner – and institutionalised property in persons and sexual pleasure, breeding jealousy, shame and inhibition. He called monogamy 'an egotism of two' and stressed that the Bible reports no couple relationships in heaven but, rather, a collective, unified 'amativeness'. Abolishing the nuclear family was thus a precondition for recovering the prelapsarian state of innocence. Noyes's theological hero was St Paul (hence the title of *The Berean*, a reference to Paul's praise for the people of Berea for testing what they heard in their synagogues against what they read in the scriptures) and his *History of American Socialisms* pointed out that 'Paul expressly places property in women and property in goods in the same category, and speaks of them together, as ready to be abolished by the advent of the Kingdom of Heaven'; hence, '*marriage is*

14 John Humphrey Noyes, *History of American Socialisms*, Philadelphia, J.B. Lippincott & Co., 1870, p. 639.

not an institution of the Kingdom of Heaven, and must give place to Communism'.[15] The principle of 'Complex Marriage', intended to institute 'free love', meant that every (post-pubescent) member of the Oneida community was married to every other, a principle founded on nature as well as scripture. Proposition XII of *Bible Communism* argued that, notwithstanding the myths perpetuated by romantic fiction and the Church:

> All experience testifies ... that sexual love is not naturally restricted to pairs ... Men and women find universally ... that their susceptibility to love is not burnt out by one honey-moon, or satisfied by one lover. On the contrary, the secret history of the human heart will bear out the assertion that it is capable of loving any number of times and any number of persons, and that the more it loves the more it can love. This is the law of nature, thrust out of sight, and condemned by common consent, and yet secretly known to all.[16]

Contrary to the Puritan ethic of frugality and productive investment, then, desire is increased, not depleted, by libidinal expenditure, and the more promiscuously a community spends or exchanges its sexual energy, the richer in libido it becomes. Exclusive couple-relationships were not permitted at Oneida: Noyes advocated brief sexual couplings, with a minimum of conversation, and arranged through third parties, to discourage couple-bonding.[17] Children were planned and raised communally, according to principles of 'Scientific Breeding', or 'Stirpiculture' (Noyes's neologism, from the Latin *stirps*, meaning stem, root, stock, or offspring), influenced both by Malthusian anxieties about over-population relative to a

15 Ibid., pp. 624-5.

16 Oneida Association, *Bible Communism: A Compilation from the Annual Reports and Other Publications of the Oneida Association*, Brooklyn, N.Y., Office of the Circular, 1853, p. 35.

17 John H. Noyes, 'Practical Suggestions for Regulating Intercourse of the Sexes' (1852), quoted in Robert S. Fogarty, *Desire and Duty at Oneida: Tirzah Miller's Intimate Memoir*, Bloomington, IN, Indiana University Press, 2000, p. 19.

community's resources and by the concerns to which Francis Galton would later (1883) give the name 'eugenics'. Oneida's principles of 'scientific breeding' were formulated at a time when Lamarckian theories of the heritability of acquired characteristics, sometimes known as 'soft inheritance', were fashionable and when science still seemed the ally of religion, a catalyst for realising heaven or 'perfection' on earth; hence Noyes envisaged rationally planned and selective mating – by contrast with subjectively desired and randomly occurring conception – as improving the human stock of a community, just as scientific farming could improve its animal and plant stock. For the Bible Communists, Stirpiculture meant breeding increasing spirituality and wisdom into the community in order to save future generations from wasting years of their lives on making the same mistakes as their forebears had made. Between 1868 and 1879, fifty-eight stirpiculturally-planned children were born into the community.[18]

What permitted Oneida's principles of 'free love' and Scientific Breeding to be compatible more than a century before the contraceptive Pill would become definitive of 1960s sexual revolution was the principle of 'Male Continence'. A staunch antebellum feminist and abolitionist, Noyes was committed to liberating women from what he called the 'conjugal slavery' of incessant, energy-depleting child-birth and mothering, but he rejected the Shakers' solution of celibacy in favour of his own, 'revolutionary' doctrine of Male Continence. Otherwise known as '*coitus reservatus*', Male Continence was the practice of non-ejaculatory sex by the commune's men, advocated as prolonging and intensifying the exchange of erotic pleasure for both sexes while preventing conception, thus eliminating the cost to women's bodies and the community's resources of constant child-bearing and child-rearing. (In the 1890s, Edward Carpenter, the gay, utopian-socialist sexual revolutionary, would press the same argument on readers of his book, *Love's Coming of Age*. Noting that 'woman objects to being a mere machine for perpetual reproduction', Carpenter recommended the practice of *karezza*, or non-orgasmic sexual intercourse, in which,

18 Fogarty, *Desire and Duty at Oneida*, p. 22.

'given abundant time and mutual reciprocity, the interchange becomes satisfactory and complete without emission or crisis by either party' and 'gives to the sexual relation an office entirely distinct from the propagative act – it is a union on the affectional plane ... '[19]). Male Continence meant that decisions about when, and by whom, children were conceived could be made both collectively and rationally, in the spiritual and economic interests of the community, without compromising its commitment to 'free love' or to maximising erotic pleasure while minimising its libidinal costs. Indispensable as it was to libidinal communists in the mid-nineteenth century, Male Continence was predictably condemned by libidinal capitalists. In 1870, a Dr John B. Ellis indicted *coitus reservatus* as a vicious 'practice of frauds' in 'sexual commerce' in his book, *Free Love and Its Votaries; or, American Socialism Unmasked. Being an Historical and Descriptive Account of the Rise and Progress of the Various Free Love Associations in the United States, and the Effects of Their Vicious Teachings Upon American Society.*[20]

Privacy was abolished along with private property at Oneida: the sexes shared common sleeping as well as living and working quarters, and sexual desire was supposed to be exchanged or circulated as freely, equally and undiscriminatingly as possible. (By contrast, the celibate Shakers slept in gender-segregated quarters and only came together in prayer and work.) Just as libido was to be 'collectivised' at Oneida, so were the contents of minds: individuals' most private thoughts and feelings were turned into communal property in regular sessions of 'Mutual Criticism' (a forerunner of the Maoists' *jiăntăo*, or autocritique) in which Oneidans were given ideological health-checks by the assembled community and received feedback on their practice of free-love socialism and their progress toward perfection. The only hierarchy recognised in the commu-

19 Edward Carpenter, *Love's Coming of Age: A Series of Papers on the Relations of the Sexes* (1896), London, Swan Schonnenheim, 1906, pp. 172-73.

20 John B. Ellis, *Free Love and Its Votaries; or, American Socialism Unmasked. Being an Historical and Descriptive Account of the Rise and Progress of the Various Free Love Associations in the United States, and the Effects of Their Vicious Teachings Upon American Society*, New York, United States Publishing Company, 1870, pp. 205-6.

nity was a spiritual one, known as 'Ascending Fellowship', which meant that those further advanced along the road to perfection assumed correspondingly greater authority and responsibility, including the responsibility of initiating the community's adolescents into Complex Marriage. Since spiritual advancement tended to come with the wisdom of age, Ascending Fellowship also served Oneida's Scientific Breeding programme. Boys were initiated into Complex Marriage by the older women, who were unlikely to become pregnant, while girls were initiated by the older men, who were more reliable practitioners of Male Continence than the younger males. Spiritual and Stirpicultural considerations notwithstanding, however, a factor in the eventual breakup of the community was reportedly the resentment felt by some of its less perfect members toward Noyes's tendency to monopolise responsibility for initiating the commune's girls into Complex Marriage. 'Ascending Fellowship' entailed an obligation to associate, not least sexually, with one's spiritual superiors in the interests of self-improvement, and the senior men were by definition the spiritually most superior members of the community, with Noyes at the apex.

As John Levi Martin has noted, two themes have invariably converged in the rhetoric of modern sexual revolution: vitalism and scientism.[21] Calls for a return to nature and spontaneity in sexuality, for an eros undistorted by a repressive culture, have converged with calls for a modern, scientific attitude toward sex and its rational organisation according to 'Darwinian' principles of selective breeding, or 'race hygiene', and Malthusian calculations of economically sustainable birth-rates and optimal population sizes. The Oneida Association was no exception: its founding texts are amalgams of theology, vitalism and scientism that offer striking illustrations of libidinal economy-in-the-making, or the process of the progressive secularisation of sexual morality during the nineteenth century as religious and moral discourse on sex was variously reinforced, challenged and displaced by a hybrid discourse drawn from the proverbially modern sciences of energy and money. Oneida's manifestoes submit the sexual

21 John Levi Martin, 'Structuring the Sexual Revolution', pp. 105-51.

precepts of scripture, tradition and superstition to the 'reality principles' of contemporary physics and economics, intermixing the language of virtue and vice, love and lust, with thermodynamic, electromagnetic and economic explanations of sexuality.

What economics contributed to Oneida's vitalist ontology is exemplified by Proposition XIX of *Bible Communism*, a lengthy exposition of the differences between 'amative' and 'propagative' sexual intercourse, the former focused on mutual pleasure, the vitalising exchange or transmission of energy, and the latter on procreation. The Proposition contrasts the 'profit' of 'amative' sex – meaning its yield of energising pleasure – with the 'costs' of 'propagative' sex, meaning the drain on the group's vital economy that reproduction could impose. Arguing for the pleasure-principle of spending energy in sexual intercourse rather than investing it in production/reproduction, the Proposition relies uncannily on the very language of profit and loss that free-love socialism was meant to transcend:

> PROPOSITION XIX – The propagative part of the sexual relation is in its nature the *expensive* department. 1. While amativeness keeps the capital stock of life circulating between two, propagation introduces a third partner. 2. The propagative act, i.e., the emission of the seed, is a drain on the life of man, and when habitual, produces disease. 3. The infirmities and vital expenses of woman during the long period of pregnancy, waste her constitution. 4. The awful agonies of child-birth heavily tax the life of woman. 5. The cares of the nursing period bear heavily on woman. 6. The cares of both parents, through the period of the childhood of their offspring, are many and burdensome. 7. The labor of man is greatly increased by the necessity of providing for children. A portion of these expenses would undoubtedly have been curtailed, if human nature had remained in its original integrity [i.e., in Eden], and will, when it is restored. But it is still self-evident, that the birth of children, viewed either as a vital or a mechanical operation, is in its nature expensive; and the fact that multiplied conception was imposed as a curse, indicates that it was so regarded by the Creator.

> *Note* 1. – Amativeness being the profitable part, and propagation the expensive part of the sexual relation, it is evident that a true balance between them is essential to the interests of the vital economy. If expenses exceed income, bankruptcy ensues. After the fall, sin and shame curtailed amativeness, thus diminishing the profitable department; and the curse increased propagation, thus enlarging the expensive department. Death, i.e. vital bankruptcy, is the law of the race in its fallen condition; and it results more from this derangement of the sexual economy, than from any other cause, except the disruption from God. It is the expression of the disproportion of amativeness to propagation – or of life to its expenses; each generation dies in giving life to its successor …
>
> *Note* 3. – The grand problem which must be solved before redemption can be carried forward to immortality is this: – *How can the benefits of amativeness be secured and increased, and the expenses of propagation be reduced to such limits as life can afford?*[22]

If the language of capitalism here returns uncannily to haunt the very doctrines of libidinal communism that were meant to end the commodification and exploitation of bodies, labour and love at Oneida, it was only one of the rhetorics in play in the community's vitalist theology. Equally insistent and secularising was the language of physics: if desire, construed as psychosexual energy, could be explained as an economic resource or liquid asset, it could also be explained by the freshly fashionable science of electromagnetism. A chapter of *The Berean* devoted to 'the curious science' of 'animal magnetism' reported that while it had been 'condemned and executed' as a pseudo-science, some fifty years earlier, by a French government commission whose membership included Benjamin Franklin, it had since 'risen from the dead' in America and was exciting even more interest than was phrenology.[23] Nor was 'raising the dead' a mere metaphor for animal magnetism, since its existence had been empirically verified by experiments in moving

22 Oneida Association, *Bible Communism*, pp. 45-46.

23 Noyes, *The Berean*, p. 65.

the muscles of dead bodies 'by the application of galvanism'. This nascent science was thus 'opening a passage from the highest point of physical science, into spiritual philosophy. It is in our view the connecting link between the sciences which treat of those subtler powers of nature, called electricity, galvanism, magnetism, &c., and the science of life, animal and eternal'.[24]

In *The Berean*, Noyes posed the question, 'What is a spirit?' and he claimed to improve on all existing dictionary definitions by explaining that 'a spirit ... is a *fluid; having many of the properties of caloric, light, electricity, galvanism and magnetism*', and he insisted that 'almost every page of the Bible' could be cited as authority for 'calling spirit a *fluid*', including some important passages of *Luke* and *Acts* 'in which one of the special characteristics of electricity – its power of passing from one point to another by material conductors – is attributed to the spiritual fluid'.[25] Subtitled *A Manual for the Help of Those Who Seek the Faith of the Primitive Church*, *The Berean* spelled out Noyes's vitalist ontology: the force that moves the world on its axis is divine love; the expression of love at all levels is sexual; God the Father manifests the male attributes, and God the Son the female attributes, of the love or life-force that animates the universe; and this force is a kind of spiritual fluid or electrical current. Like the divine love that transmitted life to Adam, human sexual love is a transmission, exchange or conducting of this 'magnetic or vital fluid', which emanates from all living bodies, albeit in different quantities and intensities. Noyes followed other Enlightenment exponents of bioelectricity in figuring male and female as the positive and negative poles of an electrical battery between which current can flow, creating a circuit of life-giving energy, like the love between God the Father and Son. The primitive church's doctrine of the 'laying-on of hands' was evidence that this love-force or life-force could be transmitted through any form of contact, bodily or spiritual; but heterosexual intercourse was the most efficient human means of conducting the vital fluid, creating the strongest electrical connection or contact for the current to flow.

24 Ibid.
25 Ibid., pp. 55-56.

In his theory of spirit, love and life as electrical energy, Noyes believed he had found the solution both to the problem or 'curse' of labour and to immortality on earth. A century after Benjamin Franklin had coined the term 'battery' for an arrangement of multiple Leyden jars, Noyes represented a 'complexly married' community as a giant battery, arguing that it was through the super-charging of the collective battery in a community of freely-loving men and women that the life-force could be maximised and hence disease defeated and immortality attained: 'Victory over death', he declared, 'will be the result of the action of an extensive battery of this kind'.[26] Noyes also literalised the trope of sexual desire as heat or flame, arguing that if sexual passion 'is a fire, which under the devil's administration burns houses, why may it not under God's administration, prepare food, warm dwellings, and drive steamboats?'[27] – thereby relieving polyamorous humanity of much hard labour.

A Digression on Electrifying Sex

As we saw in chapter one, Noyes was far from unique in invoking electricity to explain sexuality. Another mid-nineteenth-century exponent of electromagnetism as the secret of life and libidinal economy was the American phrenologist and self-styled 'Professor', Orson Squire Fowler (1809-1887), publisher of Walt Whitman's 'I Sing the Body Electric' and author of *Creative and Sexual Science: or, Manhood, Womanhood, and Their Mutual Interrelations*.[28] Fowler published his *magnum opus* in variant editions and it was evidently between the 1870 and 1875 editions that he discovered the seduc-

26 Oneida Association, *Bible Communism*, p. 44.

27 Ibid., p. 45.

28 Fowler, *Creative and Sexual Science: or, Manhood, Womanhood, and Their Mutual Interrelations; Love, Its Laws, Power, Etc.; Selection, or Mutual Adaptation; Courtship, Married Life, and Perfect Children ... as Taught By Phrenology and Physiology* (1870), Philadelphia, E. Gately & Co., n.d. [1875]. Whitman was a regular reader of Fowler's *The American Phrenological Review*. See M. Jimmie Killingsworth, *Whitman's Poetry of the Body: Sexuality, Politics, and the Text*, Chapel Hill & London, University of North Carolina Press, 1989, p. 56; and Edward Hungerford, 'Walt Whitman and His Chart of Bumps', *American Literature*, 2 (1931): 350-84.

tive explanatory power of electricity: the 'amativeness' that was interpreted phrenologically in the 1870 edition is explained electromagnetically in the 1875 edition. (The merger of mesmerism with phrenology, dubbed 'phrenomagnetism', in the 1840s, and then with spiritualism in the 1850s, in America, has been traced by Taylor Stoehr.[29]) Readers of the 1875 edition of *Creative and Sexual Science* were informed that life's 'chief organic agent and motor' is electricity; that male and female bodies are positively and negatively charged respectively, and thus when a man and woman fall in love 'their very proximity thrills each other because their electricities are exchanged through air … Both were full of this sexual electricity, which both gave off to and received from the other' – indeed, 'all Love-making interchanges this male and female magnetism', which 'then *creates* their offspring', since sperm and ova are themselves positively and negatively charged and hence mutually attractive.[30] Fowler claimed to be the first to explain the electrical basis of the experimentally-proven fact that 'reciprocating Love creates warmth. Hence no fire is ever needed to court by, even in long, cold nights … Our electrical theory shows why'.[31] The heat-generating friction of sexual love had communal as well as personal benefits: 'Active Love electrifies the entire Social Group'.[32] And, like Noyes before him, Fowler propounded the death-defeating properties of the electrical charge generated in sexual intercourse. Two decades before Freud had published a word of psychoanalysis, Fowler insisted that 'most nervous diseases have a sexual origin and cure' and he claimed to have personally proven that electricity – the essence of the life-force that sexual intercourse raised to its greatest intensity – could cure most diseases.[33]

Claims to have been the first to discover the electrical basis of sexuality have been made at least as often since the eighteenth century

29 Taylor Stoehr, *Hawthorne's Mad Scientists: Pseudoscience and Social Science in Nineteenth-Century Life and Letters*, Hamden, Conn., Archon Books, 1978, pp. 66-67.

30 Fowler, *Creative and Sexual Science*, pp. 188, 191-2.

31 Ibid., p. 250.

32 Ibid., pp. 250, 259.

33 Ibid., pp. 350, 204.

as claims to have invented libidinal economy by discovering monetary explanations of sexuality. Consider the Scottish pioneer sex therapist and medical entrepreneur, Dr James Graham (1745-1794), inventor of the notorious Celestial Electrical Bed.[34] A century before Fowler launched his own scientific 'discoveries' upon the world, Graham claimed to provide irrefutable evidence for solving the puzzle of conception and generation that had exercised philosophers, scientists and theologians since at least Aristotle's time, by demonstrating that 'the act of venery itself is an electrical operation' and the 'bewitching pleasure' of 'copulation is no other than electric strokes'.[35] Graham's 'new theory of generation', expounded in his treatise, *Eccentric Lecture on the Art of Propagating the Human Species* (1783), was that the future child is wholly contained in the ovum, awaiting only an electrical shock to bring it to life, and that this shock is delivered by semen. In copulation, the electrical charge transmitted by the semen to the vaginal nerves stimulates ovulation and the development of the foetus follows as a matter of course. The stronger the electrical stimulus or shock, the more robust the offspring; hence Graham's injunctions to both men and women (who supplied their own quantum of electrical energy to the foetus) not to dissipate their bioelectrical energy in masturbation or promiscuity, on threat of becoming sterile or producing only sickly progeny. This was where his Celestial Electrical bed came in: a twelve-foot by nine-foot 'wonder-working edifice' that cost £20,000 to build, the bed was set up in premises Graham called the Temple of Hymen in Pall Mall in 1781. Standing on glass feet, hitched up to electrical cables and an array of magnets, and accompanied by aphrodisiacal music and perfumes, the bed could be hired at £50 a time by a couple wishing to maximise the intensity of their copulative pleasure and prolong its climactic phase for up to an hour while guaranteeing conception of vigorous progeny and generally re-charging their vital economies.

34 See the discussion of Graham in chapter 2, above.

35 James Graham, *An Eccentric Lecture on the Art of Propagating the Human Species, and Producing a Numerous and Healthy Offspring, &c. Wherein is Particularly Recommended ... Temperance and Sobriety ...* [and] *the Efficacious Virtues of the ELECTRICAL BED, in the Act of Copulation, &c*, London, A. Roger et al., 1783, p. 28.

Graham had learned the principles of electricity from Benjamin Franklin's friend and collaborator, Ebenezer Kinnersley, while travelling around the American colonies as a medical appliance salesman. His explanations and advertisements of his bed were unashamedly pornographic, but his therapy also spoke to the public fascination with physics and to British anxieties about a declining birth-rate at a time of perceived need to boost the birth-rate in order to populate the British colonies. Flagging fertility was attributed to a general decline in vitality due to the life-style faults of 'self-pollution', caffeine- and alcohol-drinking and poor personal hygiene – for which a booster charge of electricity, understood as the essential currency of life and desire, could immediately help to compensate. The colonial legacy of such anxieties would be apparent 150 years later in Mahatma Gandhi's theories of the libidinal economy of Indian struggles for independence and the need for anti-colonial activists to emulate the sex-hygiene practices of the British imperialists.[36]

Neither Noyes nor Fowler, then, was the first 'sexual scientist' to argue that the currency exchanged in libidinal economy was electrical current. In fact, the fashion for electrical explanations of life in general and sexuality in particular had been the butt of ribald satire as early as the 1740s, when the botanist William Watson, known as 'Electrical Watson', demonstrated to the Royal Society his discoveries concerning the existence of a 'fluid' that he called 'electrical ether'. A lewd satire of 1746, with the mock-pedantic title, *Teague-Root Display'd: Being Some Useful and Important Discoveries Tending to Illustrate the Doctrine of Electricity, in a Letter from Paddy Strong-Cock, Fellow of Drury-Lane, and Professor of Natural Philosophy in M. King's College, Covent-Garden, to W'–m W'–n* [William Watson], *F.R.S., Author of a late Pamphlet on that Subject*,[37] offered its own investigation of the electricity of sex,

36 See above, chapter 5.

37 Anon, *Teague-Root Display'd: Being Some Useful and Important Discoveries Tending to Illustrate the Doctrine of Electricity, in a Letter from Paddy Strong-Cock, Fellow of Drury-Lane, and Professor of Natural Philosophy in M. King's College, Covent-Garden, to W'—m W'—n* [William Watson], *F.R.S., Author of a late Pamphlet on that Subject*, London, W. Webb, 1746.

coded botanically as the actions and mutual attractions of male and female 'teague-root' plants, by way of a humble homage and contribution to the 'Advancement of a Branch of Learning which the R–l S–y [Royal Society] thought worthy of their Notice' and which will be forever associated with their professor 'with the immortal Name of Electrical *W*–n' (Watson).[38] The satire's anonymous author proposes: 'let one of the nicest Ladies take a Male-Root into her Hand, and she becomes instantly Electrical, and you may observe the quick and sudden Flashes of Electrical Fire dart from her Eyes: The Flashes are more frequent, and much more discernible than those seen from the highest Electrified Tube'.[39]

Nor were Noyes and Fowler the last to discover libidinal economy's electrical currency. On 27 May, 1935, Wilhelm Reich made a one-sentence entry in his diary: 'The experiments were completely successful – the electrical nature of sexuality has been proved'.[40] Dr Graham's 'celestial or magneto electrical bed', which he imagined being one day mass-produced and supplied to every household,[41] was an early ancestor of Reich's 'orgone box' or 'energy accumulator', which he started building in 1940 and in which his patients could sit to harness the reputed health benefits of the cosmic energy that Reich called 'orgone' and that others, he said, called God – leading to newspaper stories of 'sex boxes' that cured cancer.[42] Whereas most psychoanalysts followed the pessimistic Freud – for whom repression and hence discontent were prerequisites of civilisation – in equating 'free' sexuality with chaos and social disorder, Reich observed that people who discharged their sexual energy in fact 'were more productive in their work'

38 Ibid., pp. 12-13.

39 Ibid., pp. 18-19.

40 Wilhelm Reich, *Beyond Psychology: Letters and Journals, 1934-1939*, Mary Boyd Higgins (ed.), New York, Farrar, Strauss and Giroux, 1994, p. 47. Reich's electrocardiographic experiments on orgasmic patients in Scandinavia in the mid-1930s are discussed in chapter 5, above.

41 See James Graham, *A Private Advice*, London; n.p., 1783, p. 10; and Graham, *Eccentric Lecture*, p. 28.

42 Sharaf, *Fury on* Earth, pp. 301-6. Cf. Reich, *Ether, God and Devil: Cosmic Superimposition*, New York, Farrar, Straus & Giroux, 1973, pp. 39ff, 50.

than the sexually repressed or abstinent.[43] As we have seen, in Reich's 'sex economy', spending, not saving, was the prescription for economic health.

The fashion for electrical explanations of life has persisted in the contemporary vogue of the neurosciences, themselves a development of nineteenth-century neurology, which drew on electro-magnetism to explain nerve activity and the life-force, not least as it manifests as sexual desire, attraction and generation. As the Oxford University physiologist Frances Ashcroft explains in her book *The Spark of Life* (2012): human bodies are 'electrical machines'; ions (electrically charged atoms) carry currents across cell membranes and around our bodies to keep our nerves and muscles functioning; a third of the oxygen we breathe and half of the food we eat are spent on maintaining the fine balance of positively-charged sodium, potassium, calcium and hydrogen ions and negatively-charged chloride ions within our bodies; and the electricity that our bodies generate travels through the nervous system at 0.07 miles per second.[44]

But how does the body electric connect with the body economic? The much-repeated claim to be the first to have discovered electrifying sex is itself a feature of the entrepreneurial tradition of libidinal economists, many of whom displayed a remarkable talent for converting electrical current into hard currency, electricity into money. Probably the most successful of such entrepreneurs was Dr Franz Anton Mesmer himself, the immediate inspiration of Noyes's and Fowler's electromagnetic sexology, famous for his ability to manipulate, with magnets and his own hands, the 'universal magnetic fluid' that 'could be conveyed from one body to another' and that possessed the curative effects on disease that the life-force itself could be expected to exert.[45] Mesmer's patients' experiences of 'magnetisation' were invariably described in the same terms – of sexual arousal culminating in 'convulsions', or 'the magnetic crisis',

43 See Mary Boyd Higgins, 'Introduction, Reich's Development, 1922-1934', in Reich, *Beyond Psychology*, p. xiii.

44 Frances Ashcroft, *The Spark of Life: Electricity in the Human Body*, London, Allen Lane, 2012.

45 See Anon, *Animal Magnetism: Its History to the Present Time, with a brief account of the Life of Mesmer, by a surgeon*, London, G.B. Dyer, 1841, p. 16.

experienced as pleasurable relief of tension – as Reichian therapists would describe the experience of 'discharging' accumulated energy in orgasm and as psychologists of 'retail therapy' describe their patients' experience of spending libido and money in compulsive shopping. Despite the finding of the 1784 French royal commission into animal magnetism 'that no such fluid exists as that for which the Mesmerists contend', it was reported that in that very same year, 'old and young, rich and poor, flocked to the residence of the great sorcerer, and by his mystic legerdemain many were relieved of their misery, and most of their money'.[46] The anonymous English surgeon who recounted these events in a history of animal magnetism published in 1841 went on to report that Mesmer received 400,000 francs in patient fees during 1784, and 'so spell-bound was the whole of the French nation by the artifices of this ingenious and audacious visionary, that the government, at the instance of Maurepas, the minister of the day, was at length led to offer him an annual stipend of 20,000 francs, together with 10,000 more for the erection of an establishment for patients and pupils, on condition that he would remain in France'.[47]

More pertinent to Mesmer's appeal to the Oneida sexual revolutionaries, however, was the fact that he 'actually advocated a political revolution and reorganization [of society] on magnetical principles'.[48]

Eroticising Work in Utopian Libidinal Economy

The 'disciplining' of discourse during the nineteenth century would render the vocabularies of money and electricity, economics and physics, seemingly discrete and incommensurable, but in Oneida's nascent theorising of libidinal economy they could comfortably cohabit in a single discourse, together with theology and psychology. Since it was 'the law of nature' that 'the more [one] loves, the more [one] *can* love', it followed that the more frequently the Oneida communists engaged in 'amative' sexual intercourse, the more

46 Ibid.
47 Ibid., pp. 17-18.
48 Ibid.

vital energy they would generate and hence the more economically productive the commune would become.[49] Noyes argued that 'The amative part of the sexual relation, separate from the propagative, is eminently favorable to life' – indeed, 'is the first and best *distributive* of life'[50] – and that 'amative', not 'propagative', love was also the originary function of sex, for which God created Eve as companion to cure Adam's loneliness before cursing their disobedience with the labour pains of childbirth and work. Both the Bible and Nature furnished ample evidence 'that pleasure, or amative social union, stands before propagation, as the superior function' of sex.[51] Thus Noyes envisaged a future in which a properly scientific understanding and harnessing of the vital energy released and exchanged in 'amative' love would be an insurance not only against self-alienating labour but against disease and mortality: 'In vital society, strength will be increased and the necessity of labor diminished, till work will become sport, as it would have been in the original Eden state … We can now see our way to victory over death … Vital society increases strength, diminishes work, and makes labor attractive, thus removing the antecedents of death'.[52] 'Attractive labour' (*travail attrayant*) was Charles Fourier's term for un-alienated, freely-chosen, self-rewarding work undertaken enthusiastically and pleasurably as part of a community and deriving, as Marcuse would put it, 'above all from the release of libidinal forces', which 'makes for pleasurable co-operation' and tends to 'the creation of "luxury, or the pleasure of the five senses"'.[53]

Combining productive work with erotic play in a manner that broke down the dichotomy between pleasure and labour proved 'economically as well as spiritually profitable':[54] Noyes' vision of the erotic 'mingling of the sexes' as generating, rather than

49 Noyes, *History of American Socialisms*, p. 636.

50 Ibid., p. 631.

51 Oneida Association, *Bible Communism*, p. 43.

52 Noyes, *History of American Socialisms*, pp. 635-36.

53 Charles Fourier, 'Attractive Labour', *Selections from the Works of Fourier*, Julia Franklin (trans.), London, Sonnenschen & Co., 1901, pp. 163-67. Cf. Marcuse, *Eros and Civilization*, p. 217.

54 Ibid.

wasting, libidinal energy seemed vindicated by the fact that the Oneida communists were renowned for producing large economic surpluses while reducing their work-hours to a minimum. Able-bodied Oneida men only needed to work seven hours per day, women only six hours and forty minutes, the young and invalid very much less, and even so, their work produced a thirty-three per cent surplus after all community expenses – apparently confirming Noyes's argument that when amative and industrial activities are fused rather than separated, there is more energy in circulation, and the freer the circulation, the richer the community.[55] An example of how 'work [could] become sport' in such an energy-rich economy was provided in the Oneida *Daily Journal*'s report of a special working bee convened on 14 September, 1866, to can a large consignment of peaches that had suddenly arrived from Georgia: 'the bee [was] a complete success and yielded about 800 quarts of fruit to the preserves. We have never seen anything so brilliant. It was perfectly electric. The condensation of magnetic life produced a general sparkle and flash of mirth throughout the bee'.[56]

Oneida Community pea-shelling bee, c. 1866 (OCMH B7 #4).
Courtesy of the Oneida Community Mansion House.

55 Ibid., pp. 641-45.
56 Quoted in Fogarty, *Desire and Duty at Oneida*, p. 14.

When Noyes came to publish his 600-page *History of American Socialisms* in 1870, he would review the economic, sexual and governmental policies and practices of more than fifty experiments in utopian socialist living, ranging from the early Fourierist and Owenite settlements through to his own Oneida Community, and tabulating all the available figures on their annual economic productivity and communal wealth. What his analysis showed, contrary to the 'petit-bourgeois' or Freudian model of libidinal economy and civilisation's discontents, was that the economically most successful communist experiment could also be the sexually least repressed, the one that practised the 'freest' love. By the time the Oneida Association disbanded in 1881, its assets were valued at $600,000.

Noyes's theology anticipated both the Freud who insisted on the instinctual primacy of the pleasure-principle of spending libido over the reality-principle of investing it in (re)production, and the Marcuse of *Eros and Civilization* who imagined a postmodern utopian society in which work would be transformed into pleasure and all the zones and relations of bodies would, as he put it, be 're-sexualised', or re-eroticised, on the model of the 'polymorphously perverse' sexuality of the pre-oedipal, pre-genital infant. To read Noyes's *The Berean* and *Bible Communism* beside Marcuse's *Eros and Civilization*, published more than a century later (1956) in the middle of the Cold War and McCarthyite era, is to find that Marcuse's future tense was Noyes' present tense. Marcuse's chapter on 'The Transformation of Sexuality into Eros' reads like the post-Freudian theory of the Oneida Association's practice. Peculiarly among the Frankfurt School membership, Marcuse studied and wrote in the tradition of utopian socialism and he was certainly familiar with Fourierist experiments, if not with the Oneida project.[57] As for Noyes before him, so for Marcuse, 'free love' or sexual liberation meant disarticulating eroticism from reproduction (in Marcuse's words, 'undo[ing] the channelling of sexuality in monogamic reproduction'), eroticising or 'resexualising' the whole body (not merely the generative organs) and its manifold relations with other bodies, and dismantling the opposi-

57 See Marcuse, *Eros and Civilization*, p. 217: 'The transformation of labor into pleasure is the central idea in Fourier's giant socialist utopia'.

tion between productive work-time and pleasurable, self-gratifying leisure-time – an opposition determined by the logic of energy-accumulation and energy-expenditure in an alienated libidinal economy, or unliberated society. Marcuse imagined the result of this re-sexualisation of all bodily parts, functions and relations with other bodies as not simply 'a release' or animalistic 'explosion of libido' but rather a redistribution or spreading of libido, a freer circulation of a libido that in repressive society is variously hoarded as capital or concentrated in particular accounts, relationships or activities, to the exclusion of others:

> No longer used as a full-time instrument of labor, the body would be resexualized. The regression involved in this spread of the libido would first manifest itself in a reactivation of all erotogenic zones and, consequently, in a resurgence of pregenital polymorphous sexuality and in a decline of genital supremacy. The body in its entirety would become an object of cathexis, a thing to be enjoyed – an instrument of pleasure. This change in the value and scope of libidinal relations would lead to a disintegration of the institutions in which the private interpersonal relations have been organized, particularly the monogamic and patriarchal family....
>
> [T]he free development of transformed libido within transformed institutions, while eroticising previously tabooed zones, time, and relations, would *minimize* the manifestations of *mere* sexuality by integrating them into a far larger order, including the order of work. In this context, sexuality tends to its own sublimation ...[58]

Such was the reputed achievement of the Oneida community in the mid-nineteenth century. Its manifestoes contended that once sexual pleasure was disarticulated from propagation – as it was by the practice of Male Continence – it could be cultivated for its own sake as a fine art, like conversation, musical performance and other social activities, except that its refining influence on society was superior to that of the other arts, given its greater yield of pleasure,

58 Ibid., pp. 201-202.

Oneida Community reception for visitors in Quad, c. 1867 (OCMH B7 #19, SUL 107). *Courtesy of the Oneida Community Mansion House*

or life-giving energy. In a letter of 1869, Tirzah Miller, a popular female member of the community, reported Noyes's plans to have couples perform sexual intercourse on the stage at Oneida, on the grounds both that privacy and shame were to be abolished and that 'There is no reason why it should not be done in public as much as music and dancing. It is the focus of all the fine arts, and singing, music and dancing are only valuable as they cluster around and add charm to that'.[59] Such plans would not only 'realise' the phenomena of love that had merely imaginary status in the traditional fine arts, they were also intended as a response to the Shakers' use of song and dance to celebrate their core value of celibacy in public. Oneida communalism was designed to ensure that the sexes mingled pleasurably in all daily activities and spaces, encouraging a pervasive eroticising of everyday life, in which work and pleasure were fused, labour de-alienated, and libidinal spending or exchange maximised, thus guaranteeing the health or wealth of its libidinal economy. Visitors to Oneida (an estimated 40,000 of them between 1862 and 1867),

59 Tirzah Miller, letter to George W. Noyes, 28 March, 1869, quoted in Fogarty, *Desire and Duty at Oneida*, p. 23.

including inquisitive journalists and numerous would-be new recruits to the community,[60] invariably remarked on the civility, grace, harmony and courtesy to be found among its practitioners of free love, confirming that a liberated 'sexuality tends to its own sublimation', or that a pervasively eroticised existence is the opposite of a bestial 'explosion of libido'. (Indeed, one member of the community reported to his brother in 1852 that the level of sexual activity within the group was 'scarcely one seventh' of what would be expected in 'ordinary married life in the world'.[61]) In his vision of eroticised work, Noyes was anticipating the Freud whom Marcuse quoted as saying, 'experience has shown that in cases of collaboration libidinal ties are regularly formed between the fellow-workers which prolong and solidify the relations between them to a point beyond what is merely profitable'.[62] Hence Marcuse's vision of a civilisation founded on non-repressive desublimation:

> Reactivation of polymorphous and narcissistic sexuality ceases to be a threat to culture and can itself lead to culture-building if the organism exists not as an instrument of alienated labor but as a subject of self-realization – in other words, if socially useful work is at the same time the transparent satisfaction of an individual need. In primitive society, this organization of work may be immediate and 'natural'; in mature civilization, it can be envisaged only as the result of liberation.[63]

And yet Marcuse found it hard to entertain this outcome as a practical possibility. While he endorsed Fourier's insistence that the utopian transformation of labour into pleasure depends on the eroticisation of work relations, he insisted this could never be achieved when work was administered by 'a giant organization and administration' such as Fourier envisaged in his utopia. Indeed, Marcuse seems unable logically to entertain the idea of unalienated,

60 See Fogarty, *Desire and Duty at Oneida*, p. 16.

61 John L. Skinner, letter to Alanson Skinner, 30 March, 1852, quoted in Fogarty, *Desire and Duty at Oneida*.

62 Marcuse, *Eros and Civilization*., p. 213.

63 Ibid., p. 210.

eroticised work as in any way organised or rationally planned – as it was, so effectively, at Oneida. Marcuse's insistence that 'work as free play cannot be subject to administration; only alienated labor can be organised and administered by rational routine', depended on the implausibly narrow notion, which he derived from Barbara Lintos, that 'play expresses object autoeroticism', that it serves no 'other purpose than that of instinctual gratification'.[64] Thus, while Marcuse could envisage the fusion of pleasure and labour (eroticised work) as a theoretical possibility, he seems unable to envisage it as a practicality without surplus industrial production furnishing luxury, eradicating scarcity, and essentially abolishing work altogether; in this sense, it remained, for him, the possibility only of a technologically advanced, postmodern, or 'postindustrial' utopia. By contrast, the Oneida Association represented itself as having successfully fused Fourier's ideal of 'attractive labour' with sexual liberation as early as the 1840s, ensuring that work tasks and roles were shared and exchanged in ways that avoided tedium and made work a skill-developing experience, a form of self-re-creation, while liberating erotic pleasure from its confinement to the genitals and the marriage bed and distributing it across all the dimensions of communal life.

So, why did Oneida fail? The community broke up in the late 1870s as a result of both internal dissent and external pressures, the former concentrated in a faction known as the Townerites (led by James W. Towner who had joined Oneida in 1874) and directed against Noyes for his perceived despotism and tendency to monopolise the role of 'first husband' in initiating young women into sexual experience – a monopolistic tendency Noyes justified on grounds of having received a revelation of his mission directly from God. The dissent was partly facilitated by the progressive secularisation of Noyes's own thought and his doctrinal justifications of the Oneida experiment, a secularisation that cost him some of his charismatic authority. Having reconciled with God and attained perfection, he became increasingly preoccupied during the 1860s with the nascent study of social science; wrote

64 Ibid. p. 214.

and published his *History of American Socialisms* (1870); replaced the community's religious newspaper, the *Oneida Circular*, with the secular *American Socialist* in 1876; and was no longer perceived to enjoy such direct communication with God as he had previously seemed to enjoy as a charismatic young preacher. (Noyes also simply grew older and deafer and the Oedipal sons wanted to eat the primal father)

At the same time, a group of local clergymen, led by Professor John W. Mears of nearby Hamilton college, mounted a concerted campaign and threats of violence against the 'immoral' Perfectionists.[65] In a general meeting on August 26, 1879, Noyes announced that within forty-eight hours Complex Marriage would cease to be mandatory and members would be free to marry – an announcement that apparently precipitated two days of frenzied sexual activity.[66] Threatened by the hostile Mears campaign with charges of statutory rape, Noyes himself crossed over into Canada in 1879 with a small group of supporters. The remaining Oneidans failed to agree on an effective mode of self-governance, reluctantly succumbed to the moral opprobrium of their Puritan neighbours and agreed to abandon complex marriage – a decision that reintroduced all the problems of nuclear-familial property-ownership that the utopian commune had been designed to transcend – and some of its members scattered to set up other groups, including one centred on Noyes in Clifton, on the Canadian side of Niagara Falls.

In 1881 the surviving Association appointed a commission composed of its administrative council members to manage the retreat from communalism to private property, and it was agreed that Oneida's manufacturing industries – notably its cutlery, steel trap and chain factories – could continue to be run for the benefit of the community as a joint-stock company, one of America's very first. Its assets of $600,000 were divided into $25 shares and distributed among the 226 members, whom the company continued to employ and support as stockholders. During the mid-to-late 1880s

65 See Maren Lockwood Garden, *Oneida: Utopian Community to Modern Corporation*, Syracuse, N.Y., Syracuse University Press, 1998, p. 101.
66 Fogarty, *Desire and Duty at Oneida*, p. 24.

the company's commercial development was apparently hampered by the old-fashioned business methods of elderly Oneidans and by unhelpful messages that some of them claimed to be receiving from the spirit-world – including the spirit of John Humphrey Noyes following his death in 1886 – about how the company should best be managed. After Noyes's son, Pierrepont Burt Noyes, was appointed director in January, 1894, having proven his commercial talents in a partnership called Noyes Bros., Wholesalers of Silverware and Novelties, the company was run on 'modern' principles of cut-throat competition, effective promotion and advertising, combined with progressive treatment of its employees as a community of interest. The company steadily grew through the twentieth century into the giant multinational stainless-steel tableware manufacturer that we know today as Oneida Ltd, marketing its goods under the vitalist slogan: 'Bring life to the table'.

Back-to-the-future utopian tourists can still visit the Oneida Community Mansion House, now 'A National Historic Landmark' in up-state New York, and rent a room for the night. The minimum tariff for a 'Full Bed Guest Room' at Oneida is $100 per night, while the 'John Humphrey Noyes Suite' costs $250 per night. For both types of accommodation, the management stipulates: 'Maximum Occupancy: 2'. The advertising makes no mention of an electrical bed, but it does offer the Oneida Mansion House for hire for – of all things – weddings.[67]

67 See the Oneida Community Mansion House web site: http://www.oneidacommunity.org/

7

Libidinal Communists and Sexual Revolutionaries, Part 2:

The Friedrichshof Commune (1972–1990), With a Reflection on Keynesianism

The Oneida communitarians, then, were Reichians or Keynesians in libidinal economy *avant la lettre*, believing that the more freely desire was spent and circulated between bodies, the more of it would be generated and the richer in energy the community would become. A century later, the Friedrichshof Commune, founded by the Viennese Actionist leader Otto Muehl in Burgenland, Austria, instituted an even more radical version of libidinal Keynesianism than the Bible Communists had, but without their economic success. Described by a reporter in the *Guardian* newspaper as being 'for a halcyon period between the early 70s and the beginning of the 90s … the world's most famous sex commune',[1] the Friedrichshof 'family' had 600 members at its height, and saw itself as building on millenarian experiments like Oneida, but exchanging their theology for a heady mix of Marxism, anarchism and Reichian psychoanalysis.

Like Oneida, Friedrichshof was a utopian project of sexual and economic communism galvanised around a charismatic leader. The movement began as a group flat-sharing arrangement in Vienna: the communards set about clearing out the nuclear-familial furniture from Muehl's flat and from their own psyches, issuing manifestoes that were potent cocktails of anarchism, obscenity and psychoanalytic theory, and combining communal living with odd

1 Jonathan Margolis, 'The price of free love', *The Guardian*, 8 October 1999, p. 21: http://www.theguardian.com/theguardian/1999/oct/08/features11.g21

jobs, partying, Actionist happenings and a shared vision of reinventing everything from language to the economy by turning their backs on bourgeois consumption and its cultural and political institutions.[2] In the 1960s, Viennese Actionism had staged the destruction of art and the promise of revolution, first on the canvas, later on the body. Concluding that the Actionist happening was, after all, only 'a bourgeois art form, mere art', Muehl completed

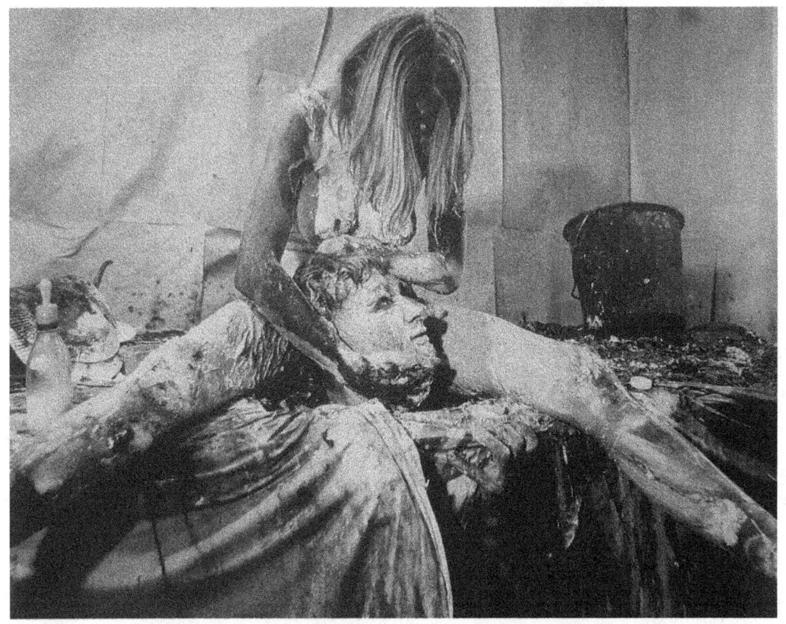

Otto Muehl, Mama and Papa, 1964. Photo by L. Hofenreich.

2 Sources of information about the Friedrichshof Commune include the following (full details are provided in the bibliography): *AAN (AktionsAnalytische-News)* (the commune's newsletter, published approximately seven times per year between Summer 1974 and Spring 1978); Theo Altenberg, *Das Paradies Experiment: Die Utopie der freien Sexualität Kommune Fridrichshof 1973-1978* (2001); Andreas Schlothauer, *Die Diktatur der freien Sexualitaet – AAO, Muehl Kommune, Friedrichshof* (1975); Frank Nordhausen and Liane von Billerbeck, *Psycho-Sekten - die Praktiken der Seelenfänger* (1999); Stefan Beyst, *De extasen van eros: Over liefde, lust en verlangen* (1997) and *Otto Mühl: From the Happening to the Commune* (2002); and Soul Purpose Productions, 'Slaves in Paradise' (UK Channel 4 TV documentary, 1999).

what he called 'the transition from art to life' in 1972 by founding the Friedrichshof community in Burgenland, where thirty members of three Viennese communes bought land with their pooled funds and established a kind of anti-society, based on the abolition of money, property, careers, romantic love, the nuclear family, the work/leisure dichotomy, the state and the police. Their politico-economic vision was of a world commune organisation, or 'WCO', which more and more people would decide to join, building up an alternative global economy and 'subverting the dominant capitalism' by refusing to consume the commodities produced by the corporations, leaving them sitting on the shelves, thereby precipitating a crisis of over-production that would bring capitalism tumbling, peacefully, to the ground.[3]

In practice, things were not so simple. The movement's limping alternative economy depended heavily on recruiting new members and their injections of fresh capital. Facing bankruptcy in 1979, a Nuremberg 'congress' of the movement's interlinked groups (there would be some twenty interlinked groups by the early 1980s, mainly in Germany, France and Scandinavia[4]) agreed to practise what they called 'a new form of dissimulation', known ironically as 'new horny capitalism', in which members donned suits, took corporate jobs and started businesses, but pooled their salaries to support the commune – thus 'externally playing along with the system and secretly building up a functioning countermodel'.[5] By 1985, thirty-five members of the commune were working 'under cover' as traders in the Amsterdam stock exchange[6] (the most successful of them, Jenny Simanowitz, who had joined Friedrichshof from Bradford in 1980, being the top earner at £2m per year).[7]

The commune's free-sex regime presupposed that the originary

3 Theo Altenberg, *Das Paradies Experiment: Die Utopie der freien Sexulität Kommune Friedrichshof 1973-1978*, Wien, Triton Verlag, 2001, p. 116. Altenberg joined Muehl's commune at the age of 21.

4 Ibid., pp. 127-28

5 Ibid., pp. 122-25.

6 Reported in the Channel 4 TV documentary film, *Slaves in Paradise*, directed and produced by Madonna Benjamin, Soul Purpose Productions, 1999.

7 Margolis, 'The price of free love'.

form of the property-relationship was sexual – property in women, institutionalised in monogamy, which, in turn, institutionalised inhibition, jealousy and repression. When Muehl's girlfriend Elke left the commune in 1973, he proclaimed the principle of 'free sexuality' and 'group marriage' and all couple relationships were dissolved. As at Oneida, so at Friedrichshof – only more so – 'group marriage' required the abolition of private space and intimacy as well as of private property, with a view to producing a fully communal or collective sexuality and subjectivity. Communards were expected to embark on a programme of subjective redevelopment – a psychical house-clearing and reconstruction – mapped out by Muehl in what he called his *Aktionsanalyse Parabola* (Action-Analysis Parabola), whose goal was to achieve what he called a stage of 'genital and social identity' in which one became a 'fully social' subject and an 'exemplary energeticist'.[8]

Sexual intercourse played a central role in this process. For Muehl, as for Reich, orgasm was the spending of an energy that could otherwise be hoarded or trapped in the body as a defence, forming an 'armour' that protected the subject against powerful emotions but blocked the natural, pleasurable impulse to discharge rather than save libido: a legacy of the patriarchal nuclear family and its taboos, such character-armour was the foundation of the fascist state. In Muehl's 'Action Analysis', which laced Reichian 'body therapy' with Janov's 'primal scream' or re-birthing therapy, the individual expelled

Otto Muehl practising Actionism.

8 Altenberg, *Das Paradies Experiment*, p. 114.

all the aggressive energy accumulated in their character-armour as a result of 'small-family damage' and was psychically released or re-born into a taboo-free 'genital and social identity', with what Reich called 'full orgastic potency' – the capacity to spend libido uninhibitedly, without reserve or return. The curve of the AA Parabola plotted the six different stages of psychic 'descent' through 'the consciousness structure' that the individual had to make, overcoming their bodily and psychic resistances and expelling their hoarded emotion in laughing, depressive crying, screaming, vomiting, excreting and blind rage against the parents. Psychic regression was to be followed by the six stages of re-ascent, through the resolution of parental transference, overcoming of the incest taboo (incestuous fantasies being a universal symptom of 'small-family damage') and liberation from jealousy or possessiveness, required for rebirth as a fully social and genital identity, or an 'exemplary energeticist'. It was commonly agreed that only Muehl himself had so far completed the journey.

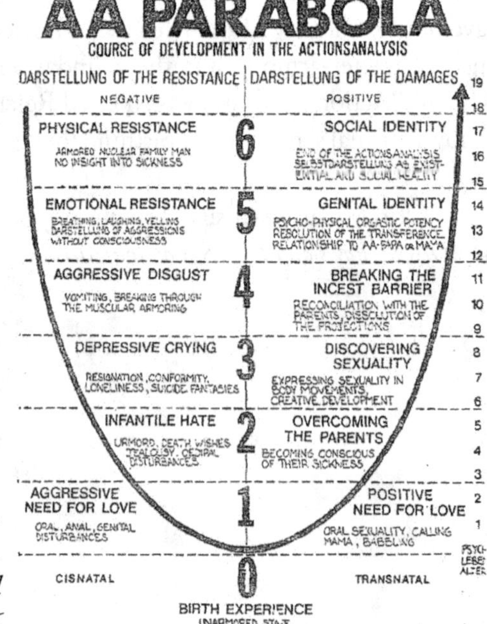

Actionsanalysis Parabola, AA News no. 1, 1975. *© ADAGP, Paris and DACS, London 2016*

Muehl explained 'genital identity' and 'social identity' in a 1975 issue of the *AktionsAnalyse-Newsletter*:

> Genital Identity *(Genitale Identität)*
>
> *The overcoming of the incest taboo opens the road to the ability of orgasm. A shudder goes through the body; an energetic discharge takes place, which is nothing else but the devolvement of all psycho-physical pressure potential. It is the creation of unity between brain and body; the conciliation of all the cells of the body. The psycho-physical orgasm is a rejuvenation just like the experience of birth, a real rebirth, a creative event.*
>
> Social Identity *(Soziale Identität)*
>
> *Whoever wants to accomplish genital as well as social identity must abandon the property of things and human beings. He/she will exchange property for consciousness. Consciousness means that all human beings will be included in his/her existence, genital as well as social.*[9]

During the commune's first year, Muehl had introduced therapeutical 'Sprechtstunden' (consultation hours), modelled on his own experience of an uncompleted Freudian analysis intermixed with his reading of Reich; in these sessions he provided disinhibiting therapy for all the other communards, regularly inviting them into his 'Analysebox', where sexual exchange would occur.[10] The demands this practice made on the analyst and his growing cohort of analysands were such that in 1973 Muehl abandoned the individualised therapy of the 'Sprechtstunden' in favour of collective 'action-analysis', with the AA Parabola serving commune members as a map through the resulting psychological chaos. Just as Oneida had its daily group therapy sessions, known as Mutual Criticism, in which individuals' thoughts and feelings were 'collectivised', so Friedrichshof staged nightly *SelbstDarstellung* or 'self-presentation' sessions, in which individuals or groups would act out emotions,

9 Quoted from the *AA-Newsletter*, 1 (1975), pp. 52-66, in Schlothauer, *Die Diktatur der freien Sexualitaet*, p. 29 (my translation).

10 Schlothauer, *Die Diktatur der freien Sexualitaet*, pp. 179-80.

Friedrichshof communards. © *ADAGP, Paris and DACS, London 2016*

Muehl and communards. © *ADAGP, Paris and DACS, London 2016*

memories and fantasies, often sexual in content, exorcising *homo œconomicus* from their psyches on the road to orgastic potency and a 'fully social' subjectivity. Muehl argued that the two fundamental human needs are communicative and sexual, and that they are essentially one and the same: a need for the exchange or transmission of psychosexual energy – and if this need were met by an economy of freely-spent and circulating libido, then '*the commune society can satisfy all the real needs of humankind and, thus, can do without most branches of industry*'.[11] Much as Noyes had envisaged

11 Otto Muehl, *AA-Newsletter* (1974) and *Commune Manifesto* (1976), quoted in Schlothauer, *Die Diktatur der freien Sexualitaet*, p. 21 (my translation). Schlothauer was a member of the commune until the mid-1980s and later involved as a prosecution witness in Muehl's trial for sexual offences. In 1992

the fire of sexual passion, fanned by Oneida's free-love ideology, supplying the heat needed to warm hearths and drive industrial machinery, so the Friedrichshoffers believed that their command-economy of free sex would generate sufficient sustaining energy to free them from alienated labour. Maintaining the circuitry by which libidinal energy flowed through and around the community with their free-love regime, they would obviate a need for more industrial modes of energy-production while simultaneously forging world peace through erotic hedonism. An issue of the *AA-Newsletter* explained: '*Only those who understand how to exchange their energy as sexual energy by fucking with others will not see enemies but sexual beings who promise sexual pleasure. This applies to individuals, states, nations, and super-powers*'.[12] Once the disinhibited spending of libido had been collectivised and universalised through the sexual recruitment of more and more contributors to the network's libidinal economy, '*the boundaries between humans caused by money, class, property and ancestry [will] have fallen, and therefore humans will be borderless and without boundaries*'[13] – re-born, in effect, as a fully communal subjects, the ideal medium for the transmission of a now de-privatised desire, or what Deleuze and Guattari woud call free-floating intensities.

To optimise the libidinal energy in circulation, communards were required to make love as often as Muslims bow to Mecca (five times a day) and with the maximum number of different partners and a minimum of romantic foreplay, to prevent what the sociologists call any dyadic disinvestment of libido from the group. The ideal was a totally non-repetitive copulation – the unremitting promiscuity of a Casanova, a Don Juan or a Cathérine Millett – which would eventually recruit the whole world's population to the libidinal economy that the communards were pioneering.[14] (The early prohibition

he published his memoir, *Die Diktatur der freien Sexualitaet* (the dictatorship of free sexuality).

12 Otto Muehl, *AA-Newsletter*, 6 (1976), p. 66.

13 *AA-Newsletter*, 2 (1976), p. 8.

14 Stefan Beyst, *Otto Mühl: From the Happening to the Commune* (2002), http://d-sites.net/english/muhl.html. Principle 6 of the 'AA Human Rights' declaration held that: 'All humans have the right to realize their sexuality as

against copulating with the same partner more than once a week, that is, once in every thirty-five copulations, was based only on the size of the commune at the time, whereas the goal was a totally non-repetitive promiscuity. As one commentator put it: 'The ideal of life-long fidelity was replaced by the ideal of absolute promiscuity'.[15]) Muehl himself proved unmatched in his power to attract new conductors to the commune's sexual circuitry. Three- to ten-minute copulations were recommended to maximise the speed of libidinal exchange, and as the commune's population expanded to 600 members, it had recourse to the notorious computer-generated *Ficklisten* (literally, 'fuck-lists' or 'fuck-registers'), posted daily, directing who should make love to whom and when, formalising what was initially supposed to be a spontaneous arrangement. (A Californian counterpart of Friedrichshof, the Haight-Ashbury-based Kerista Commune, which practised 'polyfidelity' and economic communism from 1971 to 1991, famously bought a Macintosh computer in the mid-1980s to run its own roster of nightly polyfidelity, only to develop within five years into the largest Mac consultancy and dealership in the USA, with a $35 million per year turnover. Basic bookkeeping and money-management skills were in fact one of the requirements for joining the commune.[16]) Friedrichshof's free-sex economy thus quickly became an authoritarian regime of biopolitics in which, as one commentator put it, 'the marital duty of the bourgeois couple is as nothing compared to' the compulsory sex demanded of every communard with every other communard of the opposite sex, however undesirable she or he might seem in comparison with

free sexuality without the restrictions of the couple relationship, marriage, or morality. Free sexuality can only be realized in an existential group of socially equal humans – private property prevents free sexuality' (Altenberg, *Das Paradies Experiment*, p. 162).

15 Beyst, *Otto Mühl.*

16 For information on this Californian commune, see *Kerista Village Handbook*, San Francisco, Kerista Consciousness Church, 1979; Ryam Nearing, *Loving More: The Polyfidelity Primer*, San Francisco, Pep Publishing, 1992; John Stewart Sill, 'Utopian Group Marriage in the 19th and 20th Centuries: Oneida Community and Kerista Commune', *Free Inquiry in Creative Sociology*, 18 (1990): 21-28; Grant, *Sexing the Millennium*, ch. 7: 'Sister Kerista saves the world', pp. 155-164.

other potential partners. (All reports suggest that there was intense competition among the women to be selected as a bed-mate by Muehl, who retained the privilege of choice.)

The Friedrichshof community lasted some twenty years, and during the late 1970s associated AA communes were established in Berlin, Frankfurt, Heidelberg, Krefeld, Geneva, Toulouse, Lyon, Oslo, Amsterdam, Vienna and even Boston, all living according to the six 'AA-principles': '1. Self-Expression; 2. Free Sexuality; 3. Common Property; 4. Common Work and Production; 5. Common Child-Rearing; 6. Direct Democracy'.[17] During the 1970s, *Aktionsanalytische Organisation* (AAO) teams, instantly recognisable by their identical clothing and shaven heads symbolising their secession from bourgeois culture, regularly performed on German university campuses to promote the organisation and its principles. Whereas the Oneida community had grown increasingly affluent, however, Friedrichshof often teetered on the edge of bankruptcy. And yet, despite their economic differences, the Oneida and Friedrichshof experiments ultimately failed for much

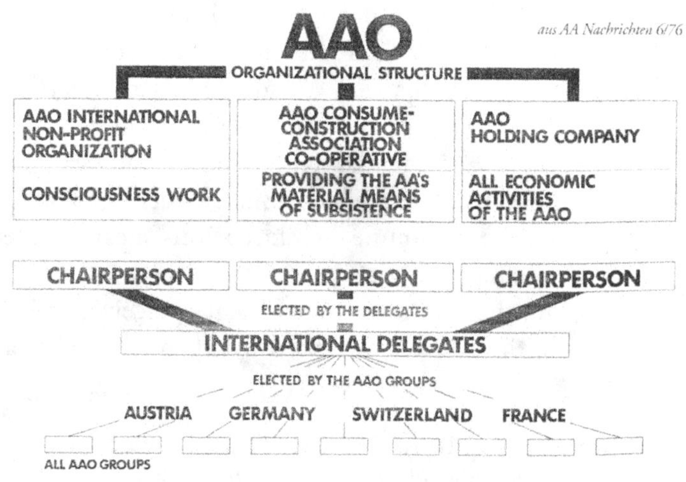

Aktionsanalytische network structure. AA News no. 1, 1977.
© ADAGP, Paris and DACS, London 2016

17 See Schlothauer, *Die Diktatur der freien* Sexualitaet, pp. 179-80, and Altenberg, *Das Paradies Experiment*, p. 148.

the same reasons. In each case, practice sooner or later began to contradict theory, some animals on their farms became more equal than others, and their charismatic leaders betrayed their own doctrines by hoarding sexual pleasure and partners for themselves, prompting oedipal challenges that eventually broke apart the communities. Both leaders were also charged with statutory rape (and in Muehl's case, incest) under laws that their communes had abolished and in relation to which they were in a revolutionary 'state of exception'. In Friedrichshof's case, the principle of collectively owned, freely circulating libido in an economy of spending without saving gave way to what one commentator called an 'inner circle' arrangement whereby 'the happy few preferred the happy few' and 'were no longer prepared to descend to the lower regions of the pyramid' – 'to the utter dissatisfaction of the wretched on the base, who so dearly wanted to gain access to the top of the pyramid'.[18] Protests against this de-facto privatisation and hoarding of libido were stifled in 1987-8 when the Friedrichshof elite closed ranks and formalised their hierarchy by proclaiming a 'monarchy', having engineered the consent of 360 of the then 400 communards. The ideal of a global network of communes was replaced by the concept of a 'Kleinfamiliengesellschaft' (small family company). Muehl married Claudia Weissensteiner; their three-year-old son, Attila, became heir apparent; and Muehl was granted *droit de seigneur*, the feudal right to initiate the commune's girl-children into sexual intercourse.[19] Since Muehl had himself fathered many of the commune's children, this meant a literal 'overcoming' of the incest taboo.[20]

Tensions within the commune over Muehl's perceived megalomania culminated in a revolt organised by Theo Altenberg, and

18 The quotations are from Beyst, *Otto Mühl.* Beyst is a critical chronicler of Viennese Actionism and author of *De extasen van Eros*, Hadewych, Antwerpen, 1997, http://d-sites.net/english/eros00.htm

19 Altenberg, *Das Paradies Experiment*, p. 139.

20 Beyst observes of this resurgence of patriarchy: 'After the collective property of the commune had been transformed into the harem of a monarch, the monarch himself turns out to be the very embodiment of Freud's primeval father, incestuously swallowing up the next generation' (Beyst, *Otto Mühl*).

when Muehl was tried and convicted in 1991 on charges of statutory rape (the legal age of consent in Austria being 14), the commune as such disintegrated. Some of its members maintained the Friedrichshof property as cooperative housing with a strong community spirit, and today (as at Oneida) the site includes a hotel and conference centre. The Seminarhotel Friedrichshof currently boasts 'modern streamlined lodging offering a gourmet restaurant, sauna and swimming pool', together with a museum, the Sammlung Friedrichshof, housing artworks of Viennese Actionists including Muehl – thus apparently completing the circle of 'the transition from art to life' and back again to art.[21]

Meanwhile, various offshoots of the Friedrichshof Commune, such as Dieter Duhm's 'Project Meiga', have continued its countercultural, anti-capitalist experiment in what Duhm describes as 'freeing the sexes from culturally conditioned prohibitions and fears that block human energy'.[22] Released from prison after six and a half years in 1997, Muehl himself moved to Fargo, in Portugal, to start a new commune experiment and, despite suffering from Parkinson disease, continued making and exhibiting art-work until his death in 2013. At a press conference before the opening of an exhibition of his work at the Leopold Museum in Vienna in 2010, Muehl read an apology for his authoritarian role in the Friedrichshof Commune, while defending its theoretical principles.

The Oneida and Friedrichshof collectives, then, were just two of the numerous experiments in libidinal communism during the past 200 years that have attempted to practise what Esposito calls a politics '*for*' life instead of '*over*' life, treating the body as 'subject', 'not object', by maximising its pleasure in exchanging or transmitting what is variously called energy, electricity, the life-force, love, desire. The communes' commitments to exorcising the petit-bourgeois *homo œconomicus* from *homo sexualis*, to de-commodifying and de-reifying bodies and libido, and to maximising the circulation of vital energy in a community of freely-loving individuals,

21 See http://www.hotel-friedrichshof.com

22 See Dieter Duhm, *Eros Unredeemed: The World Power of Sexuality*, Bad Belzig, Verlag Meiga, 2010 and Leila Dregger, 'Project Meiga: How It All Began', http://www.jugglerpress.com/jockm/zegghistory.html

meant turning the individual from an owner and entrepreneur of private libidinal capital into a compulsory exchanger or spender of a now common libidinal wealth – a collectivisation variously depicted as a return to a state of nature and as a regaining of Paradise on earth.

The chief irony of the Oneida and Friedrichshof experiments, however, is not that *homo œconomicus* eventually resurfaced to practise private enterprise where there was supposed to be libidinal socialism – not, in other words, that their charismatic leaders sooner or later betrayed their own doctrines by hoarding sexual pleasure and partners for themselves, prompting oedipal challenges that eventually broke apart the communes. Rather, the chief irony is that their ostensibly free libidinal economies turned out to be rigidly, even baroquely ordered, no less rule-bound than bourgeois sexuality is by its codes of incest, courtship, modesty, marriage, filiation and so on. In short, the biopolitics of 'free love' movements are invariably no less regulated than the putatively free market, which is sustained by innumerable tariffs, imposts, quotas, taxes and barriers. As our fiscal policy-makers kept rediscovering during the 2008-2010 'global financial crisis', there is an uncanny convergence between Keynesian policies of unconstrained spending and centralised government-control of the institutions that keep the currency of desire circulating. What the Oneida and Friedrichshof experiments in collectivising desire suggest is that there is no such thing as a 'free' or un-rule-bound sexual desire, merely different regimes of sexuality by which desire is defined, generated and channelled.

Keynesianism and Spending for Wealth

Mention of Keynesianism raises the question of in what sense my description of free-love libidinal economies as not only Reichian and utopian-socialist but also as 'Keynesian' might be defended as neither anachronistic nor simply metaphorical – no more the forcing of an analogy between the vocabularies of sex and money than is the idea of 'libidinal economy' itself. One way to approach the relation between Keynesianism and libidinal economy is via the concept of depression, a concept that has spanned the discourses of psychology and political economy since the 1790s. Written during the height of the so-called Great Depression, Keynes's *The General Theory of Employment, Interest and Money* proposed that the antidote to depression was not the self-disciplined thrift that Adam Smith advocated when arguing that private frugality is the cause of public wealth. On the contrary, Keynes argued, the cure for depression is disinhibited spending led by government example. The way to fend off depression was not to reduce wages and prices in order to alleviate unemployment, as classical economics supposed, but to increase consumption by the spending of money, not least by the state, which should be prepared to go into deficit to finance its spending. Nor was it relevant whether this spending fulfilled any desirable public or private purpose. What Keynes saw as the petit-bourgeois and working-class tendency to hoard money as cash when times got tough, rather than to spend or invest it (in other words, their 'liquidity preference') – this tendency withdraws money from circulation, and when money is withdrawn from circulation, the result is 'over-production' and unemployment: the previous output of goods cannot be sold because those who would buy them are now unemployed and penniless, and society sinks into a general depression which, Keynes contended, is capable of lasting indefinitely. Thus the antidote to depression is spending for spending's sake, irrespective of what it buys.

Keynes went so far as to denigrate saving as a destructive 'leakage' of spending-power from the economy, and he insisted that wealth should be conceived not as the amount of material goods produced within an economy but as the amount of money that flows through it, passing from person to person, spender to spender. Keynes also pointed out that each act of spending creates an additionally stimulating 'multiplier effect', since a fraction of every dollar spent is in turn re-spent, so that each act of spending creates waves of benefits throughout the economic system. Hoarding, by contrast, would show its true colours, he believed, as soon as the technological leaps of the twentieth century had satisfied all humankind's basic economic needs and thus rendered money-making no longer a plausible excuse for living. Optimistic that this could be achieved by 2030, Keynes predicted in 1930 that 'The love of money as a possession – as distinguished from the love of money as a means to the enjoyments and realities of life – will be recognised for what it is, a somewhat disgusting morbidity, one of those semicriminal, semipathological propensities which one hands over with a shudder to the specialists in mental disease'.[23] The specialists Keynes had in mind were the psychoanalysts: Freud, Ernest Jones, Sándor Ferenczi, who de-historicised and biologised money-fetishism, explaining what they called 'the capitalistic instinct'[24] of acquisitiveness as a neurotic displacement, in the potty-trained adult, of a universal, infantile anal-erotic drive. (In the chapter of his *Treatise on Money* dealing with the gold standard, Keynes cited 'the Freudian theory of the love of money and of gold in particular' as a plausible explanation of why civilisation had ended up with a gold standard rather than an iron, copper or silver standard. Referring to Freud's etymological and ethnographic investigations of the links between gold and excrement, Keynes reported: 'Dr Freud relates that there are peculiar reasons deep in our subconsciousness why gold in particular should satisfy strong instincts and serve as a symbol'.[25]) As Ferenczi made clear in his essay 'The Ontogenesis of the Interest in Money' (1914), for

23 John Maynard Keynes, 'Economic Possibilities for Our Grandchildren' (1930), *Essays in Persuasion*, New York, W. W. Norton & Co., 1963, pp. 371-72.

24 Sandor Ferenczi, 'The Ontogenesis of the Interest in Money', *Sex in Psychoanalysis: Contributions to Psychoanalysis*, preface by Ernest Jones, New York, Robert Brunner, 1950, p. 331. Summarising classical psychoanalytic theories of money, Ferenczi maintained that 'the capitalistic interest' or 'capitalistic instinct' has 'both an egoistic and an anal-erotic component', satisfying both the reality principle (i.e., serving 'practical, egoistic aims') and the pleasure principle (i.e., 'represent[ing] the symbolic displacement of, and the reaction-formation to, repressed anal erotism').

25 John Maynard Keynes, *A Treatise on Money, Volume II: The Applied Theory of Money*, London, Macmillan, 1930, pp. 289-90. In a footnote, Keynes directs his reader to papers by Freud, Ferenczi and Jones, congratulating Jones and psychoanalysis for successfully prophesying that the psychological identification of wealth with gold would lead to post-World War I efforts to reintroduce a gold currency in England. For a discussion of Keynes' relationship with Freudianism, see John Forrester, 'Freud in Cambridge', *Critical Quarterly*, 46, 2 (2004): 1-26.

orthodox Freudians such as himself the psychology of money-fetishism was not so much a mirage of capitalism – concealing a social relation behind the appearance of value-in-itself – as a neurotic displacement of the infantile 'bodily narcissism' that takes pleasure in saving or hoarding faeces. Speaking of the infant's reluctance to let go of a part of its own body, Ferenczi concludes that 'the excrementa thus held back are really the *first "savings"* of the growing child'. 'Pleasure in the intestinal contents becomes enjoyment of money', he explained; 'whatever form may be assumed by money, the enjoyment at possessing it has its deepest and amplest source in coprophilia'.[26] Hence, it would seem, the 'shudder' with which Keynes was anxious to hand over the psychology of hoarding 'to the specialists in mental disease'.

During the 2008-2010 global financial crisis, die-hard free-marketeers regularly levelled the charge of 'socialism' against governments that, having driven their hardline Friedmanite or 'monetarist' policies on a crash course, suddenly rediscovered Keynes and started extravagantly spending their way out of recession and into debt – proving, once more, that capitalism is indeed 'communism for the rich and free enterprise for the poor' (as Martin Luther King is reputed to have said) by bailing out private banks with public funds in order to fend off the sickness of depression. As we have already noted, Keynes was no socialist: a famously successful personal investor as well as a chairman of the Bank of England, he described Marxism as founded on 'an obsolete textbook' that he knew 'not only to be scientifically erroneous but without interest or application in the modern world'.[27] Nonetheless, like the ideologues of Oneida and Friedrichshof, Keynes maintained that populations could not be relied upon to keep spending freely, for spending's sake, without such spending being

26 Ferenczi, 'Ontogenesis', pp. 327-28.

27 Ibid. Keynes also indicts Marx's *Capital* because it 'exalts the boorish proletariat above the bourgeoisie and the intelligentsia, who with all their faults, are the quality of life and surely carry the seeds of all human achievement'. Quentin Bell quotes Keynes as saying Marxism 'was founded upon nothing better than a misunderstanding of Ricardo'. Quentin Bell, *Virginia Woolf, A Biography*, London, Hogarth Press, 1996, p. 177.

instituted as a principle of government. (In Part 1 of *The General Theory*, Keynes asserted that the core of his theory was his rejection of Say's Law, the doctrine that, irrespective of consumer or investor confidence, people will spend all the income they receive. Contrary to Say's Law, Keynes argued, in a monetary economy people can try to accumulate cash rather than real goods; and when everyone is trying to accumulate money at the same time, the result is an end to demand, which produces a severe recession.) Rejecting the received wisdom of neoclassical economics, which held that free markets were the best defence against depression, Keynes advocated state intervention in the economy, and he called on psychoanalysis to explain what he described as the 'irrational' impulse to hoard money rather than spend it freely – an impulse he believed needed to be guarded against by state policy,[28] much as the Friedrichshof commune conceived of its *ficklisten* as a safeguard against hoarding in its own libidinal commonwealth.

But, of course, political economy did not need to wait for Keynes's dramatic arrival on the scene in the 1930s to register the message that 'if everybody spent more, all would obtain larger incomes "and might then live more plentifully"'.[29] The latter quotation is from a seventeenth-century political economist, Cary, one of the many exponents of spending, not accumulating, as the source of communal prosperity whom Keynes cites in the historical appendix of *The General Theory*, where he tracks the changing fortunes of his own views of money and spending through the seventeenth, eighteenth and nineteenth centuries. Among other authorities Keynes cites is that insightful anticipator of twentieth-century consumerist culture, Bernard Mandeville, whose satirical *Parable of the Bees: or, Private Vices, Publick Benefits* advanced 'the doctrine that prosperity was increased by expenditure rather than by saving' as long ago as 1714 – some three centuries before George

28 See E.G. Winslow, 'Keynes and Freud: psychoanalysis and Keynes's account of the "Animal Spirits" of capitalism', *Social Research*, 53 (1986): 549-578. Cf. George Ackerlof and Robert Shiller, *Animal Spirits: How Human Psychology Drives the Economy and Why It Matters for Global Capitalism*, Princeton and Oxford, Princeton University Press, 2009.

29 Keynes, *The General Theory*, p. 359.

W. Bush suggested shopping as the most patriotic American response to '9/11', or before Australia's Labor government undertook to fend off depression during the 2008-2010 financial crisis with a $42-billion government handout of 'helicopter money' to Australians, exhorting them to take it straight to the nation's shopping malls. (In the event, the Rudd Labor Government's 'economic stimulus package', which gave $900 to every low-income tax-payer, proved a failure as most of its beneficiaries used it to service debts rather than finance retail therapy for an ailing economy.) Spending as a form of 'selflessness'– a necessary contribution to the common wealth and a refusal of the Calvinist or petit-bourgeois saver who lurks as a potentiality within us all – has been a principle contending with thrift, parsimony and prudent investment throughout the history of political economy, whether bourgeois, socialist or communist, since its inception in the Enlightenment. To describe Oneida's libidinal economics as Keynesian, then, is not as anachronistic as it may sound. As Keynes pointed out, in the 1820s even the Reverend Robert Malthus, that seminal biopolitician and key influence on Oneida's population-planning, convincingly repudiated Adam Smith's view 'that every frugal man is a public benefactor' and 'that capitals are increased by parsimony' rather than by compulsive spenders.[30]

As Proposition XIX of Oneida's *Bible Communism* illustrated, the vocabularies of money, sexual desire, love and electricity were already promiscuously in play with one another within the same discursive economy in the 1840s – along with the vocabularies of theology, politics and biology. The question thus arises: is what Esposito today calls 'life' or 'the body', the 'same' as what Noyes, in the 1840s, wrote of as love (divine and human), as vital energy, as electricity and as the 'capital stock' or economic wealth of a community? And is this same life-force or energy what Marx called 'labour-power', what Freud called 'libido', and what Reich (believing he had found the crucial common denominator of Marxism and Freudianism) called 'orgone? And is this 'life', 'energy', 'libido' or 'divine love' what poststructuralists such as Lyotard and Deleuze

30 Ibid.

sometimes call 'intensities' and sometimes 'desire'? Are they all 'really' speaking of the 'same' thing, that mysterious entity 'life', omnipresent but nowhere identifiable in itself?

Around the turn of the nineteenth century, Freud cobbled together the language of psychoanalysis with terms borrowed from mythology, neurology, physics, economics, chemistry and hydraulics – not because he lacked the inventiveness or confidence to create a distinctive psychoanalytic language, but because of his deep conviction that theoretical rigour would lead to a unified discourse incorporating psychical phenomena with the physical universe. In the words of Alphonso Lingis: 'Freud's metapsychology is a provisional effort in the way of a metaphysics, in the Aristotelian and Whiteheadian sense, a universal and unified categorical system which could function to establish translatability between the data accounted for in physical terms and those accounted for in psychic terms'.[31] *Pace* Esposito, we could say that what is needed today is not so much a new form of 'biopolitics capable of being used in favour of bodies, not on them' – such a politics has been imagined many times in the past – but, rather, a new understanding of the discursive economy in which Esposito's self-valorising concept of 'life' (for which his 'body' is a synonym) appears to function as a transcendental signifier or master-signifier that literally names a natural truth that can only be metaphorically signified by such concepts as 'divine love', 'electrical fluid', 'vital energy' or 'libidinal capital'. As I suggested in chapter one, none of these terms is inherently more literal or metaphorical than others; only history makes them appear so – the history, for example, that by the mid-nineteenth century would install the thermodynamic concept of 'energy', defined as work-power, as the literal naming of a 'life-force' that religion had previously 'mystified' as 'divine love'.

What is needed, in other words, is not a new terminology or language to resolve the Babel of politics by identifying the 'proper' subject of history (as Esposito's 'life' or 'bios' appears to do), but a

31 Alphonso Lingis, 'A New Philosophical Interpretation of the Libido', *SubStance*, 8, 4, 25 (1979): 88.

new, *historical* understanding of the politics of exchange among the currencies that compete – and sometimes collaborate – to name such a subject with their own coinages. Re-imagining the politics of 'life', in other words, means theorising a unified discursive economy in which the currencies of such terms can be freely exchanged, without such a unified theory turning into a totalitarian one.

Sexual Revolution and Consumerism

And yet, to invoke Keynesianism to characterise the libidinal economics of Oneida and Friedrichshof is also, implicitly, to make the politically depressing point that such utopian experiments in sexual and economic revolution ultimately functioned, despite themselves, as dress-rehearsals for the full-blown consumerist culture of administered enjoyment and disinhibited spending. Later in the century whose economics Keynes revolutionised and in the early years of the twenty-first century, such spending has been interpreted as a prophylactic against global depression, as proof of patriotism, or more generally as obedience to the mandatory 'enjoyment' that Slavoj Žižek and others have attributed to 'the decline of Oedipus' in postmodern consumer society.[32]

Together with Reich and Marcuse, another straight, male Freudian, Norman O. Brown, proved to be an influential ideologue of sexual revolution and libidinal spending in the 1960s. While Brown's vision of sexual liberation would turn out, disappointingly for many of his readers, to be more poetical than carnal when he published *Love's Body* in 1966, the revolutionary rhetoric of his *Life Against Death: The Psychoanalytical Meaning of History* (1959) seemed to dismiss even the need for a 'basic' repression such as Marcuse acknowledged. In *Life Against Death* Brown mustered canonical Romantic poets, Christian and oriental mystics, Marx and Nietzsche to critique the classical Freudian hypothesis of repression as indispensable to civilisation and, like Reich in the 1944 edition of *The Sexual Revolution*, announced,

32 For an elaboration of this vision of the postmodern superego, see Todd McGowan, *The End of Dissatisfaction? Jacques Lacan and the Emerging Society of Enjoyment*, Albany, NY, State University of New York Press, 2004.

under the banner of 'The Resurrection of the Body', an imminent apocalyptic ending to millennia of sublimation.[33] In Brown's version of Freudianism, repression and sublimation were primary agents of the death instinct, which 'the friends of the life instinct' were combating with their vision of life as 'play', not work, for the 'resurrected' body, 'based not on anxiety and aggression but on narcissism and erotic exuberance'.[34] Like Noyes, Reich and Marcuse before him, Brown argued that 'the abolition of repression would abolish the unnatural concentrations of libido in certain bodily organs' (the genitalia), permitting all the senses of the human body to be developed and intensified to their full potential, affording a 'consciousness which *does not negate any more*'.[35] Brown's 'resurrected' body, like Reich's and Marcuse's 're-sexualised body', was the 'polymorphously perverse' one of Freud's pre-oedipal infant, blissfully innocent of both work and shame, in a psychic Eden. Brown argued that in Jacob Boehme's concept of life as 'love-play' and his vision of 'the spiritual or paradisical body of Adam before the Fall', we can recognise 'the potent demand in our unconscious both for an androgynous mode of being and for a narcissistic mode of self-expression, as well as the corruption in our current use of the oral, anal, and genital functions'.[36]

Such calls to 'narcissistic' hedonism and polymorphous pleasures *as liberation*, and hence as a political duty to oneself and society at large, were potent rhetoric for a generation of post-war Western babyboomers growing accustomed, in the 1960s, to welfare-state-provided healthcare and higher education, the promise of full employment should it ever be wanted, and a booming consumerist culture. One of the powerful theses advanced by the minority-liberation movements of the 1960s sexual revolution was the 'sexual preference' model of sexuality. From the emergence of sexology as a discipline in the late nineteenth century through to its grappling

33 Norman O. Brown, *Life Against Death: The Psychoanalytical Meaning of History* (1959), London, Sphere, 1968, p. 269.

34 Ibid.

35 Ibid., p. 270.

36 Ibid., p. 272.

with gender-role confusion during and after World War II, sexologists had pathologised sexual 'deviance', attributing divergences from normative definitions of 'healthy', 'natural' sexuality to psychological damage or disease. Such pathologising of homosexuality, lesbianism, bisexuality, sadomasochism and transvestism had the dubious virtue of freeing the 'deviant' subject from a discourse of moral opprobrium while defining him or her as a suitable case for treatment. The 'sexual preference' model reversed this logic: while seeking 'tolerance' of a minority's right to exercise its sexual preferences, it represented sexuality as a matter of choice or taste, at once voluntary and cultivated, and not a matter of innate predisposition, insisting that anyone is potentially capable of choosing heterodox sexual practices and relationships. In doing so, the 'sexual preference' model de-naturalised what would come to be called 'heteronormativity' and de-pathologised its alternatives. The charge of pathology was pinned, instead, on the heteronormative police: it was the disease of 'homophobia' that now needed diagnosis and cure.

The Reichian stress on 'natural', 'healthy' sexuality, freed from neuroses (civilisation's discontents), had driven sex out into the open – into the countercultural Californian sun, where, for example, an invariably naked Fredrick 'Fritz' Perls offered free love and gestalt therapy at the Esalen Institute to anyone seeking a back-to-nature refuge from consumer capitalism. But the 'sexual preference' model shifted the ground from nature to choice, and hence from determinism to liberalism. Sexuality became the stuff of self-fashioning. And it was a short step from the notion of sexual identity as a self-fashioning choice or taste to the idea of the consumer as sovereign in a free market of sexual pleasures, lifestyles and identities. Sexuality thus came to seem as susceptible to manipulation by commercial fashion-cycles as any other kind of consumer choice. As Sheila Jeffreys puts it: 'Heterosexuality and homosexuality are seen as sexual preferences or choices, defined by sexual activities and feelings or even "lifestyles", but having no more to do with politics than a preference for peas or cabbage'.[37]

37 Jeffreys, *Anticlimax*, p. 289.

For the Freudo-Marxist tradition, sexual repression (and its secret agent, the superego) is a mechanism of capitalist domination, operating through the patriarchal family; and the more naive liberation campaigns – such as *Oz* magazine's in the 1960s, with its slogan, 'The destruction of all inhibition is our aim' – view the pursuit of sexual pleasure and license *per se* as a means of resisting capitalist domination. But, as Marcuse pointed out, some kinds of sexual liberalisation operate as repressive desublimation, complicit with the system they oppose.[38] And when the postmodern superego is heard issuing the command, 'Enjoy!', instead of 'Don't!', how can we be sure that obeying it will mean emancipation?

The advent of 1980s identity politics saw a shift from a politics of liberation to a politics of representation – of subaltern groups and minority subcultures demanding 'recognition' and 'respect'. Queer theory signalled another shift, in some (university-related) quarters, from a politics of representation to a politics of deconstruction. The postmodern deconstruction of representations – re-casting sexuality as a realm of plurality, ambiguity and fluidity, rather than of identities – has been seen both as a site of radical change today and as complicit with a mainstream consumer culture whose ever-changing fashion-cycles interpellate the consumer as the self-fashioning subject of an always mobile, polymorphous and insatiable desire. In Viagra-culture, desire itself is sold back to us as a desirable commodity, and the question of what might constitute an un-alienated or liberated sexuality today – and a sexual politics 'for' life, not 'over' life – seems no easier to answer than it was for the nineteenth-century utopian-socialists who finally admitted defeat by turning their revolutionary community into a joint-stock company.

38 Marcuse, *One-Dimensional Man*, p. 69.

8

Psychoanalysis, Post-Communism and the Black Economy

Some historians of psychoanalysis have suggested that the profession had become all but irrelevant to 'the spirit of capitalism' by the 1970s, 'when narcissism, as the libidinal face of egoism, replaced asceticism, the first component of the spirit of capitalism as described by Weber'.[1] Such is Eli Karetsky's reluctant conclusion in *Political Freud: A History* (2015). Karetsky follows Žižek and others in portraying psychoanalysis as a therapy closely tied to the instinctual renunciation required by capitalism ('because of the imperatives of saving') as Weber saw it in the 1900s, since when 'a new spirit of capitalism', sanctioning spending, 'the naturalness of egoism' and flexibly networked interpersonal relationships, has rendered depth psychology and its oedipal logic all but obsolete. In other words, the neoliberal spirit of capitalism has validated narcissism, universalised the *homo œconomicus* model of autonomous, 'rational' self-interest, doused interpersonal relationships in what Marx and Engels called 'the icy waters of egotistical calculation', and applied the 'bottom-line' test to every institution and occupation, including the profession of psychoanalysis, which has proved far less cost-effective than pharmaceutical and cognitive-behavioural fixes for neoliberal maladies.

By the 1990s in the USA, psychoanalysis seemed widely discredited, under pressure, as it was, from multiple quarters: the health insurance funds and pharma giants, cash-strapped state health and welfare agencies and two genres of intellectual critique. The feminist critiques of Freudianism's phallocentrism, led in the 1970s by

1 Eli Zaretsky, *Political Freud: A History*, New York, Columbia University Press, 2015, p. 180.

Kate Millett, Germaine Greer, Shulamith Firestone and Eva Figes, had converged with the critiques by such male Freudian apostates as Jeffrey Masson, Adolf Grunbaum, Frank Sulloway and Frederick Crews to fuel the so-called 'Freud Wars' and 'Freud-bashing industry' of the nineties. Such was the situation in the USA, where Crews had predicted in 1980 that 'psychoanalysis will fade away just as mesmerism and phrenology did, and for the same reason: its exploded pretensions will deprive it of recruits'.[2] But what of other parts of the world, where the spirit of capitalism was mutating at a different pace?

In fictocritical mode, this chapter is an attempt to imagine a connection between two seemingly disparate events: a Russian presidential decree of 1996 and a lavish houseboat party on the outskirts of St Petersburg on the Fourth of July, 1998, which I attended as a participant in a conference on psychoanalysis, literature and the arts, hosted by the East-European Institute of Psychoanalysis in St Petersburg and co-convened by the University of Florida's Institute for the Psychological Study of the Arts (IPSA). Like other foreign speakers at the conference, I had arrived in St Petersburg with an imagination primed by Western press coverage of the endemic official corruption and gangster-capitalism that were reportedly bankrupting Russia's economy and polity following the collapse of communism in 1991 – since when Russia's GNP had dropped by forty per cent; the national debt had risen to US$140 billion; previously state-owned industries and services, including up to eighty-five per cent of banks, were reputedly in the hands of organised crime; corporate and personal income taxes were largely uncollected; health and welfare systems were collapsing; wages and pension payments were in chronic arrears; and homelessness, beggary, suicide and assassination rates were soaring. I was therefore surprised to learn that in July 1996 Boris Yeltsin had found time to issue a presidential decree (No. 1044) entitled, 'On the Revival and Development of Philosophical, Clinical and Applied Psychoanalysis' in Russia. I knew that psychoanalysis had been officially suppressed by the Bolshevik Party in the 1930s, but

2 Frederick Crews, 'Analysis Interminable', *Commentary*, July 1980, pp. 33-34.

surely there must have been more urgent matters on President Yeltsin's political plate in 1996 than a government-sponsored revival of the highly individualised, private, expensive and hence elitist practice of psychoanalysis.

I had come to St Petersburg with a commission from Australia's ABC Radio National to compile a story and record interviews with Russian psychoanalysts and scholars for a planned programme on the history of 'Freud in Russia' (the material I gathered proved sufficient for two 50-minute programmes);[3] so my Western imagination was receptive to rumours from the political unconscious and ready to make connections where perhaps there were none. But the plot seemed to thicken when I learned that one of the drafters of the presidential decree was our conference host, Dr Mikhail Reshetnikov, whose Institute had been named in the decree as the only state-endorsed one of its kind and was housed in prime real estate in the centre of St Petersburg, where housing shortages and homelessness were probably more acute than almost anywhere else in Russia and where, even today, a psychoanalytic institute needs all the political influence and patronage it can muster – or what Russian vernacular knows as 'a roof' – to avoid being shouldered out of valuable real estate by powerful business interests. I was also told by one of my interviewees that Dr Reshetnikov had been a colonel and military psychiatrist in both the Soviet and the Russian armies, that he had close ties with the Yeltsin regime and might well (my interviewee speculated) have been a minister in Yeltsin's government, had he so wished.[4] That he had

3 'Freud in Russia, Parts I and II', broadcast in The Europeans series, ABC Radio National, 11 and 18 April, 1999.

4 Dr Reshetnikov later explained that as a colonel in the medical corps he had specialised in neuropathology, psychology and psychotherapy, researching psychical reactions to extreme situations such as wars and technologically-caused catastrophes. As a specialist in mass phenomena, he was a scientific consultant in the Administration of the Russian President, deputy chief editor of its publication *Rossiiskie vesti*, and was offered the headship of its Information Analysis department but preferred the role of scientist to that of bureaucrat in the Administration of the President. See Mikhail Reshetnikov, 'Letter to the Editor', *Journal for the Psychoanalysis of Culture and Society*, 6, 2 (2001): 358. For the common ground between psychiatry and psychotherapy in Russia, see below, n. 7.

chosen instead to become the director of a psychoanalytic institute was something of a puzzle for my interviewee. But it was later pointed out to me that military psychiatrists were in widespread disrepute and often subjects of vilification, or worse, by their ex-'patients'. As Reshetnikov himself noted in a report to a 1997 Novgorod conference (with the somewhat Soviet-sounding title of 'The Medical, Psychological, Social and Valeological Problems of Protecting the Mental Health of the Population of Russia's Regions Under Conditions of Social and Economic Reforms'): 'The traditional prejudice against psychiatrists, which has increased in the past few years because of the greatly exaggerated problem of so-called "punitive psychiatry", is enormous'.[5] The late Anatoly Sobchak, Mayor of St Petersburg (1991-1996) and mentor of Vladimir Putin and Dmitry Medvedev, deemed the problem far from exaggerated. 'The scale ... of repressive psychiatry in the USSR is testified by inexorable figures and facts', Sobchak wrote; 'in 1978, 4.5 million people were on the psychiatric register', and when the Soviet system began to founder in 1988, 'hurried covering of tracks began through mass rehabilitation of patients, some of them mentally crippled (in that year alone, 800,000 patients were removed from the psychiatric register). In Leningrad alone, 60,000 people were rehabilitated in 1991 and 1992'.[6] For reasons I shall be suggesting, then, Freudian psychoanalysis might have been seen as a preferable and legitimising new face for the Russian psychiatric profession in the post-Soviet era.[7]

5 Mikhail Reshetnikov, quoted in 'Why Sorcerers Are preferred to Psychoanalysts', *The Current Digest of the Post-Soviet Press* 49, 7 (6 August 1997): 9.

6 Anatoly Sobchak, 'Preface to the book by Nikolay Kupriyanov *GULAG-2-SN*', in A.E. Taras (ed.), *Punitive Psychiatry*, Moscow and Minsk, AST, Harvest, 2005, pp. 6-7.

7 The distinction between Soviet 'psychiatrist' and 'psychotherapist' could seem politically and ethically crucial, given the double standard manifest in the coexistence in Russia, from the mid-1970s to the 1990s, of two systems: the system of punitive psychiatry serving state power, led by the Moscow Institute for Forensic Psychiatry, and the system composed of elite, psychotherapeutically oriented clinics, led by the Leningrad Psychoneurological Institute. However, as Reshetnikov himself explained, in 2001, in a speech on 'The First Ten Years of Psychoanalysis in Russia', all psychotherapists were by definition psychiatrists:

So much for President Yeltsin's decree and the newfound solidarity between psychoanalysis and the Russian state. As for the party, the week of the conference – in which the seventy-odd Western psychoanalysts and academics among the delegates were bussed daily from our ex-Intourist hotel on the banks of the Neva, past the Summer Gardens and the Winter Palace to the East-European Institute of Psychoanalysis, where the Russians conducted their half of the conference in the basement while the Europeans and Americans conferred in English above-stairs – the week of the conference spanned American Independence Day, on the evening of which, according to our conference programme, Westerners were invited to a celebratory party at an unnamed private residence. The identity of our generous hosts, the nature of their interest in psychoanalysis, and their connections with the East-European Institute seemed to be a mystery to the Western organisers and delegates. We were told only that our hosts wished to remain incognito, and when we set off in two coach-loads through the St Petersburg suburbs on the evening of the Fourth of July, only our Russian bus drivers seemed to know where we were going.

The private residence turned out to be a multi-storey houseboat moored on a river on the outskirts of the city. (Houseboats, I was later informed by an interviewee, were the preferred operational bases of eastern European mafia, for security and surveillance reasons; but there are houseboats and there are houseboats.) Parked on the river-bank at a rakish angle to the gangplank was a gargantuan Excalibur car – retro-1930s, Al Capone-style, US$50,000-worth of gleaming black duco and chrome, with running boards and bug-eyed headlamps and a set of six gun-barrel-like air-horns mounted on its grille. Suitably impressed by this 'auto-erotic' spectacle of *nouvelle richesse*, some of the American psychoanalysts among us

since a 1985 decree that formally recognised psychotherapy as a medical profession for the first time, Russian law has required that 'a psychotherapist must be a medical doctor who specialised in psychiatry, and who has had at least three years experience in psychiatric institutions, as well as "additional training" in psychotherapy'. Mikhail Reshetnikov, 'The Time of Illusions and Hopes: The First Ten Years of Psychoanalysis in Russia', *JEP. European Journal of Psychoanalysis*, 12-13 (Winter-Fall 2001), available at http://www.psychomedia.it/jep/number12-13/reshetnikov.htm

had themselves photographed leaning gingerly on the car's wings, before we proceeded up the gangplank, watched at a discreet distance by armed security guards in fatigues. The houseboat windows were bullet-proofed and alarmed, and on the main deck we found a dance-floor with a stage, a grand piano and a band in full swing to greet us, and a spread of champagne, vodka, caviar and steak that still hadn't run out when we, the seventy-odd guests, returned, cheeks aglow, down the gangplank to our coaches at the end of the party, with the strains of The Star-Spangled Banner still ringing in our ears.

Discreet forays onto the upper decks had revealed anonymously furnished guest bedrooms but little sign of 'private residence'. Among the Russians who were already on board when we arrived were Dr Reshetnikov, his retinue of helpful students-cum-interpreters, and a good-looking thirty-something couple dressed in Western designer-gear. The couple seemed to be behaving in a vaguely host-like manner and were happy enough to make small talk in rudimentary English until I committed the *faux pas* of asking if they were indeed our hosts, whereupon they abruptly forgot how to speak English and walked away. (Reshetnikov later explained that 'the host was dressed in the costume of a waiter – this is an ordinary Russian practical joke'.[8]) Rumours circulating at the party – and reported on the IPSA conference web site by the American organisers, though later prudently deleted – to the effect that our hosts were 'New Russians', a term virtually synonymous with mafiosi in the 1990s, seemed reinforced when, as we returned to our coaches at the end of the party, the young man to whom I had been speaking fanfared our departure by sounding the air-horns on his Excalibur car, which played the theme-tune of Coppola's *The Godfather*. (Dr Reshetnikov would later comment of this fanfare: 'I, however, unlike [Bennett], have other associations with this music – primarily of aesthetic content'.[9])

I subsequently learned that our host's female companion was a part-time student at Reshetnikov's institute, hoping one day to

8 Reshetnikov, 'Letter to the Editor', p. 359.
9 Ibid., p. 360.

become a psychoanalytic art critic, and when I recounted our experience of the party to Dr Viktor Mazin, a lecturer at the East-European Institute of Psychoanalysis, he said: 'The New Russians, they are so rich; [for them] girls are ornaments for male physiology, and the more Westernised the girl, the more ornamental she is; if she can speak a foreign language, knows about Western cooking, or knows about psychoanalysis, or even better, is in analysis, she is more of an asset'.[10] Another interviewee, Dr Alexander Etkind, confirmed that it was typically only 'New Russians' who could afford psychoanalysis at that time, and while the men were more likely to be concerned about assassination than neurosis, their women – often bored, unhappy, and with only time to kill – were its principal patrons.[11] It seemed that psychoanalysis, long stigmatised in Soviet Russia as an elitist, decadent, Western bourgeois practice, had become a fashionable form of cultural capital in the (under)world of the New Russian economy. An appropriately fictional source confirms this picture: Martin Cruz Smith's novel *Wolves Eat Dogs* (2005), set in Russia and Ukraine in 2004, depicts the rare case of a 'New Russian' seeking treatment for his insomnia, fear and depression from a psychotherapist, who observes: 'He seemed typical of our new entrepreneurs. Aggressive, intelligent, adaptable; the last sort to seek psychotherapy. They are happy to send in their wives or mistresses; it's popular for the women, like feng shui, but the men rarely come in themselves. In fact, he missed his last four sessions, although he insisted on paying for them'.[12] Smith's characters reflect repeatedly on the slippage of meaning between 'New Russian', 'new entrepreneur' and 'mafia' in the early 2000s, as when his protagonist remarks of New Russians: 'They saw themselves as the robber barons of the American Wild

10 Viktor Mazin, recorded interview with the author, 6 July 1998. In addition to lecturing at the East European Institute of Psychoanalysis, Mazin is an art critic, psychoanalyst, curator and founder of the Freud Dreams Museum in St Petersburg.

11 Alexander Etkind, recorded interview with the author, 5 July 1998. By contrast, Reshetnikov observed that 'the cost for one session of analytic therapy in Russia is, on average, about 100-250 rubles … which is affordable for the middle class in Russia'. See Reshetnikov, 'Letter to the Editor', p. 360.

12 Martin Cruz Smith, *Wolves Eat Dogs*, London, Macmillan, 2005), p. 44.

West, and didn't someone say that every great fortune started with crime? Russia had already over thirty billionaires, more than any other country. That was a lot of crime'.[13] Dr Reshetnikov subsequently scotched the rumours about our St Petersburg party host, however, by explaining that the latter was simply 'a very successful businessman, in some sense a financial genius', who had bought his 'river barge' 'from the government at closeout prices' and had 'no connection whatsoever with the mafia'.[14]

I had presented my conference paper on the morning before the party, and to explain the framework in which I speculated about links between the so-called 'mafia' party and the 'party-political' decree – and to explain why several of my fellow party-goers whispered to me during the evening, 'But this is what your paper was all about!' – I should outline the paper's themes, before giving an account of psychoanalysis's shifting, often contradictory relationships with legality and criminality, the state and the underworld, in Russia since the early 1920s.

My conference paper drew on preliminary research for chapter one of this book, specifically, its re-examination of Freudian libidinal economy in the light of the neoclassical economists' concern with the need to stimulate consumer spending-desire at a time of perceived 'over-supply' of commodities. Pivotal to my paper was the long passage of *The Interpretation of Dreams* (reproduced verbatim in 'Dora', or 'Fragment of an Analysis of a Case of Hysteria') where Freud develops his elaborate analogy between repressed – because guilty – desires and unused 'capital' awaiting an 'entrepreneur' to put it to work in our dreams.[15] Quoting Freud's justification of the expense of psychoanalysis on the grounds that it could increase his bourgeois patients' work-power and hence earning-capacity, by freeing them from the incapacitating neurotic symptoms of repressed guilt, I suggested that Freud's manifest analogy between censored desire and sleeping assets screened a latent one between the analyst and the entrepre-

13 Ibid., p. 81.

14 Reshetnikov, 'Letter to the Editor', p. 357.

15 Freud, *Interpretation of Dreams*, p. 561 (quoted and discussed at length in chapter 2, above).

neur: the role played by a daytime wish in exploiting what he called the 'capital' or 'capitalist' of unconscious desire in dreams bears an uncanny resemblance to the role of the entrepreneurial analyst who knows how to turn a profit from the guilty desires locked up in his patients' dreams and neurotic symptoms. When erotic desire was so criminalised that its energy became dammed up, according to Freud, it transformed itself into pathological symptoms: civilisation's discontents. In my reading of Freud, psychoanalysis undertook to put the sleeping asset of this blocked desire, or unused 'capital', to work, freeing it from the stigma of perversion or criminality, bringing it up from the underworld, out of the closet of the unconscious, into what Hegel called 'civil society', or the market economy, where it might become profitable for analyst and analysand alike.

Such were some of the thoughts that I took to the lavish Russian party thrown for Western psychoanalysts and critics on American Independence Day, and that shaped my interviews with St Petersburg scholars on the history of the criminalisation and decriminalisation – the repression, sublimation and desublimation – of psychoanalysis in Russia.

Psychoanalysis and Russian Repression

The extraordinary popularity of Freudianism in early twentieth-century Russia is well-known and richly documented by Alexandr Etkind in *Eros of the Impossible.* Many of Freud's earliest students, colleagues and followers were Russians; his texts were translated into Russian years before they appeared in any other foreign language (beginning with *The Interpretation of Dreams* in 1906); wealthy Russian neurotics were among the favourite patrons of the analysts of Vienna, Zurich, and Berlin; and when Russian émigrés such as Sabina Spielrein, Nikolai Osipov and Tatiana Rosenthal, who had studied with Freud, Jung and Karl Abraham, returned home to found their own psychoanalytic tradition in the years immediately before and after the October Revolution, they found an eager clientele among the Russian intelligentsia and the new political elite. As Freud wrote to Jung in 1912, 'there seems to be a local epidemic of psychoanalysis' in Russia;[16] or, as Lenin put it some years later, 'Freud's theory is a kind of popular fad, nowadays'.[17]

Private medical practice, like every other private enterprise, was officially banned by the Bolsheviks in the immediate aftermath of the revolution – a ban enforced through dozens of trials of physicians who were accused of bribing their patients to obtain fees. But when Lenin announced his 'strategic retreat' from total nationalisation and collectivism with his New Economic Policy in 1921, a degree of pluralism was permitted and various experimentalist movements in science, education and the arts were allowed to compete for the right to represent the revolution and the so-called 'New Man of the masses'. In 1922, a group of Muscovite Freudians – formed the previous year by three psychologists and five professors of aesthetics, philosophy and mathematics – constituted themselves as the Russian Psychoanalytic Society, organised into three sections, concerned respectively with the psychology of artistic creativity, clinical analysis, and pedagogy. By the autumn of 1922, the Society had become an Institute for Psychoanalysis, signifying that it had the approval of Freud's institute and could offer psychoanalytic training programmes. Only two other such institutes existed at the time, one in Vienna, the other in Berlin. In establishing their institute, the Moscow society negotiated with the scientific-pedagogical section of the State Scientific Soviet, which reported directly to the Commissar of Enlightenment and Education, Anatoly Lunacharsky, who had close personal ties with Lenin. (Lenin himself, incidentally, had three volumes of Freud translations in his private library, one heavily annotated by his wife, Krupskaia, though official Party records suggest that he strongly disapproved of what he called the Freudian 'fad'. Lenin also employed a former professor of psychoanalysis as a policy adviser: Jenö Varga, who would go on to advise Stalin on his five-year plans.[18])

16 Sigmund Freud, *The Freud-Jung Letters*, W. McGuire (ed.), London, Hogarth, 1974, p. 495.

17 Quoted in Alexander Etkind, *Eros of the Impossible: The History of Psychoanalysis in Russia*, N. and M. Rubins (trans.), Boulder, Colorado, Westview Press, 1997, p. 179.

18 Several months before Hungary became a Soviet Republic in 1919, Freud's friend and colleague, Sándor Ferenczi, was instrumental in setting

The Moscow institute's largest course, directed by Sabina Spielrein (Jung's first patient and a member of the Vienna Psychoanalytic Institute), was on the psychoanalysis of children, and the institute took over a project to establish a clinical institution for children run on exclusively psychoanalytic principles. Known as the State Psychoanalytic Orphanage-Laboratory (and named in Party documents 'The International Solidarity Psychoanalytic Institute and Laboratory'), this institution is unique in the history of psychoanalysis as a state-run educational-scientific project. Its aims were to study psychological conflicts in infants on the Freudian premise that their actions were often motivated by the unconscious quest for sexual gratification and, through the supportive example of its staff (all of whom were to have been analysed and psychoanalytically trained 'in order to nullify the injurious effects of their own complexes on the work'[19]), to provide models of adult tenderness, explanation and trust, rather than guilt-inducing judgement and punishment, which would obviate sexually derived problems in the children's later lives.

When the orphanage-laboratory opened in August 1921, it had a staff of fifty-one and twenty-four children between the ages of one and five (numbers that would dwindle by 1923 to eighteen staff and twelve children). Its director, Ivan Yermakov, explained in a 1923 report that its primary scientific objective was 'methodical observation in a special institution for children' with a view to developing methods for 'educating the socially useful individual within the collective'.[20] At a time when most educational activities were already under Party control

up a Professorship of Psychoanalysis in Hungary, with Jenö Varga as the incumbent. Though the position only lasted a couple of months, Varga's talent was recognised by Lenin and Varga went on to become a close policy adviser of Stalin's, contributing to his five-year plans. See Christfried Tögel, 'Jenö Varga, Psychanalyse, Räterrepublik und Stalinismus', *Werkblatt. Zeitschrift für Psychoanalyse und Gesellschaftskritik*, 42 (1999), H. 1, S, pp. 96–113: http://freud-biographik.de/Toegel%20-%20Jen%F6%20Varga%20,%20Psychoanalyse,%20R%E4terepublik%20und%20Stalinismus%20-%20Werkblatt.pdf

19 Quoted in Etkind, *Eros of the Impossible*, p. 203.

20 Ibid.

and translations of Freud's texts were being issued in a multi-volume series by the State Publishing House, this Psychoanalytic Orphanage-Laboratory could only have been established with the approval and financial support of the highest levels of the Party. In fact, its title of 'orphanage' was belied by its clientele: among the children were the sons both of its principal, Vera Schmidt, and of the General Secretary of the Party's Central Committee, Joseph Stalin. (Apparently, the infant Vasily Stalin didn't benefit much from this special treatment. Etkind told me that Vasily went on to become a military man, an air-force general and a drunkard.[21]) Yermakov's report noted that his 'orphans' were mainly the offspring of 'Party officials who spend most of their time doing important Party work, and are therefore unable to raise their children'.[22] In other words, psychoanalysis was as fashionable and economically elitist a practice in Bolshevik Russia during the 1920s as it was in Austria or Germany, and the orphanage-laboratory provided an opportunity for Party functionaries unwilling or unable to look after their own children to hand them over for safekeeping to an organisation whose every need was met by the state.

From the outset, the school was plagued by rumours of sexual excesses among the children, allegedly encouraged by the staff, although a series of official investigations found nothing to substantiate the stories. A commission set up in 1923 to investigate the school's activities and oversee its functions passed a series of resolutions, describing it as 'the only institution in the world where the basic suppositions of psychoanalysis are applied to pedagogy',[23] and praising its methods as a model to be adapted and emulated in Soviet education at large. At the same time, however, the commission recommended that the school's mandate be expanded to include 'the study of social principles governing child development' (meaning the 'problems of social classes');[24] that it strengthen the 'proletarian contingent' among

21 Etkind, recorded interview with the author.

22 Quoted in Etkind, *Eros of the Impossible*, p. 203.

23 Quoted ibid., p. 211.

24 Quoted in Martin Miller, *Freud and the Bolsheviks: Psychoanalysis in*

its children by increasing their numbers; and that it come under the scientific leadership of a committee in which the dominant influence would be Marxist workers. Etkind's inference from his archival research is that the only person who could have written these provocative recommendations was Lenin's then-favourite and Stalin's arch-rival, Leon Trotsky.

For a brief period in the early 1920s, then, psychoanalysis and Bolshevism enjoyed a symbiotic relationship: while the Freudians needed state approval and funding for their work, the Party was seeking practical guidance in how to cope with the large problem of homeless and orphaned children victimised by the violence of the civil war – many of them sexually traumatised and psychotically disturbed. But it was in the context of a larger scientific and social programme that Freudianism's potential value to communism was widely debated in major Party organs during the 1920s. One of the projects called-for during the period of Lenin's New Economic Policy was the creation of a distinctively Marxist psychology, founded on empirical scientific principles and integrating biological and neurological science with historical materialism – what Stalin called a Soviet 'psychology of the masses and their relationships to labour' – which would help shape the new post-revolutionary society by providing an understanding of mass behaviour, and hence methods of controlling it. Party journals carried numerous articles by pro-Freudians pointing out the convergences between Marx's and Freud's interpretations of religion, the ways in which Freudian psychology could complement Pavlov's physiology of conditioned reflexes, and the potential compatibility of psychoanalysis with materialist science. Meanwhile, Communist youth organisations thought Freudianism could help justify the sexual freedom that Lenin favoured in a bid to break down the traditional bourgeois patriarchal family, while medical doctors such as Aron Zalkind planned a new form of teaching practice based on Freud's theory of sublimation, arguing that 'since human

Imperial Russia and the Soviet Union, New Haven and London, Yale University Press, 1998, p. 66.

beings possess a single form of bio-psychic energy, it should be managed in such a way as to derive the maximum benefit from eroticism for collective purposes …'[25]

What the Bolsheviks had discovered – contrary to their understanding of Marx's own theory – was that a political and economic revolution did not automatically produce a psychological one: that while the new collectivist society had been formed, the mass of Soviet citizens neither knew how to live in it nor wanted to. Broadly speaking, there were three ways of responding to this discovery. One response, associated with Lenin and his New Economic Policy, was to carry on with the economic and political reforms and let people think and live as best they knew how. Another, associated with Stalin, was to select those who thought the right way and send the rest to the Gulag. The third, most idealistic and impracticable response was to undertake a scientific remoulding of the human psyche on a mass scale – the project associated with Trotsky, who believed that if the success of the revolution was to be guaranteed, then a resistant mass unconscious would have to be systematically analysed, excavated, and reconstructed by psychological and educational experiment.

In his 1924 speech, 'A Few Words on How to Raise a Human Being', Trotsky argued that the future task of communism was 'To issue a new "improved edition" of man … But for this it is necessary as a start to know man from all sides, to know his anatomy, his physiology, and that part of his physiology which is called psychology'. 'For what is man?' he asked:

25 Aleksandr Mikhalevich, 'Russia: the revenge of subjectivity', *The Unesco Courier* March 1993, p. 37. Demonstrating the compatibility of Freudianism and Marxism was by no means an exclusively Soviet interest, of course; many in the West were also trying to demonstrate it. Freud's personal library (now in the collections of the London Freud Museum and the Library of Congress) contains several articles and books on the subject, including R. Osborn's *Freud and Marx: A Dialectical Study*, London, Victor Gollancz, 1937, which argued that many of Freud's findings on the unconscious were anticipated by Engels and that psychoanalysts 'have been talking dialectical materialism for years without knowing it' (p. 10).

> Not at all a finished and harmonious being; no, his being is still very incoherent. In him there is not only the vestige of the appendix, which is no use to him – only appendicitis comes of it – but also, if you take the psyche, then you will find there as many unnecessary 'vestiges' as you like, from which come all sorts of illnesses, all sorts of spiritual appendicitis.[26]

Seventeen years earlier, Trotsky had emigrated to Vienna, following his trial and exile to Siberia for leading a revolutionary strike movement against the tsarist government in St. Petersburg. In Vienna he mixed with the Freudians, read their work, took part in psychoanalytic seminars, became friendly with Alfred Adler (a Marxist analyst, whose Russian wife was a member of the Bolshevik party) and formed a close friendship with one of Adler's patients, Adolf Joffe, who would become a Bolshevik ambassador in Europe after the 1917 revolution.

The appeal of psychoanalysis for Trotsky lay in its Enlightenment ethos, encapsulated in Freud's phrase, 'Where Id was, there Ego shall become' – that is, the characteristic appeal, for Trotsky, of a top-down purge of the chaotic and the irrational by consciousness, reason and science. In his essay 'On the Culture of the Future', Trotsky suggested: 'As he rises, Man purges from the top down; first he rids himself of God, then the foundation of government starting with the Czar, then he purges his economy of chaos and competition, then he moves on to his internal world, driving out the dark and the unconscious'.[27] And in another of his essays:

> Psychoanalysis, with the inspired hand of Sigmund Freud, has lifted the cover of the well which is poetically called the 'soul'. And what has been revealed? Our conscious thought is only a small part of the work of the dark, psychic forces ... Human thought, descending to the bottom of its own psychic sources,

26 Leon Trotsky, 'A Few Words on How to Raise a Human Being' (1924), *Problems of Everyday Life and Other Writings on Culture and Science*, New York, Monad, 1973, pp. 139-40.
27 Quoted in Etkind, *Eros of the Impossible*, p. 236.

> must shed light on the most mysterious driving forces of the soul and subject them to reason and to will.[28]

It was Trotsky who first proposed a scientific synthesis of Freud's and Pavlov's work, which he saw as approaching essentially the same goal of a materialist explanation of the mind from different viewpoints: the Freudian hypothetical-theoretical and the Pavlovian empirical-experimental (one from the top, as it were, the other from the bottom).[29] In an open letter to Pavlov in 1923, Trotsky (then Commissar of War and Foreign Affairs and second-in-command of the Bolshevik government) mentioned his personal acquaintance with the Viennese Freudians, suggesting that their theories complemented Pavlov's own, and offering official support for research on how they could be amalgamated. Perceiving psychoanalysis as 'a scientifically based promise of the real … alteration of man, achieved through the reformation of consciousness',[30] Trotsky and other Bolsheviks like him envisaged Freud's bourgeois-individualist practice being extended to the proletarian psyche and applied on a mass scale. Such was the vision reflected in the revised brief given to the State Psychoanalytic Orphanage-Laboratory by the 1923 Party commission. As Etkind puts it: 'The Bolsheviks most likely saw Freud, with his examining couch and individual patients with whom he would have to work for years, as the forerunner of psychoanalytic factories of the future … '[31] Freud himself was not above sharing this dream of psychoanalysis for the masses. In *The*

28 Leon Trotsky, *Leon Trotsky Speaks*, New York, Pathfinder, 1972, p. 269. For conflicting Soviet perspectives on the 'dictatorship of reason', consider Evgeny Zamyatin's novel *We* (1920) and Mikhail Zoshchenko's *Before Sunrise* (1943), both of which conclude with the slogan, 'reason must conquer'. Whereas Zoshchenko's (once banned) semi-autobiographical account of his struggle with melancholia, depression and hypochondria represents rational will – informed by Pavlov's 'mathematically precise' theories – conquering neurasthenia, however, Zamyatin's novel mocks the dictatorship of reason, representing it as converting men into soulless robots, happy goons unable to feel or fantasise.

29 Leon Trotsky, 'Culture and Socialism', *The Age of Revolution: A Trotsky Anthology*, Isaac Deutscher (ed.), New York, Dell, 1964, p. 312.

30 Etkind, *Eros of the Impossible*, p. 185.

31 Ibid.

Question of Lay Analysis (1926), he called for an American millionaire to sponsor what he termed 'a new kind of Salvation Army' made up of psychoanalytically trained social workers and 'educational-analysts' whose mission would be 'combating the neuroses of civilization' on a national or international scale, with a special brief for the raising of neurosis-free children.[32] One of Freud's admirers, the American left-wing editor, poet and activist Floyd Dell, would claim that this vision was realised in America by the Mental Hygiene movement, founded by a businessman committed to bringing psychotherapy to the nation at large.[33] (The National Committee for Mental Hygiene was founded by Clifford Beers, a businessman who survived his own experience of barbaric 'treatment' in an insane-asylum and devoted the remainder of his life to promoting 'scientific' psychotherapeutic help for children and adults through the American school and college systems and in the industrial and business sectors.)

Trotsky himself, of course, was soon to follow a different kind of top-down trajectory, descending from the top of the Party structure to the realm of darkness and the unconscious – to be 'unpersoned', in Soviet parlance, airbrushed out of the history of the Bolshevik leadership. At the 13th Party Conference in January 1924, the Trotskyist opposition to Stalin was condemned as a petit-bourgeois, Menshevik-like, illegal factional deviation. Trotsky was removed from the war commissariat a year later, ousted from the Politburo in 1926, dropped from the Central Committee the following year, expelled from the Communist Party in November 1927, exiled to Central Asia in January 1928, and a year later banished from the territory of the USSR.

32 Sigmund Freud, 'The Question of Lay Analysis', *Historical and Expository Works on Psychoanalysis. The Penguin Freud Library*, Vol. 15, James Strachey (trans.), Albert Dickson (ed.), London, Penguin, 1993, pp. 352-53.

33 Floyd Dell, *Love in the Machine Age: A Psychological Study of the Transition from Patriarchal Society*, London, George Routledge, 1930, pp. 406-7. Dell's book also proposed a 'non-patriarchal method of education, dispensing with the mechanisms of compulsion, shame and parental fixation – that is to say, a kind of child-training which will enable children to grow up to psychic adulthood and fit them for love and work in the modern world' (ibid., p. 9) – a vision shared with the State Psychoanalytic Orphanage-Laboratory.

And with him, more or less, went psychoanalysis. When Stalin mounted a mass-media campaign against Trotsky's influence in state and society, a political counterattack against the proponents of so-called 'Freudo-marxism' began. In the late 1920s, a series of articles in major party journals by Soviet psychiatrists – some of them previously advocates of psychoanalysis – undertook to demonstrate the fundamental incompatibility of Freud's individualism with Marx's collectivism and economic determinism, arguing that Trotsky's efforts to broker a marriage between Pavlovian and Freudian theory were proof that he had 'capitulated to bourgeois psychology'. Psychoanalysis began to be demonised as a decadent Western bourgeois pseudo-science, as pan-sexualist, Trotskyist, and counterrevolutionary. (Freud himself seriously doubted the compatibility of psychoanalysis and Marxism. While he wrote respectfully of 'the tremendous experiment' of Russian communism,[34] he argued in *Civilization and Its Discontents* that 'the psychological premises on which the [communist] system is based are an untenable illusion', and expressed profound reservations about the future prospects of a society in which private property was abolished and the bourgeois class scapegoated as an official enemy.[35]) One of the most scalding and comprehensive critiques of the Soviet Freudians at this time was V.N. Volosinov's book *Freudianism: A Marxist Critique* (1927), which reprimanded Freud for the 'subjective' and speculative nature of his ideas, censured his 'monstrous overestimation' of the sexual component 'in life and in ideology', denounced him for failing to take account of socio-economic determinations when formulating his universalist psychological hypotheses, and concluded triumphantly with the judgement: 'Psychoanalysis is an intimate part of the decaying ideology of the bourgeoisie ...'[36]

34 Sigmund Freud, 'The Question of a Weltanschauung', *New Introductory Lectures on Psychoanalysis. The Pelican Freud Library*, Vol. 2, James Strachey (trans.), James Strachey and Angela Richards (eds), Harmondsworth, Penguin, 1973, p. 218.

35 Freud, *Civilization and Its Discontents*, p. 304.

36 V.N. Volosinov, *Freudianism: A Marxist Critique*, I. R. Titunik (trans.),

Under Stalin's policy of the systematic sovietising of science and culture, all the influences of bourgeois trends in Marxist psychology were to be completely eradicated – beginning with 'the theory of the unconscious', which Engels and Lenin had interpreted as simply the result of 'nonexistent, insufficient or distorted knowledge of the objective processes of nature or society'.[37] The Freudian notion that neurosis is a necessary condition of socialisation – that people are governed by aggressive instincts that are repressed, with pathological consequences, in a civilised society – was unacceptable to a regime that had undertaken to educate the masses scientifically in the objective processes of nature and society, thereby reconstructing the popular psyche as reason-governed, self-determining, and collectivist. The Bolshevik revolution had abolished the bourgeois distinction between public and private life (or between the state, civil society, and the family – the tripartite distinction so crucial to Freud's model of the psyche) and Stalinism could no more tolerate a personal unconscious – a hidden, private domain of desire and aggression in conflict with the rational ego – than it could officially tolerate private property, a black market or criminal underworld.

In 1926 the Bolshevik government stopped funding the Moscow Psychoanalytic Institute, its orphanage-laboratory was closed, and the Psychoanalytic Society itself was disbanded soon afterwards. The last Soviet book on clinical psychoanalysis was published in 1927. Bans were imposed on the study of childhood sexual psychology because of its association with Freud's name; sexual abuse and sexual crimes ceased to be legitimate subjects of research and publication; and after the State Publishing House issued the last of its volumes of Freud translations in 1930, the Soviet psychoanalytic movement came to a standstill, its previous work officially ceasing to exist.

The result was that a theory of the criminalising and repression of instinctual drives as a regrettable condition of civilisation was

I.R. Titunik with N.H. Bruss (eds), New York, San Francisco, London, Academic Press, 1976.

37 I.D. Sapir, quoted in Miller, *Freud and the Bolsheviks*, p. 83.

itself criminalised, repressed, and could only circulate in a kind of intellectual black market. For, during the next five or six decades, psychoanalytic texts and teachings did continue to circulate illicitly, whether in the form of contraband copies of the Freudians' texts or in the unofficial therapeutic practices of some state psychiatrists and psychologists. Alexander Etkind tells the story of a Soviet medical practitioner who had a double, reversible portrait hanging in his office. During the daytime he saw his patients under a portrait of the official guru of Soviet psychology, Ivan Pavlov, but in the evening he turned the picture around and conducted his illicit, private practice under a portrait of Sigmund Freud.[38] A similar story was told to me by one of the graduate students at the East-European Institute for Psychoanalysis, who said that when his father was working as a professional geologist in Siberia, he encountered a German prisoner who had been trained as an analyst by Karl Abraham; the prisoner had analysed his father, who went on to practice psychoanalysis himself under cover of his geological profession. The climate in which such 'feral' analysis was practised up until the end of the Soviet era is suggested by Viktor Mazin's anecdote of his first official introduction to psychoanalysis, when he was training as a biologist at Smolensk University in the 1980s. Mazin had begun reading Freud as a teenager when his texts were officially banned but photocopies were easy to obtain. A segment of Mazin's university science course was on psychology, and he was surprised and very excited to find that one of the lectures was to be devoted to psychoanalysis. In Mazin's words:

> The lecturer was a Professor of psychology, very well-known in Russia, author of many books. I knew already how complicated Freud was, so I was amazed when the Professor began by saying, 'I will tell you everything you need to know about psychoanalysis in five minutes'. And then I was even more amazed when he said, 'I address myself only to girl students here; as for men, they can close their ears, they don't need to hear it'. Of course, I didn't close my ears, I made them even bigger than

38 Etkind, recorded interview with the author.

> they were before. Then the professor said: 'Girls, please, if you meet a boy and this boy tells you the name Freud, run away immediately, because this man is bastard and sexual maniac'.[39]

And that was the sum of the eminent professor's explication of psychoanalysis. (Mazin would recount this memory in slightly different words in an interview with the *Journal for Lacanian Studies* in 2004, in which he said that the professor warned his female students that any young man who mentioned Freud's name would 'definitely be a crook'.[40] When, years after the disappointing lecture, Mazin himself graduated from the East-European Institute of Psychoanalysis, he did so with a psychologist's diploma, since there was, and today (in 2016) remains, no such profession as psychoanalyst in the Russian state register of occupations.)

Official Soviet interest in Freudianism was dramatically revived during the Cold War period, albeit in the inverted or sublimated form of theoretically sophisticated critique and condemnation. Cold War competition with the US on the scientific and philosophical fronts meant engaging in systematic analysis and criticism of Western scientific disciplines, and Soviet intellectuals who were interested in psychoanalysis learned that the way to gain access to its censored texts was to become a critic of Freud. The 1920s Freudo-Marxist enemy within had become the Western enemy without. Characteristic of this period of official Freud-bashing was a conference held in Moscow in 1958 by the Soviet Academy of Medical Sciences under the title 'Problems of Ideological Struggle with Modern Freudism'. The conference proceedings represented psychoanalysis as the dominant influence in Western psychology and described it as an imperialistic doctrine that had set out 'to explain the causes and nature of neuroses, but later began to lay claim to the role of a universal doctrine, extending its influence beyond the medical and biological sciences to the field of socio-economic and historical disciplines'. The report continued: 'Freudism, a typical product of bourgeois ideological reaction in

39 Mazin, recorded interview with the author.

40 Victor Mazin, 'Interview: On the Status of Psychoanalysis in Russia', *Journal for Lacanian Studies*, 2, 1 (2004): 105.

the era of imperialism, was used by the bourgeois ideologists to dupe the masses in the interests of imperialism and as an ideological weapon in the fight against Marxism'.[41] In one of the conference papers, S.A. Sarkisov, a member of the Presidium of the Academy of Medical Sciences, explained how, in the United States, 'Freud's reactionary followers try to persuade the worker that all the difficulties of his existence have their root cause in himself and not in bourgeois society, that they are not the consequence of the relationships of production which exist in an exploiter society'.[42]

By the 1970s, 'Freudism' (as it was called by analogy with Marxism) had become a state-sponsored field of criticism in the Soviet Union. Graduate students were launching their careers as Freud critics in a range of disciplines and psychoanalysis's legal status had become farcically paradoxical. In Martin Miller's words:

> psychoanalytic works could be read but not published, discussed but not approved, presented in a paper at a scientific meeting but not practised in a hospital or psychiatrist's office. A substantial number of specialists in the philosophy, history and sociology of psychoanalysis were at work, but the subject could not be taught in university or medical school courses.[43]

Meanwhile, as far as the imperialist West was concerned, official Soviet psychiatry had lost most of its own credibility during the Brezhnev phase of the Cold War (1964-82), when parts of the psychiatric profession were tied more directly to state political interests than at any time since the Bolsheviks had outlawed private medical practice following the October Revolution. Psychiatrists were required to play the role of a punitive judiciary, diagnosing dissidents as suffering from psychiatric disorders and sending them for 'treatment' to the Serbskii Institute of Forensic and General Psychiatry in Moscow. When news of these internments and the clinical abuse of dissidents filtered through to the West in the late

41 Quoted in Miller, *Freud and the Bolsheviks*, p. 128.

42 Ibid.

43 Ibid., p. 146.

1970s, the British delegates of the World Psychiatric Association led a campaign against their Soviet colleagues, culminating in the forced resignation of the Soviets from the WPA in January, 1983. The Russian Federation formally acknowledged the 'problem' of Soviet punitive psychiatry by making indemnity payments to persons committed to compulsory psychiatric treatment for their political views – incarcerations justified by diagnoses of such mental disorders as 'philosophical intoxication' (in cases where dissenters criticised the leadership by quoting the works of Marx, Engels and Lenin), 'paranoiac states with delusion of reformism', and 'sluggish schizophrenia' (supposedly a non-psychotic type of schizophrenia whose symptoms were often only apparent to the psychiatrically-trained eye).

Psychoanalysis's own public profile began to change – 'Freudism' began to be decriminalised – in Russia in the late 1980s, under Gorbachev's twin policies of *perestroika* and *glasnost* (political restructuring and cultural openness). Favourable commentaries, tributes, and stories about Freud – and indictments of the regime that, as one writer put it, had deprived the USSR of the work of the man 'who defined the face of world psychology' in the twentieth century – started appearing in Soviet newspapers, magazine articles, and even a film: Andrei Zagdanzky's *Interpretation of Dreams*, which juxtaposed graphic documentary footage from the savage history of imperialism, warfare, revolution and totalitarianism with interpretive quotations from Freud's texts, and ended with a single sentence projected on the screen: 'From 1929 to 1989, Freud was not published in the USSR'.

In the same year as Zagdansky's film was made (1989), the Russian Psychoanalytic Association was re-established in Moscow by Aaron Belkin, director of the National Psychoendocrinology Centre at the Ministry of Public Health, who had been introduced to Freudianism in the 1950s by two psychiatrists in Eastern Siberia who were covertly using psychotherapy to treat patients with neurotic disorders. A return of the repressed began to be staged, culminating in Boris Yeltsin's 1996 presidential decree, which promised to do for psychoanalysis what his government did for the Church of Christ the Saviour in Moscow: rebuild, from the ground up, what the Bolsheviks had demolished some six decades earlier.

But if psychoanalysis was resurfacing from the intellectual black market in the late 1980s and 1990s, and recovering from the super-egoistic form of punitive self-criticism into which it was forced during the Cold War, it was returning in several, seemingly contradictory guises and paradoxical relations to criminality and legality – guises that help to explain the 'unhomely' alliances apparently forming between the state, the 'mafia' and the psychoanalytic profession.

In the first place, psychoanalytic literature was rehabilitated in Russia as pornography, or eroticised commodity, which translates repressed desire directly into rubles. Under the puritanical regime of Soviet Socialist realism, sexually explicit writing was taboo, eroticism being regarded as a distraction of valuable energies from the meeting of the Party's productivity targets. (The heroes of Soviet Socialist Realist novels rarely find love, but they always find the approval of the Party; hence the vernacular term, previously cited, for the Stalin Prize novel: 'Boy Meets Tractor' fiction.) Following *glasnost*, in the five-year period 1992-97 the texts of the classic psychoanalytic writers and their followers were republished in Russian editions totalling some fifty million copies[44] – a figure unimaginable in the West – which Viktor Mazin glossed for me:

> At the end of the '80s, people were highly interested in everything which was prohibited before, in avant-garde painting, in genetics, in psychoanalysis, whatever … Even more importantly, for the general public, the interest came from sexual issues, because the name of Freud in the general knowledge of people is always connected with sex, so, to know everything about this secret area, people need to read Freud. That is why one of the first books I discovered on the shelves here in the bookstores was *Three Essays on the Theory of Sexuality* – and it's very possible it was published in five million copies because, when people saw the word 'sex' together with the name 'Freud', they would immediately buy it to understand what's going on … Nowadays, people understand that Freud is not so easy to read, he's not such

44 Reshetnikov, recorded interview with the author.

> a popular writer … and as for young people who're interested in sexual issues, it's much easier now to go and buy *Playboy*.[45]

At the same time, psychoanalytic theory has been legitimised as a discourse for criminalising the regime that suppressed it. Long an object of state scorn and attack – long counted by Soviets among those Western capitalist 'theories that are anti-scientific and that drag human reason backward' (to quote D. Fedotov, Director of the Institute of Psychiatry of the Ministry of Health of the USSR)[46] – it was converted in the late 1980s into a critical weapon against the one-party state. This was the new – and newly respectable – sociological and academic face of Freudianism, which aligned it with political liberalism and free-market economics against the communist state during the late Gorbachev period. Two major publications of the Gorbachev years used Freudian theory to explain the Soviet population's complicity in – not merely its victimisation by – totalitarianism. Aaron Belkin, in the introduction to his 1989 edition of Freud's collected works, explained the institutionalisation of totalitarianism in Russia and Nazi Germany in the 1930s in terms of what he called 'the social Oedipus': a process in which the sons join with the father to kill themselves. According to Belkin's analysis, the ego 'was filled with totalitarian values of the regime', and the critical role of the superego was reversed to accept what would normally be considered immoral or criminal; hence citizens could commit crimes on behalf of the state, free from either punishment or psychic guilt.[47] To rebel against the system was to act criminally in terms of state-defined values, while to behave loyally, carrying out the demands of the totalitarian regime, was to act criminally in moral terms. The only other choice – a common one – was apathy and indifference. The result, according to Belkin, was a pervasive disrespect for all norms and laws:

45 Mazin, recorded interview with the author.

46 D. Fedotov, 'The Soviet View of Psychoanalysis' (1957), reprinted in Paul A. Baran, *Marxism and Psychoanalysis*, New York, Monthly Review Pamphlet Series No. 14, 1960, pp. 55-60.

47 A.I. Belkin, 'Zigmund Freud: Vozrozhdenie v SSSR?', S. Freud, *Izbrannoe*, A.I. Belkin (ed.), Moscow, Vneshtorgizdat, 1989, pp. 5-35, cited in Miller, *Freud and the Bolsheviks*, p. 161.

a dangerous situation for a Russia trying to emerge, in the 1990s, from the Soviet experience of broken or empty government promises. Belkin optimistically suggested that a revival of Freudianism might help counter this pervasive amorality and contribute to a renewed sense of the difference between criminality and legitimacy.

In the same genre of sociological re-legitimations of psychoanalysis, Leonid Gozman and Alexander Etkind's *The Psychology of Post-Totalitarianism in Russia* (1992) offered an anatomy of the disease of post-*perestroika* 'political depression' among Russian youth, a legacy, in part, of Brezhnevite corruption and dissident-smashing. Regarding all forms of ethical or political action as senseless or useless, and lacking any respect for the property-rights of others or the state, Russia's 'politically depressed' youth were/are irresistibly attracted to the amoral economy of black-market entrepreneurship and organised crime. Writing during the last years of the Gorbachev government, Gozman and Etkind commented:

> Complete merger of power and property is what the political programme of the mafia boils down to – Sicilian, Colombian, Uzbek or any other. The mafia form of government, if it won, would be indistinguishable from real socialism. In the power system there are no effective means of fighting the mafia simply because the system itself is one enormous mafia that has swallowed all its competitors.[48]

Meanwhile, psychoanalysis also resurfaced as part of a panoply of so-called 'alternative therapies' – alternative, that is, to state-administered mental health services – all the more popularly appealing and marketable for having been stigmatised as 'unscientific' and outlawed by the Soviet regime. In the 1990s the Russian press reported an explosion of demand for 'alternative' healers: psychics, sorcerers, wizards, 'astrologer-psychoanalysts', bioenergetic therapists, occultist healers of various kinds – some operating under an Orthodox Church front, using prayers, icons and crosses in

48 Leonid Gozman and Alexander Etkind, *The Psychology of Post-Totalitarianism in Russia*, London, Centre for Research into Communist Economies, 1992, p. 95.

rituals promising to heal by 'casting out evil spirits'. Advertising publications were chock-full of their announcements: 'We Get Rid of the Evil Eye and Wasting Diseases Caused by Spells'; 'Relief From All Sickness and Problems'.[49] As Etkind put it in his interview with me: 'Obviously, there's a huge market for psychotherapies in Russia today: millions of people have lost their statues, their jokes, and they're looking for external support and guidance'. By the end of the 1990s there was reportedly one occultist-healer for every 500 residents of Moscow, charging anything up to ten thousand dollars for each hour-long session.[50] Given what Reshetnikov described as 'the greatly exaggerated problem of so-called "punitive psychiatry"' in Russia, the appeal of 'countercultural' therapies that by-pass state-monitoring and state institutions is obvious. As the head of the Kazan Psychotherapy Centre, Gumar Ziyatdinov, commented in a Moscow press interview in 1997: 'A person fears that a traditional physician might put him on an official register and send him to a "nuthouse"'.[51] And riding on the wave of this new demand for 'alternative' therapies was psychoanalysis itself. In his 1997 report to the Novgorod conference, Reshetnikov calculated that 'the army of so-called "uncredentialed analysts," who are essentially taking parasitic advantage of the popularity of psychoanalysis and the absence of legal guidelines for its application, totals tens of thousands of people'.[52] Among these practitioners were self-taught analysts offering curbside consultations to shoppers and pedestrians on the streets of Moscow and St. Petersburg.[53] In an odd twist to the logic of free-market legitimacy, Reshetnikov presented estimates of general-public expenditure on these 'uncredentialed' therapies indicating that 'the least possible direct losses to the state budget of this "activity" total about 1 trillion rubles a year, not counting the "indirect" economic damage from the harm

49 Alevitina Pechereskaya, 'Sorcerers Under the Icons', *The Current Digest of the Post-Soviet Press* 49, 7 (6 August 1997): 10.

50 Reshetnikov, quoted in 'Why Sorcerers', p. 9.

51 Quoted ibid., p. 10.

52 Quoted ibid., p. 9.

53 Felicity Barringer, 'In the New Soviet Psyche, A Place Is Made for Freud', *New York Times* 18 July 1988, pp. 1 and A7.

done to patients by this "treatment" ... We need a law on the protection of patients' rights'.[54] Similar calls were coming from Orthodox Churchmen. In other words, the claims being made by 'alternative' therapists on the psyches, souls and purses of the population – its unconscious desires and unused capital – were now being contested by interest groups like the Orthodox Church and Reshetnikov's Institute for Psychoanalysis, which base their own claims to legitimacy on a new affinity or alliance with the state.

As I implied in speculating that directorship of a psychoanalytic institute might offer a useful image-makeover for an ex-Soviet military psychiatrist, psychoanalysis is also returning from the criminal underworld as a new, legitimate face for the Russian psychiatric profession. This was certainly how the *New York Times* saw the apparent revival of psychoanalysis in the USSR when it reported a full-page article by Aaron Belkin in *Literaturnaia gazeta* in 1988, announcing a return of Freudianism to the public domain in the Soviet Union. The *Times* gave front-page prominence to Belkin's article, but explained it as follows: 'Dr Belkin did not say so, but by giving intellectual respectability back to Freud, Soviet psychiatry would be earning back a measure of international respectability for itself. Its image has been badly marred by persistent reports of the wide use of psychiatric confinement as a method of repressing dissidents'.[55]

From this perspective, President Yeltsin's 1996 decree of a state-backed revival of psychoanalysis makes at least two kinds of sense. My interviewees (Dr Reshetnikov excepted) confirmed that the decree itself could only have been politically motivated – not medically, scientifically or philosophically inspired. The decree was one of many gestures (Number 1044!) by which Yeltsin could distance his government from the Soviet era, notwithstanding his own past as a top-ranking member of the *nomenklatura*, or Communist Party elite. By embracing a previously outlawed practice, one perceived in Russia as highly important and influential in the West, Yeltsin signalled that his government was anti-Soviet, liberal, Westernised,

54 Reshetnikov, quoted in 'Why Sorcerers', p. 9.
55 Barringer, 'In the New Soviet Psyche'.

or interested in bridge-building with the West – which is what the international conference hosted by Reshetnikov's Institute in 1998 was largely about. (While the Western conferees were converting their economic capital into pleasure as tourists in St Petersburg, the Institute was converting their presence into cultural capital, bidding for professional recognition by the International Psychoanalytic Association, which regards Russian analytical training in general as unprofessional and has yet to give its imprimatur to state-endorsed institutes such as Dr Reshetnikov's.) A double process of legitimisation is at work here, in the new alliance between psychoanalysis and the Russian government. While the state seeks to legitimise itself – as anti-authoritarian, liberal, democratic, Westernised – by association with a previously criminalised psychoanalysis, psychoanalysis seeks legitimacy for itself by association with the state – with government-credentialed and sponsored programmes by which it can stake its claim to market share and distinguish itself from what Reshetnikov argued should be a re-criminalised underworld of 'folk' or 'alternative' therapies.

At the same time, the main 'private' patrons of state-endorsed analysts and their institutes, the only ones who could afford their services and fund their houseboat parties, were reputed to be quasi-underworld figures themselves, so-called New Russians – except that the very terminology of legitimacy and criminality seems barely applicable in post-Soviet Russia, where the boundaries between the state and the underworld, between legitimate government and organised crime, have been so blurred as to be imperceptible. (During 1999, American and Swiss authorities were investigating evidence of massive bribe-taking and money-laundering rackets by the Yeltsin inner circle, known to the Russian press as 'The Family', who had allegedly siphoned some US$15 billion of public funds out of Russia into private bank accounts in the West. The Duma, or parliament, was meanwhile repeatedly throwing out proposed measures for clamping down on money-launderers and organised crime in Russia.[56]) The official 'criminalising' of the so-called 'Stalin era' of

56 Peter Willan and James Meek, 'Yeltsin family "took bribes"', *The Guardian* 28 August 1999, available at http://www.theguardian.com/world/1999/aug/26/russia.philipwillan

Soviet government, which began to peak in Gorbachev's last years in power with almost daily revelations of what had become the 'crimes' and corruption of the communist regime – years when the collective unconscious of the country's repressed past seemed to be unlocked and its guilty contents were being purged – was followed in the late 1990s with almost daily revelations of the crimes and corruption of the new regime that 'discredited' communism, the regime of former Party bureaucrats-turned-gangster-capitalists and oligarchs. The repressed corruption of socialism has returned as the unashamed 'entrepreneurship' of racketeer-capitalism.

Which brings me to the final paradoxical twist in psychoanalysis's uncanny relationships with legitimacy and criminality in Russia – one that returns us to Freud's image of censored desire as unused capital and libidinal economy as a black economy. For the so-called New Russians, psychoanalysis became at once a commodity – a designer fashion accessory (therapy-chic), a purchasable form of Western cultural capital, all the more desirable for being beyond the means of most law-abiding Russians – and also a way of re-inventing their own subjectivities as orthodox Western-style capitalists.[57] As the studies by Belkin, Gozman and Etkind suggest, where there is no distinction between legitimate and criminal, there is no guilt and therefore, it would follow, no repression or neurosis. To undergo analysis is to discover or acquire guilt – a hitherto unconscious resource of censored desires – and thereby, we could say, to become Westernised. For the New Russian 'mafiocrats', to acquire the cultural capital of guilt is to become legitimate, neurotic, Western-style capitalists, at once apparently in need of therapy and

57 In a 2004 interview with the *Journal for Lacanian Studies*, Viktor Mazin said: 'The collaboration with the authorities has also a less obvious side than bureaucratization. I mean all these endless seminars, summer schools, and conferences dedicated in Russia to the questions of how psychoanalysis might help develop business, marketing, and commercials. Just recently I got an invitation from the Russian Association for Applied Psychoanalysis in Moscow to take part in a seminar called "Applied Psychoanalytic Technologies in Politics, Business, and Consulting". Psychoanalysis is now a marketable commodity, and in this sense it is paradigmatic of the relations between analysts and the "neoliberal oligarchy", to use Castoriadis's term' (Mazin, 'Interview: On the Status of Psychoanalysis in Russia', p. 112).

yet able to flaunt their 'criminal' desires guiltlessly to American psychoanalyst party-guests, in a now universal lingua franca, by playing the theme-tune of *The Godfather* on their carhorns. To misquote Hamlet: 'Thus conscience doth make capitalists of us all' – 'tis a consummation devoutly to be wish'd'.

On 'the Mafia' as/and Business as Usual

The Russian 'mafia' is neither a new nor a distinctively post-communist development. The term became common currency in the Soviet Union as early as the 1970s, when it described the combination of underground economic enterprises and the Party bureaucrats and officials who were their protectors and beneficiaries (no connection with the Italian mafia was implied). By most accepted sociological definitions, 'mafia' designates a form of large-scale business enterprise claiming a monopoly on supply of illegal goods and services to the public, protecting its monopoly by corrupting government bureaucracies, and competing with the state's official monopoly on the use or threat of violence in order to control market access and exclude competitors.[58] The blurring of boundaries between state and underworld is thus a defining feature of mafias, which perform governmental functions – law-enforcement, criminal justice, 'taxation' – in spheres where the legal judicial system is either unwilling or unable to exercise power, as in nineteenth-century Sicily, or in Soviet Russia where the market economy as such was officially criminalised and hence not subject to contract law or state regulation. The mafia thus amounts to a form of monopoly capitalism in the black economy – or a shadow corporate state.

Studies of the Soviet economy indicate that the mafia-system or 'criminal' economy was in practice indispensable to the state from the 1930s onwards, sustaining the command economy as 'the obscene underside of the Law', to borrow Žižek's phrase. (Describing a 'splitting of the law into the written public Law and its underside, the "unwritten", obscene secret code', Žižek has

58 Annelise Anderson, 'The Red Mafia: A Legacy of Communism', in Edward P. Lazear (ed.), *Economic Transition in Eastern Europe and Russia: Realities of Reform*, Stanford, Hoover Institution Press, 1995, pp. 340-66.

suggested that 'What "holds together" a community most deeply is not so much identification with the Law that regulates the community's "normal" everyday circuit, but rather *identification with a specific form of transgression of the Law, the Law's suspension* ... '[59]) Bribery and extortion, illegal productions and fraudulent stock-keeping were systemic features of the Soviet economy. In order to meet their state-defined productivity targets, factory managers had to rely on systems of bribery to obtain raw materials and services, which were invariably in short supply; almost all Soviet citizens stole from state enterprises to supplement their incomes; and because of excessive bureaucratic power, bribes were necessary to secure everything from goods to drivers' licences to medical care and higher education. At the same time, lucrative official positions were sold or rented out to individuals by the Party bureaucracy in what has been described as a form of mercantilism: 'an economy where the central government sells strategic rent-generating positions within the economy for the purpose of raising revenue'.[60]

In the Gorbachev era, two new laws significantly affected the underground economy: the Law on Individual Labour Activity (1987) and the Law on Cooperatives (1988), which legalised some degree of private business. By the beginning of 1990, some 200,000 cooperatives were in operation: some were former underground enterprises that became legal; some were fronts for racketeers; others were spontaneous new business ventures; but the majority were created within state-owned enterprises by their managers. Under the Soviet state, all profit-making was 'profiteering' – putatively immoral and illegal – hence all business people were suspect as such, but the most cynical view of the privatisation process was that it was a convenient cover for the *nomenklatura*'s hijacking of state enterprises and property. President Yeltsin himself publicly recognised the problem in a speech in December 1992: 'Bribery, privatisation for the sake of and by the *nomenklatura*, the plunder of natural resources, and *nomenklatura* separatism threaten the

59 Slavoj Žižek, *The Metastases of Enjoyment*, London, Verso, 1994, pp. 54-57.
60 Peter S. Boettke and Gary M. Anderson, 'Socialist Venality: A Rent-Seeking Model of the Mature Soviet-Style Economy', Stanford, Hoover Institute Working Papers, 1992, p. 6.

disintegration of Russia'.[61] The Party 'kleptocrats', however, were not alone. The *Vorovskoi Mir* (Thieves' Community), which reportedly grew up inside Soviet prison camps (their 'university and parliament') and whose blackmarketeering accounted for fifteen per cent of all trade in goods and services in Russia in 1991 (US$1.5 billions' worth), held a convention at Vedentsovo, outside Moscow, in December of 1991 to discuss their response to the economic transition.[62] By 1995, the Russian Academy of Sciences' Institute of Sociology was reporting that criminal organisations had established control over 35,000 economic entities, including 400 banks, forty-seven currency exchanges and 1,500 state enterprises, and that by accepting shares of stock as tribute and securing seats on boards of directors, the mafia had taken control of eighty per cent of all stock and thirty per cent of all capital in Russia.[63]

As the revelations of Yeltsin's own alleged mafia activities suggest, speeches and political campaigns against corrupt business in Russia are widely regarded with the same cynicism as 'biznesmen' themselves are. Acquiring legitimacy is thus often perceived as a matter of performance for Western eyes (including Western lending banks and potential business-partners). Hence my speculation that the minor role psychoanalysis might play in this performance of legitimacy consists in a 'rationalising' of resources that is the ironic inverse of the one Freud offered to his neurotic bourgeois clients: psychotherapy, in this case, can convert business-as-usual into a form of (unconscious) guilt, which, as 'moral capital', can in turn be cashed-in by Russian mafiocrats seeking credible commercial and institutional partnerships in the West. As the 'outward' sign or social signifier of self-repression, and hence of a certain interiority, psychotherapy can be worn as a badge of honour, adding a 'depth'-dimension to the superficial lifestyle markers of the new Russian entrepreneurs described by Rose Brady in her book *Kapitalizm: Russia's Struggle to Free Its Economy* (1999):

61 Joseph R. Blasi, Maya Kroumova and Douglas Kruse, *Kremlin Capitalism: The Privatisation of the Russian Economy*, Ithaca and London, Cornell University Press, 1997, p. 35.

62 Ibid., p. 118.

63 Ibid., pp. 115, 117.

> They dressed in Versace jackets and drove Mercedes 600s. 'Do I look like a *solidol*?' a biznesman would ask. 'Solidol' was slang for 'a solid-looking person'. The appearance was far more important than what was underneath.
>
> 'The Russian person is standing on the first step of change', my friend Elena explained. 'He understands that capitalism is much more complicated than socialism … For the person brought up in socialism, today it is very difficult for him to reject hypocrisy, to reject the show for outside effect. It's very hard for him to get away from the idea that he wants an outward beautiful shine and it's not as important what he is made of inside'.[64]

The subtitle of Brady's book, 'Russia's Struggle to Free its Economy', must have seemed uncontentious and transparent to its author as the Moscow bureau chief of *Business Weekly* in 1999. And no doubt it would have seemed equally inspirational to the New Russians portrayed by the novelist Martin Cruz Smith (another American) as avatars of the 'robber barons' of nineteenth-century America, who practised 'free enterprise' as expropriation, uninhibited by ethics or the state. Brady's borrowed assertion that 'it is very difficult' for post-communist Russian entrepreneurs 'to reject hypocrisy' – that is, to feel guilty – implicitly claims ethical superiority for the 'Western' *homo œconomicus* who makes a cost-for-benefit calculation and accepts repressed guilt as the price of profit – with neurotic consequences, according to Freud, on which psychoanalysts can capitalise.

And yet, it seems pertinent to ask, does this model of the capitalist subject as a conscience-troubled exploiter retain any currency today, even in the West? Eli Zaretsky's verdict, quoted at the start of this chapter, suggests not. And all the evidence of how bankers have behaved and governments have rewarded them since the 'global financial crisis' of 2008-10 would seem to confirm that verdict.

64 Rose Brady, *Kapitalizm: Russia's Struggle to Free Its Economy*, New Haven and London, Yale University Press, 1999, p. 149.

Coincidentally, however, psychoanalysis has been enjoying a resurgence of interest in China in recent decades, with the establishment of clinical training institutes, state-approved university courses in psychoanalytic studies, and the biennial International Psychoanalytical Association-endorsed 'Chinese Psychoanalytic Congress'.[65] But if Gozman and Etkind's analysis of the psychology of post-totalitarianism can be transposed from Russia in the 1990s to China in the 2010s, then we can assume that the so-called 'New Chinese' 'kleptocrats', or twenty-first-century robber barons, are no more inclined to feel spontaneously guilty for being the blunt instruments of China's 'struggle to free its economy' from communism — a struggle otherwise known as capitalistic expropriation — than their Russian counterparts have been before them. Western press commentary on China today is replete with all the themes that have typified press coverage of the Russian economy since the 1980s. 'China is a mafia state'; 'China is a kleptocracy of a scale never seen before in human history'; 'the children and relatives of CPC Central Committee members are amongst the beneficiaries of the wave of stock fraud in the US';[66] 'over 182,000 "corrupt" officials punished in China' but 'no systemic measures have been brought in to curb endemic graft';[67] 'prominent Chinese anti-corruption activist sentenced to jail'.[68] While socialism might once have posed as the conscience of capitalism, such press commentary on China today ensures that capitalism's economic defeat of 'actually existing socialism' (the Brezhnev-era term for the best show a

65 See, e.g., American Psychoanalytic Association, 'Psychoanalysis in China: An International Exchange' (press release), *Newswise*, 18 April, 2002: http://www.newswise.com/articles/psychoanalysis-in-china-an-international-exchange; and the web site of the 4th Chinese Psychoanalytic Congress (2015): http://www.jiankangle.com/conference/index.htm.

66 John Hempton, 'The Chinese Kleptocracy Is Like Nothing In Human History', *Business Insider Australia*, 10 June 2012: http://www.businessinsider.com.au/how-the-chinese-kleptrocracy-works-2012-6 (accessed 28/01/2014).

67 'Over 182,000 corrupt officials punished in China', *The Nation*, 28 January 2014: http://www.nation.com.pk/international/11-Jan-2014/over-182-000-corrupt-officials-punished-in-china (accessed 28/01/2014).

68 'China court sentences Xu Zhiyong to four years in jail', BBC News China, 26 January 2014: http://www.bbc.co.uk/news/world-asia-china-25900272 (accessed 28/01/2014).

socialist nation could put on in globally hostile circumstances) has been followed by the resounding moral defeat of socialist ideals *tout court*, as the Soviet and Maoist Party-faithful 'inheritors' of those ideals make a shameless spectacle of lining their pockets with the proceeds thereof.

And the result may well be an emptying-out of the latent superego of 'Western' *homo œconomicus*. For, there was a time when Marxism proposed an even more radical vision of social justice than did Adam Smith's liberalism, with its vision of mutually beneficial exchange between free individuals as the paradigmatic social relation, whose freedom it was the business of government to underwrite. *Contra* Smith's vision of free-and-equal exchange, Marx proposed for communism the more radical vision: 'From each according to his ability, to each according to his needs!' Having enunciated this ideal in his *Critique of the Gotha Programme*, Marx went on to complain: 'what a crime it is to attempt ... to force on our Party again, as dogmas, ideas which in a certain period had some meaning but have now become obsolete verbal rubbish' – the ideas in question being those of '"equal right" and "fair distribution"'.[69] With the moral and economic defeat of communism in both of its super-power incarnations in the East, any talk of capitalist conscience or guilt in the West comes increasingly to seem 'obsolete verbal rubbish'. The contemporary West's robber barons – its Bernie Madoff-style pyramid scheme-builders and its casino-capitalist bankers who count on neoliberal governments to pay their gambling debts and bonuses with the expropriated pensions and wages of PAYE tax-payers – show little sign of the conscience that might make capitalists of psychoanalysts.

Indeed, the very mindset with which I began researching the history of psychoanalysis in Russia and imagining hidden, guilty links between a Russian presidential decree and a houseboat party on American Independence Day (a mindset all too hospitable to rumours from the political unconscious) may now be as obsolete as guilt and shame are on the stock market floor. Freud predicated

69 Karl Marx, *Critique of the Gotha Programme*, Peking, Foreign Language Press, 1972, p. 17.

psychoanalysis on crime, either imagined or actual, in so far as its key postulate is repression of outlawed desires. Where, as in the economy of periods such as *perestroika*, the legitimate and illegitimate are indistinguishable – where, as Derrida would say, the 'state' and the 'rogue' are one and the same and 'a state of nonlaw' prevails[70] – it is hard to imagine what, if anything, psychoanalysis might have left to say to 'economic man'. In the neoliberal era of capital, with its 'greed is good' spirit, its globalised financial crashes, its state 'bailouts' of 'rogue' bankers, its 'blackmailing' or 'hijacking' of democratic governments by guiltless plutocrats or private banking elites, the question of psychoanalysis's future relationship with *homo œconomicus* is a moot one.

70 See Jacques Derrida, 'The Last of the Rogue States: The "Democracy to Come", Opening in Two Turns', *South Atlantic Quarterly*, 103, 2/3 (2004): 323-41.

Bibliography

AAN (AktionsAnalytische-News). Friedrichshof commune newsletter. Published Summer 1974-Spring 1978. Cited as *AAN* by volume, year, and page no.

Abelson, Elaine S. *When Ladies Go A-Thieving: Middle-Class Shoplifters in the Victorian Department Store.* New York and Oxford: Oxford University Press, 1989.

Abernethy, John. *An Inquiry into the Probability and Rationality of Mr. Hunter's Theory of Life, Being the Subject of the First Two Anatomical Lectures Delivered before the Royal College of Surgeons of London in the Year 1814*. London: Longman & Co., 1814.

Abraham, Karl. 'Notes on the Psycho-analytical Investigation and Treatment of Manic-Depressive Insanity and Allied Conditions. *Selected Papers on Psychoanalysis.* [1927] New York: Basic Books, 1953. 137-156.

——. 'On the Psychogenesis of Agoraphobia in Childhood'. *Clinical Papers and Essays on Psycho-Analysis.* [1913] London: Maresfield Reprints, 1979.

——. 'Review of C.G. Jung's *Versuch einer Darstellung de Psychoanalytischen Theories*'. *Clinical Papers and Essays on Psychoanalysis.* Vol. 2. Ed. Hilda Abraham. Trans. Hilda Abraham and D.R. Ellison. New York: Basic Books, 1955. 101-115.

——. 'The Spending of Money in Anxiety States'. *Selected Papers of Karl Abraham, M.D.* Trans. Douglas Bryan and Alix Strachey. Introd. Ernest Jones. London: Hogarth Press and Institute of Psycho-Analysis, 1927.

Ackerlof, George and Robert Shiller. *Animal Spirits: How Human Psychology Drives the Economy and Why It Matters for Global Capitalism.* Princeton and Oxford: Princeton University Press, 2009.

Acton, William. *Prostitution, considered in its moral, social and sanitary aspects in London and other large cities.* London: John Churchill, 1857.

Altenberg, Theo. *Das Paradies Experiment – Die Utopie der freien Sexualitaet Kommune Fridrichshof 1973-1978.* Wien: Triton, 2001.

'Amen'. *The Pearl, a Journal of Facetiae* [sic] *Voluptuous Reading*. 1 July 1879: 32.

American Psychiatric Association. *Diagnostic and Statistical Manual of Mental Disorders*. Fifth Edition, DSM-5. Washington, D.C. and London: American Psychiatric Publishing, 2013.

American Psychoanalytic Association, 'Psychoanalysis in China: An International Exchange' (press release), *Newswise*, 18 April, 2002: http://www.newswise.com/articles/psychoanalysis-in-china-an-international-exchange.

Anderson, Annelise. 'The Red Mafia: A Legacy of Communism'. In *Economic Transition in Eastern Europe and Russia: Realities of Reform*. Ed. Edward P. Lazear. Stanford: Hoover Institution Press, 1995. 340-66.

Anderson, William L. 'Say's Law: Were (Are) the Critics Right?'. In *Austrian Scholars Conference 7: Proceedings*. Auburn, Alabama: Ludwig von Mises Institute, 2001. http://www.mises.org/upcomingstory.aspx?Id=15

Angell, Jeanette. *Callgirl: Confessions of a Double Life*. Sag Harbour, NY: Permanent Press, 2004.

Anon. *Animal Magnetism: Its History to the Present Time, with a brief account of the Life of Mesmer, by a surgeon*. London: G.B. Dyer, 1841.

Anon. *A Supplement to the Onania, Or the Heinous Sin of Self-Pollution, And all its frightful Consequences, in the two Sexes, consider'd, Etc. … to be bound up with either the 7th, 8th, 9th, or 10th Editions of that Book*. London: T. Crouch and J. Isted, n.d. [1720s?]

Anon. *My Secret Life*. [first published in 11 volumes, 1888–1895] Abr. edition with an introduction by G. Legman. New York: Grove, 1996.

Anon. *Onania; Or the Heinous Sin of Self-Pollution, And All its Frightful Consequences, in both Sexes, Consider'd, with Spiritual and Physical Advice to those who have already injur'd themselves by this abominable Practice*. 4th edn. London: printed for the author, and sold by N. Crouch, P. Varenne, and J. Isted; n.d. [1711 or 1718?].

Anon. 'Sub-Umbra, or Sport Amongst the She-Noodles'. *The Pearl, a Journal of Facetiae*, 2, (August 1879): 34-35.

Anon. 'The Passenger's Story'. *Swivia; or, the Briefless Barrister. The Extra Special Number of* The Pearl, *Containing a Variety of Complete Tales, with Five Illustrations, Poetry, Facetiae, Etc.* Christmas 1879. 46.

Anon. *Teague-Root Display'd: Being Some Useful and Important Discoveries Tending to Illustrate the Doctrine of Electricity, in a Letter from Paddy Strong-Cock, Fellow of Drury-Lane, and Professor of Natural Philosophy in M. King's College, Covent-Garden, to W—m W—n* [William Watson], *F.R.S., Author of a late Pamphlet on that Subject.* London: W. Webb, 1746.

Arendt, Hannah. 'Social Science and the Study of Concentration Camps'. *Jewish Social Studies*, 12, 1 (1950): 232-47.

Armstrong, John. *The Œconomy of Love: A Poetical Essay* [1736]. Third edition. London: M. Cooper, 1739.

Armstrong, R.H. 'The Archaeology of Freud's Reading'. *International Review of Modernism*, 3, 1 (1999): 16-20.

Ashcroft, Frances. *The Spark of Life: Electricity in the Human Body.* London: Allen Lane, 2012.

Baker, Ronald. 'Some Reflections on Humor in Psychoanalysis'. *International Journal of Psychoanalysis*, 74, 5 (1993): 951-60.

Bargh, John A. 'Losing Consciousness: Automatic Influence on Consumer Judgment, Behavior, and Motivation'. *Journal of Consumer Research*, 29, 2 (2002): 280-86.

Barker-Benfield, G.J. *The Culture of Sensibility: Sex and Society in Eighteenth-Century Britain.* Chicago and London: University of Chicago Press, 1992.

——. *The Horrors of the Half-Known Life: Male Attitudes Toward Women and Sexuality in Nineteenth-Century America.* New York: Harper and Row, 1976.

——. 'The Spermatic Economy: A Nineteenth-Century View of Sexuality'. *The American Family in Social-Historical Perspective.* Ed. Michael Gordon. Second edition. New York: St Martin's Press, 1978. 374-402.

Barringer, Felicity. 'In the New Soviet Psyche, A Place Is Made for Freud'. *New York Times*, 18 July 1988: 1 and A7.

Bartos, Rena. 'Ernest Dichter: Motive Interpreter' (interview with Dichter). *Journal of Advertising Research*, 26, 1 (Feb/Mar 1986): 15-20.

Bataille, Georges. *Erotism: Death and Sensuality.* Trans. M. Dalwood. San Francisco: City Lights, 1986.

——. *The Bataille Reader.* Ed. Fred Botting and Scott Wilson. Oxford: Blackwell, 1997.

——. 'The Meaning of General Economy'. *The Accursed Share.* Trans. Robert Hurley. Vol. 1. New York: Zone Books, 1991. 19-26.

——. 'The Notion of Expenditure'. [1933]. *Visions of Excess: Selected Writings, 1927-1939*. Ed. Allan Stoekl. Trans. Allan Stoekl with Carl R. Lovitt and Donald M. Leslie, Jr. Minneapolis: University of Minnesota Press, 1985. 116-29.

Baudrillard, Jean. *The Consumer Society: Myths and Structures.* London: Sage, 1998.

Baumeister, Roy F. and Kathleen D. Vohs. 'Sexual Economics: Sex as Female Resource for Social Exchange in Heterosexual Interactions'. *Personality and Social Psychology Review*, 8, 4 (2004): 339-363.

Becker, Robert O. and Gary Selden. *The Body Electric: Electromagnetism and the Foundation of Life.* New York: William Morrow, 1985.

Belk, Russell W., Güliz Ger and Søren Askegaard. 'The Missing Streetcar Named Desire'. In S. Ratneshwar, David Glen Mick and Cynthia Huffman. Eds. *The Why of Consumption: Contemporary Perspectives on Consumer Motives, Goals, and Desire.* London and New York: Routledge, 2000. 98-103.

Belkin, A.I. 'Zigmund Freud: Vozrozhdenie v SSSR?' S. Freud, *Izbrannoe.* Ed. A.I. Belkin. Moscow: Vneshtorgizdat, 1989. 5-35

Bell, Quentin. *Virginia Woolf, A Biography.* Revised edition. London: Hogarth Press, 1996.

Belle de Jour. *The Intimate Adventures of a London Call Girl.* London: Weidenfeld & Nicolson, 2005.

Benjamin, Walter. *The Arcades Project* (1927-1940). Ed. Rolf Tiedemann. Trans. Howard Eiland and Kevin McLaughlin. Cambridge, MA: Harvard University Press, 2002.

Bennett, David. 'Getting the Id to Go Shopping: Psychoanalysis, Advertising, Barbie Dolls, and the Invention of the Consumer Unconscious'. *Public Culture*, 17, 1 (January 2005): 1-25.

——. 'May '68, ÉVÉNEMENTS'. In Stuart Sim. Ed. *The Lyotard Dictionary.* Edinburgh: Edinburgh University Press, 2011. 138-41.

——. '*Homo Œconomicus* vs *Homo Psychologicus*: A Critique of Pure Reason in Economics and Psychoanalysis'. In David Bennett. Ed. *Loaded Subjects: Psychoanalysis, Money and the Global Financial Crisis.* London: Lawrence & Wishart, 2012. 7-33.

Beyst, Stefan. *De extasen van eros: Over liefde, lust en verlangen.* Antwerpen: Hadewijch, 1997.

——. *Otto Mühl: From the Happening to the Commune.* Stefan Beyst Texts. 2002. http://d-sites.net/english/muhl.html.

Birken, Lawrence. *Consuming Desire: Sexual Science and the Emergence of a Culture of Abundance, 1871-1914*. Ithaca and London: Cornell University Press, 1988.

Blanchflower, David D. and Andrew J. Oswald, 'Money, Sex and Happiness: An Empirical Study'. Working Paper 10499, National Bureau of Economic Research. Cambridge, MA. May 2004. http://www.nber.org/papers/w10499.

Bland, Lucy and Laura Doan. Eds. *Sexology Uncensored: The Documents of Sexual Science*. Cambridge: Polity Press, 1998.

Blasi, Joseph R., Maya Kroumova and Douglas Kruse. *Kremlin Capitalism: The Privatisation of the Russian Economy*. Ithaca and London: Cornell University Press, 1997.

Blechschmidt, Aike and Michael Pfister. *Kommune, Frauenrolle und Utopie – Der Friedrichshof: Versuch einer historischen Standortsbestimmung*. Freiburg: Dreisam Verlag, 1982.

Boettke, Peter S., and Gary M. Anderson. 'Socialist Venality: A Rent-Seeking Model of the Mature Soviet-Style Economy'. Stanford: Hoover Institute Working Papers, 1992.

Boire, Richard Glen. 'Laced Media', *The Journal of Cognitive Liberties*, 1, 3 (2000): 72-76.

Borneman, Ernst. *Sex im Volksmund. Die sexuelle Umgangssprache des deutschen Volkes*. Hamburg: Rowohlt, 1971.

Bottomley, J.H. *A Popular Lecture of Socialism, Atheism, and Free Love, Explained and Exposed by J.H. Bottomley, Esq*. St Helens: St Helens and Prescot Reporter Ltd., 1907.

Bourdieu, Pierre. 'The Essence of Neoliberalism'. *Le Monde diplomatique*. English edition. December 1998. http://mondediplo.com/1998/12/08bourdieu.

——. 'The forms of capital'. In J. Richardson. Ed. *Handbook of Theory and Research for the Sociology of Education*. New York: Greenwood, 1986. 241-258.

Bowlby, Rachel. *Shopping With Freud*. London and New York: Routledge, 1993.

Boyer, John W. 'Freud, Marriage, and Late Viennese Liberalism: A Commentary from 1905'. *Journal of Modern History*, 50, 1 (March 1978): 72-102.

Brady, Rose. *Kapitalizm: Russia's Struggle to Free Its Economy*. New Haven and London: Yale University Press, 1999.

Breuer, Josef and Sigmund Freud. *Studies on Hysteria. Standard Edition of the Complete Psychological Works of Sigmund Freud*. Ed. James Strachey. Vol. 2. London: Vintage, 2001.

Brewis, Joanna and Stephen Linstead. *Sex, Work and Sex Work: Eroticizing Organization*. London: Routledge, 2000.

Brigham, Amariah. *Remarks on the Influence of Mental Cultivation and Mental Excitement upon Mental Health*. [1832] Boston: Marsh Capen and Lyon, 1833.

Brome, Vincent. *Freud and His Early Circle: The Struggles of Psychoanalysis*. London: Heinemann, 1967.

Brown, Norman O. *Life Against Death: The Psychoanalytical Meaning of History*. [1959] London: Sphere, 1968.

Bruni, Luigino and Robert Sugden. 'The Road Not Taken: How psychology was removed from economics, and how it might be brought back'. *The Economic Journal*, 117 (January 2007): 146-73.

Buchholz, Michael B. Ed. *Metaphernanalyse*. Göttingen: Vandenhoeck & Ruprecht, 1993.

Budd, Alan. 'General Introduction'. *John Armstrong's The Art of Preserving Health: Eighteenth-Century Sensibility in Practice*. Ed. Alan Budd. Farnham: Ashgate, 2011.

Burstyn, Barbara Sumner. 'Hooker Look in Fashion as Porn Becomes de Rigueur'. *Dissident Voice*, 3 November , 2003. http://www.dissidentvoice.org/Articles9/Burstyn_Hooker-Look.htm.

Caldwell, Gail. 'Major Barbie: She's the plastic miniature of everything good, bad and ugly about American culture'. *Boston Globe*, 27 November 1994, A13.

Campbell, Colin. *The Romantic Ethic and the Spirit of Modern Consumerism*. Oxford: Blackwell, 1987.

Carden, Maren Lockwood. *Oneida: Utopian Community to Modern Corporation*. Syracuse, NY: Syracuse University Press, 1998.

Carleton, Gregory. *Sexual Revolution in Bolshevik Russia*. Pittsburgh: University of Pittsburgh Press, 2005.

Carpenter, Edward. *Love's Coming of Age: A Series of Papers on the Relations of the Sexes*. [1896] London: Swan Schonnenheim, 1906.

Carrington, Penelope M. 'Hooker look is out'. *Potomac News*, 28 January, 2005. http://www.insidenova.com/servlet/Satellite?pagename=WPN/HTMLPage/WPN_HTMLPage&c=HTMLPage&cid=1031777505020&tacodalogin=no

Caygill, Howard. 'Life and Energy'. *Theory, Culture & Society*, 24, 19 (2007): 20-28.

Chaker, Anne Marie. 'For Antidepressant Makers, Shopaholics Are a New Market'. *The Wall Street Journal*, 2 January 2003: http://www.wsj.com/articles/SB1040671904659951873.

Cheskin, Louis. *Why People Buy: Motivation Research and Its Successful Application* [1959]. Second edition. Introd. Howard D. Hadley. London: Business Publications Ltd, 1960.

'China court sentences Xu Zhiyong to four years in jail'. BBC News China, 26 January 2014: http://www.bbc.co.uk/news/world-asia-china-25900272

Corbin, Alain. *Women For Hire: Prostitution and Sexuality in France after 1850*. Trans. Alan Sheridan. Cambridge, MA and London: Harvard University Press, 1990.

Crews, Frederick. 'Analysis Interminable'. *Commentary*. July 1980: 33-34.

Cullen, William. *Lectures on Materia Medica*. Dublin: Whitestone, 1761.

——. *The Works of William Cullen, M.D.* [1772]. Ed. John Thomson. Vol. 1. Edinburgh: Blackwood; London: Underwood, 1827.

Darmon, Pierre. *Trial by Impotence: Virility and Marriage in Pre-Revolutionary France*. Trans. Paul Keegan. London: Chatto & Windus, 1985.

Dean, Carolyn. *Sexuality and Modern Western Culture*. New York: Twayne Publishers, 1996.

Decker, Hannah S. *Freud, Dora, and Vienna 1900*. New York: Free Press, 1991.

Deleuze, Gilles and Félix Guattari. *Anti-Oedipus: Capitalism and Schizophrenia*. Trans. Robert Hurley, Mark Seem and Helen R. Lane. Preface by Michel Foucault. Minneapolis: University of Minnesota Press, 1983.

Dell, Floyd. *Love in the Machine Age: A Psychological Study of the Transition from Patriarchal Society*. London: George Routledge, 1930.

Derrida, Jacques. 'The Last of the Rogue States: The "Democracy to Come," Opening in Two Turns'. *South Atlantic Quarterly*, 103, 2/3 (2004): 323-41.

——. *Writing and Difference*. Trans. Alan Bass. Chicago: University of Chicago Press; London: Routledge and Kegan, 1978.

Desmaze, Charles. *Le crime et la débouache à Paris: Le divorce*. Paris: G. Charpentier, 1881.

Dichter, Ernest. *Getting Motivated by Ernest Dichter: The Secret Behind*

Individual Motivations by the Man Who Was Not Afraid to Ask 'Why'. New York: Pergamon Press, 1979.

——. *Packaging, the Sixth Sense? A Guide to Identifying Consumer Motivation.* Boston: Cahners Books, 1975.

——. *The Psychology of Everyday Living.* New York: Barnes & Noble, 1947.

——. *The Strategy of Desire.* Garden City, New York: Doubleday, 1960.

Draaisma, Douwe. *Metaphors of Memory: A History of Ideas About the Mind.* Cambridge: Cambridge University Press, 1999.

Dregger, Leila. 'Project Meiga: How It All Began'. http://www.juggler-press.com/jockm/zegghistory.html.

Dreuw, Wilhelm Heinrich. *Die Sexual-Revolution: Der Kampf um die staatliche. Bekämpfung der Geschlechtskrankheiten.* Leipzig: Ernst Bircher Verlag, 1921.

Dubuisson, Paul. 'Les Voleuses des grands magasins'. *Archives d'Anthropologie Criminelle: De criminologie et de psychologie normale et pathologique*, Vol. 16 (1901): 1-20.

Drucker, Peter F. *Adventures of a Bystander.* London: Heinemann, 1979.

Du Camp, Maxime. *Paris: ses organes, ses fonctions et sa vie dans la seconde moitié du XIX siècle.* Vol. 3. Paris: Hachette, 1872.

Duhm, Dieter. *Eros Unredeemed: The World Power of Sexuality.* Bad Belzig: Verlag Meiga, 2010.

Dyer, Alfred S. *Facts for Men on Moral Purity and Health, Being Plain Words to Young Men Upon an Avoided Subject; Safeguards against Immorality, & Facts that Men Ought to Know.* London: Dyer Brothers, 1884.

Edgeworth, Francis. *Mathematical Psychics.* [1881] New York: Kelley, 1967.

Ellis, Bret Easton. *American Psycho.* New York: Vintage, 1991.

Ellis, Havelock. 'Analysis of the Sexual Impulse'. *Studies in the Psychology of Sex.* Philadelphia: Davis, 1908. 1-55.

——. *Psychology of Sex.* London: Heinemann, 1933.

——. *Studies in the Psychology of Sex.* Third edition. Vol. 1. Philadelphia: Davis, 1910.

Ellis, John B. *Free Love and Its Votaries; or, American Socialism Unmasked. Being an Historical and Descriptive Account of the Rise and Progress of the Various Free Love Associations in the United States, and the Effects of Their Vicious Teachings Upon American Society.* New York: United States Publishing Company; San Francisco: A.L. Bancroft & Co., 1870.

Engels, Frederick. *The Origin of the Family, Private Property and the State.* [1884] Introd. E.B. Leacock. New York: International Publishers, 1972.

Erikson, Erik H. *Gandhi's Truth: On the Origins of Militant Nonviolence.* London: Faber & Faber, 1970.

Esposito, Roberto. 'Totalitarianism or Biopolitics? Concerning a Philosophical Interpretation of the Twentieth Century'. Trans. Timothy Campbell. *Critical Inquiry*, 34, 4 (Summer 2008): 633-44.

Etkind, Alexander. *Eros of the Impossible: The History of Psychoanalysis in Russia.* Boulder, CO: Westview, 1997.

Faivre, Antoine. *Access to Western Esotericism.* Albany, NY: State University of New York Press, 1994.

Farmer, John S. Ed. *Slang and its analogues past and present: a dictionary, historical and comparative, of the heterodox speech of all classes of society for more than three hundred years; with synonyms in English, French, German, Italian, etc.* London: Printed for subscribers, 1890-1904.

Federn, Paul. 'Factors in the World Depression'. *The Journal of Nervous and Mental Disease*, 79, 1 (1934): 43-58.

Fenichel, Otto. 'The Drive to Amass Wealth'. *Psychoanalytic Quarterly*, 7 (1938): 69-95.

Fernihough, Anne. *D.H. Lawrence: Aesthetics and Ideology.* Oxford: Clarendon, 1993.

Fedotov, D. 'The Soviet View of Psychoanalysis' (1957). Appendix in Paul A. Baran, *Marxism and Psychoanalysis.* New York: Monthly Review Pamphlet Series No. 14, 1960: 55-60.

Ferris, Paul. *Sex and the British: A Twentieth Century History.* London: Michael Joseph, 1993.

Fleck, Robert. *Die Muehl Kommune. Freie Sexualitaet und Aktionismus. Geschichte eines Experiments.* Koeln: Verlag Walter Koenig, 2003.

Fogarty, Robert S. *Desire and Duty at Oneida: Tirzah Miller's Intimate Memoir.* Bloomington, IN: Indiana University Press, 2000.

——. Ed. *Special Love, Special Sex: An Oneida Community Diary.* Syracuse University Press, 1994.

Foster, Lawrence. *Women, Family, and Utopia: Communal Experiments of the Shakers, the Oneida Community, and the Mormons.* Syracuse, NY: Syracuse University Press, 1991.

Foucault, Michel. *The History of Sexuality, Volume 1: An Introduction.* Trans. Robert Hurley. Harmondsworth: Penguin, 1981.

Fourier, Charles. 'Attractive Labour'. *Selections from the Works of Fourier.* Trans. Julia Franklin. London: Sonnenschen & Co., 1901. 163-67.

Fowler, Orson Squire. *Creative and Sexual Science: Or, Manhood, Womanhood, and Their Mutual Interrelations; Love, Its Laws, Power, Etc. … as Taught By Phrenology and Physiology.* Philadelphia: E. Gately & Co., n.d. [1870].

Frank, Thomas. *One Market Under God.* London: Vintage, 2002.

Franklin, Benjamin. 'On Luxury, Idleness, and Industry' (from a letter of 1784). *The Works of Benjamin Franklin: Containing Several Political and Historical Tracts Not Included in Any Former Edition, and Many Letters, Official and Private, Not Hitherto Published; with Notes and a Life of the Author, by Jared Sparks, Volume II.* Boston: Hilliard, Gray, 1840. 448-49.

Frederick, J. George. *Introduction to the New Science and Art of Motivation Research.* Liverpool: Bell Press, n.d. [1958].

Frégier, H.A. *Des classes dangereuses de la population dans les grandes villes, et des moyens de les rendre meilleures.* Vol. 2. Paris: J.B. Baillière, 1840.

Freud, Sigmund. 'An Autobiographical Study'. *Standard Edition of the Complete Psychological Works of Sigmund Freud.* Ed. James Strachey. Vol. 20. London: Vintage, 2001. 7-74.

——. 'Beyond the Pleasure Principle'. *Standard Edition of the Complete Psychological Works of Sigmund Freud.* Ed. James Strachey. Vol. 18. London: Vintage, 2001. 7-64.

——. 'Character and Anal Erotism'. *Standard Edition of the Complete Psychological Works of Sigmund Freud.* Ed. James Strachey. Vol. 9. London: Vintage, 2001. 167-76.

——. *Civilization and Its Discontents. Standard Edition of the Complete Psychological Works of Sigmund Freud.* Ed. James Strachey. Vol. 21. London: Vintage, 2001. 59-243.

——. *Complete Letters of Sigmund Freud to Wilhelm Fliess 1887*-1904. Ed. Jeffrey Masson. Cambridge, MA: Harvard University Press, 1985.

——. 'Fragment of an Analysis of a Case of Hysteria' ('Dora'). *Standard Edition of the Complete Psychological Works of Sigmund Freud.* Ed. James Strachey. Vol. 7. London: Vintage, 2001. 7-122.

——. 'Group Psychology and the Analysis of the Ego'. *Standard Edition of the Complete Psychological Works of Sigmund Freud.* Ed. James Strachey. Vol. 18. London: Vintage, 2001. 65-143.

——. 'Inhibitions, Symptoms and Anxiety'. *Standard Edition of the Complete Psychological Works of Sigmund Freud.* Ed. James Strachey. Vol. 20. London: Vintage, 2001. 77-175.

——. 'On Beginning the Treatment'. *Standard Edition of the Complete Psychological Works of Sigmund Freud.* Ed. James Strachey. Vol. 12. London: Vintage, 2001. 121-44.

——. 'Project for a Scientific Psychology'. *Standard Edition of the Complete Psychological Works of Sigmund Freud.* Ed. James Strachey. Vol. 1. London: Vintage, 2001. 283-389.

——. 'Psycho-Analysis'. *Standard Edition of the Complete Psychological Works of Sigmund Freud.* Ed. James Strachey. Vol. 20. London: Vintage, 2001. 259-70.

——. 'The Dissection of the Psychical Personality'. *New Introductory Lectures on Psychoanalysis. Standard Edition of the Complete Psychological Works of Sigmund Freud.* Ed. James Strachey. Vol. 22. London: Vintage, 2001. 57-80.

——. *The Freud—Jung Letters.* Ed. W. McGuire. London: Hogarth, 1974.

——. *The Future of an Illusion. Standard Edition of the Complete Psychological Works of Sigmund Freud.* Ed. James Strachey. Vol. 21. London: Vintage, 2001. 5-56.

——. *The Interpretation of Dreams. Standard Edition of the Complete Psychological Works of Sigmund Freud.* Ed. James Strachey. Vols 4 and 5. London: Vintage, 2001.

——. *The Origins of Psychoanalysis, Letters to Wilhelm Fliess, Drafts and Notes: 1887–1902.* Ed. Marie Bonaparte, Anna Freud, Ernst Kris. New York: Basic Books, 1954.

——. 'The Question of Lay Analysis'. *Historical and Expository Works on Psychoanalysis. The Penguin Freud Library.* Trans. James Strachey. Ed. Albert Dickson. London: Penguin, 1993.

——. 'The Question of a Weltanschauung'. *New Introductory Lectures on Psychoanalysis. The Pelican Freud Library.* Vol. 2. Trans. James Strachey. Ed. James Strachey and Angela Richards. Harmondsworth: Penguin, 1973.

——. 'The Unconscious' (1915). *Standard Edition of the Complete Psychological Works of Sigmund Freud.* Ed. James Strachey. Vol. 14. London: Vintage, 2001. 159-215.

——. 'Three Essays on the Theory of Sexuality'. *Standard Edition of the Complete Psychological Works of Sigmund Freud.* Ed James Strachey. Vol. 7. London: Vintage, 2001. 123-245.

Friedan, Betty. *The Feminine Mystique*. London: Victor Gollancz, 1963.

Fuller, Francis. *Medicina Gymnastica: or, A Treatise Concerning the Power of Exercise, with Respect to the Animal Œconomy, etc.* Second edition with additions. London: Robert Knaplock, 1705.

Fullerton, Ronald A. '"Mr. MASS motivations himself": Explaining Dr. Ernest Dichter'. *Journal of Consumer Behavior*, 6 (2007): 369-82.

Fullerton, Ronald A. and Barbara B. Stern. 'The Rise and Fall of Ernest Dichter'. *Werbeforschung und Praxis*, 35, 6 (June 1990): 208-11.

Gandhi, M.K. 'On the Necessity of Continence'. *Self-restraint versus Self-indulgence*. Third edition. Ahmedabad: Navajivan Press, 1930. 66-76.

——. 'Towards Moral Bankruptcy'. *Self-Restraint versus Self-Indulgence*. Third edition. Ahmedabad: Navajivan Press, 1930. 1-49.

Gans, Jerome S. 'Money and psychodynamic group therapy'. *International Journal of Group Psychotherapy*, 42, 1 (1992): 133-152.

Gay, Peter. *Freud: A Life for Our Time*. London: Macmillan, 1989.

Gesell, Silvio. *The Natural Economic Order*. Trans. Philip Pye. Berlin: NEO-Verlag, 1906.

Goldman, Emma. 'Marriage and Love'. *Anarchism and Other Essays*. New York: Mother Earth Publishing, 1910. 233-45.

Goodwin, Jeff. 'The Libidinal Constitution of a High-Risk Social Movement: Affectual Ties and Solidarity in the Huk Rebellion, 1946 to 1954'. *American Sociological Review*, 62 (February 1997): 53-69.

Goux, Jean-Joseph. 'General Economics and Postmodern Capitalism'. *Yale French Studies*, 78 (1990): 206-24.

Gozman, Leonid, and Alexander Etkind. *Psychology of Post-Totalitarianism in Russia*. London: Centre for Research into Communist Economies, 1992.

Graham, James. *An Eccentric Lecture on the Art of Propagating the Human Species, and Producing a Numerous and Healthy Offspring, &c. Wherein is Particularly Recommended…Temperance and Sobriety…* [and] *the Efficacious Virtues of the ELECTRICAL BED, in the Act of Copulation, &c.* London: A. Roger, G. Lister and other Booksellers, 1783.

——. *A Private Advice*. London; n.p., 1783.

Grant, Linda. *Sexing the Millennium: A Political History of the Sexual Revolution*. London: HarperCollins, 1993.

Green, Jonathon. *The Cassell Dictionary of Slang.* London: Cassell, 1998.

Green, Malcolm. Ed. and trans. *Brus, Muehl, Nitsch, Schwarzkogler: Writings of the Vienna Actionists.* London: Atlas Press, 1999.

Griffin, Susan. *Pornography and Silence: Culture's Revenge Against Nature.* New York: Harper and Row, 1982.

Grose, Francis. *A Classical Dictionary of the Vulgar Tongue.* London: S. Hooper, 1785.

Guiraud, Pierre. *Dictionnaire Erotique.* Paris: Editions Payot & Rivages, 1993.

Hakim, Catherine. *Honey Money: The Power of Erotic Capital.* London: Allen Lane, 2011.

——. *The New Rules: Internet, Playfairs and Erotic Power.* London: Gibson Square, 2012.

——. 'The recipe for happiness? An enduring marriage and an affair with lots of sex'. *The Telegraph*, 20 August, 2012. http://www.telegraph.co.uk/women/sex9486351/The-recipe-for-happiness-An-enduring-marriage-and-an-affair-with-lots-of-sex.html.

Hare, E.H. 'Masturbatory Insanity: The History of an Idea'. *Journal of Medical Science*, 108, 452 (January 1962): 1-21.

Haste, Cate. *Rules of Desire—Sex in Britain: World War I to the Present.* London: Chatto & Windus, 1992.

Haug, Wolfgang Fritz. *Critique of Commodity Aesthetics: Appearance, Sexuality and Advertising in Capitalist Society.* Trans. Robert Brock. Cambridge: Polity, 1971.

Hegel, G.W.F. 'Civil Society'. Part 3, Section 2 of *The Philosophy of Right. The Philosophy of Right, The Philosophy of History.* Trans. T.M. Knox and J. Sibree. Chicago, London, Toronto: Encyclopaedia Britannica, 1952. 64-80.

Hemyng, Bracebridge. 'Prostitution in London'. In Henry Mayhew, *London Labour and the London Poor.* Vol. IV. 1861. Rpt London: Frank Cass & Co., 1967.

Hempton, John. 'The Chinese Kleptocracy Is Like Nothing In Human History'. *Business Insider Australia*, 10 June 2012: http://www.businessinsider.com.au/how-the-chinese-kleptrocracy-works-2012-6.

Hennessy, Rosemary. 'Queer Theory, Left Politics'. *Rethinking Marxism* 7, 3 (1994): 85-111.

Holden, Kate. *In My Skin: A Memoir.* Melbourne: Text Publishing, 2005.

Holland, Eugene. 'Schizoanalysis'. In *Marxism and the Interpretation of*

Culture. Ed. L. Grossberg and C. Nelson. Urbana and Chicago: University of Illinois Press, 1988. 405-16.

Hopkins, Jim. 'Psychoanalysis, Metaphor, and the Concept of Mind'. M. Levine. Ed. *The Analytic Freud.* London: Routledge, 2000.

Horowitz, Daniel. 'The Émigré as Celebrant of American Consumer Culture'. In *Getting and Spending: American and European Consumer Society in the Twentieth Century*. Ed. Susan Strasser et al. Cambridge: Cambridge University Press, 1999. 149-66.

Hume, David. *A Treatise of Human Nature*. Ed. L. A. Selby-Bigge and P. Neddich. Second edition. Oxford: Clarendon, 1978.

Huneman, Philippe. '"Animal Economy": Anthropology and the Rise of Psychiatry from the *Encyclopédie* to the Alienists'. Larry Wolf and Marco Cipollini. Eds. *The Anthropology of the Enlightenment.* Stanford, Ca.: Stanford University Press, 2007. 262-76.

Hungerford, Edward. 'Walt Whitman and His Chart of Bumps'. *American Literature*, 2 (1931): 350-84.

Hunold, Günther. *Sexualität in der Sprache: Lexikon des obszönen Wortschatzes*. München: Heyne, 1978.

Hunt, Lynn. Ed. *The Invention of Pornography, 1500–1800*. New York: Zone Books, 1993.

Huxley, Julian. *Essays of a Biologist.* New York: Alfred A. Knopf, 1923.

Jameson, Jenna. *How to Make Love Like a Porn Star*. New York: William Morrow, 2004.

Janet, Pierre. 'La Kleptomanie et la depression mentale'. *Journale de psychologie, normale et pathologique*, 8ème Année (1911): 97-103.

Jeannel, Julien F. *De la prostitution dans les grandes villes au XIXe siècle et de l'extinction des maladies vénériennes*. Paris: J.B. Baillière, 1862.

Jeffreys, Sheila. *Anticlimax: A Feminist Perspective on the Sexual Revolution.* London: Women's Press, 1990.

Jeffries, Stuart. 'The sex issue: Is monogamy dead?' *The Guardian*, 10 November 2012. http://www.guardian.co.uk/lfeandstyle/2012/nov/10/sex-is-monogamy-dead.

Jevons, W. Stanley. *The Theory of Political Economy*. [1871] London: Penguin, 1970.

Jones, Ernest. *Sigmund Freud: Life and Work, Volume III, the Last Phase, 1919–1939*. London: Hogarth Press, 1957.

Jung, C.G. *Contributions to Analytic Psychology*. Trans. H.G. and Cary F. Baynes. London: Kegan, Trench, Trubner, 1928.

——. 'On Psychical Energy'. *Contributions to Analytical Psychology.* Trans. H.G. and Cary F. Baynes. London: Kegan Paul, Trench, Trubner, 1928. 1-76.

Kay-Shuttleworth, James Phillips. *The Moral and Physical Condition of the Working Classes employed in the Cotton Manufacture in Manchester.* 1832. Rpt. Manchester: E.J. Morten, 1969.

Kern, Louis J. *An Ordered Love: Sex Roles and Sexuality in Victorian Utopias – The Shakers, the Mormons, and the Oneida Community.* Chapel Hill: University of North Carolina Press, 1981.

Keynes, John Maynard. 'Economic Possibilities for Our Grandchildren' (1930). *Essays in Persuasion.* New York: W.W. Norton & Co., 1963. 358-73.

——. *The General Theory of Employment, Interest and Money.* London: Macmillan, 1936.

Killingsworth, M. Jimmie. *Whitman's Poetry of the Body: Sexuality, Politics, and the Text.* Chapel Hill & London: University of North Carolina Press, 1989.

Klaw, Spencer. *Without Sin: The Life and Death of the Oneida Community.* New York: Penguin Books, 1993.

Kofman, Sarah. *Camera Obscura of Ideology.* Ithaca, NY: Cornell University Press, 1999.

Kon, Igor S. *The Sexual Revolution in Russia: From the Age of the Czars to Today.* Trans. J. Riordan. New York: Free Press, 1995.

Koran, Lorrin M., Ronald J. Faber, Elias Aboujaoude, Michael D. Large and Richard T. Serpe. 'Estimated Prevalence of Compulsive Buying Behavior in the United States'. *American Journal of Psychiatry,* 163 (1 October, 2006): 1806-1812.

Kraepelin, Emil. *Psychiatrie: Ein Lehrbuch Für Studierende und Ärzte.* Leipzig: Verlag von Johann Ambrosius Barth, 1915.

Krafft-Ebing, R. v. *Psychopathia Sexualis with especial reference to Antipathic Sexual Instinct: A Medico-Forensic Study.* Translation of the tenth German edition. London: Rebman, 1899.

Krueger, David W. *The Last Taboo: Money as Symbol and Reality in Psychotherapy and Psychoanalysis.* New York: Brunner and Mazel, 1986.

Lacan, Jacques. *Écrits: A Selection.* Trans. Alan Sheridan. London: Tavistock Publications, 1982.

——. *The Seminar of Jacques Lacan, Book II: The Ego in Freud's Theory and in the Technique of Psychoanalysis, 1954–1955.* Ed. Jacques-Alain

Miller. Trans. Sylvana Tomaselli. Notes by John Forrester. New York and London: W.W. Norton, 1991.

Laqueur, Thomas W. 'Credit, Novels, Masturbation'. In *Choreographing History*. Ed. Susan Leigh Foster. Bloomington and Indianapolis: Indiana University Press, 1995. 119-28.

——. 'Sexual Desire and the Market Economy During the Industrial Revolution'. *Discourses of Sexuality: From Aristotle to AIDS*. Ed. Donna C. Stanton. Ann Arbor: University of Michigan Press, 1992. 185-215.

——. *Solitary Sex: A Cultural History of Masturbation*. New York: Zone Books, 2003.

Lawrence, D.H. *Fantasia of the Unconscious and Psychoanalysis and the Unconscious*. London: Heinemann, 1961.

——. 'Introduction to These Paintings'. *Phoenix: The Posthumous Papers of D.H. Lawrence*. Ed. Edward D. McDonald. London: Heinemann, 1936. 551-84.

——. *Lady Chatterley's Lover and A Propos of Lady Chatterley's Lover*. Ed. Michael Squires. Cambridge: Cambridge University Press, 1993.

——. 'Pornography and Obscenity'. *Phoenix: The Posthumous Papers of D.H. Lawrence*. Ed. Edward D. McDonald. London: Heinemann, 1936.

——. *The Letters of D.H. Lawrence, Vol. II*. Ed. George J. Zytaruk and James T. Boulton. Cambridge: Cambridge University Press, 1981.

——. 'The Rocking-Horse Winner'. *The Woman Who Rode Away and Other Stories*. Ed. Dieter Mehl and Christa Jansohn. Cambridge: Cambridge University Press, 1995. 230-43.

——. *The Symbolic Meaning: The Uncollected Versions of Studies in Classic American Literature*. Ed. A. Arnold. Fontwell, Arundel: Centaur, 1962.

Leigh, Carol. 'Inventing Sex Work'. In Jill Nagle. Ed. *Whores and Other Feminists*. New York and London: Routledge, 1997.

Levine, Robert. 'Would You Like an Extra Shot of Music with that Macchiato'. *New York Times*, 3 November 2004: E3.

Lingis, Alphonso. 'A New Philosophical Interpretation of the Libido'. *SubStance*, 8, 4, 25 (1979): 87-97.

Lipkis, J.M. 'Historians and the History of Economic Thought: A Response to Lawrence Birken'. *History of Political Economy*, 25, 1 (1993): 85-113.

Locke, John. *Two Treatises of Government*. Ed. Peter Laslett. Cambridge: Cambridge University Press, 1988.

Loewenthal, Del. 'Editorial: Sex, Shit, Money and Marxism – The Continued Demise of the "Third Way"'. *European Journal of Psychotherapy and Counselling*, 11, 4 (2009): 349-53.

Lord, M.G. *Forever Barbie: The Unauthorized Biography of a Real Doll.* New York: William Morrow & Co., 1994.

Lowndes Sevely, J. and J.W. Bennett. 'Concerning Female Ejaculation and the Female Prostate'. *The Journal of Sex Research*, 14, 1 (February 1978): 1-20.

Luscombe, Richard. 'Anti-Depressant Drug on Offer to Shopaholics'. *The Scotsman*, 18 July 2003. http://www.news.scotsman.com/index.cfm?id=778492003 .

Lyotard, Jean-François. *Économie libidinale.* Paris: Les Éditions de Minuit, 1974.

——. *Just Gaming.* Trans. Wlad Godzich. Minneapolis: University of Minnesota Press, 1985.

——. *Libidinal Economy.* Trans. Iain Hamilton Grant. London: Athlone Press, 1993.

——. 'March 23'. *Political Writings.* Trans. Bill Readings and Kevin Paul Geiman. Foreword by Bill Readings. London: UCL Press, 1993. 60-67.

——. 'On a Figure of Discourse'. *Toward the Postmodern.* Ed. R. Harvey and M.S. Roberts. Atlantic Highlands, NJ: Humanities Press, 1993. 12-26.

MacDonald, Robert H. 'The Frightful Consequences of Onanism: Notes on the History of a Delusion'. *Journal of the History of Ideas*, 28, 3 (1967): 423-24.

McCloskey, Donald N. *The Rhetoric of Economics.* Madison: University of Wisconsin Press, 1985.

McGowan, Todd. *The End of Dissatisfaction? Jacques Lacan and the Emerging Society of Enjoyment.* Albany, NY: State University of New York Press, 2004.

Mairowitz, D.Z. *Reich for Beginners.* London: Unwin, 1986.

Malinowski, Bronislaw. *Argonauts of the Western Pacific.* New York: E.P. Dutton & Co., 1922.

Mandeville, Bernard. *The Fable of the Bees: Or, Private Vices, Publick Benefits.* Fifth edition. London: J. Tonson, 1728.

Mackenzie, Compton. *My Life and Times: Octave Five (1915–1923).* London: Chatto and Windus, 1966.

Marcuse, Herbert. *Eros and Civilization.* [1955] Boston: Beacon Press, 1966.

——. *One-Dimensional Man.* London: Sphere Books, 1968.

Margolis, Jonathan. 'The price of free love'. *The Guardian,* 8 October 1999. 21.

Marshall, Alfred. *Principles of Economics.* London: Macmillan, 1890.

Martin, John Levi. 'Structuring the Sexual Revolution'. *Theory and Society,* 25, 1 (February 1996): 105-51.

Marx, Karl. *Capital: A Critique of Political Economy.* [1867] Ed. F. Engels. Third edition. Vol. 1. Chicago: Charles H. Kerr, 1919.

——. *Critique of the Gotha Programme.* Peking: Foreign Language Press, 1972.

——. 'Economic and Philosophical Manuscripts'. *Early Writings.* Harmondsworth: Penguin, 1974.

——. *Economic and Philosophic Manuscripts of 1844.* Fifth edition. Moscow: Progress Publishers, 1977.

——. *Grundrisse.* New York: Penguin Classics, 1993.

——. 'Private Property and Communism'. *Karl Marx Selected Writings.* Ed. David McLellan. Oxford: Oxford University Press, 1977. 87-96.

Mazin, Viktor. 'Interview: On the Status of Psychoanalysis in Russia'. *Journal for Lacanian Studies,* 2, 1 (2004): 105-17.

McClure, Samuel M., et al. 'Neural Correlates of Behavioral Preference for Culturally Familiar Drinks'. *Neuron,* 44, 2 (October 2004): 379-87.

McKendrick, Neil. 'Introduction' and 'The Consumer Revolution of Eighteenth-Century England'. *The Birth of a Consumer Society: The Commercialization of Eighteenth-Century England.* Ed. Neil McKendrick, John Brewer and J.H. Plumb. Bloomington and Indianapolis: Indiana University Press, 1985.

McNair, Brian. *Striptease Culture: Sex, Media and the Democratisation of Desire.* London: Routledge, 2002.

Menger, Carl. *Principles of Economics.* Trans. J. Dingwall and B.F. Hoselitz. New York and London: New York University Press, 1981.

Micale, Mark S. *Approaching Hysteria: Disease and Its Interpretations.* Princeton: Princeton University Press, 1995.

Mikhalevich, Aleksandr. 'Russia: the revenge of subjectivity'. *The Unesco Courier,* March 1993. 37.

Mill, John Stuart. 'On the Definition of Political Economy; and on the Method of Investigation Proper to It' [first edition October 1836, *The London and Westminster Review*]. *Essays on Some Unsettled Questions of Political Economy by John Stuart Mill.* London: Parker, 1844.

Miller, Jacques-Alain. 'On Perversion'. Richard Feldstein, Bruce Fink and Maire Jaanus. Eds. *Reading Seminars I and II: Lacan's Return to Freud.* Albany, NY: SUNY Press, 1996. 306-20.

Miller, Martin. *Freud and the Bolsheviks: Psychoanalysis in Imperial Russia and the Soviet Union.* New Haven and London: Yale University Press, 1998.

Moll, Albert. *Libido Sexualis: Studies in the Psychosexual Laws of Love Verified by Clinical Sexual Case Histories.* New York: American Ethnological Press, 1933.

Monro. Alexander. Ed. *Medical Essays and Observations.* London: T. Cadell, 1773.

Mostyn, Barbara. *Motivational Research, Passing Fad or Permanent Feature?* Bradford, UK: MCB Books, 1977.

Nietzsche, Friedrich. 'On Truth and Lie in an Extra-Moral Sense'. *The Portable* Nietzsche. Ed. and trans. Walter Kaufmann. Harmondsworth: Penguin, 1976. 42-47.

Nordhoff, Charles. *American Utopias.* Ed. Robert Fogarty. Stockbridge, MA: Berkshire House Publishers, 1993. Originally published in 1875 as *The Communistic Societies of the United States.*

Nordhausen, Frank and Liane von Billerbeck. *Psycho-Sekten – die Praktiken der Seelenfänger.* Fischer Verlag, 1999.

Noyes, John Humphrey. *Essay on Scientific Propagation.* Oneida, N.Y.: Oneida Community, n.d. [1875].

——. *Male Continence.* Oneida, N.Y.: Office of the American Socialist, 1872.

——. *History of American Socialisms.* Philadelphia: J.B. Lippincott & Co., 1870.

——. *The Berean: A Manual for the Help of Those Who Seek the Faith of the Primitive Church.* Putney, VT: The Spiritual Magazine, 1847.

——. *The Way of Holiness: A Series of Papers Formerly Published in the* Perfectionist *at New Haven.* Putney, VY: J.H. Noyes & Co., 1838.

Noyes, George W. *The Religious Experience of John Humphrey Noyes, Founder of the Oneida Community.* New York: Macmillan, 1923.

Nunberg, Herman and Ernst Federn. Eds. *Minutes of the Vienna Psychoanalytic Society, Volume 1: 1906–1908.* Trans M. Nunberg. New York: International Universities Press, 1962.

——. *Minutes of the Vienna Psychoanalytic Society, Volume II: 1908–1910.* Trans. M. Nunberg. New York: International Universities Press, 1967.

Oneida Association. *Bible Communism: A Compilation from the Annual Reports and Other Publications of the Oneida Association and Its Branches; presenting, in connection with their history, a summary view of their Religious and Social Thoughts.* Brooklyn, N.Y.: Office of the Circular, 1853.

——. *Handbook of the Oneida Community; with a Sketch of Its Founder and an outline of its Constitution and Doctrines.* Wallingford, Conn.: Office of the Circular, 1867.

Osborn, R. *Freud and Marx: A Dialectical Study.* London: Victor Gollancz, 1937.

'Over 182,000 corrupt officials punished in China'. *The Nation,* 28 January 2014: http://www.nation.com.pk/international/11-Jan-2014/over-182-000-corrupt-officials-punished-in-china.

Packard, Vance. *The Hidden Persuaders.* New York: McKay; London: Longmans, Green, 1957.

——. *The Hidden Persuaders* [revised edition]. Harmondsworth: Penguin, 1981.

Parent-Duchâtelet, A.J.B. *De la prostitution dans la ville de Paris considérée sous le rapport de l'hygiène publique de la morale et de l'adminstration ouvrage appuyé de documents statistiques.* Paris: J.B. Baillière, 1836.

——. *Prostitution in Paris, Considered Morally, Politically and Medically: Prepared for philanthropists and legislators from statistical documents, translated from the French by an American physician.* Boston: C.H. Brainard, 1845.

Pareto, Vilfredo. *Manual of Political Economy.* [1909] New York: Kelley, 1971.

Pechereskaya, Alevitina. 'Sorcerers Under the Icons'. *The Current Digest of the Post–Soviet Press,* 49, 7 (6 August 1997): 10.

Persky, Joseph. 'The Ethology of *Homo Economicus*'. *Journal of Economic Perspectives,* 9, 2 (Spring 1995): 221-31.

Peters, Tom. 'The Brand Called You'. *Fastcompany Magazine,* August 1997. http://www.fastcompany.com/28905/brand-called-you.

Picture, Bill. 'X-tina's image makeover'. *San Francisco Examiner,* July 7, 2004. http://www.examiner.com/article/index.cfm/i/070704c_scoop

Pigou, A.C. Ed. *Memorials of Alfred Marshall.* London: Macmillan, 1925.

Platen, P.M. *Livre d'Or de la Santé.* Trans. and expanded by Dr. L. Deschamps. *Volume spécial.* Paris, 1902.

Posner, Richard A. *Sex and Reason*. Cambridge, MA and London: Harvard University Press, 1992.

Philo-Castitatis. *Onania Examin'd, and Detected; or, The Ignorance, Error, Impertinence, and Contradiction of a Book call'd ONANIA, Discovered, and Exposed.* London: Joseph Marshall, 1723.

Radin, Margaret Jane. *Contested Commodities: The Trouble with Trade in Sex, Children, Body Parts, and Other Things*. Cambridge, Mass: Harvard University Press, 1996.

Ray, Isaac. *Conversations on the Animal Economy: Designed for the Instruction of Youth and the Perusal of General Readers*. Portland, OR.: Shirley and Hyde, 1829.

——. *Mental Hygiene*. Boston: Ticknor and Fields, 1863. Rpt New York: Hafner, 1968.

Reich, Wilhelm. *Beyond Psychology: Letters and Journals, 1934–1939*. Ed. Mary Boyd Higgins. New York: Farrar, Strauss and Giroux, 1994.

——. *Ether, God and Devil: Cosmic Superimposition*. New York: Farrar, Straus & Giroux, 1973.

——. *Geschlechtsreife, Enthaltsamkeit, Ehemoral* [sexual maturity, abstinence and marital fidelity]. Vienna: Muensterverlag, 1930.

——. *People in Trouble*. Trans. Philip Schmitz. New York: Farrar, Strauss and Giroux, 1976.

——. *The Bioelectrical Investigation of Sexuality and Anxiety*. Ed. Mary Higgins and Chesterfield M. Raphael. Trans. Marion Faber with Derek and Ince Jordan. New York: Farrar, Straus and Giroux, 1982.

——. *The Bion Experiments*. [1938] New York: Farrar Straus and Giroux, 1979.

——. *The Function of the Orgasm: Sex-economic Problems of Biological Energy*. Trans. Vincent R. Carfagno. New York: Farrar, Straus and Giroux, 1973.

——. 'The Problem of Sexual Economy'. *Sex-Pol: Essays 1929–1934*. Ed. Lee Baxandall. Introd. Bertell Ollman. Trans. Anna Bostock, Tom DuBose and Lee Baxandall. New York: Random House, 1972. 226-49.

——. *The Sexual Revolution: Toward a Self-Governing Character Structure*. Revised edition. Trans. Theodore P. Wolfe. New York: Farrar, Straus and Giroux, 1969.

——. *The Sexual Struggle of Youth. The Invasion of Compulsory Sex Morality*. [1932] London: Socialist Reproduction, 1972.

——. *Wilhelm Reich Speaks of Freud.* Ed. Mary Higgins and Chester M. Raphael. Harmondsworth: Penguin, 1975.

Reshetnikov, Mikhail. Letter to the Editor. *Journal for the Psychoanalysis of Culture and Society,* 6, 2 (2001): 357-60.

——. 'The Conceptual Approaches of National Psychoanalytical Federation to the Problem of Psychoanalytical Education and Training in Russia'. Report to the European Psychoanalytic Federation seminar, Moscow, May 29, 1998. Unpublished English transcript provided by the author.

——. 'The Time of Illusions and Hopes: The First Ten Years of Psychoanalysis in Russia'. *JEP. European Journal of Psychoanalysis,* 12-13 (Winter-Fall 2001), available at http://www.psychomedia.it/jep/number12-13/reshetnikov.htm

Richter, Alan. *Dictionary of Sexual Slang: Words, Phrases, and Idioms from AC/DC to Zig-zig.* New York: John Wiley, 1993.

Riesman, David. *The Lonely Crowd.* New Haven: Yale University Press, 1950.

Ruthven, K. K. 'Keats and *Dea Moneta*'. *Studies in Romanticism,* 15, 3 (Summer 1976): 445-59.

Samuel, Lawrence R. *Freud on Madison Avenue.* Philadelphia: University of Pennsylvania Press, 2010.

Say, Jean-Baptiste. *Traité d'Economie Politique.* Paris: Horace Say, 1803.

Schlothauer, Andreas. *Die Diktatur der freien Sexualitaet – AAO, Muehl Kommune, Friedrichshof.* Wien: Verlag fuer Gesellschaftskritik, 1992. http://www.agpf.de/Schlothauer-AAO-Muehl.htm

Schopenhauer, Arthur. 'On Women'. *Essays and Aphorisms.* Introd. and trans. R.J. Hollingdale. Harmondsworth: Penguin, 1973.

Schwartzkopf, Stefan and Rainer Gries. Eds. *Ernest Dichter and Motivation Research: New Perspectives on the Making of Post-war Consumer Culture.* Basingstoke: Palgrave Macmillan, 2010.

Sharaf, Myron. *Fury on Earth: A Biography of Wilhelm Reich.* London: Hutchinson, 1983.

Shattuc, Jane M. *The Talking Cure: TV Talk Shows and Women.* New York and London: Routledge, 1997.

Shaw, George Bernard. *Mrs Warren's Profession* [1894]. *Plays Pleasant and Unpleasant.* Vol. 1. London: Constable, 1931.

Shklovskij, Viktor. 'Art as Technique'. Julie Rivkin and Michael Ryan. Eds. *Literary Theory: An Anthology.* Malden: Blackwell Publishing, 1998.

Sill, John Stewart. 'Utopian Group Marriage in the 19th and 20th Centuries: Oneida Community and Kerista Commune'. *Free Inquiry in Creative Sociology*, 18, 1 (May 1990): 21-28.

Slater, Philip E. *Footholds: Understanding the Shifting Family and Sexual Tensions in Our Culture*. Ed. Wendy Slater Palmer. Boston: Beacon Press, 1977.

——. 'On Social Regression', *American Sociological Review*, 28, 3 (June, 1963): 339-64.

Smith, Martin Cruz. *Wolves Eat Dogs*. London: Macmillan, 2005.

Sobchak, Anatoly. 'Preface to the book by Nikolay Kupriyanov *GULAG-2-SN*'. In A.E. Taras. Ed. *Punitive Psychiatry*. Moscow and Minsk: AST, Harvest, 2005. 67.

Soul Purpose Productions. 'Slaves in Paradise' (TV documentary film). Prod. and dir. by Madonna Benjamin. UK Channel Four Television Corporation, 1999.

Spears, Richard A. *Slang and Euphemism: A Dictionary of Oaths, Curses, Insults, Sexual Slang and Metaphor, Racial Slurs, Drug Talk, Homosexual Lingo, and Related Matters.* New York: Jonathan David Publishers, 1981.

Spence, Donald P. *Narrative Truth and Historical Truth.* New York: W.W. Norton, 1984.

Spitz, René A. 'Authority and Masturbation: Some Remarks on a Bibliographical Investigation'. *Psychoanalytic Quartlerly* 21 (1952): 490-526.

Stekel, Wilhelm. *The Autobiography of Wilhelm Stekel.* Ed. Emil A. Gutheil et al. New York: Liveright, 1950.

——. *Auto-erotism: A Psychiatric Study of Masturbation and Neurosis.* Introd. Frederic Wertham. Trans. J.S. Van Teslaar. London: Peter Nevill, 1951.

——. *Conditions of Nervous Anxiety and Their Treament.* Trans. Rosalie Gabler. London: Kegan Paul, Trench, Trubner, 1923.

——. 'The Sexual Root of Kleptomania'. *Journal of the American Institute of Criminal Law and Criminology*, 2, 2 (July 1911): 239-46.

Stengers, Jean, and Anne Van Neck. *Masturbation: The History of a Great Terror.* Trans. K. Hoffmann. New York: Palgrave, 2001.

Stepansky, Paul E. *Freud, Surgery, and the Surgeons.* New York: The Analytic Press, 1999.

Stiegler, Bernard. 'Constitution and Individuation'. *Ars Industrialis.* n.d. http://arsindustrialis.org/node/2927.

——. 'Pharmacology of Desire: Drive-Based Capitalism and Libidinal

Dis-economy'. David Bennett. Ed. *Loaded Subjects: Psychoanalysis, Money and the Global Financial Crisis*. London: Lawrence & Wishart, 2012. 232-45.

Stoehr, Taylor. *Hawthorne's Mad Scientists: Pseudoscience and Social Science in Nineteenth-Century Life and Letters*. Hamden, Conn.: Archon Books, 1978.

Stopes, Marie. *Married Love: A New Contribution to the Solution of Sex Difficulties*. London: Putnam, 1918.

'Sub-Umbra, or Sport Amongst the She-Noodles'. *The Pearl, a Journal of Facetiae,* 2 (August 1879): 34-35.

Sulloway, Frank J. *Freud, Biologist of the Mind: Beyond the Psychoanalytic Legend*. Cambridge, MA: Harvard University Press, 1992.

'The Passenger's Story'. *Swivia; or, the Briefless Barrister. The Extra Special Number of* The Pearl, *Containing a Variety of Complete Tales, with Five Illustrations, Poetry, Facetiae, Etc.* Christmas 1879: 46.

Thompson, Craig J. 'Postmodern Consumer Goals Made Easy!' In S. Ratneshwar et al. Eds. *The Why of Consumption: Contemporary Perspectives on Consumer Motives, Goals, and Desire.* London and New York: Routledge, 2000. 120-21.

Tissot, Samuel Auguste David. *Diseases Caused by Masturbation.* Introd. C.V. Ruisdael. Philadelphia and New York: Gottfried and Fritz, 2015.

——. *L'Onanisme. Dissertation sur les maladies produites par la masturbation.* Fourth edition. Lausanne: Marc Chapius et Co., 1773.

'To Ask Freud to Come Here'. *New York Times,* 21 December 1924, sec. 7, 3.

Todd, John. *The Student's Manual.* Northampton: Hopkins, Bridgman, 1835.

Tögel, Christfried. 'Jenö Varga, Psychanalyse, Räterrepublik und Stalinismus', *Werkblatt. Zeitschrift für Psychoanalyse und Gesellschaftskritik,* 42 (1999), H. 1, S: 96-113: http://freud-biographik.de/Toegel%20-%20Jen%F6%20Varga%20,%20Psychoanalyse,%20R%E4terepublik%20und%20Stalinismus%20-%20Werkblatt.pdf.

Trachtman, Richard. 'The Money Taboo: Its Effects in Everyday Life and in the Practice of Psychotherapy'. *Clinical Social Work Journal,* 27 (1999): 275-88.

Trotsky, Leon. 'A Few Words on How to Raise a Human Being' [1924]. *Problems of Everyday Life and Other Writings on Culture and Science.* New York: Monad, 1973.

——. 'Culture and Socialism'. *The Age of Revolution: A Trotsky Anthology*. Ed. Isaac Deutscher. New York: Dell, 1964. 305-14.

——. *Leon Trotsky Speaks.* New York: Pathfinder, 1972.

Turner, John F. 'The Perversion of Play in D.H. Lawrence's "The Rocking-Horse Winner"'. *The D.H. Lawrence Review*, 15, 3 (Fall 1982): 249-70.

Vaneigem, Raoul. *The Revolution of Everyday Life: Survival and false opposition to it.* [1967]. Situationist International Text Library: http://library.nothingness.org/articles/SI/en/display/60.

Volosinov, V.N. *Freudianism: A Marxist Critique*. Trans. I.R. Titunik. Ed. I.R. Titunik with N.H. Bruss. New York, San Francisco, London: Academic Press, 1976.

'Why Sorcerers Are preferred to Psychoanalysts'. *The Current Digest of the Post-Soviet Press*, 49, 7 (6 August 1997): 9-10.

Whyte, William H. *The Organization Man.* New York: Simon & Schuster, 1956.

Willan, Peter and James Meek. 'Yeltsin family "took bribes"'. *The Guardian*, 28 August 1999: http://www.theguardian.com/world/1999/aug/26/russia.philipwillan.

Williams, Gordon. *A Dictionary of Sexual Language and Imagery in Shakespearean and Stuart Literature*. Vols I–III. London and Atlantic Highlands, NJ: Athlone Press, 1994.

Williams, Rosalind H. *Dream Worlds: Mass Consumption in Late Nineteenth-Century France*. Berkeley and Los Angeles: University of California Press, 1982.

Winslow, E.G. 'Keynes and Freud: psychoanalysis and Keynes's account of the "Animal Spirits" of capitalism'. *Social Research*, 53 (1986): 549-78.

Woodmansee, Martha and Marc Osteen. Eds. *The New Economic Criticism: Studies at the Intersection of Literature and Economics*. London: Routledge, 1999.

Wrong, Dennis H. *The Problem of Order, or What Unites and Divides Society*. Cambridge, MA: Harvard University Press, 1995.

Wulfeck, Joseph W. and Edward M. Bennett. *The Language of Dynamic Psychology As Related to Motivation Research*. New York, Toronto, London: McGraw-Hill, 1954.

Xenos, Nicholas. *Scarcity and Modernity*. London and New York: Routledge, 1989.

Zaltman, Gerald. *How Customers Think: Essential Insights into the Mind of the Market.* Boston: Harvard Business School Press, 2003.

Zaretsky, Eli. *Political Freud: A History*. New York: Columbia University Press, 2015.

——. *Secrets of the Soul: A Social and Cultural History of Psychoanalysis*. New York: Alfred A. Knopf, 2004.

Žižek, Slavoj. *The Metastases of Enjoyment*. London: Verso, 1994.

Index

www.ingramcontent.com/pod-product-compliance
Lightning Source LLC
Chambersburg PA
CBHW071639270326
41928CB00010B/1984